COUNSELING

Helping Women and Men Redefine Their Roles

Cecelia H. Foxley

University of Iowa

KENDALL/HUNT PUBLISHING COMPANY

2460 Kerper Boulevard, Dubuque, Iowa 52001

HQ
1075
.F69

81070131

Printed in the United States of America

C   401969   01

NONSEXIST COUNSELING

NONSEXIST

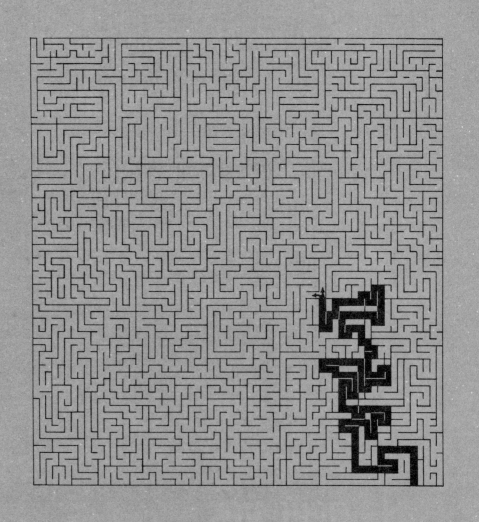

Dedicated to my daughter, Stacy Kay Smith . . .
with the hope that she and her contemporaries
will not be restricted by sex roles.

Contents

Preface

Traditional sex roles and stereotypes are being challenged and changed as women demand that they be allowed to define their own roles—to choose among the widest possible range of opportunities in their education, employment, and personal life styles. Ambiguity and frustration are two terms which describe the present state of affairs as women of all ages are struggling to define new roles for themselves and as men are trying to understand the impact this is having on their own lives.

In reviewing the literature on counseling and changing sex roles, it became increasingly clear that while the changing role of women has been focused on, few authors have given much thought to what it all means for men. Also lacking in the literature are the implications which new or redefined roles for both men and women have for counselors and counselor educators. *Nonsexist Counseling: Helping Women and Men Redefine Their Roles* was written to help fill this important gap in the present literature.

The main purpose of *Nonsexist Counseling: Helping Women and Men Redefine Their Roles* is to help counselors, counselor educators, and others in the helping professions become more aware of the detriments of sex role stereotyping for both sexes and to provide them with models/programs/suggestions/activities they can use in working with a wide variety of clients—girls and boys, women and men who find themselves living in a time of rapidly changing roles.

The scope of the book is purposefully broad in an effort to cover three major content areas. These content areas, which correspond with the three major sections of the book are: (1) Stereotyping of Sex Roles, (2) Counselors and Social Change, and (3) Training for Nonsexist Counseling. Section I—Stereotyping of Sex Roles—describes the basic problem from several approaches so that the reader gains a full understanding and awareness of the detriments of sex role stereotyping. Socialization and how sex roles are developed is the focus of chapter 1. Chapter 2 is a discussion of counselors' and therapists' views of mental health as they relate to men and women. Chapters 3 and 4 describe the sex role stereotyping that is reinforced and perpetuated in our educational institutions and in the work world. Chapter 5 is an overview of present federal laws and regulations which prohibit discrimination on the basis of sex.

Section II—Counselors and Social Change—suggests ways in which counselors in a variety of settings can promote social change and assist in alleviating the problems caused by detrimental sex typing described in section I. Chapter 6 explores androgyny as a model of psychological health for men and women. Chapters 7 and 8 describe ways in which counselors can (a) help student and employee clients and fellow professionals deal with sexism and (b) work to omit institutional sex typing and discrimination in school, employment, and community settings.

Section III—Training for Nonsexist Counseling—discusses the types of training necessary for nonsexist counseling. Chapter 9 presents a rationale for and an outline of a new nonsexist counseling curriculum for counselor education programs. In-service and professional development training programs for the practitioners and paraprofessionals already in the field is the focus of chapter 10. The final chapter, chapter 11, suggests ways in which all individuals affiliated with the helping professions—as student, trainee, educator, practitioner, or paraprofessional—can improve their awareness of sex role stereotyping and sexism in their own attitudes and behaviors and can design and implement a plan for change, self-improvement, and personal growth.

It is hoped that *Nonsexist Counseling: Helping Women and Men Redefine Their Roles* will prove to be a useful resource for all individuals affiliated with the helping professions—students, trainees, educators, practitioners, and paraprofessionals—as we work together to reevaluate the respective status of men and women in our society and strive for a more meaningful and equitable balance, a more androgynous society where boys and girls, women and men can develop according to their own individual interests and abilities rather than according to restrictive roles determined by their sex.

I would like to express my gratitude to several individuals who helped make this book possible: Members of the University of Iowa Administration, for granting me a leave from my teaching responsibilities so that I could complete the book; Rita Litton, Ginny Volk, and Linda Carter for their expert typing; my father for his careful proofreading of the manuscript.

Stereotyping of Sex Roles

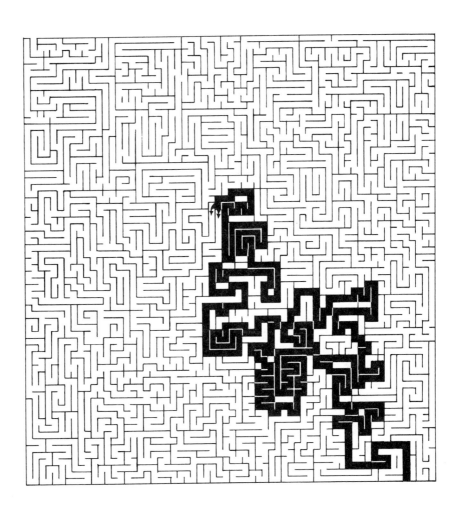

1 Sex Role Development and Socialization

An individual's sex role is the most salient of her or his many social roles. No other social role affects more of a person's behavior, attitudes, emotional reactions, cognitive functioning, and general psychological and social adjustment. As Linton (1945) put it, "The division of the society's members into age-sex categories is perhaps the feature of greatest importance for establishing participation of the individual in culture."

In recent years, much as been written about the limiting effect, particularly regarding women, of traditional sex roles in American culture. Outdated sex role stereotypes of "appropriate" behavior and attributes are still used to differentiate between women and men. In their article "Sex Role Stereotypes: A Current Appraisal," Broverman and associates (1972) summarize the sex role stereotypes for men and women which exist despite "the phenomenon of 'unisex' currently touted in the media":

Women are perceived as relatively less competent, less independent, less objective, and less logical than men; men are perceived as lacking interpersonal sensitivity, warmth, and expressiveness in comparison to women. Moreover, stereotypically masculine traits are more often perceived to be desirable than are stereotypically feminine characteristics. Most importantly, both men and women incorporate both the positive and negative traits of the appropriate stereotype into their self-concepts. Since more feminine traits are negatively valued than are masculine traits, women tend to have more negative self-concepts than do men. The tendency for women to denigrate themselves in this manner can be seen as evidence of the powerful social pressures to conform to the sex-role standards of the society.

Core aspects of the female role are described by Keller (1974) as:

1. a concentration on marriage, home, and children as the primary focus of feminine concern.
2. a reliance on a male provider for sustenance and status. This important component of the wife role is symbolized by the women taking her husband's name and sharing her husband's income.
3. an expectation that women will emphasize nurturance and life-preserving activities, both literally as in the creation of life and symbolically, in taking care of, healing, and ministering to the helpless, the unfortunate, the ill. Preeminent

qualities of character stressed for women include sympathy, care, love, and compassion, seemingly best realized in the roles of mother, teacher, and nurse.

4. an injunction that women live through and for others rather than for the self. Ideally, a woman is enjoined to lead a vicarious existence—feeling pride or dismay about her husband's achievements and failures or about her children's competitive standing.

5. a stress on beauty, personal adornment, and eroticism, which, though a general feature of the female role, is most marked for the glamour girl.

6. a ban on the expression of direct assertion, aggression, and power strivings except in areas clearly marked woman's domain—as in the defense of hearth and home. There is a similar ban on women taking the direct (but not indirect) sexual initiative.

In discussing this traditional role for women, Keller (1974) outlines some costs and benefits. Although she says the advantages may be viewed from a different perspective as disadvantages, she lists these benefits: economic security, emotional security, the cult of beauty ("a socially sanctioned narcissism that feeds the ego"), the lack of pressure to achieve, and a number of other qualities usually ascribed to the female role, such as nurturance, warmth, and sympathy, which are pleasant to acquire and to exercise. She lists the costs of the female role as: lesser autonomy, ignorance and lack of training, and categorical subordination to men.

Similarly, core aspects of the male role have been compiled by Canavan and Haskell (1977). According to Canavan and Haskell, "Men must deal with the conflict that is generated between the realities of their lives and the stereotype of the Great American Male," which they describe as:

1. successful in business—has a high corporate position with a great deal of responsibility, power, etc.

2. financially productive—owns a house, has a car for himself and wife, has good clothes.

3. sexually attractive—physically in good condition and attractive so that women other than his wife find him physically desirable.

4. physically productive—can build things, repair cars, etc., as well as be capable of producing physically attractive offspring.

5. knowledgeable—about the business world, the state of the economy, the political situation, and his own personal and professional goals and directions.

Canavan and Haskell also list costs and benefits of pursuing this role. The benefits they include are: power, feeling of security, satisfaction, access to quality goods, attractive surroundings (including people), popularity, happiness, and sexual pleasure. The costs they list are: failure, few intimate or collaborative relationships, frustration, anger, hostility, fatigue, alcoholism, drug dependency, cigarette smoking, obesity, high blood pressure, ulcers, heart disease—all of which may result in physical disability or early death. While Canavan and Haskell don't discuss the lack of involvement with family and the lack of sharing in the rearing of children as a cost of the male stereotypic role, for an increasing number of men today it is a cost that is too high.

How can these sex role differences be explained? Are men and women born with these characteristics, or does our society socialize the sexes into these roles? While the nature-nurture controversy continues in some circles, research has found very few sex differences. After reviewing hundreds of research studies on sex differences in children, Maccoby and Jacklin (1974), found only a few behaviors which were different: males were more aggressive and better at spatial and mathematical tasks, while girls showed earlier verbal facility. Just how hormones and learning interact to produce these differences is now known.

Anthropologists who study sex roles cross-culturally have demonstrated that sex role differences are not biologically determined. Rather, characteristics, attitudes, tasks, and activities are assigned differently to women and men in different cultures. Margaret Mead's (1935) classic study of three New Guinea tribes impressively demonstrates cross-cultural variation in assigned sex roles. Among the Mundugumor tribe, both women and men are aggressive, unresponsive, severe, and ruthless. In contrast, she found the Arapesh men and women to be unaggressive, cooperative, and responsive to the needs of others. Neither of these tribes ascribe differing personality characteristics to men and women. In the third tribe, the Tchambuli, women are dominant, impersonal, and managing, while the men are less responsible and emotionally dependent— the reversal of the typical sex roles found in Western cultures. Since there is no cross-cultural variation in hormonal or biological sex, these sex role differences must be culturally determined—they must be learned.

In another very different kind of research—the work of Dr. John Money (1965) and his associates on hermaphrodites—the powerful impact of the environment and cultural factors is dramatically demonstrated. The true sex of hermaphrodites— persons who possess complete sets of both female and male genitalia and reproductive organs—is difficult to determine. Some hermaphroditic infants may appear to be male but are biologically female and vice versa. After following the life histories of these babies for twenty years, Dr. Money and his associates found that those who were assigned one sex at birth and were later found to belong biologically to the opposite sex identified with the assigned sex rather than the biological sex. For example, babies who were biologically male but reared as girls followed the typical "feminine" pattern of development—they preferred playing with dolls and domestic toys, preferred marriage over a career, and saw their future fulfillment in the traditional women's role. The reverse was also true: infants assigned as males at birth (but who were later found to be genetically and hormally female) were raised as boys by their parents and thought of themselves as boys—played boys' sports, developed male sex fantasies, and fell in love with girls.

The cross-cultural research on sex roles and the research on hermaphrodites illustrate the great influence of socialization, of learned determinants, on sex role behavior. The primary purpose of this chapter is to briefly present the three major theories of sex role development or sex role socialization—(1) social-learning theory, (2) cognitive-developmental theory, and (3) identification—and to discuss some of the relevant empirical data on sex typing and sex role development. The discussion focuses on the early phases of sex role development (infancy through preschool age) because the first few years are of critical importance and because sex typing and socialization of school age children, adolescents, and adults are discussed in subsequent chapters.

Before going into the socialization theories, defining some terms may be useful. Gender refers to the gonadal, chromosomal, and hormonal characteristics which identify a person to being either male or female. "Masculine" and "feminine" are sex role terms rather than gender terms. Socialization is the process by which someone learns the ways of a given society or social group so that she or he can function within it. Sex typing refers to the process by which a person develops the attributes (behaviors, attitudes, beliefs, and personality characteristics) considered appropriate for his or her sex in a particular culture. "This process is the link between the ascriptive act by the society (namely the parents, at first) and the role performance by the child. . . . There is nothing automatic about the connection between ascription and role adoption; sex typing is a complex process" (Sears, 1965). Sex typed behaviors and sex roles are the products or outcomes of this complex process. Sex roles, then, consist of behaviors which are socially defined and expected of a person because of his or her gender.

Studies have shown that by nine months of age, infants can differentiate others on the basis of gender, and gender identity is established within the first two years of life (Lewis and Weinraub, 1974). There is also substantial evidence that sex typing begins very early and becomes crystallized during the first few years of the child's life (Kagan, 1964; Reeves, 1971). By the age of three or four, boys express distinct preferences for masculine toys, objects, and activities (Brown, 1957; Hartup and Zook, 1960; Kagan and Moss, 1962; Rabban, 1950), while sex typed preferences for girls are more variable and less distinct. Most girls' behavior, interests, and activities fit the feminine stereotypes; however, many girls between the ages of three and ten demonstrate preferences for masculine toys, objects, games, and other activities (Brown, 1957; Hartup and Zook, 1960). While almost all boys prefer same sex friends during the early school years, many girls that age prefer male friends. In addition, a considerable number of girls wish they were boys or "daddies," but very few boys want to be girls or "mommies" (Brown, 1957). It seems that even preschool children sense that the valued sex role in our society is male.

Sex typed behaviors become more firmly established with age (Rabban, 1950) and are relatively stable from childhood to maturity (Kagan and Moss, 1962). In their study of the subjects in the Fels Research Institute's longitudinal population, Kagan and Moss (1962) found that girls high in dependence and passivity during childhood manifested these characteristics as adults, and boys with high levels of aggression and heterosexual behavior demonstrated a strong sexual orientation and anger arousal in adulthood. Passive, dependent boys and aggressive girls were not likely to retain these characteristics, illustrating that "behavioral stability depended on congruence with sex role standards" (Kagan, 1964).

It should be pointed out that there are some differences in the degree and training of sex typing among subgroups within our society. For example, girls and boys of the lower socioeconomic class become aware of their expected sex role behaviors earlier than their middle class peers, and their toy and activity preferences conform more closely to the traditional female and male stereotypes (Rabban, 1950). While ethnic and racial variation in sex role standards has been pretty much ignored in the socialization literature, Ladner's (1971) research on sex roles in the black community suggests that black girls are encouraged to be more independent than white girls, aspiring to the image of the "strong black woman"—resourceful, hardworking, and economically independent. Certainly, further study of ethnic and racial differences in perceptions of appropriate behavior for women and men would be very beneficial.

Sex Role	The three major sex role development theories presented here are
Development	identification, the social-learning theory, and the cognitive-develop-
Theories	mental theory.

Identification   The concept of identification originated within the framework of psychoanalytical theory. Freud (1921) first introduced the term as the process which "endeavors to mold a person's own ego after the fashion of one that has been taken as a model." Freud believed that children "introject" parts of the same sex parent's personality into their own in order to reduce the anxiety and conflict caused by Oedipal desires. Most present-day theories of identification do not focus so centrally on sexual motivation; rather they emphasize the child's desire to be like someone of the same sex, enjoying their status vicariously, or to reproduce the feelings they experienced when the model gave the child attention and love. Identification in sex typing socialization theories has come to mean the "spontaneous duplication of a model's complex, integrated pattern of behavior (rather than simple, discrete responses), without specific training or direct reward but based on an intimate relationship between the identifier and model" (Mussen, 1969). From the child's viewpoint, such identification is evident by the belief that he or she possesses some of the model's feelings and attributes. As Kagan (1964) explains:

If a six-year-old boy is identified with his father, he necessarily regards himself as possessing some of his father's characteristics, one of which is maleness or masculinity. Moreover, if a child is identified with a model, he will behave, to some extent, as if events that occur to the model are occurring to him. If a child is identified with his father, he shares vicariously in the latter's victories and defeats; in his happiness and in his sorrow; in his strengths and in his weaknesses.

Obviously, if a child identifies with the same sex parent, his or her sex typing is enhanced considerably. As pointed out by Kagan (1964):

The boy with a masculine father gains two products from an identification with him—the vicarious power and strength that faciliate future attempts to master sex-typed skills, and the continued exposure to sex-typed behavior. This exposure facilitates the acquisition of sex-typed responses.

What happens when the child identifies with the parent of the opposite sex? Some studies support the Freudian hypothesis that male homosexuals show stronger identification with their mothers than with their fathers (Bieber et al., 1962; Chang and Block, 1960; Mowrer, 1950). But homosexuality does not necessarily result when a child identifies with the parent of the opposite sex. Other research shows that some nontraditional career women identified with (felt closer to) their fathers rather than their mothers (Tangri, 1972). And after finding no significant correlations between parental nurturance and power and nursery school students' sex role behavior, Sears et al. (1965) contend that "the primary identification theory as an explanation of gender role is poor."

Part of the problem is that personality is hard to measure, and it is difficult to say with certainty when identification has occurred. And while the general concept of identification is plausible, it is defined variously by theorists and researchers. For some it means that a child wants to be like a parent; for others that a child feels closest to the parent; and for still others that a child behaves like the parent. With such multiple meanings it is difficult to interpret the concept. For whatever reasons, developmental identification does not appear to be an adequate and complete explanation of sex typing and sex role development.

Social-learning
Theory

Social-learning theory explanations of sex typing and sex role development form the basis of most of the contemporary research in the area and thus are the best known and most widely accepted. A product of the behavioralist school of psychology, social-learning theory is based on well-known, experimentally verified principles of learning. The major learning principle is that behavior is controlled by its consequences. Differential and selective rewards and punishments, generalization, mediation, modeling, and vicarious learning are factors central to the principles of learning. An explanation of sex typing and sex role development according to social-learning theory would go something like this. Sex appropriate responses (e.g., girls playing with dolls) are rewarded by parents (e.g., "What a good little mommie you make!"), and thus are repeated. On the other hand, sex inappropriate responses (e.g., boys playing with dolls) are likely to be punished (e.g., "Only sissies play with dolls"), and thus diminish and finally become extinguished. Parents say they want their sons to be aggressive and independent and their daughters to be nurturing, passive, and dependent, and thus, most parents punish dependency and passivity in their sons and aggression in their daughters (Aberle and Naegele, 1968; Kohn, 1959; Mussen, Conger, and Kagan, 1963; Sears, Maccoby, and Levin, 1957). Because the typical child seeks the acceptance of parents and peers and wants to avoid rejection from them, he or she is predisposed to shun inappropriate activities and to choose responses which are congruent with sex role standards (Kagan, 1964).

Since reinforcement alone cannot explain everything that children learn about what their sex is expected to do and not to do, social-learning theorists contend that children learn the nuances of sex roles through imitation (or modeling). Imitation and identification are very similar concepts; so similar in fact that Bandura and Walters (1963) deny that they can be differentiated from each other:

> . . . Observational learning is generally labeled "imitation" in experimental psychology and "identification" in theories of personality. Both concepts, however, encompass the same behavioral phenomena, namely the tendency for a person to reproduce the actions, attitudes, or emotional responses exhibited by models.

Most empirical studies of imitation have been done in laboratory rather than real life settings, and the types of models children choose to imitate can often be predicted by laboratory psychologists. For example, Bandura and Huston (1961) found that children tend to imitate adults who are warm, attentive, and friendly. Children have also been found to imitate powerful adults—those who control resources important to them such as toys, candy, or privileges (Bandura, Ross, and Ross, 1963; Mischel and Grusec, 1966). Since parents are considered to be the most powerful and nurturant people to a child, they are assumed to be effective models. As was mentioned earlier, however, when tested in real life settings, Sears and associates (1965) found no data supportive of a "modeling" hypothesis that "if the father is more nurturant and more powerful than the mother, the child will use him as the more-to-be imitated model, and will thus be more masculine." Therefore, Sears and associates (1965) contend:

> There is no evidence that the feminine girls' mothers were warm or set high standards (except for table manners) or used love-oriented discipline, or specified themselves as models. The masculine boys' parents, in the home, were not warm, nor did they use love-oriented discipline or refer to themselves as models . . . the primary identification theory as an explanation of gender role is poor.

More rigorous, systematic observation of child-parent and child-significant others interactions and relationships is needed to fully test the social-learning theory as it relates to sex typing and sex role development. In commenting on the social-learning approach to the sex typing of dependency and aggression, Mischel (1966) also indicates the present status of the social-learning theory as it applies to sex typing and sex role development in general:

The greater incidence of dependent behaviors for girls than boys, and the reverse situation with respect to physically aggressive behavior, seems directly applicable in social-learning terms. Dependent behaviors are less rewarded for males, physically aggressive behaviors are less rewarded for females in our culture and consequently there are mean differences between the sexes in the frequency of such behaviors after the first few years of life.

Unfortunately, present evidence that the sexes are indeed treated differentially by their parents with respect to the above behaviors is far from firm, and much more detailed investigations are needed of the differential reward patterns and modeling procedures used by mothers, fathers, and other models with boys and girls in the natural setting. The current empirical evidence is equivocal, although consistent with a social-learning view.

Cognitive-developmental Theory

Cognitive-developmental theory applied to sex role development contrasts sharply with social-learning theory. While social-learning theorists view the child from the outside and believe that the acquisition of sex roles is accomplished through reinforcement and modeling, cognitive theorists believe that all children pass through certain stages of development, and sex roles are developed through the "child's cognitive organization of his world along sex-role dimensions" (Kohlberg, 1966). Proposed by Kohlberg (1966, 1969), the cognitive-developmental theory of sex typing is linked to both the work of Piaget and the current stress on motives like exploration, curiosity, competence, and mastery. "The development of sex typing is conceived as an aspect of cognitive growth which involves basic, qualitative changes with age in the child's modes of thinking and concomitantly, in his perceptions of the physical and social world, including his sense of self, and of his sex role. Learning, particularly observational learning, plays some role in sex-role acquisition, but the most significant factor is the child's *cognitive activity*—his active selection and organization (structuring of his perceptions, knowledge and understanding)" (Mussen, 1969).

Sex typing begins with the labeling of the child "boy" or "girl" and with the child hearing and learning these labels. As has been mentioned earlier, children know their own sex labels as early as two years of age. As Kohlberg (1966) explains, the child's first conception of sex role originates from

important, "natural" components of patterning; i.e., aspects of sex-role attitudes which are universal across cultures and family structures and which appear relatively early in the child's development. This patterning of sex-role attitudes is essentially "cognitive" in that it is rooted in the child's conceptions of physical things, the bodies of himself and of others, as he relates body concepts to his conceptions of a social order which makes functional use of sex categories in quite culturally universal ways. Rather than biological instinct, it is the child's cognitive organization of social role concepts around universal physical dimensions that accounts for the existence of universals in sex-role attitudes.

Once the child learns her or his sex identification, it becomes the main determinant and organizer of the child's attitudes, values, interests, and activities. The sex identification of the child becomes stabilized in the fifth or sixth year and is "maintained by a motivated adaptation to physical-social reality and by the need to preserve a stable and positive self-image" (Kohlberg, 1966). Mussen (1969) effectively outlines Kohlberg's five mechanisms by which sex role concepts become converted into masculine-feminine values:

1. The first, an expression of Piaget's notion of *assimilation,* is the child's "tendency to respond to new activities and interests that are consistent with old ones.". . . By the age of two, there are clear-cut sex differences in interests, activities, and personality characteristics. New objects or activities consistent with established interests and preferences are assimilated, while discrepant ones are not.
2. Children make value judgments consistent with their self-concepts of sex role. The three-year-old has a "naive or egocentric tendency to value anything associated with or like himself" as best, and hence values and seeks objects and activities that are representative of his own sex.
3. Young children tend to associate positive, self-enhancing values with sex-role stereotypes and these values are motivating. For example, masculinity is associated with values of strength, competence, and power, and for the boy, acquiring this stereotype produces a motivation to enact a masculine role, to conform to the stereotype. According to Kohlberg, this is true regardless of the rewards associated with the role.
4. The child perceives his gender role as normative and hence generates judgments that conformity is morally right and deviations are morally wrong.
5. Modeling or identification is the fifth mechanism, but Kohlberg's analysis of the process is strikingly different from the psychoanalytic or learning interpretations discussed earlier. Sex typing is not conceived as a *product* of identification; quite contrary, identification is a consequence of sex typing. Boys model themselves after males because they already have masculine interests and values; "for the boy with masculine interests and values, the activities of a male model are more interesting and hence more modeled.". . .

While the cognitive-developmental theory of sex typing and sex role development has not been fully tested, it shows promise for explaining questions and problems neglected by other theories. As Lewis and Weinraub (1974) conclude in their brief review of the theoretical positions used to discuss the etiology of sex differences.

We feel that the cognitive view of sex differences in infancy has, in fact, some support. At leat the notion of gender saliency should be carefully considered. We are discovering that the infant is a more sophisticated information-seeking and information-processing organism than we have imagined. We should not be misled into believing that its intellectual capacities all await the display of language.

Each of the theories on sex role development and sex typing—identification, social-learning theory, and cognitive-developmental theory—gives us some good ideas of how sex typing and sex role acquisition occur in general, but no one theory by itself can explain every aspect of this complex process for every individual.

No two individuals develop in precisely the same way. And whatever the outcome or end result, the social-learning theorist would point to the rewards and punishments experienced by the child, the identification theorist would look to see which parent the child resembled most, and the cognitive theorist would assess the child's mental processes and ways of assimilating information. All are valuable approaches. Thus, the student, theorist, and practitioner gain a more comprehensive understanding of sex-role development by combining the elements of all three approaches.

Regardless of theoretical approach, research has shown that sex-role development begins early in the life of the child and the child's environment is filled with sex role messages. Much of the research focuses on the child-parent relationship and the parents' attitudes and values regarding sex roles. The remainder of this chapter discusses the parents and television as two early sources of socialization of sex roles. Other sources, such as peers, teachers, counselors, and other adults, picture books, teaching materials, and the like are discussed in chapters that follow.

Some Early Sources of Socialization

Parents

As Elkin (1960) says, "Many agencies share in teaching a child the expected behavior of his sex, but the family is pre-eminent." And parents seem to sex type their infants at birth. Within twenty-four hours of the birth of their first baby, thirty sets of parents (fifteen of girls and fifteen of boys) were asked by Rubin, Provenzano and Luria (1974) to describe their baby as they would to a close relative or friend. The infants did not differ in their average birth weight, length, or characteristics of good health and normalcy, yet they were differentially perceived and described. Both fathers and mothers described their daughters as soft, small, delicate, beautiful, and weak, while sons were described as larger featured, better coordinated, more alert, firmer, stronger, and hardier than the girl infants.

In a study by Will and associates (1976) a six-month-old boy was dressed as a girl and presented to some mothers under the name of "Beth" and was later dressed as a boy and presented to other mothers as "Adam." The mothers were directed to hold the infant and play with her or him for several minutes. During the experiment, the mothers handed a train more often to "Adam" and a doll more often to "Beth"; they also smiled more often when they believed they were holding a female. All of the mothers had small children of both sexes of their own, and had reported earlier that they perceived no differences in the behaviors of female and male infants, and that they encouraged doll play with their own sons and roughouse play with their daughters. Yet in the experimental situation, they were unaware of their stereotypic treatment of the infants.

Consciously, or unconsciously, parents supply their children with sex stereotypic toys and encourage sex stereotypic play activity. But girls are granted a wider choice of toys and play activities than the boys, as parents seem to tolerate girls playing with boys' toys but strongly discourage boys from playing with girls toys or doing "girlish" things (Fling and Manosevitz, 1972; Lansky, 1967).

Studies of the interaction between parent and infant also show some differential treatment on the basis of sex. Moss (1967) observed that mothers with infants at three weeks and three months old were consistently reinforcing "appropriate" behavior. He found that mothers talk to boy infants less after the first three months, and they talk to girl infants more and more often after this three-month period. Based on his observations, Moss (1967) tentatively suggested that parents selectively encouraged patterns leading to aggression in boys and verbal ability in girls. Similarly, Kagan and Lewis (1965) found that mothers of six-month-old girl babies talked to, touched, and handled their daughters more often than did mothers of the same age infant boys. In observing the same children when they were thirteen months old, Goldberg and Lewis (1969) found that the girls clung to, looked at, and talked to their mothers more often than the boys. The authors link the behavioral differences to the differential treatment by the mother when the babies were younger.

According to Bronfenbrenner (1961) different methods of child training are used for girls and boys, with boys more often being subjected to physical punishment and girls more often being subjected to psychological punishment, such as the threat of withdrawal of love. These different methods of child training have been found to differentially influence self-reliance and independence. Children trained with psychological punishment have been shown to be typically more obedient and dependent, while those trained with physical punishment are usually more self-reliant and independent (Bronfenbrenner, 1961; Schachter, 1959). The two methods of training and their supposed causal relationship with personality traits definitely fit sex role stereotyped characteristics of women and men.

While data are diverse when it comes to the question of which parent plays the greater role in influencing sex role stereotypic behavior and attitudes in children, several studies point to the father.

A study by Fagot (1973) showed that the father appears to be the one who holds the more definite opinions about sex stereotypes. She presented a list of thirty-eight behaviors to fathers and mothers of two-year-olds and asked them to rate the behaviors as masculine or feminine. For example, all of the fathers considered playing roughhouse to be a masculine activity and playing with dolls to be feminine. All of the mothers did not agree with this stereotyping of activities; many of them viewed the activities as common to both girls and boys.

Another differential treatment by fathers was found by Rebelsky and Hanks (1971). In observing the times fathers engaged in caretaking (feeding, diapering) and in noncaretaking activities, they found that 62 percent of the father's interactions with girl babies occurs during caretaking activities and 38 percent occurs during noncaretaking. With boy babies the father's interaction pattern is reversed; 34 percent of the interaction occurs during caretaking and 66 percent during noncaretaking. The investigators suggest that fathers relate caretaking to "mothering" and may feel that it is worse for a man to mother a male than a female.

A study by Margolin and Patterson (1975) showed that fathers gave twice as many positive responses (approval, attention, compliance, laugh, play, talk, and touch) to their sons as to their daughters, whereas mothers gave nearly the same number of positive responses to their daughters and sons. In another study regarding parental praise, Fagot (1974) found that mothers gave more praise than fathers, and both parents gave girls more praise as well as more criticism. They also found that parents joined boy's play more actively than they joined girl's play. The Fagot (1974) study also showed that mothers physically punished their children of both sexes more than fathers. The different findings of the two studies may be due in part to the ages of the children. In the Fagot (1974) study the children were toddlers, while in the Margolin and Patterson (1975) study the ages of the children observed ranged between five and eight years.

While many studies show that parents think of their sons and daughters in stereotypic ways and treat them accordingly, not all research shows differential parental treatment of girls and boys. After reviewing the research literature, Maccoby and Jacklin (1974) conclude that parents generally treat boys and girls similarly. However, boys tend to receive more intense and directive interactions from parents than girls. Boys receive more criticism, but also more direct praise and encouragement, while girls are given more generalized approval. Thus, knowingly or unknowingly, parents encourage "sex-appropriate" behavior, and children respond to this encouragement.

Television   Another influential source of sex role socialization for young children is television since they spend so much time watching it. In a national sample of television viewers, Gerbner and Gross (1976) found that half of the twelve-year-olds in this country watch an average of six or more hours each day. Parents of younger children tend to rely on television to entertain them while they go about their household chores. What are the messages children get from television about sex roles? In an analysis of ten popular children's programs during the 1971–72 season, Sternglanz and Serbin (1974) found that males were depicted as aggressive, constructive, helpful, and were rewarded for their actions. Females on the other hand were shown as differential, passive, and sometimes punished for being too active. When they did have an impact on the course of events, they usually used magic. Four of the five female title-role stars were witches of some sort.

The popular children's TV program "Sesame Street," which has succeeded so well in avoiding racial stereotypes has been criticized for maintaining sex role stereotypes. In commenting on the show's depiction of "appropriate" work for men and women, Gardner (1970) says:

On one program, Big Bird (having said that he would like to be a member of a family and having been told that Gordon and Susan would be his family) is told that he will have to help with the work and that since he is a boy bird, he will have to do men's work—the heavy work, the "important" work and also that he should get a girl (bird) to help Susan with *her* work arranging flowers, redecorating, etc. There was more and virtually all of it emphasized that there is men's work and then there is women's work—that men's work is outside the home and women's work is in the home. (This in spite of the fact that 17 *million* children under eighteen have mothers who are employed outside the home; of these 4.5 million are under six.)

Prime time TV programs also show men and women in stereotyped roles. Three-fourths of the leading characters are male (Women on Words and Images, 1975), and adventure shows depict men as freewheeling cowboys, cops and secret agents, while the women are interested in romance, their families, and the welfare of their boss. Mary Tyler Moore was one of the few women to hold a responsible job and who was not portrayed as dumb. More recently, Charlie's Angels, Police Woman, Wonder Woman, and the Bionic Woman have helped balance the statistics somewhat. However, they still take orders from a man, are often bailed out of trouble by a man, or succeed because of supernatural powers. In addition the TV heroines are beautiful, slender, and young, while the heroes may be bald (Kojak), fat (Cannon), old (Barnaby Jones), or paralyzed (Ironside).

In comedy series, men and women appear in almost equal numbers, and men as well as women are depicted as dingbats. "In fact, often it is the wives who are wise, witty, and patient, and who end up deflating their husbands' puffed-up egos. Possibly men get their comeuppance in situation comedies because sitcoms ridicule everybody, or because the family is the female's domain and the male role at home is ambiguous and changing, an easy target" (Tavis and Offir, 1977).

Commercials also show men and women in stereotyped roles. Chafetz (1974) reported a study of 100 TV commercials aired during children's shows in February, 1971. The majority of the narrators (seventy-nine of eighty-three) were male. Men were more physically active than women and were portrayed in provider roles. Women were shown as economically dependent and responding to social pressure. In husband-wife relationships, "the male was invariably pictured as independent and intelligent. He almost always had the competitive drive, the self-confidence, and the judgment necessary to control the life of his mate. The female, however, submits to the male authority and assumes a dependent posture." When pictured as parents, the mother usually stayed at home watching the younger children, while the father took the older children outside to play. More recently commercials have started to break away from these stereotypes, showing men who cook and women who work outside the home and girls who play baseball. But overall, commercials do not show either sex as especially likable or intelligent.

Conclusion The process of sex role acquisition and sex role development is complex. Sex "appropriate" behavior and attitudes appear to be learned early in life, long before a child enters school. While there are many assumptions about how this process occurs, no one has all the answers. Three prominent theories of sex role development have been presented—identification, social-learning theory, and cognitive-developmental theory. Each contribute to the understanding of sex role acquisition, but none is able to account for all of the observed phenomena and data on sex typing. Thus, a comprehensive theory of sex role development must include aspects of all three theories and perhaps some concepts not yet thought of.

While there are many sources of socialization in a child's environment, two—parents and television—were discussed here because of their salience in the child's preschool years. Other sources of sex role socialization, such as peers, teachers and other adults, books and instructional materials, and the like, are discussed in subsequent chapters.

References   Aberle, D., and Naegele, K. Middle class father's occupational role and attitudes toward children. In N. W. Bell and E. F. Vogel (eds.), *The family.* New York: Free Press, 1968.

Bandura, A., and Huston, A. C. Identification as a process of incidental learning. *Journal of Abnormal and Social Psychology,* 1961, *63,* 311–318.

Bandura, A.; Ross, D.; and Ross, S. A. A comparative test of the status envy, social power, and secondary reinforcement theories of identification learning. *Journal of Abnormal and Social Psychology,* 1963, *67,* 527–534.

Bandura, A., and Walters, R. H. *Social learning and personality development.* New York: Holt, Rinehart & Winston, 1963.

Bieber, I.; Dain, H. J.; Dince, P. R.; Dreblich, M. G.; Grand, H. G.; Gundlach, R. H.; Kremer, M. W.; Rifkin, A. H.; Wilbur, C. B.; and Bieber, T. B. *Homosexuality.* New York: Basic Books, 1962.

Bronfenbrenner, U. The changing American child: A speculative analysis. *Merrill-Palmer Quarterly,* 1961, *7,* 73–83, 9.

Broverman, I. K.; Vogel, S. R.; Broverman, D. M.; Clarkson, F. E.; and Rosenkrantz, P. S. Sex-role stereotypes: A current appraisal. *Journal of Social Issues,* 1972, 28, *2,* 59–78.

Brown, D. G. Masculinity-femininity development in children. *Journal of Consulting Psychology,* 1957, *21,* 197–202.

Canavan, P., and Haskell, J. The great american male stereotype. In C. G. Carney and S. L. McMahon (eds.) *Exploring contemporary male/female roles.* La Jolla, Calif.: University Associates, Inc., 1977.

Chafetz, J. S. *Masculine/feminine or human? An overview of the sociology of sex roles.* Itasca, Ill.: F. E. Peacock Publishers, 1974.

Chang, J., and Block, J. A study of identification in male homosexuals. *Journal of Consulting Psychology,* 1960, *24,* 307–310.

Elkin, F. *The child and society.* New York: Random House, 1960.

Fagot, B. I. Sex differences in toddlers' behavior and parental reaction. *Developmental Psychology,* 1974, *10,* 554–558.

Fagot, B. I. Sex-related stereotyping of toddlers' behavior. *Developmental Psychology,* 1973, *9,* 429.

Fling, S., and Manosevitz, M. Sex typing in nursery school children's play interests. *Developmental Psychology,* 1972, *7,* 146–152.

Freud, S. *Group psychology and the analysis of the ego.* London: Hogarth Press, 1921.

Gardner, J. A. "Sesame Street" and sex role stereotypes. *Women,* Spring 1970, 1, 3.

Gerbner, G., and Gross, L. The scary world of TV's heavy viewer. *Psychology Today,* April, 1976, *9,* 41–45.

Goldberg, S., and Lewis, M. Play behavior in the year-old infant; early sex differences. *Child Development,* 1969, *40,* 21–30.

Hartup, W. W., and Zook, E. A. Sex-role preferences in three- and four-year-old children. *Journal of Consulting Psychology,* 1960, *24,* 420–426.

Kagan, J. Acquisition and significance of sex typing and sex role identity. In L. W. Hoffman and M. L. Hoffman (eds.), *Review of child development research,* Vol. I. New York: Russell Sage Foundation, 1964.

Kagan, J., and Lewis, M. Studies of attention in the human infant. *Merrill-Palmer Quarterly,* 1965, *2,* 95–127.

Kagan, J., and Moss, H. A. *Birth to maturity.* New York: Wiley, 1962.

Keller, S. The female role: Constants and change. In V. Franks and V. Burtle (eds.) *Women in therapy.* New York: Brunner/Mazel, 1974.

Kohlberg, L. A cognitive-developmental analysis of children's sex-role concepts and attitudes. In E. Maccoby (ed.), *The development of sex differences.* Stanford, California: Stanford University Press, 1966.

Kohlberg, L. Stage and sequence: The cognitive-developmental approach to socialization. In D. A. Goslin (ed.), *Handbook of socialization theory and research.* Chicago: Rand McNally, 1969.

Kohn, M. L. Social class and parental values. *American Journal of Sociology,* January 1959, *64,* 337–351.

Ladner, J. A. *Tomorrow's tomorrow: The black woman.* New York: Doubleday, 1971.

Lansky, L. M. The family structure also affects the model: Sex-role attitudes in parents of preschool children. *Merrill-Palmer Quarterly,* 1967, *13,* 139–150.

Lewis, M., and Weinraub, M. Sex of parent x sex of child: Socioemotional development. In R. Friedman and Vande Wide (eds.), *Sex differences in behavior.* New York: John Wiley, 1974.

Linton, R. *The cultural background of personality.* New York: Appleton-Century-Crofts, 1945.

Maccoby, E., and Jacklin, C. N. *The psychology of sex differences.* Palo Alto, California: Stanford University Press, 1974.

Margolin, G., and Patterson, G. Differential consequences provided by mothers and fathers for their sons and daughters. *Developmental Psychology,* 1975, *11,* 537–538.

Mead, M. *Sex and temperament in three primitive societies.* New York: Morrow, 1935.

Mischel, W. A social learning view of sex differences in behavior. In E. Maccoby (ed.), *The development of sex differences.* Stanford, California: Stanford University Press, 1966.

Mischel, W., and Grusec, J. Determinants of the rehearsal and transmission of neutral and aversive behaviors. *Journal of Personality and Social Psychology,* 1966, *3,* 197–205.

Money, J. *Sex research: New developments.* New York: Holt, Rinehart, & Winston, 1965.

Moss, H. A. Sex, age, and state as determinants of mother-infant interaction. *Merrill-Palmer Quarterly,* 1967, 13, *1,* 19–36.

Mowrer, O. H. *Learning theory and personality dynamics.* New York: Ronald Press, 1950.

Mussen, P. H. Early sex-role development. In D. A. Goslin (ed.), *Handbook of socialization theory and research.* Chicago: Rand McNally, 1969.

Mussen, P. H.; Conger, J. U.; and Kagan, J. *Child development and personality,* 2nd ed. New York: Harper and Row, 1963.

Rabban, M. Sex-role identification in young children in two diverse social groups. *Genetic Psychology Monographs,* 1950, *42,* 81–158.

Rebelsky, F., and Hanks, C. Fathers' verbal interaction with infants in the first three months of life. *Child Development,* 1971, *42,* 63–68.

Reeves, N. *Womankind.* New York: Aldinee-Atherton, 1971.

Rubin, J.; Provenzano, F.; and Luria, Z. The eye of the beholder: Parents' views on sex of newborns. *American Journal of Orthopsychiatry,* 1974, *44,* 512–519.

Schachter, S. *The psychology of affiliation.* Stanford, California: Stanford University Press, 1959.

Sears, R. R. Development of gender roles. In F. A. Beach (ed.), *Sex and behavior.* New York: Wiley, 1965.

Sears, R. R.; Maccoby, E.; and Levin. *Patterns of child rearing.* Evanston, Ill.: Row, Peterson, 1957.

Sears, R. R.; Rau, L.; and Alpert, R. *Identification and child rearing.* Stanford, California: Stanford University Press, 1965.

Sternglanz, S. H., and Serbin, L. A. Sex role stereotyping in children's television programs. *Developmental Psychology,* 1974, *10,* 710-715.

Tangri, S. S. Determinants of occupational role innovation among college women. *Journal of Social Issues,* 28, *2,* 177-199.

Tavis, C., and Offir, C. *The longest war; Sex differences in perspective.* New York: Harcourt Brace Jovanovich, 1977.

Will, J. A.; Self, P. A.; and Datan, N. Maternal behavior and perceived sex of infant. *American Journal of Orthopsychiatry,* 1976, 46, *1,* 135-139.

Women on Words and Images. *Channeling children: Sex stereotyping on prime time TV.* Princeton, N.J.: Women on Words and Images, 1975.

2 Sex Typing and Judgments of Mental Health

The Double Standard of Mental Health

During the nineteenth century, mental disorder was considered sex related (Veith, 1965). Even in the early part of this century, for example, hysteria was thought to affect women almost exclusively, while hypochondriasis affected men almost exclusively. Today neither condition is considered sex related. There is, however, a growing concern that a double standard of mental health exists—that the therapist's view of health is different for men and women and that these differences parallel stereotypic sex differences assumed by society. Along with this concern about a double standard of mental health, Freud has been focused on as a primary influence in helping establish and perpetuate present-day stereotyped sex roles. His early ideas about the female role and his view of the psychology of women in general are thought by his many critics to have affected women, and especially women patients, very negatively (Bengis, 1972; Chisler, 1972; Cummings, 1972; Gilman, 1971; Green, 1970; Roche Report, 1971; Roipke, 1973; Stevens, 1971; West, 1972). As Figes (1970) states:

Of all the factors that have served to perpetuate a male-oriented society, that have hindered the free development of women as human beings in the Western world today, the emergence of Freudian psychoanalysis has been the most serious. . . . Psychoanalysis, whatever individual therapists may say, does tend to encourage conformity which may amount to something like brainwashing.

Some of the most frequently quoted statements of Freud and other psychoanalysts which imply a double standard of mental health are these:

Sigmund Freud (1956):
[Women] refuse to accept the fact of being castrated and have the hope of someday obtaining a penis in spite of everything. . . . I cannot escape the notion (though I hesitate to give it expression) that for woman the level of what is ethically normal is different from what it is in man. We must not allow ourselves to be deflected from such conclusions by the denials of the feminists who are anxious to force us to regard the two sexes as completely equal in position and worth.

Carl G. Jung (1928):

But no one can evade the fact, that in taking up a masculine calling, studying, and working in a man's way, woman is doing something not wholly in agreement with, if not directly injurious to, her feminine nature. . . . [Female] psychology is founded on the principle of Eros, the great binder and deliverer; while age-old wisdom has ascribed Logos to man and his ruling principle.

Joseph Rheingold (1964):

. . . woman is nurturance . . . anatomy decrees the life of a woman. . . . When women grow up without dread of their biological functions and without subversion by feminist doctrines and therefore enter upon motherhood with a sense of fulfill-ment and altruistic sentiment we shall attain the goal of a good life and a secure world in which to live.

Eric Erickson (1965):

For the student of development and practitioner of psychoanalysis, the stage of life crucial for the understanding of womanhood is the step from youth to maturity, the state when the young woman relinquishes the care received from the parental family and the extended care of institutions of education, in order to commit herself to the love of a stranger and to the care to be given to his or her offspring . . . young women often ask whether they can "have an identity" before they know whom they will marry and for whom they will make a home. Granted that something in the young woman's identity must keep itself open for the peculiarities of the man to be joined and of the children to be brought up, I think that much of a young woman's identity is already defined in her kind of attractiveness and in the selectivity of her search for the man (or men) by whom she wishes to be sought.

Bruno Bettelheim (1965):

. . . as much as women want to be good scientists and engineers, they want first and foremost, to be womanly companions of men and to be mothers.

In defense of Freud and his followers, feminist Juliet Mitchell (1974) argues that a full understanding of his total work and life, rather than popularized Freudianism, is necessary "for challenging the oppression of women. . . . However it may have been used, psychoanalysis is not a recommendation for a patriarchal society, but an analysis of one." Be that as it may, too few people (including therapists, it seems) have a full understanding of Freud, and such terms as "penis envy," "anatomy is destiny," "castrating female," and the like are used commonly in reference to the lower status of women when compared to men. And certainly, opinions regarding the inequality of women and men, such as those expressed by the above theorists, are congruent with the limiting sex role stereotypes and behavior believed to be appropriate by our larger society as discussed in chapter 1.

But few psychoanalysts today would consider themselves true Freudians, holding to every tenet of his theories. Indeed, many theorists and clinicians critical of Freud argue sex differences are largely sociological. I have selected three theorists—an earlier one,

Karen Horney, and two present-day ones, David Cooper and Harvey Kaye—to discuss here.

Horney, in rebuttal to Freud, emphasized "the actual subordination of women," or the real disadvantages endured by women as they are usually economically dependent on men and psychologically dependent on the family for their self-esteem and fulfillment. While she does not deny that anatomical differences have psychological consequences, she felt the social facts regarding the status of women must be considered in order for there to be a complete psychology of women and psychoanalysis which is more than an ideology which reinforces the existing patriarchal establishment. In her 1935 paper entitled, "The Problem of Feminine Masochism" (*Feminine Psychology,* 1970), she states:

> . . . there may appear certain fixed ideologies concerning the "nature" of woman; such as doctrines that woman is innately weak, emotional, enjoys dependence, is limited in capacities for independent work and autonomous thinking. One is tempted to include in this category the psychoanalytic belief woman is masochistic by nature. It is fairly obvious that these ideologies function not only to reconcile women to their subordinate role by presenting it as an unalterable one, but also to plant the belief that it represents a fulfillment they crave, or an ideal for which it is commendable and desirable to strive. The influence that these ideologies exert on women is materially strengthened by the fact that women presenting the specified traits are more frequently chosen by men.

Cooper (1970) is another theoretician who recognizes the effects of female socialization. In his book, *The Death of the Family,* he states:

> A little girl, before she can be her own baby is plied with object-babies, so that she can learn to forget her experiences of birth and childhood and become not her own child but childlike; so that if later in life, she wants to return to this area, she can become childish, . . . she was educated to be a mother like her mother, like all other mothers who are educated not to be themselves but to be "like mothers."

In his cleverly and humorously written *Male Survival: Masculinity without Myth* (1974), Kaye calls Freud "one of the few authentic geniuses of the past century" but "being human, Freud was not infallible." In generalizing from his patients who were "nurtured in an oppressive Victorian-like atmosphere, and were largely suffering from hysteria and pseudo-hysterical illnesses," Freud assumed all women were "fated to strive hopelessly for a penis of their own." According to Kaye, the concept of male superiority has developed into a full-blown "masculine mystique," and "the mystique, never turning down a succulent plum, has heralded this dictum as a scientific verification for its grandiose pretensions." The "Masculine Mystique" is a combination of quasi-mystical attitudes and expectations of society regarding the male which begin at birth:

A cursory examination of the pubic area reveals the presence of a penis, and the exhausted mother and nail-biting father are informed that they have a son. From that moment, the cultural indoctrination begins.

The blue blanket, the miniature boxing gloves, the blue Superman tights with accompanying cape, subtly inform this newly-hatched amorphous bit of protoplasm of the great and impossible expectations which constitute the essence of his recently acquired humanity. He is to become the embodiment of heroism and courage, and aggressivity and aptitude, an amalgamation of the fantasies of Hemingway and Mailer. The roughhouse play with adults, the injunction that "little boys don't cry," and "did you win?" when he returns home after his first pugilistic encounter with the boy next door, nose bloodied and tears only barely contained: the message is received, the boy is trained to be a "man." Vulnerability is a vice, emotionality is odious, and stoicism connotes strength.

Unconscious conspirators, parents, and society weave the Mystique into the psyche of the developing boy.

Throughout his book, Kaye discussed the problems caused by this "Masculine Mystique" and states at the end that it "should be regarded as a dysfunctional and distorted vestige, a collective remnant of social exigencies which have outlined their utility."

Having taken a brief look at a theoretical basis for what has been called the double standard of mental health, I now turn to a discussion of the attitudes of clinicians—those practicing psychotherapy.

In a study conducted by Neulinger (1968), psychiatrists, psychologists, and social workers were asked to rank twenty paragraphs according to how descriptive they were of a mentally healthy male and again for a mentally healthy female. The results showed that while the two rankings were highly correlated, there were significant differences in the mean rankings of male and female on eighteen of the twenty paragraphs. For example, characteristics such as sentience, nurturance, play, succorance, deference, and abasement were rated higher for the mentally healthy female; and dominance, achievement, autonomy, counteraction, and aggression were rated higher for the mentally healthy male. In interpreting his findings, Neulinger states that "the sex orientation of this society is not only shared, but also promoted by its clinical personnel."

Clearly the best known and most frequently quoted study regarding sex role stereotypes and clinicians' judgments of mental health is the one by Broverman and associates (1970). In this study, seventy-nine practicing clinicians—clinical psychologists, psychiatrists, and psychiatric social workers—including forty-six men and thirty-three women, were sent a set of 122 bipolar adjectives describing behavior traits or characteristics such as: "very aggressive . . . not at all aggressive" and "doesn't hide emotions . . . always hides emotions." The clinicians were divided into three groups. One group was asked to "think of normal adult men, and then indicate on each item that pole to which a mature, healthy, socially competent adult man would be closer." One group was asked to do the same for a "mature, healthy, socially competent adult woman"; and the third group was asked to do the same for a "healthy, mature, socially competent person," sex unspecified. The results of the study showed that men and women clinicians did not differ from each other in their descriptions of men, women, and adults, sex unspecified. However, while the concepts of the mature, healthy man were not different from the mature, healthy adult, the clinicians were significantly less likely to ascribe to healthy women the same traits and characteristics they ascribed to the healthy adult. In effect the clinicians viewed healthy women as different from healthy men by being more submissive, less independent, less adventurous, less objective, more easily influenced, less aggressive, less competitive, more excitable in minor crises, more emotional, more conceited about appearance, and having their feelings hurt more easily. Broverman and associates thus confirmed their hypothesis that a double standard of health exists for men and women. The general standard of health for adults is actually applied only to men, while women are viewed as significantly less healthy. The authors note that such a double standard places women in a difficult position:

Acceptance of an adjustment notion of health, then, places women in the conflictual position of having to decide whether to exhibit those positive characteristics considered desirable for men and adults, and thus have their "feminity" questioned, that is, be deviant in terms of being a woman; or to behave in the prescribed feminine manner, accept second-class adult status, and possibly live a lie to boot.

The Broverman et al. article ends with this observation: "The cause of mental health may be better served if both men and women are encouraged to a maximum realization of individual potential, rather than to an adjustment to existing restrictive sex roles."

In summarizing the Broverman et al. work and concluding from her own research and clinical work, Chesler (1971) makes the following observations:

1. For a number of reasons, women "go crazy" more often than men, and this craziness is more likely to be self destructive than other destructive. . . .

2. Most female "neuroses" are a result of societal demands and discrimination rather than the supposed mental illness of the individual. . . .
3. The therapist-patient relationship reinforces a system of beliefs and attitudes that is psychologically damaging to the patient and psychologically rewarding to the doctors. . . .

In another study Abramowitz et al. (1973) gave clinicians a psychological and educational history of college students and were asked to make a judgment of mental health of the subject. The case histories were identical except for sex of subject (identified as either John or Joan) and political orientation (left or right politically active). The results showed the clinicians viewed the left-involved female as significantly more maladjusted than her male counterpart, and their verdicts for her were more severe than for the conservative youth of either sex.

Fabrikant (1974) reports some studies he did with his research associates which are essentially replications of the Broverman work with more focus on the background, training, and attitudes of the therapist. When therapists were asked to respond to an adjective checklist describing sex role characteristics as applied to either men or women, the traits they ascribed to each sex are comparable to the lists found in earlier studies. For example, there was statistically significant agreement between the female and male therapists in describing men as aggressive, assertive, bold, breadwinner, chivalrous, crude, independent, and virile; and women as decorative, dependent, domestic, fearful, flighty, fragile, generous, irrational, maturing, overemotional, passive subordinate, temperamental, and virtuous.

However, in responding to specific questions, the psychotherapists indicated a somewhat more liberal view (and seemingly contradictory to their response on the adjective checklist) than those reported in earlier studies. For example, there was agreement among male and female therapists that:

1. Women need not be married to have a full life.
2. Marriage should be run as a co-equal partnership.
3. Women cannot be completely satisfied or fulfilled in only the wife/mother role.
4. Women's sexual satisfaction is a necessary part of marriage. . . .
5. A woman can experience a fulfilling sexual relationship with someone other than her husband.
6. A woman should exercise the freedom to choose life roles other than those of marriage and a family.

In discussing the results of his studies, Fabrikant admits they are complex, confusing, and often contradictory. While therapists still stereotypically view male characteristics or traits as positive and female traits as negative, they show a tempering of the magnitude of sex bias in responding to specific sex role questions. Based on this Fabrikant feels that ". . . the reported strongly negative feelings against current psychoanalytic therapists as perpetuators of male chauvinism are open to question." He states that the majority of the therapists he studied consider themselves analytically oriented, causing Fabrikant to hypothesize that ". . . it may be that the younger male or female analytic therapist is not as tradition-bound as has been so forcibly stated in the feminist literature."

Another replication of the Broverman et al. study was done by Maslin and Davis (1975) with counselors-in-training rather than practicing therapists. Of the ninety counselors-in-training studied there was an equal number of males and females, with twenty-two at the doctoral level and sixty-eight at the master's level of training. Like the earlier studies, both the males and females agreed that healthy males had the same stereotypic characteristics as healthy adults, sex unspecified. Unlike the earlier studies, however, the female counselors-in-training viewed a healthy female as having approximately the same traits as a healthy adult or healthy male. The male counselor-in-training viewed the healthy female as generally not having the same characteristics as the healthy male and healthy adult. In their discussion of the results, Maslin and Davis suggest that an explanation for the difference between their findings and those of earlier studies might be the time which has elapsed between the studies and the impact of the feminist movement on perceptions held by women today of the healthy female.

In a review of her extensive program of research regarding the female role, Steinmann (1974) reports discrepancies in male-female role expectancies for professional men and women in psychology. The findings of her studies relevant to our discussion here show that male psychologists view the ideal woman as more self-oriented than the women professionals in psychology predicted they would, but less self-oriented than the female psychologists viewed themselves and their ideal woman.

The instrument used was the MAFERR Inventory of Feminine Values, consisting of thirty-four statements expressing particular values or value judgments related to women's activities and satisfactions. Half of the items delineate a family-oriented woman who sees her family responsibilities as taking precedence over any potential personal occupational activity and who ranks her own satisfaction as second to those of her husband and family. Examples of such items are: "I believe the personal ambitions of a woman should be subordinated to the family as a group," and "I will have achieved the main goal of my life if I rear normal, well-adjusted children." The other half of the items depict a self-achieving woman who sees her own satisfactions as equally as important to those of husband and family, and who desires to have opportunities to utilize her abilities and talents. "I would like to create or accomplish something which would be recognized by everybody," and "I would rather not marry than sacrifice some of my essential beliefs and needs in order to adjust to another person" are examples of this type of item.

The fifty-four female subjects of this investigation were feminist women members of an association for women in the field of psychology. They were asked to fill out three forms of the MAFERR Inventory: one on their own self concept, one on their concept of the ideal woman, and one on their concept of man's ideal woman. The fifty-one male psychologists were asked to respond to the items, first, as their ideal woman would, and then as they felt women's ideal woman would answer.

In summarizing her findings regarding the perceptions of male and female psychologists, Steinmann says:

Discrepancies in male-female role expectancies for professional men and women in psychology appear to run along the same lines as those of most men and women in our society, but this sample of male psychologists perceived their ideal woman as more self-achieving than the national composite of males. . . . So that while the present study supports earlier findings regarding female role perceptions among women in general, it also illustrates the severity of the conflict for these professional women. These women were acting in accord with their own activist ideas toward role behaviors, but not in accord with the familial orientation they perceived men to desire in women. And while the male psychologists stated that they wanted a self-achieving, creative woman, it is vital to underscore the fact that there exists a large discrepancy between the female psychologists' concept of women's active role, and the male's concept of women's active role.

Steinmann attributes such discrepancies in part to a failure in communication between men and women, and in the case of the sample of professional feminist women, their attitudes "may reflect the system's failure to fulfill the promises of women's education, which seem to assure the possibility of combining home and career."

In an article arguing that there is no clear evidence of sexism in therapy, Stricker (1977) criticizes the methodology used and assumptions made in much of the research done to date concerning the psychotherapeutic treatment of women. He then goes on to report the research findings of doctoral dissertation studies of two of his students.

In the first one (Maxfield, 1976), approximately 250 members of the American Psychological Association's Division of Psychotherapy were given the Rosenkrantz Stereotype Questionnaire and a set of specially constructed vignettes describing people at four levels of psychopathology as well as people with stereotypic male and female traits. The therapists were asked to respond to eleven questions regarding diagnostic and therapeutic implications for each of the vignettes.

Stricker reports that there were no differences between the responses of the male and female therapists in the Maxfield study. On the stereotype questionnaire, the means for healthy males and females were on the same side of the neutral point on over 90 percent of the items, "so that any differences were quantitative rather than qualitative." Regarding the vignette data, the only item differentiating males from females was one dealing with expected earning ability, and the therapists indicated that they expected men to earn more money than women. Stricker quotes Maxfield's conclusions:

The major implication of this study is that there is not an overall bias against women by either men or women psychotherapists. . . . Although the sex of the therapist and the sex of the patient may make a meaningful difference on an individual basis, there is no evidence of an across-the-board effect. The cry for feminist therapists and different treatment of women psychotherapy patients may have important political and social implications, but the result of this study would suggest that male patients need liberation as much or as little as female patients.

In the second doctoral dissertation study (Oppendisano-Reich, 1976) Stricker refers to, mental health professionals were given a series of vignettes of patients who differ in their symptoms, social class, race, and sex and were asked to make diagnostic and prognostic judgments. The investigator found many differences based on symptoms, some based on class, and no main effects of race or sex. Some interactions involving sex were found: the females were considered less mentally ill than the males by social workers and psychologists but not by psychiatrists; male professionals preferred treating female psychotics rather than male psychotics; and neurotic females were judged by psychiatrists as less likely to improve than neurotic males.

While these studies have import (as do all the others discussed in this chapter) for the serious question of whether or not there is a double standard of mental health, Stricker makes some of the same mistakes he criticizes in other authors; e.g., not presenting the data in "sufficient detail to allow for adequate evaluation and critique," and not seeming to apply the same standards of research methodology to the two doctoral dissertation studies as he does to the other studies he reviews.

Two surveys which polled members of professional associations in psychology and counselor education deserve mention here. In the first one, Bingham and House (1975) sent a questionnaire dealing with attitudes and facts regarding the occupational status and opportunities of women to 358 randomly selected members of the Association of Counselor Educators and Supervisors (ACES). With a 54 percent return, male counselors were found to be less well informed in general than female counselors, especially in areas such as the discrepancy between women's and men's salaries for similar work, the proportion of women working for income, and the ability of women to perform well as both homemaker and worker. On the other hand, female ACES members were found to have more unfavorable or stereotyped attitudes than male members. For example, the women more often felt that working women feel guilty and that no man prefers a female boss.

The other survey was conducted by the American Psychological Association's Task Force on Sex Bias and Sex-Role Stereotyping (1975). A sample of 2,000 female psychologists was asked to respond to an open-ended questionnaire regarding actual circumstances and incidents which illustrate sexism in psychotherapy with women. While only 16 percent of the sample returned the questionnaire, making it difficult to generalize the results, five areas of sexist behavior were identified as areas of common concern by those who responded. It was felt that sexism in psychotherapy exists as a result of psychotherapists (1) fostering traditional sex roles, primarily by emphasizing the role of wife and mother and de-emphasizing the rewards from a career, (2) having lower expectations for female clients and devaluing them, as shown through demeaning comments and the encouragement of dependency and passivity, (3) using psychoanalytic concepts, e.g., penis envy, in a sexist way, (4) viewing women as sex objects, and (5) sexually exploiting female clients.

While no single study reported here, or anywhere else for that matter, contains enough evidence to prove that sexism in therapy is widespread, it is the cumulative data provided by all the studies combined, as imperfect as they may be, which are alarming. Granted, this area of research is still in its infancy, and better designed studies need to be carried out with larger samples. But therapists, like everyone else, have been reared and educated in a society which has encouraged and perpetuated stereotyped roles for men and women. That mental health professionals have escaped this indoctrination or sexist attitudes is not likely. That their own attitudes and values affect their professional work with clients is likely.

Sex Differences in Mental Illness

National figures on mental illness can be considered only rough estimates due to the difficulties in collecting such data (see Chesler, 1972, for a full explanation of the difficulties), and the fact that many persons with mental and emotional problems do not seek professional help. The statistics which are available, however, show higher rates of psychiatric disturbance among women than men. Table 2-1, adopted from Gove and Tudor (1973) by Williams (1977), presents the proportions of males and females in various mental health facilities by diagnostic category of mental disorder.

The diagnostic categories of mental disorder in the table are based on the classification system devised by the American Psychiatric Association (1968) and are defined by Williams (1977) as follows:

Functional psychosis is a general term for serious mental disorders characterized by some degree of personality disorganization, loss of ability to evaluate reality, and inability to relate effectively to others. The term functional means that there is no known pathology of the central nervous system related to the psychosis. The most common of the functional psychosis is schizophrenia, whose outstanding characteristics are the affected person's disordered thought processes which sometimes make behavior and speech incomprehensible and the inability to express feelings and emotions appropriately.

The psychoneuroses are milder forms of mental disorder than the psychoses. Their chief characteristic is anxiety, either overtly manifested or concealed in other symptoms. Common neurosis symptoms include anxiety, irrational fears, obsessions and compulsions, and depressions without the disorganization of psychotic reactions. Many neurotics experience periods of impaired function owing to their symptoms, but many whose symptoms are milder continue to function adequately without treatment.

Psychophysiological and psychosomatic disorders are characterized by physical symptoms that appear to result from emotional tension or prolonged stress.

Table 2-1 Females Per 100 Males by Psychiatric Diagnosis and Facility*

| Diagnosis | Facility** | | |
	Mental Hospital	General Hospital	Outpatient Psychiatric Clinic
Functional Psychosis	110	144	121
Psychoneurosis	146	189	173
Transient Situational Disorder	81	162	163
Psychophysiological and Psychosomatic Disorder	100	169	135

*Adopted from Gove and Tudor (1973) by Williams (1977)
**Includes Veterans Administration, state, county, and private hospitals and clinics.

Events which affect the person psychologically lead to malfunction of body systems and actual tissue damage. Examples are gastrointestinal reactions such as duodenal ulcers, and respiratory reactions such as asthma. While these are not always caused by emotional stress, they are often exacerbated by it.

Transient situational disorders are acute symptom responses to an overwhelming stress situation where there is no underlying pathology. When the stress diminishes, the symptoms do also. This diagnosis is used with people of all ages, though unlike the others, it is more frequently used for children and adolescents. An example is an acute but transient depression brought about by loss of a loved one or a job.

As can be seen in table 2-1, women substantially outnumber men in all categories except for transient situational disorders and psychophysiological and psychosomatic disorders in mental hospitals.

Sex differences by specific type of mental disorder are more clearly seen in table 2-2. The incidence of all disorders are much higher in women than men, except for transient situational disorders in mental hospitals and alcohol addiction, alcohol intoxication, and drug addiction in all psychiatric settings—disorders which men are more likely to suffer from than women.

While literally hundreds of thousands of men and women are treated for mental disorders each year in mental hospitals, general hospitals, and outpatient psychiatric clinics, it is estimated that the majority of individuals receiving treatment for mental illness are treated by physicians in nonpsychiatric settings, and that approximately two of every three patients are female (Gove and Tudor, 1973).

Table 2-2 Admissions to Inpatient Psychiatric Facilities in the U.S.A. by Sex and Selected Diagnoses, for 1970

Selected Diagnosis	State & Co. Ment. Hosp. Number/100,000 same sex in the pop. of U.S.		Women/ 100 Men	Type of Facility General Hospital Number/100,000 same sex in the pop of U.S.		Women/ 100 Men	Community Ment. Hlth. Ctr. Number/100,000 same sex in the pop. of U.S.		Women/ 100 Men
	Women	Men		Women	Men		Women	Men	
Psychotic Depressive Disorder	3.55	2.05	198	2.95	1.49	228	11.50	5.07	260
Manic-Depressive Disorder	10.23	5.13	229	3.99	2.13	215	2.01	9.86	233
Psychoneurotic (Incl. Depr.)	20.78	14.36	166	18.66	11.90	180	123.35	95.24	149
Other and Undiagnosed Psychosis	2.59	1.52	196	1.59	.81	225	9.36	6.59	163
Schizophrenia	66.76	72.47	106	11.15	7.87	162	43.62	31.87	157
Transient Sit. Disorder	5.08	6.58	88	1.70	1.30	151	11.30	8.31	156
Alcohol Addiction	3.34	18.00	21	.64	1.94	38	2.73	8.44	37
Alcohol Intoxication	11.54	79.06	17	1.60	4.60	40	11.76	42.45	32
Drug Addiction	4.74	15.24	36	.61	1.21	57	4.13	7.90	60

Source: Howard, E. M. and Howard, J. L. Women in Institutions: Treatment in Prisons and Mental Hospitals. In Franks, V., and Burtle, V., eds., *Women in Therapy.* New York: Brunner/Mazel, 1974.

Though not defined as mental illness, a word should be said about suicide since suicide and attempted suicide clearly reflect severe personal distress. Persons suffering intolerable pressures of depression, anxiety, or psychotic distortions of reality often, in combination with severe environmental stress, may view suicide or attempted suicide as a solution to their problem. As with mental illness, there are marked differences in the suicide and attempted suicide rates of men and women. Women make about four times as many attempts to commit suicide, but men commit nearly three times as many suicides as women (Garai, 1970). While the rate of suicide among men has not increased in recent years, the rate for women has increased considerably. Congruent with stereotypic traits of men and women in our society, men are more likely to use violent methods like firearms and knives, while women use less aggressive methods like gas or pills. In addition, women are more likely to use suicide attempts to appeal to or manipulate others (Stengel, 1964).

Why the higher rate of mental illness in women? While no one has argued that genetic differences between men and women are a contributing factor, "the decline of estrogen premenstrually and during the climacterium seems to be related to mood changes as well as to somatic symptoms in some women, and the high incidence of depression, especially in older women, may reflect a contribution from this source" (Williams, 1977). However, as Williams explains, if depressive disorders in women were caused mainly by the involution of the ovarian function, the incidence would be much higher than it is.

Some theorists contend that the higher rates of psychiatric disturbance among women do not reflect real sex differences in freqency of disturbance but rather the reluctance of men to complain and admit to certain unpleasant sensations and feelings (Gurin et al., 1960; Phillips and Segal, 1969; and Cooperstock, 1971). Phillips and Segal suggest this reluctance among men could be due to the belief that it is "more culturally appropriate and acceptable for women to be more expressive about their difficulties." In explaining the results of studies which show that psychotherapeutic drugs are much more likely to be prescribed for women than for men, Cooperstock argues that "contemporary Western women are permitted greater freedom than men in expressing feelings, and that she feels freer to bring her perceived emotional problems to the attention of a physician." Certainly it is acceptable for women in our society to admit weaknesses, ask for help, and to express grief, pain, sorrow, concern, joy, excitement, and a whole host of emotions while men are expected to be more stoic and approach difficult situations with an objective, problem-solving orientation. As Kagan (1972) explains, "take it like a man" means don't cry, but *do* something about the situation; doing something about it, the issuance of an instrumental response, is one way to handle feelings, especially fear and anxiety.

Another sociological explanation for the differences in mental health between women and men having to do with sex differentiated socialization practices and stereotypic sex roles focuses on marital status. After an extensive analysis of studies dealing with the relationship between sex, marital status, and mental illness in industrial societies since World War II, Gove (1972a) noted that ". . . it is the relatively high rates of mental illness in married women that account for the higher rates of mental illness among women." In summarizing his findings on marital status, sex, and mental health, Gove (1972b) states:

Married women do tend to have much higher rates of mental illness than married men. But when single men are compared with single women, divorced men and divorced women, and widowed men with widowed women it is found that these women do not tend to have higher rates than their male counterparts. In fact, if there is a difference, it appears to be that women in these categories tend to have lower rates. The data thus suggest that the role explanation accounts for the differences between the sexes.

In summary, the married of both sexes have lower rates of mental illness than the unmarried. This relationship would appear to be due to both the nature of the roles of the married and the unmarried and to selective processes which kept unstable persons from marrying. When we look at the differences between the sexes it appears that, at least in terms of mental illness, being married is considerably more advantageous to men than it is to women, while being single is, if anything, slightly more disadvantageous to men than to women.

As early as 1942, Jessie Bernard proposed what she termed the "shock theory of marriage" to explain the frequently reported phenomenon of the deterioration of mental health among married women. Much of the shock was due to the realization that after attaining the much sought-after status of being married, the woman became a housewife—a low status role involving menial labor. More recently, Bernard (1971a) includes the fallacy of sex stereotypes as part of her shock theory. She feels that the expectations of the marital relationship are built on stereotypes; and when women actually experience marriage, dissonance and disillusionment result. For example, the wife discovers the dependencies and weaknesses of her husband and realizes that he is not the strong, infallible person the male stereotype pictures him to be. She finds that she herself must be the strong one in the relationship. This situation may be too much for someone who has been raised to believe that she is the "weaker sex" and needs to be protected and supported by her husband. In referring to similar dilemmas experienced by women and the fact that many married women suffer depression, Bernard (1971b) concludes that the mental health of housewives is "public enemy number one."

In an often quoted article on adult sex roles and mental illness, Gove and Tudor (1973) delineate the following reasons for women being more likely to have emotional problems because of their sex roles:

1. The role of housewife, which may include being a mother, is the single major role of most women, while men have two roles—head of the household, which may include being a father, and worker or provider. Although a large percentage of women work outside the home, most of them are employed in low-level jobs which do not contribute to their self-esteem and sense of identity. If the woman does find her role of housewife gratifying, she typically has no other major source of gratification.
2. Most activities of the housewife do not require a high level of skill or training; many are just plain boring, causing frustration to many women who are over qualified for the job.
3. The role of the housewife is diffuse and poorly defined, without the structure and evaluation which go along with most jobs.
4. The married woman who works outside the home is usually in a less satisfactory position than the married man. She generally earns less, holds a less fulfilling/rewarding job, and usually still does most of the household chores.
5. The expectations society has for women are unclear and oftentimes contradictory. Their lives appear to be contingent upon the lives of others—especially members of their family. Though women receive the same education as men, they are still not treated as equals but remain in stereotyped, institutionalized positions.

MacLennan (1972) ties in this differential treatment of women with their mental health when he says, "Discriminating limitations on women with their attendant effects are often not consciously felt by women, but are expressed instead in apathy, anxiety, and depression and in very dependent childlike behavior."

Conclusion   Except for alcoholism, drug addiction, and some transient situational disorders, women experience a higher rate of mental illness than men in our society. Women attempt to commit suicide more than men, but more men are successful in committing suicide than women. The precise effect which sex roles, and what has been termed a double standard of mental health, have on the mental health of men and women is not completely clear. But there is growing evidence that both sexes suffer from the pressures and limitations placed on them by society's restricted sex roles.

To what extent therapists participate in the perpetuation of sex-role stereotypes when working with their clients is also not certain. However, the attitudes of mental health professionals toward what is "healthy" for adult men and what is "healthy" for adult women indicate that a double standard of mental health may exist. Anything which restricts choice cannot be considered good therapy; and sexism and sex role stereotyping, to whatever extent it occurs, prescribes behaviors for women and men, and thus reduces their number of choices and the likelihood that therapy will be beneficial to them.

Professional associations, educational training programs, and individual mental health workers have an obligation to ensure that sexism and sex role stereotyping do not enter into the psychotherapeutic process. Such an obligation has implications for the preparation of new professionals, in-service training, and the self-education and self-awareness efforts of practicing professionals. Suggestions as to how this obligation can be met are contained in section III of this volume.

References   Abramowitz, S. I.; Abramowitz, C. V.; Jackson, C.; and Gomes, B. The politics of clinical judgment: What nonliberal examiners infer about women who don't stifle themselves. *Journal of Consulting and Clinical Psychology,* 1973, *41,* 385–391.

American Psychiatric Association. *Diagnostic and Statistical Manual,* 1968.

American Psychological Association. Report of the task force on sex bias and sex-role stereotyping in psychotherapeutic practice. *American Psychologist,* 1975, *30,* 1169–1175.

Bengis, I. *Combat in the Erogenous Zone.* New York: Knopf, 1972.

Bettelheim, Bruno. The commitment required of a woman entering a scientific profession in present day American society. In *Woman and the Scientific Professions,* M.I.T. Symposium on American Women in Science and Engineering, Cambridge, Mass., 1965.

Bernard, J. The paradox of the happy marriage. In Gornick, V., and Moran, B. K., eds., *Woman in Sexist Society.* New York: Basic Books, 1971(a).

Bernard J. *Women and the Public Interest: An Essay on Policy and Protest.* New York: Aldine-Atherton, 1971(b).

Bingham, W. C., and House, E. W. ACES' members attitudes toward women and work. *Counselor Education and Supervision,* 1975, 14, *3,* 204–214.

Broverman, I. K.; Broverman, D. M.; Clarkson, F. E.; Rosenkrantz, P.; and Vogel, S. R. Sex-role stereotypes and clinical judgments of mental health. *Journal of Consulting Psychology,* 1970, *34,* 1–7.

Chesler, P. Men drive women crazy. *Psychology Today,* 18, July 1971.

Chesler, P. *Women and Madness.* New York: Doubleday, 1972.

Cooper, David. *The Death of the Family.* New York: Pantheon Books, 1970.

Cooperstock, R. Sex differences in the use of mood-modifying drugs: An explanatory model. *Journal of Health and Social Behavior,* 1971, *12,* 238–244.

Cummings, L. What psychiatrists say about women's liberation. *Family Weekly,* 4, July 2, 1972.

Erickson, Erick H. Inner and outer space: Reflections on womenhood. *Daedalus,* Vol. 3, 1965.

Fabrikant, B. The psychotherapist and the female patient. In V. Franks and V. Burtle (eds.), *Women in Therapy.* New York: Brunners/Mazel, 1974.

Figes, Eva. *Patriarchal Attitudes.* New York: Stein and Day, 1970.

Freud, Sigmund. Some psychological consequences of the anatomical distinction between the sexes. *Collected Papers,* Vol. 5, London: Hogarth Press, 1956.

Garai, J. E. Sex differences in mental health. *Genetic Psychology Monographs,* 1970, *81,* 123-142.

Gilman, R. The femlib case against Sigmund Freud. *New York Times Magazine,* Jan. 31, 1971, 10-47.

Gove, W. R. The relationship between sex role, marital status, and mental illness. *Social Forces,* 1972(b), 51, *1,* 34-44.

Gove, W. R. Sex, marital status, and suicide. *Journal of Health and Social Behavior,* 1972(a), *13,* 204-213.

Gove, W. R., and Tudor, J. F. Adult sex roles and mental illness. *American Journal of Sociology,* 1973, *78,* 812-835.

Greer, G. *The Female Eunuch.* New York: McGraw Hill, 1970.

Gurin, G.; Veroff, J.; and Feld, S. *Americans View Their Mental Health.* New York: Basic, 1960.

Horney, Karen. *Feminine Psychology,* New York: Norton, 1967.

Howard, E. M., and Howard, J. L. Women in Institutions: Treatment in Prisons and Mental Hospitals. In Franks, V., and Burtle, V. (eds.), *Women in Therapy.* New York: Brunner/Mazel, 1974.

Jung, Carl G. *Contributions to Analytical Psychology.* New York: Harcourt, Brace, 1928.

Kagan, J. The emergence of sex differences. *School Review,* 1972, *80,* 217-227.

Kaye, Harvey E. *Male Survival: Masculinity Without Myth.* New York: Grosset and Dunlap, 1974.

MacLennan, B. *Mental Health and the Status of Women.* Unpublished report for the Prince George County Task Force on the Status of Women, October, 1972.

Maslin, A., and Davis, J. L. Sex-role stereotyping as a factor in mental health standards among counselors-in-training. *Journal of Counseling Psychology,* 1975, 22,*2,* 87-91.

Mitchell, J. *Psychoanalysis and Women,* New York, New York, Pantheon, 1974.

Neulinger, J. Perceptions of the optimally integrated person: A redefinition of mental health. Proceedings of the 76th Annual Convention of the American Psychological Association, 1968, 553-554.

Phillips, D., and Segal, B. Sexual status and psychiatric symptoms. *American Sociological Review,* 1969, *34,* 58-72.

Rheingold, Joseph. *The Fear of Being a Woman.* New York: Grune and Stratton, 1964.

Roche Report. Women's lib: What is its impact on female and male psychology? *Roche Report: Frontiers of Psychiatry,* 11, *1,* 1971.

Roiphe, A. What women psychoanalysts say about women's liberation. *New York Times Magazine,* 10, February 13, 1973.

Steinmann, A. Cultural values, female role expectancies and therapeutic goals: Research and interpretation. In V. Franks and V. Burtle (eds.), *Women in Therapy.* New York: Brunner/Mazel, 1974.

Stengel, E. *Suicide and Attempted Suicide.* Baltimore: Penguin, 1964.

Stevens, B. The psychotherapist and women's liberation. *Social Work,* 1971, *11,*8 12–18.

Stricker, G. Implications of research for psychotherapeutic treatment of women. *American Psychologist,* 1977, 32,*1,* 14–22.

Veith, I. *Hysteria: The History of a Disease.* Chicago: University of Chicago Press, 1965.

West, A. G. A women's liberation or exploding the fairy princess myth. *Reflections,* 1972, *7,* 20–32.

Williams, Juanita H. *Psychology of Women: Behavior on a Biosocial Context.* New York: W. W. Norton & Co., 1977.

3 Sex Typing in the Schools

The schools have been focused on as one of the major socializing institutions in America which have perpetuated traditional sex role stereotypes (Frazier and Sadker, 1973; Grambs and Waetjen, 1975; Lewis, 1972; National Education Association, 1973; Richardson, 1974; Rossi and Calderwood, 1973; Stacey, et al., 1974; and Tavis and Offir, 1977). Through sex segregated curricular and extracurricular programs, differential school policies and rules, sexist textbooks and teaching materials, and stereotyped attitudes and behaviors of school personnel, students have been restricted on what they can and cannot learn and what they can and cannot do largely because of their sex rather than their individual abilities. In introducing her bill on women's education (which later became the Women's Educational Equity act; see chap. 5) Representative Patsy T. Mink of Hawaii summarized the severity of the problem, particularly as it relates to women, when she said:

Our educational system has divided the sexes into an insidious form of role-playing. Women provide the services and men exploit them. Women are the secretaries, nurses, teachers, and domestics, and men are the bosses, doctors, professors, and foremen. Textbooks, media, curricula, testing, counseling, and so forth, are all based on the correctness of this division of labor, and serve to reinforce the sex-role stereotype that is so devastating for our postindustrial society. More importantly, this division of labor according to sex is a totally false assumption of roles.

Women are no longer going to accept being forced into a secondary role. Demands of family life in this century just are not all-consuming any more. Given the fact that our life expectancy is well into the seventies, that women live longer than men, they have fewer children than in an agricultural society, and the women will spend more than half their adult lives in the work force outside the home, it is essential to the existence of our country that sincere and realistic attention to the realignment of our attitudes and educational priorities be made. I suggest that education is the first place to start in a reexamination of our national goals.

Despite passage of federal laws and regulations which prohibit sex discrimination in educational institutions (see chap. 5), inequities still abound in our schools. Many feel this is due to the lack of effective enforcement of such regulations by the responsible federal agencies (Project on Equal Education Rights, 1978). Whatever the reasons, we know that changes in attitudes and behaviors do not happen quickly. Thus, in many of our schools today, girls and boys, young men and women are still being channeled into educational programs and activities which encourage only the development of interests and abilities concurrent with outmoded and unrealistic sex roles.

Elementary and Secondary Schools— Impact on Girls and Boys

American elementary and secondary schools shortchange both girls and boys, but in very different ways. All of the ways cannot be discussed here, so I have selected those which appear to be most salient.

Boys in a Feminine Environment— Behavior and Reading Problems

To begin with, the elementary school has been criticized for being too "feminine" an environment for little boys who have been encouraged at home to be independent and active (Goldman and May, 1970; McFarland, 1968; Palardy, 1969; and Trippot, 1968). Thus, they do not fit into a situation where docility, neatness, and good manners appear to determine success. In expressing her concern for the development of the young boy in the elementary school, Sexton (1965) asks, "are schools emasculating our boys?" In her opinion:

Boys and the schools seem locked in a deadly and ancient conflict that may eventually inflict mortal wounds on both. . . . The problem is not just that teachers are too often women. It is that the school is too much a woman's world, governed by women's rules and standards. The school code is that of propriety, obedience, decorum, cleanliness, physical and, too often, mental passivity.

The result of this mismatch of school environment and male student is that he does not perform as well academically as his female classmates, and he is much more likely to present behavior problems for the teacher.

During the first grade, the boy is referred eleven times as often as a girl for social and emotional immaturity, a syndome characterized by a high rate of absenteeism, fatigability, inability to attend and concentrate, shyness, poor motivation for work, underweight, inability to follow directions, slow learning, infantile speech patterns, and problems in the visual-motor and visual-perception areas. As a school child, he is referred to the school clinic for stuttering (4 to 1), reading difficulty (5 to 1), and eventually to the psychiatric clinic for personality disorders (2.6 to 1), behavior problems (4.4 to 1), school failure (2.6 to 1), and delinquency (4.5 to 1). (Anthony, 1970)

Reading difficulty in grade school appears to be linked to behavior problems in many cases. Students who do not read well are less likely to be promoted, and those who are not promoted are more likely to become delinquent (Glueck and Glueck, 1934). Boys experience reading difficulties much more than girls and are found below the expected grade level more often than girls (White House Conference on Children, 1970).

Girls in Elementary School—Too Comfortable a Fit

Judging from the above comparison of grade school male and female students, it would appear the elementary school environment facilitates learning for girls much more effectively than for boys. Granted, the school environment is comfortable for the girls, because it is similar to their home environment. The treatment they have received in the home is like that which they receive in school. In both settings they are taught to be polite, passive, and dependent. Bruner (1966) explains the detrimental effect of this too comfortable fit of the elementary school environment for girls:

> Observant anthropologists have suggested that the basic values of the early grades are a stylized version of the feminine role in society, cautious rather than daring, governed by a lady-like politeness. . . . Girls in the early grades who learn to control their fidgeting earlier are rewarded for excelling in their feminine values. The reward can be almost too successful in that in later years it is difficult to move girls beyond the orderly virtues they learned in their first school encounters. The boys, more fidgety in the first grades get no such reward, and as a consequence may be freer in their approach to learning in the later grades.

By reinforcing and rewarding girls for their neatness, conformity, and silence, our schools may be thwarting their ability to learn. A study with fifth-grade children illustrated the detrimental effects that reward-seeking behavior can have on intellectual curiosity (Silberman, 1970). When students were anxious to get good grades and praise from the teacher, they hid their academic weaknesses from the teacher and avoided intellectually challenging situations. Thus, young girls who are conditioned to depend on rewards, are more likely to avoid academically challenging problems with the possibility of failure and loss of teacher approval. In doing so, they also avoid the potential for greater academic growth and intellectual stimulation.

This avoidance of challenging situations and what may be called a passive approach to learning has a disturbingly negative effect on intellectual growth. Research has shown that during the formative childhood years, some children's IQ's remain constant, and some decline, while others increase. In describing the six-year-old children whose IQ's are likely to increase by the time they are ten years of age, Maccoby (1963) says they are "competitive, self-assertive, independent, and dominant in interaction with other children." She describes those children whose IQ's are likely to decrease as "passive, shy, and dependent." Sadly, these are the same stereotypic terms used to differentiate girls and boys. By reinforcing girls (and boys who are willing) to be passive and dependent, schools may be running the risk of limiting or decreasing students' intellectual ability.

Some will argue that there are indeed sex differences when it comes to ability. As was discussed in chapter 1, there is no convincing evidence to demonstrate that one sex is brighter or more creative than the other. Maccoby and Jacklin (1974) reviewed hundreds of studies of sex differences in children and found only a few behaviors which appeared to be different for males and females: girls showed an earlier verbal facility; boys tended to be better at spatial and mathematical tasks and were more aggressive than girls. That such differences are sex linked characteristics determined by genes and hormones has not been proven. However, we do know that the environment plays a major role in encouraging and facilitating the development of certain interests and abilities in girls and certain others in boys, and discourages those which society has viewed as inappropriate for the members of each sex. While male elementary students in America experience reading difficulties to a much greater degree than females, this is not true in Europe (Entwisle, 1971). In Germany, for example, boys have been found to have higher reading skills while girls have superior mathematical skills—just the reversal from American children (Preston, 1957).

Since mastery of reading is so crucial to later school success, the fact that many boys have severe reading difficulties is of grave concern to parents and educators. While for the most part boys eventually catch up in reading ability with their female classmates (Good and Brody, 1969), the impact on the boy's self-concept of early defeats and the effect of overall school achievement cannot be ignored. (Austin, et al., 1971).

Studies show that the, elementary school is viewed as a "feminine" environment by the students. Reading is regarded as a feminine activity, a classification which "has the effect of lessening boys' motivation to excel in reading" (Dwyer, 1973). Both girls and boys regard school objects such as the blackboard, books, and desks as feminine rather than neuter or masculine (Kagan, 1964). And both sexes generally perceive their teachers as favoring girls over boys (Lee and Gropper, 1974).

Girls and Boys
and Math

While the elementary school is viewed as a feminine environment which does not encourage boys to excel, boys gain ground in the secondary school. One area in which they clearly gain is in scientific and mathematical training. Since math and science are considered more appropriate for boys than girls, it is not surprising that boys are expected to excel in these areas, and more boys than girls are enrolled in such courses. Although girls learn to count at an earlier age and there are no consistent sex differences in arithmetic computation skill or preference patterns for mathematics throughout the elementary years, boys begin to excel at higher level mathematics early in high school, and the difference between girls and boys continue to accelerate (Guttentag and Bray, 1976; Ernest, 1976). This is demonstrated over and over again with aptitude and achievement tests. For example, large sex differences have been found in favor of males on the Scholastic Aptitude Test—Mathematics (SAT-M) (Astin, 1974; Fox, 1975). While Stafford (1972) claims "that in general there is an underlying hereditary component for a proficiency in quantitative reasoning which fits the sex linked recessive model fairly well," and Page (1976) agrees, such a hypothesis has received very little acceptance. Rather than give credence to the idea that intrinsic biological differences are the major reasons for the sex differences in mathematical ability, most studies emphasize environmental and cultural influences (Aiken, 1976; Astin, 1974; Fox, Fennema, and Sherman, 1977; Poffenberger and Norton, 1963; Unkel, 1966).

After studying how sexual stereotyping affects attitudes and proficiency in mathematics, Fennema and Sherman (in press) conclude: "There is, then, an accumulation of evidence which points to the conclusion that sexual stereotyping of mathematics as a male domain operates through a myriad of subtle influences from peer to parent and within the girl herself to eventuate in the fulfillment of the stereotyped expectation of a 'female head that's not much for figures.' " As a result of this stereotyping of mathematics as a male domain, girls avoid taking other than required mathematics courses. Kagan (1965) summarizes the effect of cultural bias on girls' achievement in mathematics:

It is well documented that problems requiring analysis and reasoning, especially spatial reasoning, science, and mathematics problems, are viewed by both sexes as more appropriate for boys than for girls. As might be expected, girls perform less well on such materials. . . . The typical girl believes that the ability to solve problems in geometry, physics, logic, or arithmetic is a masculine skill, and her motivation to persist with such problems is low. Her decreased involvement reflects the fact that her self-esteem is not at stake in such problems. In such cases she is potentially threatened by the possibility that she might perform with unusual competence on such tasks, for excellence is equated with a loss of femininity.

By the time students have completed their high school education and are ready to enter college, the sex difference in differential course taking in mathematics is marked. A study of entering freshmen at the University of California at Berkeley found that 57 percent of the boys had taken four full years of mathematics, including the trigonometry-solid geometry sequence, compared with 8 percent of the girls (Sells, 1973 and 1976). Another study conducted at the University of California Santa Barbara campus also found marked sex differences in mathematics course taking, althouh the findings were not as extreme (36 percent of the males and 16 percent of the females had taken four years of high school mathematics) as the earlier study at Berkeley (Ernest, 1976). Such differential course taking is thought to be the major reason for sex differences in mathematics achievement, rather than any inability on the part of women to learn mathematics (Fox, Fennema, and Sherman, 1977). Studies which show sex differences on mathematics tests usually do not control for the number of courses taken. Thus, boys with three or four years of math courses are compared with girls who have only one to two years of mathematics training. Fennema (Fox, Fennema, and Sherman, 1977) contends that most of the sex differences in math achievement would be eliminated if girls' enrollment in mathematics courses were increased to match boys' enrollment.

Why all the fuss about girls and math? Researchers and educators have identified mathematics as a critical skill which is directly related to educational and occupational choices and achievement (Ernst, 1977; Fox, Fennema, and Sherman, 1977; Sells, 1976; Tobias, 1977). Indeed, mathematics has been termed the "critical filter in the job market" (Sells, 1973). For example, most of the mathematics-related fields, such as engineering, physics, statistics, computer science, accounting, navigation, etc., are male dominated and are higher paying than most of the female dominated fields, such as nursing, teaching, and secretarial science. Thus, girls and women preclude themselves from considering a whole host of occupations when they avoid mathematical training. The Carnegie Commission on Higher Education has identified poor math training as one of the main barriers to the advancement of women in today's society. In a report on women in higher education, the Carnegie Commission (1973) points to the importance of mathematical studies in the following recommendation:

> The first priority in the nation's commitment to equal educational opportunity for women should be placed on changing policies in preelementary, elementary, and secondary school programs that tend to deter women from aspiring to equality with men in their career goals. This will require vigorous pursuit of appropriate policies by state and local boards of education and implementation by school administrators, teachers, and counselors.
>
> For example, high school counselors and teachers should encourage women who aspire to professional careers to choose appropriate educational programs. They should also encourage them to pursue mathematical studies throughout high school, because of the increasing importance of mathematics as a background, not only in engineering and the natural sciences, but also in other fields, such as the social sciences and business administration.

Other "Inequitable" High School Offerings

Higher level math courses are not the only part of the high school curriculum which have uneven male and female enrollments, and thus help perpetuate sexual stereotypes. While it is now illegal for schools to offer sex segregated courses, except for sex education courses, or to require different courses for male and female students, there are still relatively few girls taking auto mechanics and few boys taking home economics, although skills in both areas contribute to self-reliant adulthood. Similarly, although typing and other office business courses may be open to members of both sexes, the few boys who enroll feel less able, clumsy, and out of place (Mead, 1971). Yet, skills learned in such courses can facilitate getting through college by typing one's own papers and enabling part-time employment in office settings. Vocational training programs are also for the most part voluntarily sex segregated and continue the perpetuation of vocational sex role stereotypes. For example, in 1975, 42 percent of the 4.6 million girls registered in vocational education programs throughout the country were enrolled in what is termed "non-gainful" homemaker courses, which do not develop marketable skills (U.S. Department of Health, Education, and Welfare, undated). Even in classes specifically designed to prepare students for paid employment, the majority of high school girls are enrolled in courses which prepare for a narrow range of jobs in which women and low salaries predominate.

Sex education courses were hoped by some feminists to be a vehicle in the high school curriculum to promote equality between the sexes by providing a forum for frank discussion among students about sex role stereotypes, and an exploration of new ways for increasing the options of both males and females. However, many of these courses have instead tended to endorse the traditional sex roles portraying women as weak and submissive and men as strong and dominant (Doubrousky, 1971).

In high school extracurricular activities, the most glaring sex differences in student participation is of course in athletics. In a 1977 report of the National Federation of State High School Associations, the following information is revealed: in 1971, boys' participation in high school sports was twelve times that of girls'. In some school districts, expenditures on boys' athletics have been as much as ten times greater than those spent for girls' athletic programs. The picture has improved somewhat recently, however, due to Title IX and the impetus of the women's movement. For example, girls' participation in varsity high school athletic programs increased 460 percent between 1971 and 1976. Disparities still exist, however, as on a national average high schools still offer boys more than twice as many chances to play team sports as girls. In addition to encouraging students to keep physically fit, such athletic programs provide an opportunity for students to learn such qualities as sportsmanship, self-discipline, self-confidence, and what it means to be a team member rather than a prima donna—all qualities which are as important for girls to learn as they are for boys.

School leadership roles deserve attention here as such experiences also provide students with opportunities to develop personal qualities for their adult lives as well as sometimes leading to educational and occupational interests. Here too boys predominate. Far more boys than girls are elected student body president, appointed editor of the newspaper or yearbook, and selected as band leader (Grambs and Waetjen, 1975). Girls compete for these leadership positions, but it is usually a boy who gets appointed or elected.

What Are the Causes?

What happens in American schools so that boys become the troublemakers in the early grades and have difficulty reading, high school girls avoid math and science courses, and boys enter professions and trades while girls with similar abilities become housewives and secretaries? The answer is that it doesn't all happen in the schools. Long before a young child enters school, she or he learns what is appropriate behavior for girls and boys and women and men from family members, playmates, television, picture books, and the like. By age three, children know their gender label (Kagan, 1969) and they tend to choose sex typed toys, activities, and games. Boys especially are likely to prefer "boy-toys" and avoid "girl-toys" (Maccoby and Jacklin, 1974). By the preschool years children know the behavior patterns, play preferences, and psychological characteristics expected of them (Kohlberg, 1966). Teachers can only work with what they get.

Student Perceptions of Sex Roles   By the time children are six or seven years of age, they present a clear division of sex role definitions. The interests, attitudes, and activities of girls and boys differ dramatically. When asked about differences between girls and boys, boys complained that girls didn't play rough games or sports but instead preferred jump rope or playing with dolls. And yet girls who preferred active, strenuous, muscular activities are usually considered tomboys or loners with little group support for their preferences (Guttentag and Bray, 1976). Grade school boys have positive feelings about being male and are confident and assertive. Girls, on the other hand, are not particularly enthusiastic about being female and are less confident about their adequacy, accomplishment, and popularity (Minnchin, 1966). As girls and boys progress through school, their opinions of boys become higher, and at the same time, their opinions of girls become lower (Smith, 1939). Stein and Smithells (1969) found that children's attitudes become more sex role stereotyped as they get older. For example, when children at the second, sixth, and twelfth grades were asked what they thought was "a more boyish or girlish thing to do," young girls rated arithmetic and athletic skills as feminine while older girls did not.

Such sex typed preferences affect achievement on tasks which are thought to be sex typed (see earlier discussions on reading and math). Stein et al. (1969) found that on tasks defined as masculine, boys' achievement scores improved while their scores dropped on tasks defined as feminine. Girls' achievement scores did not increase when tasks were defined as feminine, but their scores decreased when when performing tasks which they were told were masculine.

Girls have less confidence and tend to underestimate their ability and chances of success more than boys (Brandt, 1958; Crandall, 1969). Although high school girls get better grades than boys, they are less likely to believe that they have the ability to do college work (Cross, 1968).

Students' perceptions of appropriate sex role attitudes, interests, and behaviors also influence the way they view possible future occupations for themselves. A study conducted in the early 1960s (O'Hara, 1962) found that by the time they reach the upper elementary grades, girls viewed their future occupations as limited to teacher, nurse, secretary, or mother—a very stereotyped list. Boys of the same age did not limit their future occupations but instead listed a large variety of occupations (also sex role stereotypic) from fire fighter and professional football player to doctor and engineer. In studying the occupational fantasy life of adolescents, Douvan and Adelson (1966) found that "the bulk of girls' choices (95 percent) fall into the following four categories: personal aide, social aide, white collar traditional, and glamour fashion." The boys' choices covered a much broader range of possible occupations, although they too were sex stereotypic. While girls are now beginning to consider a variety of careers, they are not able to describe specifically what it would be like to have a particular career. In contrast, boys are able to describe in considerable detail the activities which their chosen careers might entail (Iglitzin, 1972). At the high school level, a decline in career commitment has been found in girls. This decline was related to their feelings that male classmates disapproved of a woman using her intelligence (Harvly, 1971).

The equation of intellectual success with a loss of femininity appears to be common among high school peer groups. As Keniston (1964) puts it:

Girls soon learn that "popularity"—that peculiar American ecstasy from which all other goods flow—accrues to her who hides any intelligence she may have, flatters the often precarious maleness of adolescent boys, and devotes herself to activities that can in no way challenge their sex. The popular girls in high school are seldom the brilliant girls; or if they are, it is only because they are so brilliant they can hide their brilliance from less brilliant boys. . . . Most American public schools (like many private schools) make a girl with passionate intellectual interests feel a strong sense of her own inadequacy as a woman, feel guilty about these "masculine" outlooks, perhaps even wonder about her own normality.

Similarly, Pierce (1961) found high achievement motivation for young women related to success in marriage, not to academic success, as it is for men. According to Pierce, high school girls think that to achieve in life they need to excel in nonacademic ways, such as physical attractiveness, desirable social status, and "marrying the right man." While such attitudes may be less prevalent and overt among high school students in the late 1970s, they nevertheless are still in their thinking.

Teacher Expectations and Perceptions of Sex Roles   Due to their professional socialization, teachers have perceptions and expectations which interact with the sex of their students (Lee and Gropper, 1974). In a study in which junior high school teachers were asked to select adjectives they felt would describe good female students and good male students, Kerner (1965) found the teachers' responses to be stereotypes in miniature of the male and female sex roles:

Adjectives Describing Good Female Students	Adjectives Describing Good Male Students
Appreciative	Active
Calm	Adventurous
Conscientious	Aggressive
Considerate	Assertive
Cooperative	Curious
Mannerly	Energetic
Poised	Enterprising
Sensitive	Frank
Dependable	Independent
Efficient	Inventive
Mature	
Obliging	
Thorough	

In another study (Levitan and Chananie, 1972) using hypothetical girls and boys who showed characteristics of dependency, aggression, or achievement, teachers were asked how much they approved of the students (reflecting professional values), how much they liked the student (indicating personal values), and how typical the student was (depicting realistic evaluations). Findings indicate that the dependent female received more approval than the dependent male, and the aggressive male and dependent female were acknowledged to be fairly typical. Also, the teachers liked the dependent girl, the achieving girl, and the independent boy more than the dependent boy. While direct and indirect expectations and approval are communicated to the dependent girl, it is independence which later correlates with creative intellectual ability. The results of a survey by Ricks and Pyke (1973) showed that more teachers prefer male students to female students, because they felt male students were more open and outspoken, willing to exchange ideas, active, honest, and easier to talk with. The lack of causing discipline problems was the only reason they gave for preferring female students.

Although teachers are currently aware of the concerns about sexism and many report no differences in their feelings about or treatment of boys and girls (Donovan, 1974), classroom observations reveal some clear differences in teacher-female student and teacher-male student interaction patterns. In a study of teachers and children in nursery school classrooms conducted by Serbin and O'Leary (1975), trained observers found that teachers rewarded boys for being aggressive by responding over three times as often to boys who misbehaved as to girls who misbehaved. Their scoldings to the girls were brief and soft so that other children did not hear, while they called public attention to the boys' naughty actions—which reinforced the boys' behavior. The observers also found that the teachers rewarded the girls for being dependent, by responding more often to girls when they were close by than when they were out of arm's reach, and by rarely sending girls off to work on their own. In contrast, the teachers encouraged boys to do independent work and paid the same amount of attention to them whether they were nearby or not. All of the teachers paid more attention to male students. Boys were twice as likely to get individual instruction; they received more verbal and tangible rewards for academic work; and they got more assistance from the teacher when they requested it. As a result of their findings, Serbin and O'Leary contend that the teachers' unwitting encouragement of the boys' aggressive behavior explains why more boys than girls have learning disabilities and reading problems—their rowdiness prevents them from paying attention when they should. On the other hand, the encouragement of independent behavior and the extra instruction they receive from teachers helps boys develop problem-solving skills.

Similar results were found in an earlier study by Spaulding (1963) in looking at achievement, creativity, and self-concept correlates of teacher-pupil transactions at the elementary level. He found that teachers not only disapproved more of boys but gave them more attention in general, especially in terms of listening to them and giving them more direct instruction. In basic agreement with Serbin and O'Leary, Sears and Feldman (1966) suggest that the impact of this differential attention may result in "a cumulative increase in independent and autonomous behavior by boys as they are disapproved, praised, listened to, and taught more actively by the teacher."

A study conducted at the junior high level (Good, Sikes, and Brophy, 1973) indicates that teacher-student interaction patterns are fairly consistent regardless of the level of education. The results of the behavior observations showed that male and female teachers have similar patterns in their treatment of girls and boys. Students' level of achievement, as well as sex, were the main effects looked at. High achieving boys, relative to other students, received the most favorable teacher treatment; while low achieving boys, relative to other students, received the poorest contact patterns. Interactions with high achieving girls, middle achieving girls and boys, and low achieving girls fall in between. "In summary, boys were provided more opportunities to respond in the classroom and more teacher affect (both positive and negative) was directed at them. Boys were also found to create more response opportunities for themselves." The study also pointed out that teachers asked boys a higher percentage of "process questions," while girls were asked a higher proportion of "product and choice questions"; thus, encouraging problem-solving behavior in boys to a greater extent.

Such sexist attitudes and behaviors, along with teachers' knowledge of sex differences on aptitudes and achievement tests may very well create the "self-fulfilling prophecy effect"—a term coined by Rosenthal and Jacobson (1968)—to explain the phenomenon of the effect of teachers' expectations on students' performance. In a study where boys were described to a group of teachers as being superior learners, the teachers rejected this information and instead continued to operate "on the basis of developed attitudes and knowledge about children and tests" (Felming and Anttonen, 1971). In another study, teachers who expected boys to read well did in fact get better performance from boys than teachers who felt that girls would be more successful readers (Palardy, 1969). Another positive result of teacher expectations was found by Casserly (1975) in her study of twelve schools which had twice the usual percentage of girls enrolled in advanced placement calculus and physics courses. The teachers of these courses actively recruited girls to enroll and expected and encouraged high levels of achievement.

Research findings, such as those discussed in this section, are consistent with my own experiences with practicing public school teachers and students training to be teachers enrolled in a course I have been teaching at a midwestern university during the last eight years. The course is entitled "Sex Role Stereotyping and Socialization in Education," and was first viewed as radical women's lib indoctrination sessions to which only the bravest souls would venture, since many feared recrimination from their colleagues and school administrators. But as time passed and the public became more informed about the concerns regarding sexism and sex role stereotyping, those who enrolled in the course found it to be a bona fide academic approach to studying a legitimate societal problem and exploring strategies for constructive change.

Over the years, the class participants have come into the course more and more aware and informed of the detrimental effects of

sex role stereotyping in the schools. They can recite abundant research evidence, trends, and educational and employment statistics.
They espouse the philosophy of treating all students alike—as individuals, rather than as members of a particular sex. It is only
through role-play and simulation exercises, that some of the
stereotypic attitudes begin to surface. Once this happens, frank
discussions of their own behaviors and attitudes as teachers usually
take place. They are surprised, sometimes shocked, to learn that
even the "most aware" individuals still unconsciously, as a matter
of habit and their own socialization, reinforce sex role stereotypic
behavior in their classrooms. Complimenting girls on their appearance, asking a "big, strong boy" to help move some audiovisual
equipment, expecting boys to do better than girls in math and
sciences, expecting boys to be rowdy and girls to be "little ladies,"
admitting a preference of working with boys . . . and the list goes
on.

Grading and Academic Achievement   The bias against boys in grading
has been documented for almost seventy years (Ayres, 1909; Judd,
1916). While boys may achieve better than girls in many subjects,
their grades do not show it. Grambs and Waetjen (1975) report a
study conducted in the Virginia public schools of the relationship
between grades students earn and their scores on standardized tests.
Boys who earned an A in chemistry achieved at the 92nd percentile
on the standardized test, while girls who received an A were at the
86th percentile. A girl achieving at the 64th percentile received a C
grade, while a boy only a few percentile points lower would get a D.
Of particular note, is the fact that boys who earned D grades in
chemistry were, according to national norms, scoring better than 61
percent of the students in the country taking chemistry, while girls
who got D grades were in the lowest third of the national group. In
English, boys who earned an A achieved at the 92nd percentile, while
girls receiving A's scored only at the 76th percentile. Girls who got
A's in history only scored at the 64th percentile, while boys who
received A's were in the 84th percentile.
    Part of the reason for the differential performance of girls and
boys on the standardized tests may be due to test bias. Many tests of
achievement and aptitude have been found to be biased in favor of
one sex or the other (Grambs and Waetjen, 1975; Tittle, 1974). The
bias could be inherent in the test itself (e.g., the types of questions
asked or the examples or language used), or it could be derived from
the way in which the test scores are interpreted. For example, the

Academic Promise Test Manual (Psychological Corporation, 1962) allows the combining of scores for girls and boys into one table of norms in the areas of language usage, verbal, numerical, and abstract reasoning, despite the manual's statement that at every grade level girls score higher than boys in language usage. Clark (1959) used the California Achievement Test and the California Test of Mental Maturity to assess whether there were differences in achievement and abilities of children in grades three, five, and eight. While the California Test of Mental Maturity was not supposed to be sex biased, an analysis of the test scores in language, English mechanics, and yielding revealed consistently higher scores for girls, even after removing differences due to mental age and chronological age.

Tittle (1973) analyzed eight of the most frequently used major achievement test batteries: the California Achievement Tests, the Iowa Tests of Basic Skills, the Iowa Tests of Educational Development, Metropolitan Achievement Tests, Sequential Tests of Educational Progress, SRA Achievement Series, Stanford Early School Achievement Test, and the Stanford Achievement Test. She found that educational achievement tests reflect the general bias in school instructional materials. Content bias was found in a higher frequency of usage of male nouns and pronouns than female nouns and pronouns (as high as fourteen times as many in some of the batteries). Most of the tests contain numerous sex role stereotypes. "Women are portrayed almost exclusively as homemakers or in the pursuit of hobbies (e.g., 'Mrs. Jones, the president of the Garden Club . . .'). Young girls carry out 'female chores' and boys are shown playing, climbing, camping, hiking, and taking on roles of responsibility and leadership. Girls help with the cooking, buy ribbons and vegetables, and in any active pursuit take a back seat to the stronger, more qualified boys."

Most mathematics tests contain biases in favor of males. In a study of the items on the Scholastic Aptitude Test—Mathematics (SAT-M), Donlon (1971) found that the items heavily favored males. In fact, only two of the items favored females. An analysis of the items by content led Donlon to conclude that the nearly forty-point difference between the sexes on this test is due to the biased content formula.

Since many standardized tests are sex biased, they may not provide a good comparison with grades to determine if teachers are biased in favor of girls in grade giving. But the fact remains that girls get better grades than boys (Jackson, Getzels, and Xydis, 1960), whether or not it's because teachers reward girls for achievement alone or a combination of achievement and behavior.

There are of course very negative results of a biased grading system. Good grades lead to recognition (honor rolls), opportunity to participate in extracurricular school activities (students with low grades are not allowed to participate in sports, interest clubs, or hold leadership positions), and the chance to continue one's education (many colleges and universities will not admit students with low grades). Students with low grades in junior high may find themselves "tracked" in a low ability group throughout high school. Because of their lower grades, boys occupy the lower ranks in class standings (Hunt and Dopyera, 1966). Grambs and Waetjin (1975) effectively sum up the damage done to boys and girls by biased grading:

> If school were not such a destiny shaping institution, one could discount the grades given by teachers, but school is critically important as the gateway to adult achievement. The grading bias does a disservice to girls as well as boys. The boys may feel angry, cheated, or stupid. The girls may gain a spurious sense of achievement, or may not know that the grade is phoney; either way they have been as poorly served by the system as have boys.

Textbooks and Instructional Materials One of the most easily documented forms of sex role stereotyping in the schools is found in the textbooks and instructional materials. While the study of the sexist contents of children's books has received considerable public attention in recent years, it is not a recent phenomenon. As early as the 1940s, Child and associates (1946) were involved in analyses of children's textbooks. They found that girls were portrayed as passive and showed greater affiliation needs than boys. Boys were portrayed as active and had a problem-solving orientation. In the author's words, female characters were depicted as "sociable, kind, and timid . . . inactive, unambitious, and uncreative." A few years later, Tannenbaum (1954) pointed out the racist and sexist stereotypes in Textbook Town.

One of the most frequently quoted studies of sexism in textbooks in recent years is the one conducted by Women on Words and Images (1972), a New Jersey group of interested parents and educators. After surveying 134 children's readers from fourteen publishers, which total 2,750 stories, the group discovered these discouraging ratios:

Boy-centered to girl-centered stories   5:2
Adult male to adult female main characters   3:1

Male biographies to female biographies	6:1
Male animal stories to female animal stories	2:1
Male folk or fantasy stories to female folk or fantasy stories	4:1

In a 1975 update the group surveyed books published after 1972 and found that the overall picture had not changed much. Although the ratio for biographies had improved to 2:1, the ratio of boy-centered to girl-centered stories had become worse (7:2).

The very uneven numbers of male and female characters in children's stories was not the only alarming finding of the Women on Words and Images group. Perhaps even more alarming is the way females are portrayed compared to males in children's readers. Girls and women are portrayed as incompetent, emotional, and fearful, relying on others to solve their problems and comfort them. They are constantly concerned about how they look and spend most of their time baking cookies and sewing or looking on as boys make things, play sports, solve problems, or experience adventure. Boys are depicted as brave, curious, clever, and adventurous. Girls often demean themselves and accept ridicule and humiliation from boys:

"We are willing to share our great thoughts with mankind. However, you happen to be a girl." (*Ventures,* Book 4, Scott Foresman, 1965).

"Look at her, mother, just look at her. She is just like a girl. She gives up." (*Around the Corner,* Harper and Row, 1966).

"Women's advice is never worth two pennies. Yours isn't worth even a penny." (*Lippincott Basic Reading Series,* Book H, 1970).

Many other investigators (Feminists on Children's Literature, 1971; Feminists on Children's Media, 1971; Jacklin, 1972; Nilson, 1971; U'Ren, 1971; Weitzman and Rizzo, 1975; and Weitzman, et al., 1972) have documented the same discouraging stereotyped portrayals of the sexes in children's books, indicating the expansiveness of the problem.

Weitzman et al. (1972) chose to examine how sex roles are treated in those children's books which have been identified as the "very best"—the winners of the Caldecott Medal, given by the Children's Service Committee of the American Library Association for the most distinguished picture book each year. Caldecott Medal winners are ordered by almost all children's libraries in the country; and librarians, teachers, and parents alike encourage children to read them. Weitzman and her colleagues found that in the Caldecott winners from 1953 through 1971, there is a ratio of eleven pictures of males for every picture of a female. The ratio of pictures of male to female animals is even greater—an overwhelming ninety-five to one. In the more recent Caldecott winners, from 1967 through 1971, only two of the eighteen books are stories about females. In one of these stories, *The Emperor and the Kite* (Yolen, 1967), the heroine is a foreign princess, and in the other one, *Sam, Bangs, and Moonshine* (Ness, 1967), the girl has a boy's name. When there are female characters in the other books, they are usually unnoticeable or insignificant. Boys are presented in active, exciting, adventuresome, independent roles, while girls are passive and immobile, and are most often found indoors involved in service activities. A sense of camaraderie is evident with the boys as their adventures with each other, while girls are rarely shown doing things with other girls. The same passive-active dichotomy is evident with the adults in the stories: men lead and women follow; men rescue others; women are rescued; men are involved in outside activities; women perform service functions in the house.

The Weitzman et al. (1972) study also examined three other groups of children's books: the Newberry Award winners, recognized by the American Library Association as the best books for school age children who can read, and thus are directed at children in grades three through six; Little Golden Books sold in grocery, toy, and game stores; and "prescribed behavior" or etiquette books for children. Discouragingly, the findings from these samples strongly parallel those from the Caldecott sample. In concluding their article, the authors summarize the very negative female stereotype portrayed in children's books and suggest how they could be changed for the benefit of young readers of both sexes:

Through picture books, girls are taught to have low aspirations because there are so few opportunities portrayed as available to them. The world of picture books never tells little girls that as women they might find fulfillment outside of their homes or through intellectual pursuits. Women are excluded from the world of sports, politics, and science. Their future occupational world is presented as consisting primarily of glamour and service. Ironically, many of these books are written by prizewinning female authors whose own lives are probably unlike those they advertise.

. . . .

The simplified and stereotyped images in these books present such a narrow view of reality that they must violate the child's own knowledge of a rich and complex world.

. . . .

More flexible definitions of sex roles would seem to be more healthful in encouraging a greater variety of role possibilities. Stories could provide a more positive image of a woman's potential—of her physical, intellectual, creative, and emotional capabilities.

Picture books could also present a less stereotyped and less rigid definition of male roles by encouraging boys to express their emotions as well as their intellect.

Books might show little boys crying, playing with stuffed toys and dolls, and helping in the house. Stereotypes could be weakened by books showing boys being rewarded for being emotional and supportive, and girls being rewarded for being intelligent and adventuresome.

In a study of the most widely used elementary school textbooks, in grades one through six, Weitzman and Rizzo (1974) again found males and females portrayed stereotypically and in uneven proportions. One of the major foci of the study was textbook illustrations. In social studies texts, females were in only 33 percent of the illustrations; and only 26 percent of the science book pictures included girls or women. Stereotyped images such as the mathematically competent boy and the "dumb girl" were common in mathematics texts; the social studies texts showed fathers instructing sons in vocational and recreational skills, while mothers instructed daughters in domestic skills. In the reading series, 102 stories were about boys and only 35 were about girls. Even the spelling series depicted stereotypic sex roles. The consonants were shown as males, and the vowels were shown as females. The female vowels were treated in an antagonistic and derogatory manner as they were pushed around, yelled at, kicked out, told to shut up, and used as puppets. The authors point out that while the function of textbooks is to convey information about particular subject areas, they also convey what sociologists call "latent content," or information on ethical prescriptions, a picture of the good life, and how to attain it. As has been illustrated, this "latent content" includes limiting and in many cases negative images (especially for females) of what are considered to be "appropriate" sex roles.

Secondary school texts are not any better. In her analysis of twelve of the most used history texts in American public schools, Trecker (1971) found that heroic women are not included—not even in areas where women have made their greatest contribution, such as dance, theater, music, and day-to-day life in homes. For example, in a two-volume text, there are only two sentences describing the women's suffrage movement. Another text spends five pages discussing the six-shooter and barely five lines describing the frontier woman. A similar study of fourteen currently used textbooks was conducted by Arlow and Froschl (1976). They correlated their findings with those of other surveys and studies, in effect compiling research on thirty-six textbooks. The portrait they found of the treatment of women in high school history is as follows. The typical history text devotes only one of its 500 to 800 pages to women and their contributions. When women are included, they are made to appear supplemental to history rather than an integral part of it—placed under separate headings and in special sections. Few women appear in illustrations, and when they do they are not the central focus but instead appear as someone's wife or as part of the background. Oftentimes famous women meriting a full explanation of their accomplishments are mentioned only in relationship to their husbands. For example, the only mention of Eleanor Roosevelt in one book occurs under a picture captioned "President and Mrs. Franklin D. Roosevelt." Madame Curie is depicted in one text as just a helpmate for her husband in his research. And in another, Abigail Adams is mentioned as the wife of John Adams and the mother of John Quincy Adams; nothing is said of her writings and letters on reform. A more subtle form of sex bias is in the language used in history textbooks—an exclusive use of male pronouns and generic terms, and an inclusion of stereotypic and demeaning terms for women. In four key areas, where women have made considerable contributions to American history—the colonial period, the rights and reform movements, women and work, and contemporary America—there is an abundance of information available to historians. Yet very little appears in U.S. history textbooks. The little that is commonly included about women is summarized by Trecker (1971):

Women arrived in 1619. They held the Seneca Falls Convention on Women's Rights in 1848, During the rest of the nineteenth century, they participated in reform movements, chiefly temperance, and were exploited in factories. In 1923 they were given the vote. They joined the second World War and thereafter have enjoyed the good life in America. Add the names of the women who are invariably mentioned: Harriet Beecher Stowe, Jane Adams, Dorothea Dix, and Frances Perkins, with perhaps Susan B. Anthony, Elizabeth Cady Stanton and almost as frequently, Carry Nation, and you have the basic 'text' . . . a pattern which presents the stereotyped picture of the American Woman—passive, incapable of sustained organization or work, satisfied with her role in society, and well supplied with material blessings.

With such a scant view of women in U.S. history textbooks, it is not surprising that students see American history as a history of American men.

High school English literature textbooks are also male-centered. Few female authors are included in presently used anthologies. Arlow and Froschl (1976) report that one survey of 171 anthologized selections included 147 male authors and only 24 female authors; another survey of 400 selections revealed 306 male authors and 74 female authors. Language used in anthologies is sexist. Editors use "he" and "man" exclusively in their editorial comments and questions to students. Theme and characterization in the selections are also male-dominated. Popular themes such as sports, war, and nature have traditionally excluded the participation of women. Many stories are void of female characters or have minor female characters which are not fully developed. When women characters are included, they are usually depicted in the traditional roles of wife and mother, or a young woman in search of someone to marry. Distasteful stereotypes such as the nagging mother, the vain and silly sex object, the pushy, interfering status-seeker, or the bitter and jealous spinster abound. The few nonconforming female characters occasionally included are the tomboy and the proud and tough grandmother.

Beaven (1972) conducted a study to ascertain the responses of high school students to female characters in their literature books. Both girls and boys pointed to the lack of favorable women characters. Some said they could not recall reading anything at all about females; others said they were unimpressed with those they had read about. One boy commented: "We have read about so few women in English class that they are hardly worth mentioning. The few we have read about I wouldn't care to have for a wife or mother." In summarizing her results, Beaven (1972) states:

For the most part, women in the literature read and discussed in high school English classes play minor, unpleasant roles. The few major feminine characters tend to be either passive and insipid or vicious. And the result of the survey indicated that boys and girls can relate to few of these feminine characters.

The sex bias that is so obvious in history textbooks and literature anthologies also pervades texts in the social and mathematical sciences. After viewing sociology and psychology texts, Freeman (1971) comments: "One soon realizes that when the author talks about 'man' he means male. Major research has been done . . . from which women were systematically excluded . . . and there was no curiosity why this was so. Major books have been written, on such relevant topics as the occupational structure . . . but only a footnote [is given] to women (one-third of the labor force)." In commenting on the treatment of women in psychological theories and writings, Weisstein (1970) says, "There isn't the tiniest shred of evidence to indicate that those conclusions have anything to do with women's real potential." She indicates that personality theory literature dealing with women is largely based on Freud's work involving a relatively small sample of women who underwent years of intensive psychotherapy. Another major flaw is that much of the psychological literature is based on the concept of innate traits, with insufficient emphasis given to the effects of the social environment. Recent books (e.g., Donelson and Gullahorn, 1977; Maccoby and Jacklin, 1974; Mednick et al., 1975; Williams, 1977), while more appropriate for use at the college level rather than at the high school level, have made an effort to treat the topic of the psychology of women in a more complete, realistic fashion.

After examining ten randomly selected introductory sociology texts, Kirschner (1973), concluded, "The analysis of the role of women in American society is an area which the introductory texts leave impressively unexplored." In five of the books, no reference to women was indexed. Five of the texts referred to the egalitarian structure of the contemporary American family, and none of the other five books discussed the factors which contribute to family inequality. Only two of the books mentioned occupational wage differentials, and neither attempted to quantify or explain the reasons for the differential. Texts in the area of marriage and family still show that the authors think women belong in the home (Ehrlich, 1971), and home economics manuals too often teach women to assume characteristics and traits that will be pleasing to others rather than develop behaviors and attitudes which satisfy a self-determined standard (Lee, 1963).

As was pointed out in an earlier discussion, elementary school math books are sexist, and secondary school math texts follow suit. Rogers (1975) examined eight widely used algebra texts and found that men were depicted as active, alert, and scientific, while women were pictured as dull and insignificant and rarely were involved in career situations. In science textbooks, boys control the action and girls watch the action (Trecker, 1973), and adult women are almost never presented in scientific roles.

In summary, while publishers are making an effort to remove sexist elements from textbooks and improve the stereotyped images of both sexes, but particularly of girls and women, much still remains to be done. Presently there are far too few female role models—other than the traditional ones of wife and mother—in textbooks and instructional materials in all subject areas at all grade levels.

Counseling and Guidance   In chapter 2 we discussed the double standard of mental health for men and women as perceived by clinically trained psychiatrists, psychologists, social workers, and other mental health professionals. Is there also a "double standard" or sex bias among public school counselors?

In a 1969 study of high school counselors' attitudes toward the educational and vocational plans of high school girls, Friedersdorf (unpublished study cited in Schlossberg and Pietrofesa, 1973) instructed 106 counselors to role-play a high school girl while completing a Strong Vocational Interest Blank for women. A college-bound high school girl was role-played by twenty-seven male and twenty-nine female counselors, while a non-college-bound high school girl was role-played by twenty-three male and twenty-seven female counselors. Some of the results of the study are: the counselors responded differently when role-playing a college-bound and non-college-bound girl; they perceived the college-bound girl, but not the non-college-bound girl as identifying with cultural activities and skills involving verbal ability. Male counselors tended to think of women in feminine roles and associated college-bound girls with traditionally feminine occupations at the semiskilled level. Female counselors tended to expand the traditional image of female work roles somewhat although they still projected women into careers and occupations in which women predominate.

Thomas and Stewart (1971) looked at the perceptions of secondary school counselors toward female client case histories in an effort to determine whether they respond more positively to girls with traditionally feminine (conforming) goals than to girls with traditionally masculine (deviate) goals. Results showed that both male and female counselors rated conforming goals as more appropriate than deviate goals and felt that girls with deviate career goals were more in need of counseling than those with conforming goals. A sex difference was found among the counselors in that female counselors gave higher acceptance scores to both deviate and conforming clients than did male counselors. In discussing the implications of their study, the authors state that it is very likely that counselors' personal biases are communicated either openly or covertly to their clients, thus ". . . the female client who holds a deviate career goal over which she may already have ambivalent feelings may find herself in a more untenable position as a result of counseling. . . . The route to greater approval would be through greater conformity. This assumption places the counselor in the role of urging conformity to the culturally defined norms rather than aiding her to identify her uniqueness and nurture growth and self-development through independent decision making."

Hipple (1975) compared the perceptions of high school counselors and first-year college students toward career versus family orientation of the ideal woman. The instrument used in the study consisted of thirty-four items on a five-point Likert-type scale, with half of the items assessing intrafamily (home-oriented) tendencies and the other half assessing extrafamily (career-oriented) tendencies. Results showed no significant differences between high school counselors and college freshmen in their perceptions of the ideal woman, and "the direction of the scores indicates that each group holds concepts of the ideal women which place women in the balanced position, but slightly toward the out-of-home, extrafamilial, or career direction." Other studies (Englehard, Jones, and Stiggins, 1976; Hawley, 1975; Shapiro, 1975) also indicate that high school counselors are beginning to accept broader sex role definitions. In the Englehard et al. (1976) six-year longitudinal study, an eighteen-item Likert attitude questionnaire (five-point scale: strongly agree to strongly disagree) was constructed to tap school counselors' attitudes in three areas: attitudes regarding the dual role of mother and worker, perceptions of sex role definition, and expectations regarding the societal impact of women. While sex differences were found, changes of counselor attitudes from 1968 through 1971 to 1974 suggest more acceptance of the dual role and broader sex role definitions. The Working Mother factor yielded the lowest cluster of scores of the three factors, indicating the most conservative counselor attitudes; and male (average score 3.0) and female (average score 3.9) counselors are farther apart in their attitudes on this factor (with females approving of working mothers to a greater degree). Counselors' attitudes about sex roles changed significantly from an average cluster score of 3.5 in 1968 to 4.2 in 1974, with women (average score 4.3) much more open to diverse sex role definition than men (average score 3.7). The Societal Impact factor, which entails attitudes regarding the unique contributions women can make to society, remained fairly stable over the six-year period, with men decreasing slightly from an average score of 4.1 in 1968 to 4.07 in 1974, and women increasing slightly from an average score of 4.47 to 4.48. In commenting on this factor and its relationship to the other two factors, the authors state, ". . . men and women counselors agree that women are valuable to society. But, considering the changes taking place in the other two factors, guidance counselors are reassessing and redefining the true nature of that value."

While there are signs of attitude change regarding sex roles on the part of counselors, they still view the female career role as incompatible with the home-oriented role, thus creating a home-career conflict (Akrons, 1976). In a study "designed to shed light on the images that counselors hold about career vis-a-vis other female roles,'' Akrons (1976) examined and compared school counselors' perceptions of female and male social and vocational roles. A specially constructed two-page personal data form and a twelve-page Semantic Differential questionnaire mailed to over 300 school counselors revealed that "the career man concept is perceived as more similar in value to all other role concepts while the career woman concept is only perceived similar in value to career man and nurse." In discussing the results of her study Akrons states: "A comparison of the career woman-career man concept pair contributes further support to the data on female role conflicts. The career man concept links with all other male concepts. In sharp contrast, the career woman concept was not perceived as similar to the other female concepts. . . . This isolation of the career woman concept suggests that the counselors in this study perceive career goals as incompatible with the traditional female roles of wife and motherhood."

Not only are school counselors biased in their perceptions of the sex roles, but many of the materials they use contain sex bias. In the earlier discussion on grading and academic achievement, the sex bias in many standardized achievement tests was pointed out. Interest inventories such as the Strong Vocational Interest Blank (SVIB) and the Kuder Occupational Interest Survey have also been viewed as biased since they provide a more restricted range of occupations for women than for men (Cole, 1972; Harman, 1973; Schlossberg and Goodman, 1972; Tittle et al., 1974). In response to the growing awareness of bias inherent in many written materials used in counseling, the Association for Measurement and Evaluation in Guidance (AMEG, 1973) developed guidelines for the elimination of sex bias. The National Institute of Education (NIE) Career Education Program also developed guidelines for the assessment of sex bias and sex fairness in career interest inventories (Diamond, 1975), and defined sex bias in career guidance as ". . . any factor that might influence a person to limit—or might cause others to limit— his or her considerations of a career solely on the basis of gender."

Another positive response to the problem of sex bias in interest measurement has been the development of improved instruments. For example, Campbell (1974) combined the best items from the male and female forms of the SVIB into a single inventory, the Strong Campbell Interest Inventory (SCII). Each individual who takes the SCII is scored on all scales, male and female. In an effort to provide an interest inventory with sex balanced interest items and thus "sex-fair career suggestions to both men and women," test specialists at the American College Testing Program developed the Unisex ACT Interest Inventory (UNIACT) (Hanson et al., 1977). Crites' Career Maturity Inventory (CMI) is another instrument designed to eliminate sex bias (Crites, 1973). The vignettes contained in the CMI Competence Test include young women and men with nontraditional interests and career aspirations, and the items on the CMI Attitude Scale are equally applicable to either sex.

In addition to the problem of sex bias in interest instruments, career and education materials commonly used by counselors and their clients are also biased. Birk, Cooper, and Tanney (1973, 1975) found that compared to their numbers in the labor force, women are underrepresented in both the 1972 and 1974 *Occupational Outlook Handbook* (OOH). The career illustrations in the OOH convey subtle but pervasive impressions of sex appropriate career aspirations. While occasionally, women are portrayed in nontraditional professions, men are too rarely shown in nontraditional occupations. The authors assert that these illustrations may limit the horizons of the young women and men who use the OOH. Vetter (1975) found similar results in an analysis of student career guidance materials in the *Vocational Guidance Quarterly's* career literature bibliography and two other bibliographies of commercial and noncommercial materials. In all of the materials considered, 61 percent of the illustrations were of men, 21 percent of women, and 18 percent of both. Again, similar results were found by Harway (1977) in an analysis of the 1974–75 *Encyclopedia of Careers and Vocational Guidance* (ECVG) and the OOH. Eleven percent of the ECVG and 17 percent of the OOH illustrations are of women; another 14 percent of the pictures in the ECVG and 10 percent in the OOH represent both sexes. In observing how the women were portrayed, Harway (1977) commends, ". . . women are often stereotypically represented as helpful, pleasant, and attractive."

College and vocational school catalogs often comprise a large portion of the guidance materials in high school counseling and guidance offices. The information students obtain from these catalogs helps them form perceptions of the academic environment they will encounter if they go on to a postsecondary institution. Harway (1977) analyzed a random sample of catalogs from 100 colleges and 19 proprietary schools and found that a far greater proportion of college catalog content is devoted to men than to women, and both sexes are represented in a stereotypic fashion. For example, half-pages were tallied and a percentage was calculated for the half-pages devoted to men and those devoted to women:

	Percent of half-pages devoted to men	Percent of half-pages devoted to women
four-year colleges and universities	23	less than 1
two-year institutions	16	2
proprietary schools	14	9

The illustrations in the catalogs stereotype both sexes. Professors and administrators are usually male; men are shown in technical laboratories, and women are shown in nursing pictures; men are pictured in contact sports, and women are pictured alone in exercise and dance activities. While the majority of the institutions have an affirmative action statement in their catalogs, few describe programs specifically designed to meet the needs of women. In summary, Harway (1977) surmises the impact that such catalogs have on women students: "It is probable that the limited vistas for women shown in the college catalogs will convince many high school students that the options for women are also limited in colleges themselves."

Staffing Patterns and Role Models   The teacher stereotype is usually a woman, neatly groomed, very conservative, and caught up in routine. The love-starved, syrupy old maid school teacher in *Good Morning, Miss Dove* (Patton, 1954) is one version of the stereotype. Saltz (1960) presents another:

In the public mind the teacher is an ambitious, domineering, managing, fussy, tyrannical woman who has powers that enable her to see more of people's motives than they wish to reveal. She has few friends; she is not interested in people's problems; social mingling is not to her liking. When things go wrong, she rarely blames herself. Set in her ways, bound up in routine, she hesitates to do the unconventional.

Sociologist-educator Waller (1932) views the male teacher as assimilated into the "female character ideal" which isolates him from the usual male activities. On the status of the male teacher, Waller comments: "It has been said that no woman and no Negro is ever fully admitted to the white man's world. Possibly we should add men teachers to the list of the excluded."

"Like the stereotypes of the old maid school teacher and of the classroom dominated by a female, there is a reverse stereotype which identifies all administrators as males. The ogre male principal who stands ten feet tall and is ready to inflict swift punishment on some shivering boy culprit, is a standard theme of cartoons" (Grambs and Waetjen, 1975).

While these stereotypes have altered somewhat over the years, there is good reason for the teacher to be viewed as female and the administrator to be viewed as male since school staffing patterns reflect this sex difference in school personnel positions. For example, in 1973, 66 percent of the nation's public school teachers were women, including a dominant 84 percent of the elementary schools teachers and a not-so-dominant 46 percent of the secondary school teachers. Men on the other hand made up 80 percent of the elementary school principals, 97 percent of the juior high school principals, and 99 percent of the high school principals (Fishel and Pottker, 1974). Relatively recent increases in male school teachers have been accompanied by a decline in female teachers and administrators. For example, from 1958 to 1968 male teachers increased at the elementary level from 12.8 percent to 14.6 percent and at the secondary level from 50.5 percent to 52.9 percent. During the same period women principals decreased 16 percent, and the proportion of female secondary school teachers declined from 68 percent of the total in the 1920s to their present 46 percent (Clement, 1975).

Since few women are principals, it is not surprising that even fewer become superintendents. Of the 13,037 local superintendents in the United States, only 65 are women; and of the 19,227 superintendents, deputy superintendents, associate superintendents, and assistant superintendents in the nation, 401 or a mere 2 percent are women (Fishel and Pottker, 1974). Women are also not well-represented on local and state boards of education. In 1972, only 12 percent of local school board members and 20 percent of state board of education members in the country were women. During the same year, only one state had a woman chief state school officer, and only four states had either a woman deputy superintendent, or associate or assistant superintendent (Fishel and Pottker, 1974).

Since women are preponderant in the teaching ranks from which school administrators are recruited, why are there so few women in these decision-making roles? In trying to answer this question, Estler (1975) proposes three possible explanatory models: the Woman's-Place Model, the Discrimination Model, and the Meritocracy Model. The Meritocracy Model—that the most competent people are promoted according to their ability and women are not as qualified as men—is discounted with documentation of a "fairly even distribution of men and women in the eligibility pool for the principalship, based on academic credentials, and . . . the average years of teaching experience are similar for both men and women teachers." In reviewing studies on administrative competence of male and female administrators as perceived by their superiors and subordinates Estler (1975) found that the "perceived effectiveness of women as leaders is certainly as high as the perceived effectiveness of their male counterparts, if not higher." With her Meritocracy Model discounted, Estler is left with the Woman's-Place Model—that leadership traits are usually defined as male characteristics; therefore most women will not seek positions of leadership and responsibility—and the Discrimination Model—that there is a sex bias which limits opportunities for women to reach leadership positions. In commenting on the possible interaction of these two models, she states: "The existing research begins to fail us . . . in attempting to distinguish between the woman's-place and the discrimination models. While it clearly shows that women aspire to leadership to a lesser extent than do men, it does not make it clear whether these aspirations are a response to the limited opportunity accompanying discrimination or whether it is a choice on the part of the woman in response to society's expectations for her role."

For whatever reasons, and I agree with those who assert that it is a combination of socialization and discrimination factors, women outnumber men in teaching positions in elementary schools, and men far outnumber women in administration positions at all levels. Such an imbalance of the sexes in staffing is not only unfair in the sense of providing equal employment opportunities for women and men alike, but it is also restrictive in providing role models for the students. Students who never see a woman in a leadership position have a hard time believing that women can be leaders. Students who never experience a male teacher in the lower grades have a difficult time believing that anyone but "mother images" can effectively teach the very young.

The College Experience Prior to Title IX of the Education Amendments of 1972, which did not go into effect until 1975 (see chap. 5) it was not illegal for educational institutions to treat men and women differently. As a result of this differential treatment, women students were not given equal educational opportunity in institutions of higher education. Rather, they were discouraged from pursuing an education, discriminated against in admissions, and those who persisted were at best tolerated. As recent as 1971, the Newman Task Force stated in its *Report on Higher Education* (Newman, 1971), "Our study found that discrimination against women, in contrast to that against minorities, is still overt and socially acceptable within the academic community." And in 1973, the Carnegie Commission on Higher

Education (*Opportunity for Women in Higher Education,* 1973) concluded, "A substantial proportion of the intellectual talent of women has been and is being lost to society as a result of cultural circumstances. . . . Historically, women in higher education have been and still often are disadvantaged as individuals compared to the level of their potential abilities." How have women students been disadvantaged and discriminated against in our colleges and universities? Some of the more blatant ways will be discussed here. While such unfair practices are now illegal, they were prevalent in institutions of higher education until only recently, and it will be some time before their effects are no longer felt.

Some Discriminatory Practices

Admissions In testimony before the Special Subcommittee on Education of the Committee on Education and Labor (91st Cong., 2nd Sess., H. Rept. 16098, part 2, July, 1970) discriminatory practices in admissions was a central topic:

> We know that many colleges admit fixed proportions of men and women each year, resulting in a freshman class with fewer women meeting higher standards than it would contain if women were admitted on the same basis as men. At Cornell University, for example, the ratio of men to women remains three to one from year to year; at Harvard/Radcliffe, it is four to one. The University of North Carolina at Chapel Hill's fall 1969 "Profile of the Freshman Class" states, "admission of women on the freshman level will be restricted to those who are especially well qualified." They admitted 3,231 men, or about half the male applicants, and 747 women, about one-fourth the female applicants.

In March of 1971, Dr. Bernice Sandler (1971) cited the following examples of discriminatory admissions policies in testimony before the House Judiciary committee:

> For the last decade at the University of Michigan, according to G. C. Wilson, Executive Associate Director of Admissions, the Office of Admissions has "adjusted" requirements to insure that an "overbalance"—that is, a majority—of women would not occur in the freshman class for a number of years, despite the fact that in terms of grades and test scores, there are more qualified female applicants than males. At Pennsylvania State University, an artificial ratio of 2.5 men to every female is deliberately maintained. . . . In graduate school, the quota system is even more vicious. At Stanford, for example, the proportion of women students has declined over the last ten years, even though more and equally or better qualified women have applied for admission to graduate school. (One out of every 2.8 men who applied was accepted; only 1 woman out of 4.7 applicants was accepted.)

To illustrate how institutions have required female applicants to be better qualified than male applicants in order to be admitted to college, Cross (1974) computed the following table (3-1) from in-

Table 3-1 Percentages of Acceptance to a Selective Four-Year Liberal Arts College

Criterion	Percentage of Applicants Accepted*	
	Male	Female
High School Class Rank		
Top fifth	92	62
Second fifth	58	18
Third fifth and below	36	4
SAT Score, Verbal		
700-800	92	93
600-699	87	75
500-599	73	32
Below 500	35	6
SAT Score, Mathematical		
700-800	91	85
600-699	81	68
500-599	59	33
Below 500	19	11

*Applications were received from 1,037 men and 1,097 women. Overall rates of acceptance were 68 percent for men and 45 percent for women.

formation contained in the *College Handbook* (College Entrance Examination Board, 1969).

Even those colleges and universities which appear to have a more sex balanced undergraduate admissions profile may still be discriminating by admitting more women than men to schools of nursing and education and more men than women in the sciences.

While discrimination against women in graduate admissions is more difficult to document, some researchers contend that discrimination is a more serious problem at the graduate level than it is at the undergraduate level. After interviewing presidents, chancellors, and faculty members at ten leading graduate schools for her study of graduate education, Heiss (1970) concludes:

Not excluding academic qualifications, sex is probably the most discriminatory factor applied in the decision whether to admit an applicant to graduate school. It is almost a foregone conclusion that among American institutions women have greater difficulty being admitted to doctoral study and, if admitted, will have a greater difficulty being accepted than will men. Department chairmen and faculty members frankly state that their main reason for ruling against women is "the probability that they will marry."

In discussing the rationale most frequently given for differential admissions to graduate education, Cross (1974) lists three interrelated factors; cost effectiveness, completion rates, and productivity. She quotes Lewis (1968) who shows the relationship of these factors as viewed by many educators:

Sex Typing in the Schools   **69**

Many graduate and professional programs for which members of both sexes commonly apply tend to discriminate against women, and many authorities believe they have good reason. Women are poorer bets than men to finish such a program, and those who do are less likely to use their education productively. A university feels some obligation not only to educate individuals but also to be of benefit to society; thus, if an admissions committee must choose between a capable man and a capable woman for a place in its program, the choice can logically be made in favor of the man. The woman who is thereby rejected may, of course, be the exception who would have finished and who would have made a worthwhile contribution, but her more casual sisters have prejudiced the committee against her.

While evidence is scanty, it appears that women graduate students do have a higher dropout rate and take longer to complete their degrees than men. For example, while women constituted roughly half of the graduate students enrolled in master's degree programs, they received only 35 percent of the master's degrees awarded in 1968. At the doctoral level 25 percent of the enrollees were women, but only 13 percent received degrees (Ferriss, 1971). The Ferriss (1971) study also found the median time lapse from the baccalaureate to the doctorate to be 11.2 years for women and 7.9 years for men. This correlates with Astin's (1969) data which showed that women took approximately twelve years to complete their doctorates and were about four years older than their male counterparts. That women are slower in getting their degrees than men may indicate that their dropout rate is not permanent, but rather a temporary "stop out." Since longitudinal studies of graduate student progress by discipline are not available, it cannot be assumed that women are poor risks because they do not complete their graduate training.

In countering the charge that women who get graduate degrees are less productive than men, Astin (1969) found that 91 percent of the women who received doctorates in 1957 and 1958 were working in 1966. Eighty-one percent were working full time, and 79 percent of the women had never interrupted their careers. Robinson (1971) quoting Mitchell's study of women who received doctorates from Oklahoma Ph.D.-granting institutions reports that 99 percent of the women who received doctorates were working and 98 percent were working full time. Such evidence of women using their graduate education and training nullifies the idea that graduate training for women is a waste of time and resources.

Financial Aid Not only have parents been less willing to finance their daughter's college education than their son's, but women students at the undergraduate level have received less institutionally administered financial aid. In a nationwide survey of college sophomores, Haven and Horch (1972) found the average financial aid to women was $786 while the average for men was $1,000. In addition, the average institutionally administered scholarship or grant was $515 for women and $671 for men.

While athletic scholarships are available to only a small proportion of a school's student body, they deserve mention here because of the dramatic sex difference in the recipients of such scholarships. Until recently, athletic scholarships for women were almost unheard of, while men—many from lower-income families—received substantial "full-ride" athletic scholarships. It has only been during the last few years (and largely due to Title IX) that colleges and universities have begun to offer athletic scholarships for women, although they are usually considerably less in number and dollar amount than those offered men on the same campus.

Regarding financial assistance to graduate students, Cross (1974) and Creager (1971) contend that there is little or no evidence of sex discrimination. Their argument is that while men are a little more likely to derive primary support from assistantships or fellowships, the differences are not large considering the higher levels of student assistance available in the sciences. But the proportion of women graduate students who receive financial aid still is considerably less than the proportion of male graduate students who do. Astin (1969) found that only 46 percent of women doctoral candidates received financial assistance from the government or their institutions compared to 58 percent of the men.

School Policies and Rules   While colleges and universities no longer have differential policies and rules for men and women regarding such things as dress codes, parietal regulations in dormatories, and the like, some institutions still have restrictive policies regarding part-time study which are far more serious in impact and which affect women to a greater degree than men. According to the Carnegie Commission on Higher Education (1973): "Probably the most important factor tending to discriminate against women in admission to graduate study is a variety of rules and informal policies discouraging admission of students who wish to study on a part-time basis. Faced with a choice between a married woman planning to study part-time and a student who plans full-time graduate work, a department is highly likely to favor the full-time student." This has been particularly true in the professional schools such as medicine and law. Similarly, many institutions have a rule against giving financial aid to part-time students.

Such policies and practices regarding part-time study put women in a particularly difficult bind and make the continuation of their education an impossible task. According to a National Institute of Health (1968) study, the major obstacles to graduate study for women are financial limitations and family responsibilities—either of which generally necessitates part-time rather than full-time study.

Due to stable and in many instances decreasing enrollments, institutions are reviewing and many are dropping their restrictive policies regarding part-time study. Thus, educational opportunities for the part-time student, male and female, are more of a reality today than ever before.

Curriculum and Instructional Materials   Sexism and stereotyping in the curriculum and instructional materials has already been described in some detail in the earlier discussion of elementary and secondary schools. Patterns are very similar at the college level. For example, an American Psychological Association task force examined thirteen of the most frequently used textbooks in clinical psychology, child development, and tests and measurement to see "whether, and if so, in what manner there exist erroneous and harmful conceptions and representations of either sex" (Birk and others, 1974). The task force concluded that such texts show limited career roles for women and thereby restrict women's career options. Women are infrequently used as subject material or as subjects of psychological research, there is little discussion of sex roles or sex differences, and the pronoun "he" appears to refer to men specifically rather than used in the generic sense to refer to mankind.

Harway (1977) found similar results in a content analysis of the three most frequently assigned texts in graduate counseling programs: Shertzer and Stone's (1971) *Fundamentals of Guidance,* Tyler's (1969) *Work of the Counselor,* and Gazda's (1971) *Group Counseling: A Developmental Approach.* Half-pages devoted to men and half-pages devoted to women were tallied, and the results were as follows:

Text	Percent of half-pages devoted to men	Percent of half-pages devoted to women
Gazda	37	11
Shertzer and Stone	52	4
Tyler	94	4

The texts showed both men and women in stereotyped roles. The Shertzer and Stone text depicts high school girls as valuing dating, dancing, clothes, physical beauty, and manners, while boys are shown as valuing cars and athletics. Tyler depicts men as colleagues and women as clients and students. Women are seen as secretaries or receptionists, dependent and needing a man to love, or contemplating divorce and seeking career options. Men are shown entering the military service as immature boys and emerging as mature men, trying to decide between medicine, dentistry, and engineering careers. While Gazda is more egalitarian, referring to both men and women as colleagues, he still shows females as Girl Scouts, insecure students, and mothers, while males are shown as group leaders.

Similar treatment of the sexes is found in most texts and instructional materials regardless of the field of study. Women are either omitted, as is the case in history, business, mathematical, and biological science textbooks, or they are depicted stereotypically (as are men) in literature and social science books.

As an effort to counter the male curriculum of colleges and universities, women's studies courses and programs began to appear on campuses throughout the country in the late 1960s and early 1970s (see chap. 7 for more discussion). To date, approximately 15,000 courses have been developed by 8,500 teachers at 1,500 different institutions. Over 250 women's studies programs have been formed, some offering master's and Ph.D. degrees (Howe, 1977). While individual programs in the early years had diverse purposes, they shared some common ones: "(1) to raise the consciousness of the campus on the question of the male-centered curriculum by organizing such courses as 'Images of Women in Literature' and the 'Sociology of Sex Roles'; (2) to supplement the curriculum by adding such new women's studies courses as the 'History of Women in the U.S.' or 'Women in the Workforce'; and (3) to establish women as a legitimate topic for study and research." In describing the early overall mission of women's studies as a curricular strategy for change, Howe (1977) comments:

Women's studies was to be a major route to establishing educational equity for women: omitted from the curriculum, women could not know their history or understand with accuracy their present condition; admitted to the curriculum, women could then share a history and identity that would allow them to envisage and to move toward an equitable future. The presence of women in the curriculum would allow women to aspire and men to understand those aspirations.

While the early purposes and overall mission of women's studies are still apparent in present programs, they have been transformed into more specific strategies (Howe, 1977):

to transform disciplines (through a consideration of women), with regard to curriculum, research focus, and methodology;

to develop interdisciplinary curricula focused on women (or on the issues of sex and gender), along with a pedagogy that is suitable, and research methodology that is supportive;

to open additional career options for students through the development of coherent academic programs;

to affect the educational community off campus through efforts to change the preservice and inservice education of teachers.

Counseling and Academic Advising In the earlier section of this chapter on counseling and guidance in the elementary and secondary schools, counselors' sexist attitudes regarding sex roles and the sex bias in many of the instruments and materials they use in counseling with students were discussed. Counselors on the college level have also been found to have sexist attitudes, and they too use many of the biased instruments discussed previously.

Collins and Sedlacek (1974) set out to delineate areas in which male and female clients in a university counseling center are viewed and treated differently. Using an in-house data sheet ("Codebook of Counseling Categories") with "satisfactory" reliability, 565 female and 645 male clients at the University of Maryland Counseling Center were rated. Ratings were made by thirteen Ph.D. level counselors, four female and nine male. Results indicated the following client sex differences: Males were more likely to be viewed as having vocational-educational problems, while females were more often rated as having emotional-social problems. Females were more likely to be given an appointment or placed on a waiting list than males. Males terminated by mutual agreement with their counselors more frequently than did females. And females were considered to have made improvement in overall adjustment more often than were males. Such findings echo the discussion in chapter 2 of clinicians's double standard of mental health for men and women. In discussing the results, the authors explained:

The differences found between counselor ratings of male and female clients may be explained in several ways. One could say, for example, that the differences in ratings reflect "real" differences in male and female clients. Or, taking a radical stance, one might suggest that the differences are a reflection of the counselors' expectations and sexual stereotypes about differences between male and female students' problems and do not actually relate to "real" differences. A third explanation might suggest some interaction of the first two—that is, that clients have a tendency to differ according to sex and that counselors have a tendency to respond differentially to male and female clients. The data do not offer any sound rationale for explaining the differences, nor do they preclude any particular explanation.

Pietrofesa and Schlossberg (cited in Schlossberg and Pietrofesa, 1973) and Abramowitz and others (1975) found college counselors to have biased attitudes toward women students who select a nontraditional occupational choice. The Abramowitz and others (1975) study looked at counselor perceptions of the psychological adjustment of potential medical students. The counselors were given a male and female case history to evaluate and completed a psychological adjustment scale for each case history. In general, the results showed that "traditional" counselors judged psychoeducational histories of female medical school applicants as showing less psychological adjustment than male histories.

The Pietrofesa and Schlossberg study found similar results. Counseling-practicum students interviewed a coached female client who was beginning her junior year in college and could not decide between a career in education and one in engineering. The interviews were tape-recorded and were examined for counselor bias. Results indicated that counselor bias exists against women entering engineering. Typical biased counselor statements addressed the "masculinity" of the field.

College counselors' attitudes regarding nontraditional fields of study and occupational choice for students seem to be changing slowly, however, as employment practices change and as counselors are becoming sensitized to appearing sexist. Hill and others (1977) for example, found that college counselors perceived no differences between the dilemmas faced by women considering traditional (social work) and nontraditional (engineering) college majors. More studies are needed to determine if in fact counselors' attitudes are changing regarding not only nontraditional occupational choices of women but of men.

An indication of changing attitudes of counselor trainees was found by Burlin and Pearson (1978). Counselor trainees were given a description of a client seeking assistance with a personal-educational choice conflict (to remain close to a fiance/fiancee or to accept a fellowship for graduate study at a distant university). Half of the counselor trainees were told their client was male, and the other half were told their client was female. Subjects were asked to indicate their personal view of the most appropriate action for the client (opinion measure) as well as the counseling strategy that they would use were they actually working with the client (strategy measure).

While different response patterns were found between male and female counselors on the opinion measure (most of the female counselors felt the client—whether male or female—should take the fellowship; male counselors felt the client should choose the alternative he or she believed to be best), the results were not in the direction of traditional sex role stereotyping. The majority of both the male and female counselors chose the facilitative option on the strategy measure—that as counselors they would strive to help the client develop or implement her or his own solution. While the authors found no consistent indication of sex role bias with their sample of 127 counselor trainees, they caution that the results may be situation specific and recommend further research with a variety of clients in several choice situations. They also recommend similar studies done with counselors of different age groups.

Academic advising and the student-advisor relationship has received little attention in the literature on sex role stereotyping and sex bias. Yet, being admitted, financed, tested, and housed are not the only kinds of support needed by students. Faculty sponsorship and tutelage provide not only intellectual stimulation but emotional support for students which affects their self-esteem, motivation, and perseverence. Self-reports from women students, particularly those at the graduate level, would indicate that they do not receive this kind of support and encouragement from their faculty advisors. Instead, many of them are treated as if they have no business pursuing their education. For example, the following statements were made by professors to their female students (Harris, 1970):

"A pretty girl like you will certainly get married; why don't you stop with an M.A.?"

"The girls at [X university] get good grades because they study hard, but they don't have any originality."

"We expect women who come here to be competent, good students, but we don't expect them to be brilliant or original."

"Women are intrinsically inferior."

"How old are you anyway? Do you think that a girl like you could handle a job like this? You don't look like the academic type."

"Why don't you find a rich husband and give all this up?"

"Our general admissions policy has been if the body is warm and male, take it; if it's female, make sure it's an A—from Bryn Mawr."

"Somehow I can never take women in this field seriously."

At a special conference on the graduate and professional education of women sponsored by the American Association of University

Women, the Association of American Colleges, and the Cooperative College Registry, several speakers recounted the negative attitudes they encountered while they were graduate students (AAUW, 1974). Before becoming a sociologist, Muriel Cantor applied to the UCLA political science program and was told by a professor: "Well I guess we are going to have to take you. We don't like older women, we don't think you are worth our investment, but this is a state school, you have the grades and you have the letters of recommendation, so we are going to have to take you." Assistant Professor of Law Jane Dolkart described her experience in applying for a teaching job after completing her legal education: ". . . one person on the hiring committee said: 'We can't possibly hire this woman to teach because all the men in the class are going to think about when they look at her up there is whether they can go to bed with her.'" And, Associate Provost of Wesleyan University Sheila Tobias described her graduate school experience as "the only time I ever understood what it was to 'hate school.'" She described her Ph.D. seminar professor as "openly hostile" and, "over the years, his stark indifference to my work undermined me. In fact, no one ever seemed interested in my concerns and doubts. The university was prepared to invest money in me, but not time or interest. Again and again, 'it doesn't matter one way or the other' was communicated to me."

With such a lack of support from professors and advisers, it is no wonder that fewer women than men complete graduate degrees. In an analysis of data on graduate students from a Carnegie Commission survey, Holmstrom and Holmstrom (1973) found the negative attitudes of faculty toward women students contributed to the emotional stress felt by at least one in three women and also decreased their commitment to stay in graduate school. The same study revealed that substantial proportions of graduate students agreed with the statement "professors in my department don't really take female students seriously," and approximately one-fourth to one-third (depending on the type of institution and field of study) of the male faculty members agreed with the statement "the female graduate students in my department are not as dedicated as the males." As expected, fewer women faculty agreed with the statement (approximately 10 to 15 percent). In a follow-up study conducted by Trow (1976) for the Carnegie Council on Policy Studies in Higher Education, faculty were found to be only a little more liberal in their attitudes toward women students. One out of six (compared to one in five in 1969) agreed that "female graduate students in my department are not as dedicated as the males," and more than one-third of the faculty felt women were not as likely as men to complete their graduate study and make important contributions to the field. Commenting on the results of the survey, Trow concluded, ". . . if a significant proportion of college and university teachers have reservations about the likelihood of women graduate students finishing their degrees and doing important work, then they are not as likely to give them the kind of attention and challenge they give men."

Academic Ability: Are There Sex Differences?

Judging from the preference of many faculty to teach, advise, sponsor, and work with men rather than women, one would expect to find large differences in academic ability and aptitude. But such is not the case. Granted, there are some small differences which will be discussed here, but the overall potential for academic accomplishment of men and women is comparable.

Studies going back as far as the 1920s have shown that women receive markedly better grades than men from elementary school through college. The 1969 Carnegie Commission Survey of Faculty and Student Opinion (reported in *Opportunities for Women in Higher Education,* Carnegie Commission on Higher Education, 1973) showed that percentages of women with averages of B or better exceeded those of men, and percentages of men with averages of B − or lower exceeded those of women. This was true regardless of the field of study, so the argument that women have higher averages because they major in less difficult disciplines has no grounds. Data collected at the University of California at Berkeley during the 1970 spring semester show a similar pattern. Forty-six percent of the freshman women made first semester grade averages of B or above, compared with 39 percent of the men. The same proportions hold for seniors—45 percent of the women and 38 percent of the men achieved grade averages of B or better (American Council on Education, 1971). While grades are being increasingly criticized as a measure of academic prowess, they are still the best single predictor of future academic performance in educational institutions.

As has been mentioned in an earlier section of this chapter, on other measures of academic achievement and aptitude, men outperform women on quantitative tests, while women score better on tests of verbal abilities. Data for mean scores on tests administered by the American College Testing Program indicate that women perform somewhat better than men on English tests, while men perform somewhat better on mathematics and natural sciences tests and slightly better on social sciences tests. However, the overall performance of women is only slightly below that of men (Carnegie Commission on Higher Education, 1973).

Cross (1974) effectively summarizes the sex stereotypes regarding abilities and their lack of validity when she says:

Chauvinists of both sexes feel that men are better able to deal with big ideas and abstractions, whereas women handle day-to-day problems in a more practical manner. But research measuring the personality trait called "intellectuality" fails to support the stereotype. Evidence indicates that women are slightly more interested in esthetics and in working with ideas and abstractions, whereas men are more interested in theory and the use of the scientific method. Although cultural expectations may push males and females toward emphases in academic choices and behavior, the research on academic interests, abilities, and personality characteristics indicates no important differences between men and women in their potential for academic accomplishment.

Students' Views of Themselves: Sexist but Changing

College students, a group of which tends to be critical of traditional social norms and conventions, show ambiguity when it comes to conceptions of sex roles. One indication of the behaviors and roles students view as appropriate for men and women can be found by looking at the student leadership positions on campus. A survey of 454 colleges conducted by the American Association of University Women (Oltman, 1970) showed that students elected to leadership positions were invariably males. When women held student leadership positions, they were usually appointed rather than elected by their peers. In coeducational colleges, 84 percent of the student body presidents and 76 percent of the class presidents were male. Men were far more likely than women to hold such offices as judicial board chairman, student union board chiarman, freshman orientation committee chairman, and debate team captain. Women, on the other hand, held 49 percent of the yearbook editorships. While women were more likely to have an opportunity for leadership in small colleges, the majority of the positions were still held by men. Although a present update of student positions is not available, casual observation leads one to believe that women students are becoming more active in such leadership positions but still do not hold the top positions in the same proportions as do male students.

Additudinal research indicates that college women and men still believe that certain existing sex role stereotypes are desirable (Broverman et al., 1972; Elman et al., 1970; Katz, 1977; and Rosenkrantz et al., 1968). "Pluralities of men view themselves as more aggressive and objectively rational and less emotional than women. Women tend to view themselves as more emotional and sensitive and less aggressive than males" (Katz, 1977). Rosenkrantz and associates (1968) found that while college men and women perceive themselves as differing significantly along a dimension of stereotypic sex differences, the women's self-concepts were considerably less feminine than their perceptions on the "average" women, and the men's self-concepts were considerably less masculine than their perceptions of men in general.

While male and female college students tend to describe themselves using sex role stereotypic terms, their attitudes regarding equality for women have undergone considerable change in recent years. In annual surveys of large national samples of college freshmen, Astin (1977) has traced this change in college student attitudes. For example, in 1977, only 19.8 percent of the women and 35.5 percent of the men felt "women's activities should be confined to the home," compared to over one-third of the women and approximately half of the men in the early 1970s. Ninety-six percent of the women and 88 percent of the men in the 1977 sample felt that women should have job equality; changes in this attitude have pretty much paralleled changes in the laws to ensure equal employment opportunities for women.

One of the most dramatic changes in attitudes, particularly those of women, is in the sexual area. Two out of three men and one out of three women in the 1977 sample agreed that "If two people really like each other, it's all right for them to have sex even if they have known each other for only a very short time." Forty-two percent of the women and 54.5 percent of the men felt that couples should live together before deciding to get married. Sexual behaviors of college students, again particularly those of women, have changed along with their attitudes. While studies of sexual experience of female college students in the 1950s and 1960s reported low incidence (usually under 25 percent) of premarital intercourse and then usually "confined to her future spouse" (Ehrmann, 1960), more recent studies report that 50 percent of the freshman women and 76 percent of the junior women have experienced sexual intercourse, compared to 61 percent of the male freshmen and 76 percent of the male juniors (Katz, 1977). The double standard regarding sexual behavior appears to be declining.

Regarding objectives which the students consider essential or very important, almost equal amounts of men and women (58.8 and 58.9 percent, respectively) listed "raising a family." Also, similar proportions of males and females (77.5 percent of the men and 72.1 percent of the women) listed the goal of "becoming an authority in my field" (Astin, 1977). The juxtaposition of these two objectives—"raising a family" and "becoming an authority in my field"—tempts one to hypothesize about increased sharing of home and work responsibilities for future couples. McMillin (1972), however, found that of a sample of over 2,000 unmarried male students, 12 percent preferred that their future wives not work after marriage; 38 percent preferred that their future wives worked only until the time of children; 40 percent said they would like their wives to work after marriage until the time of children, devoting full time to family during the children's early years, and then returning to work as the children grow older; 4 percent said they preferred that their future wives worked continuously after marriage, taking off only short periods of time as required for family matters; and 7 percent said they did not plan to marry. But there is also some evidence that college men are willing to face up to the consequences of changed attitudes and occupational aspirations of women. According to Katz (1977), men are willing to divide domestic tasks equally, and 86 percent of the men and 96 percent of the women feel that fathers should spend as much time raising the children as mothers. However, traditional male attitudes still prevail when it comes to who earns the money. Only 44 percent of the men view it as a joint task, compared to 76 percent of the women. A majority of both sexes (96 percent of the women and 76 percent of the men) agree that "young women today must make more independent plans for their lives than their mothers did."

How have these changing attitudes affected the educational aspirations of college students? Most high school graduates today, male and female, aspire to go to college. The dividing line between the educational aspirations of young women and men has in recent years fallen between the junior college and the four-year college degree, with over half the women being content with two years of college or less and over half the men aspiring to four years of college or more (Cross, 1971). But this is changing as more women are seeking bachelor's and graduate degrees (see discussion in the section below on trends in enrollment and earned degrees). Among 1976 students, two out of every five students seeking advanced degrees were women, compared with one out of five in 1966 (Astin, 1976). While the majority of college students indicate majors and occupational plans in fields which are traditional ones for their sex, an increasing number of women are showing an interest in traditionally "male" occupations. For example, among women entering college in 1976, 19.4 percent indicated they plan a career in law, medicine, business, or engineering (Astin, 1976). In 1966, only 5.9 percent of the entering women students anticipated careers in those fields.

While women's educational aspirations are increasing and they are showing more interest in nontraditional fields, it remains to be seen whether their numbers will be sufficient enough to significantly impact the traditionally "male" fields. In the past, fewer women than men have completed their degrees (Bernard, 1964; Davis, 1963). Moreover, between the freshman and senior years of college, many women students forego their initial career goals and switch to traditionally female fields such as teaching, nursing, home economics, and social work (Karmen, 1972; Katz et al., 1968; Schwenn, 1970; Tangri, 1969).

Several explanations have been given for this gravitation of women students to traditionally feminine occupations. According to Astin (1967), "These career changes occur as a result of both personal development and educational experience enabling women to define their vocational goals more realistically." Ginzburg (1966) proposes that college women make educational and occupational plans on a contingency basis, moving to social work or teaching because these occupations provide flexibility. Epstein (1970) found that many women place self-imposed limitations on their career choice and development—choosing shortrun social and economic advantages and failing to explore real motivations and abilities. Horner's (1968, 1970, 1972) "motive to avoid success" is frequently quoted as the reason for women not completing their education or switching from nontraditional to traditional fields of study. According to Horner, women are faced with a conflict between their feminine image and developing their abilities and expressing their competences—two desirable but mutually exclusive goals of women in our society. Thus, college women, fearful that intellectual achievement is viewed as "unfeminine" and will have a negative effect on their eligibility for marriage, will adjust their behavior to their internalized sex role stereotype. Such adjustment may mean switching to traditionally "feminine" career goals or dropping out of college altogether. While critics of Horner assert that men fear success too (Hoffman, 1974; Levine and Crumrine, 1975), there appear to be different "motives to avoid success" for men and women: for females it is the fear of affiliative loss because of success, while for males it is the questioning of the value of achievement (Hoffman, 1974).

It may be that any one or a combination of the above explanations could be the cause of women altering their educational aspirations. But there is also the interrelated factor of sexist and discriminatory treatment that college women have experienced which cannot be overlooked. There has been little motivation for a woman to succeed in an academic environment which discourages or ignores her and which is void of female role models. As the educational environment changes, so, hopefully, will the aspirations of women students . . . and there are indications of both.

Trends in Enrollment and Earned Degrees

The educational aspirations and changing sex role attitudes of young men and women are reflected in the statistics of college enrollment and earned degrees. An historical perspective is especially useful in seeing the growth of female degree recipients.

Between 1900 and 1940 the proportion of women graduates increased steadily (table 3-2). A sharp decline in women graduates between 1940 and 1950 was largely due to the increase in male World War II veterans and the impact of early marriage. Since 1950, the number of women graduating from college at all three degree levels (bachelor's, master's, doctor's) has been gradually increasing and the trend is predicted to continue.

While more women are obtaining college degrees, the majority still study fields which have been traditionally women's areas, such as education, nursing, the social sciences, English, library science, and the arts (table 3-3). There are, however, increasing numbers of women earning degrees in the health professions, the biological sciences, business and management, computer and information sciences, mathematics, architecture and environmental design, public affairs and services, foreign languages, and psychology.

Table 3-2 Proportion of College and University Degrees Earned by Women and Men

Year	Bachelor's Women	Men	Master's Women	Men	Doctor's Women	Men
1900	19.7	80.3	19.1	80.9	6.0	94.0
1910	22.7	77.3	26.4	73.6	9.9	90.1
1920	34.2	65.8	30.2	69.8	15.1	84.9
1930	39.9	60.1	40.4	59.6	15.4	84.6
1940	41.6	58.4	38.3	61.7	13.0	87.0
1950	23.9	76.1	29.2	70.8	9.7	90.3
1960	37.6	62.4	31.6	68.4	10.5	89.5
1970	43.1	56.9	39.7	60.3	13.3	86.7
1975	45.3	54.7	44.8	55.2	21.3	78.7
1980*	48.4	51.6	46.9	53.1	29.7	70.3

*Projected

Sources: *Historical Statistics of the United States*, Bureau of the Census, 1960, and U.S. Department of Health, Education, and Welfare, National Center for Educational Statistics, *Earned Degrees Conferred: 1974-75* and *Projections of Education Statistics to 1985-86.*

Table 3-3 Bachelor's Master's, and Doctor's Degrees Conferred in Institutions of Higher Education, by Sex of Student, and Discipline Division: Aggregate United States, 1974-75

Discipline Division	Bachelor's Degrees Requiring 4 or 5 Years			Master's Degrees			Doctor's Degrees (Ph.D., FD.D., etc.)		
	Total	Men	Women	Total	Men	Women	Total	Men	Women
1	2	3	4	5	6	7	8	9	10
ALL DISCIPLINE DIVISIONS	931,663	508,424	423,239	293,651	162,115	131,536	34,086	26,819	7,267
Agriculture and Natural Resources	17,573	15,101	2,472	3,076	2,712	364	991	958	33
Architecture and Environmental Design	8,238	6,803	1,435	2,953	2,354	599	69	58	11
Area Studies	3,066	1,376	1,690	1,140	648	492	166	128	38
Biological Sciences	52,236	34,820	17,416	6,591	4,615	1,976	3,384	2,641	743
Business and Management	135,455	113,232	22,223	36,450	33,370	3,080	1,011	970	41
Communications	19,249	11,456	7,793	2,796	1,619	1,177	165	119	46
Computer and Information Sciences	5,039	4,083	956	2,299	1,961	338	213	199	14
Education	168,749	45,046	123,703	120,233	45,500	74,733	7,443	5,147	2,296
Engineering	47,303	46,266	1,037	15,359	14,984	375	3,108	3,042	66
Fine and Applied Arts	41,061	15,627	25,434	8,363	4,448	3,915	649	446	203
Foreign Languages	18,172	4,181	13,991	3,826	1,265	2,561	857	455	402
Health Professions	49,476	11,000	38,476	10,842	4,145	6,697	618	441	177
Home Economics	16,873	680	16,193	1,901	203	1,698	156	51	105
Law	436	374	62	1,245	1,145	100	21	21	—
Letters	57,933	24,760	33,173	11,873	4,893	6,980	2,498	1,648	850
Library Science	1,069	80	989	8,123	1,726	6,397	56	33	23
Mathematics	18,346	10,646	7,700	4,338	2,910	1,428	975	865	110
Military Sciences	390	390	—	—	—	—	—	—	—
Physical Sciences	20,896	17,058	3,838	5,830	4,982	848	3,628	3,326	302
Psychology	51,436	24,333	27,103	7,104	4,059	3,045	2,442	1,688	754
Public Affairs and Services	28,597	15,559	13,038	15,505	8,587	6,918	285	216	69
Social Sciences	136,773	85,580	51,193	16,942	11,856	5,086	4,209	3,332	877
Theology	4,818	3,499	1,319	3,230	2,232	998	872	839	33
Interdisciplinary Studies	28,479	16,474	12,005	3,632	1,901	1,731	270	196	74

Source: U.S. Department of Health, Education, and Welfare, National Center for Education Statistics, *Earned Degrees Conferred: 1974-75*, 1976.

In a fact sheet on female degree recipients, Eiden (1976) uses National Center for Education Statistics data to compare degrees earned by women in 1974–75 with those earned a decade ago. He points out some interesting changes in certain fields of study. For example, at the bachelor's degree level, women increased their proportion of degrees awarded in architecture and environmental design from 4.6 percent in 1964–65 to 17.4 percent in 1974–75. In computer and information sciences, women received 4.6 percent of the bachelor's degrees in 1964–65 and 18.9 percent in 1974–75. At the master's level, women's share of the degrees in architecture and environmental design and in mathematics increased by 12.5 percentage period to reach 20.3 and 32.9 percent respectively. In communications (including advertising, journalism, and radio/television) received 25.5 percent of the degrees in 1964–65 and 42.1 percent—an increase of 16.6 percentage points.

While the numbers are relatively small in some fields, the proportion of doctor's degrees awarded women has nearly doubled in

Table 3-4 Percentage of Women Among Doctor's Degree Recipients, by Discipline Division: Aggregate United States, 1970-71 through 1974-75

Discipline division	1970-71	1971-72	1972-73	1973-74	1974-75	1970-71 through 1974-75
ALL DISCIPLINE DIVISIONS	14.3	15.8	17.9	19.1	21.3	17.7
Agriculture and natural resources	2.9	2.7	2.6	3.5	3.3	3.0
*Architecture and environmental design	8.3	14.0	6.9	5.8	15.9	10.3
Area studies	17.4	18.2	29.1	27.6	22.9	23.2
*Biological sciences	16.3	17.0	19.5	20.3	22.0	19.0
Business and management	2.8	2.2	5.7	5.1	4.1	4.0
**Communications	13.1	13.5	18.0	16.6	27.9	18.2
Computer and information sciences	2.3	7.2	7.7	4.5	6.6	5.9
*Education	21.2	23.6	24.8	27.1	30.8	25.6
Engineering	.6	.6	1.5	1.7	2.1	1.3
*Fine and applied arts	22.2	25.2	27.1	24.8	31.3	26.2
Foreign languages	38.0	37.5	40.3	43.7	46.9	41.3
**Health professions	16.5	18.1	24.9	22.7	28.6	22.8
Home economics	61.0	71.2	75.8	66.2	67.3	68.6
Law	.0	2.5	2.7	3.7	.0	2.1
**Letters	23.5	27.2	30.1	32.1	34.0	29.4
**Library science	28.2	43.8	41.2	40.0	41.1	39.9
Mathematics	7.8	7.9	9.6	9.7	11.3	9.1
Physical sciences	5.6	6.7	6.8	7.0	8.3	6.8
*Psychology	24.0	24.8	29.0	29.5	30.9	28.0
Public affairs and services	24.2	21.8	19.2	22.2	24.2	22.4
*Social sciences	13.9	14.7	15.6	18.0	20.8	16.7
Theology	1.9	4.8	3.3	2.9	3.8	3.4
**Interdisciplinary studies	15.4	14.9	17.1	26.0	27.4	21.6

*Indicates a gain of 5 or more percentage points.
**Indicates a gain of 10 or more percentage points.

Source: U.S. Department of Health, Education, and Welfare, National Center for Education Statistics, *Analysis of Doctor's Degrees Awarded to Men and to Women, 1970-71 through 1974-75*, 1977.

the last ten years. In just five years (from 1970–1975), the number of women receiving doctorates increased 59 percent, while the doctorates awarded to men decreased 2.6 percent (Roark, 1977). The following table illustrates the growth of doctor's degrees by discipline awarded to women during just the five-year period from 1970–71 through 1974–75. In eleven of the twenty-three discipline divisions, the increase exceeded 5 percentage points, and five of the discipline divisions experienced a gain of over 10 percentage points.

A dramatic increase (184 percent) in the number of women receiving first-professional degrees is also evident during the same five-year period, 1970–71 through 1974–75, while the number of men receiving such degrees increased 37.4 percent (Roark, 1977). While the numbers of women receiving these degrees increased dramatically, their proportion of the total degrees granted still remains relatively low, although considerable gains are evident, as is illustrated in the table below. Medicine, veterinary medicine, law, and the theological professions received the largest increases in women professionals.

Sex Typing in the Schools

Table 3-5 Percentage of First-Professional Degrees Conferred on Women by Institutions of Higher Education, by Profession: Aggregate United States, 1970-71 through 1974-75

| Profession | Percentage Women by Year | | | | | 1970-71 through 1974-75 |
	1970-71	1971-72	1972-73	1973-74	1974-75	
Dentistry (D.D.S. (R.D.M.C.)	1.2	1.2	1.4	2.0	3.1	1.8
Medicine (M.D.)	9.2	9.1	9.0	11.2	13.2	10.5
Optometry (O.D.)	2.4	2.2	2.6	4.2	5.1	3.4
Osteopathic Medicine (O.D.)	2.3	3.5	2.9	2.3	5.3	3.4
Podiatry or Podiatric Medicine	2.1	0.4	0.4	1.1	1.1	1.0
Veterinary Medicine (D.V.M.)	7.8	9.4	10.2	11.2	15.9	11.0
Law, General (LL.B. or J.D.)	7.3	7.0	8.1	11.5	15.1	10.2
Theological Professions, General	2.3	1.9	3.4	5.5	6.8	4.0
Other	21.2	20.8	11.8	26.1	11.0	16.2
First Professional Degrees, total	6.5	6.3	7.2	9.9	12.5	8.7

Source: U.S. Department of Health, Education, and Welfare, National Center for Education Statistics, *Women's Representation Among Recipients of Doctor's and First-Professional Degrees, 1970-71 Through 1974-75*, 1976.

Present enrollments would indicate that the increase in the percentage of women obtaining college degrees is likely to continue. A national survey conducted by the U.S. Census Bureau found that the enrollment of women in graduate and professional schools increased approximately 75 percent between 1970 and 1975, while the five-year increase for men was only 23 percent (Roark, 1977). The upward trend in the number of women students accounted for 93 percent of enrollment growth at American colleges and universities from 1976 to 1977 (Magarrell, 1978). While many of the new women students are over 25 years of age, college women now outnumber college men in the eighteen- and nineteen-year old population group. "This year, 49 percent of all American college students are women. Ten years ago, 40 percent were women; 20 years ago, 35 percent; 30 years ago, 20 percent" (Magarrell, 1978). Scoring significant gains in both the part-time and full-time categories, women now constitute 52 percent and 46 percent respectively.

Faculty and Staff Profiles

With more women receiving doctorates, one would think that there would be a considerable increase in the number of women faculty members at institutions of higher education. But this is not the case. Depending on whose statistics one looks at and which institutions are included, the numbers may vary somewhat, but the overall gain of women faculty members during the last fifteen years has been small, as tables 3-6 and 3-7 illustrate.

Since the 1975–76 percentages in table 3-5 include two-year institutions, which tend to hire more women faculty than other types of institutions of higher education, the figures cannot be directly

Table 3-6 Percentage of Women Faculty by Rank, In Four-year Colleges and Universities, 1959-60, 1965-66, 1971-72, and 1975-76

Rank	1959-60	1965-66	1971-72	1975-76*
Full Professor	9.9	8.7	8.6	10
Associate Professor	17.5	15.1	14.6	17
Assistant Professor	21.7	19.4	20.7	29
Instructor	29.3	32.5	39.4	41
All Ranks	19.1	18.4	19.0	24

*Two-year institutions are included in the 1975-76 percentages
Sources: National Education Association, 1972; National Center for Education Statistics, as
reported in *The Chronicle of Higher Education*, February 9, 1976.

Table 3-7 Women's Share of Faculty Jobs
(Figures given are percent)

Type of Institution	1975-76 All Ranks	Prof.	Assoc. Prof.	Assist. Prof.	Instructors	Lecturers
Public Total	25	10	16	29	39	39
Universities	19	6	13	26	49	38
Four-year Institutions	24	12	17	30	50	39
Two-year Institutions	33	22	25	35	34	45
Private Total	23	10	18	29	48	42
Universitites	16	5	14	25	43	36
Four-year Institutions	26	13	20	30	48	47
Two-year Institutions	42	37	24	41	53	69
All Institutions	24	10	17	29	41	40

Source: National Center for Education Statistics, as reported in
The Chronicle of Higher Education, February 9, 1976.

compared with those of previous years. A breakdown by this type of institution gives a clearer picture of where the women faculty are employed. As table 3-7 shows, there is a tendency for ratios of women to men to be much smaller in universities, and particularly private institutions, than in other types of institutions.

Tables 3-6 and 3-7 show that women faculty are more likely to be in the lower ranks which are generally not tenured and often do not lead to promotion opportunities to regular or "ladder" faculty positions. Only the assistant professor level can be viewed as leading to promotion and tenure possibilities. Instructors are generally junior faculty members who have not completed their Ph.D. degrees, and lecturers oftentimes have part-time or adjunct appointments.

As predicted, the small numbers of women faculty are not distributed evenly throughout the various fields but are concentrated in the humanities, fine arts, education, and new fields such as women's studies. There are very few women faculty in the sciences, engineering, medicine, and law. And although more women are receiving doctorates in nontraditional disciplines such as chemistry and mathematics, the graduate departments which train them have not hired more women faculty (Project on the Status and Education of Women, 1977). For example, from 1975 to 1976 there was an increase in the percentage of women among new doctorates from 10 percent to 11 percent. During the same period of time, there was a decrease in women faculty in mathematics departments from 6.3 percent to 5.9 percent. Similarly, while 10.4 percent of the doctorates in chemistry were granted to women in 1974–75, women comprised only 2.2 percent of the chemistry faculties. It appears that affirmative action programs to hire more women in areas where they are "underrepresented" are not being implemented.

There is also a consistent general pattern of lower salaries for women faculty when compared to their male counterparts, despite the 1972 extension of the Equal Pay Act to cover teachers and other professionals. Indeed, salary inequities between men and women faculty are increasing rather than decreasing. The National Center for Education Statistics reported that in 1974–75 women faculty members earned $2,820 less than men, and in 1975–76 the salary differential increased to $3,096 (Magarrell, 1976). As table 3-8 shows, the difference in percentage increases was largest at the instructor level, where men's salaries rose an average of 8.2 percent and women's rose 7.2 percent. Only the full professor and lecturer levels are the percentage increases larger for women than for men (and then only .2 of a percent), and the dollar differential between the two sexes is still substantial.

There are many reasons given for the differences in rank and salary of men and women faculty. Some of the more frequently stated reasons are these: women do not do as much scholarly writing required for promotion and salary increases; women have not been as willing as men to move to another institution (or play the bargain-

Table 3-8 Average Faculty Salaries

Rank	Total			Men			Women		
	1974-75	1975-76	Change	1974-75	1975-76	Change	1974-75	1975-76	Change
All ranks	$15,611	$16,634	+ 6.6%	$16,290	$17,388	+ 6.7%	$13,470	$14,292	+ 6.1%
Professors	21,263	22,611	+ 6.3%	21,518	22,866	+ 6.3%	19,012	20,257	+ 6.5%
Associate professors	16,128	17.026	+ 5.6%	16,261	17,167	+ 5.6%	15,481	16,336	+ 5.5%
Assistant professors	13,290	13,966	+ 5.1%	13,452	14,154	+ 5.2%	12,857	13,506	+ 5.0%
Instructors	12,691	13,682	+ 7.8%	13,351	14.440	+ 8.2%	11,740	12.580	+ 7.2%
Lecturers	12,575	12,887	+ 2.5%	13,231	13,577	+ 2.6%	11,543	11,870	+ 2.8%
Undesignated rank	13,532	15,201	+12.3%	14,008	15,764	+12.5%	12,619	14,098	+11.7%

Source: National Center for Education Statistics.

ing game of obtaining offers to move to enhance their prestige at their own institution) to improve their rank and salary; as secondary earners in the family, women have not needed to strive for salary increases as rigorously as men; many women have preferred part-time teaching appointments or have taken considerable time out for family-related reasons. A full explanation is complex and varies from institution to institution, from department to department within a single institution, and among individual women faculty members. Generally, there is not a single reason for a woman faculty member's salary and rank being lower than her male counterparts but a combination of reasons, all of which are not due to the woman's personal choice or lack of productivity. In separate studies using data from the 1969 Carnegie Commission Survey of Faculty and Student Opinion, Astin and Bayer (1972) and Scott (reported in Carnegie Commission on Higher Education, 1973) strongly suggest that there is discrimination against women in status and compensation in higher education. Such early common practices as retaining women in the position of lecturer or instructor while moving men up the tenure ladder ranks have impacted the present status of women, affecting not only their rank but their salary as well. Nepotism clauses, which prevented members of the same family from being appointed to the same academic department, caused many women to interrupt their careers or be reassigned to an unlikely department in a field which was not their specialty. Not considered ''full colleagues'' along with the men, many women were ignored or overlooked when it came time for assignment of research funds and promotion and salary decisions. While these things are less likely to happen today because of equal employment opportunity laws and affirmative action programs, women discriminated against in the past have yet to catch up with their male colleagues.

Just as women are sparsely represented on most faculties, their representation in top academic administrative positions is also sparse—only even more so. Two recent surveys of women in administrative jobs at colleges and universities show the extent to which women have failed to achieve equity, either in proportion of positions or salary. The first study (Van Alstyne and Withers, 1977), supported by the Ford Foundation and published by the College and University Personnel Association, found that among more than 18,000 administrators at 1,037 institutions:

—79 percent of the key administrative positions are held by white males, 14 percent by white females, 5 percent by minority males and 2 percent by minority females.

—Women are paid approximately four-fifths as much as men with the same job titles at the same type of institution.

—Women hold 52 percent of the administrative positions at women's colleges and only 14 percent at white coeducational institutions.

—The proportion of white women administrators ranges from a low of 8 percent at large research universities to a high of 19 percent at liberal arts colleges.

—The only administrative position in which men and women, minorities and non-minorities all have sizable representations is "affirmative action officer," and even here men are paid more than women.

The other study by Astin (1977–b) compared American Council on Education data collected from major schools and colleges in 1973 and again in 1977. The study results show "clearly that the situation remains virtually unchanged" regarding women in academic administration. For example, in both years studied, only 1 percent of all the presidents of public four-year colleges and public and private universities are women. Of the public four-year colleges, only 3 of the 309 presidents are women, and 2 of the 3 are at schools which formerly were exclusively or primarily for women. Of the presidents at public universities, only 2 of the 113 are women, with 1 of those at a women's institution. The study reveals that when women are in administrative posts, they are most likely to be in middle- and low-level positions. For example, women occupy seven of the eight lowest-paying administrative positions on campus, including such titles as book store manager, registrar, and director of housing. In commenting on the consequences that such an imbalance of women administrators has for students who attend college, Astin says, "The absence of women in top administration can create an environment that lacks not only role models for women who might ultimately become administrators, but also the unique perspective that women might bring to the varied tasks of administering a college."

College and university governing boards—which are gaining increasing power in determining policies for our institutions of higher education—also contain few women members. A 1976 survey conducted by the American Council on Education's Higher Education Panel and funded by the Association of Governing Boards of Universities and Colleges found that of the more than 47,000 trustees and regents who serve on governing boards for the nation's 3,036 colleges and universities, only 15 percent are women (Gomberg and Atelsck, 1977). The proportion of women trustees ranges from 18 percent on public single-campus boards to 13 percent on private multi-campus boards. Nearly one-fourth of the trustees are lawyers, doctors, or clergymen, and two-thirds of them are over fifty years of age.

Stereotyping of Sex Roles

Just as male and female students in elementary and secondary schools need role models of both sexes in teaching and other professional positions, so do college students. It is difficult for a young woman to imagine herself as a chemistry professor or a college administrator if she has never seen one and if the male faculties and administrators continue to operate as "boys' clubs."

Conclusion This chapter has discussed sex typing in our educational institutions at all levels—elementary and secondary schools, and colleges and universities. Sex typing exists in many forms, from attitudes of teachers, counselors, and the students themselves to the curriculum, textbooks, and instructional materials. In addition, staffing patterns demonstrate an imbalance of women, except for teachers at the elementary school level. The lack of women in administrative positions at all levels and in teaching positions, particularly at the college level, gives the message to students that only men have the capabilities for such responsible positions.

The result of such sex typing in the schools is the encouragement and perpetuation of stereotypic sex roles rather than the full development of each person's interests and abilities regardless of his or her sex. Suggestions for what can be done to promote change in the schools to better facilitate the learning of students of both sexes are contained in chapter 7.

References Abramowitz, S. I.; Weitz, L. J.; Schwartz, J. M.; Amira, S.; Gomes, B.; and Abramowitz, C. V. Comparative counselor inferences toward women with medical school aspirations. *Journal of College Student Personnel,* 1975, *16*(2), 128–130.

Ahrons, C. R. Counselors' perceptions of career images of women. *Journal of Vocational Behavior,* 1976, *8,* 197–207.

Aiken, L. R., Jr. Update on attitudes and other affective variables in learning mathematics. *Review of Educational Research,* 1976, *46*(2), 293–311.

American Association of University Women. Graduate and professional education of women. *Proceedings of a Special Conference,* Washington, D.C., May 9–10, 1974.

American Council on Education, Office of Research. *The American freshman: National norms for Fall 1971.* Washington, D.C.: American Council on Education, 1971.

Anthony, E. J. The behavior disorders of childhood. In P. H. Mussen (ed.), *Charmichael's manual of child psychology.* New York: John Wiley & Sons, 1970.

Arlow, P., and Froschl, M. Women in the high school curriculum: A review of U.S. history and English literature texts. In C. Ahlum, J. Fralley, and F. Howe (eds.), *High school feminist studies.* Old Westbury, New York, 1976.

Association for Measurement and Evaluation in Guidance. AMEG Commission report on Sex bias in interest measurement. *Measurement and Evaluation in Guidance,* 1973, *6*(3), 171–177.

Astin, A. W. The American freshman: National norms for Fall, 1976. Los Angeles: Cooperative Institutional Research Program of the American Council on Education and the University of California at Los Angeles, 1976.

Astin, A. W. The American freshman: National norms for Fall, 1977. Los Angeles: Cooperative Institutional Research Program of the American Council on Education and the University of California at Los Angeles, 1977(a).

Astin, A. W. *The hard core of sexism in academe.* Los Angeles: Higher Education Research Institute, 1977(b).

Astin, H. S. Patterns of career choice over time. *Personnel and Guidance Journal,* 1967, *45,* 541–546.

Astin, H. S. Sex differences in mathematical and scientific precocity. In J. C. Stanley, D. P. Keating, and L. H. Fox (eds.), *Mathematical talent: Discovery, description and development.* Baltimore, Md.: The Johns Hopkins University Press, 1974.

Astin, H. S. *The women doctorate in America.* New York: Russell Sage Foundation, 1969.

Astin, H. S., and Bayer, A. E. Sex discrimination in academe.*Educational Record,* Spring 1972, *53,* 101–118.

Austin, D.; Clark, V.; and Fitchett, G. *Reading rights for boys: Sex role in language experience.* New York: Appleton-Century-Crofts, 1971.

Ayres, L. P. *Laggards in our schools.* New York: Russell Sage Foundation, 1909.

Beaven, M. H. Responses of adolescents to feminize characters in literature. *Research in the Teaching of English,* Spring 1972.

Bernard, J. *Academic women.* University Park, Penn.: Pennsylvania State University Press, 1964.

Birk, J. M.; Barbanel, L.; Brooks, L.; Herman, M. H.; Juhasy, J. B.; Seltzer, R. A.; and Tangri, S. S. A content analysis of sexual bias in commonly used psychology textbooks. Journal Supplement Abstract Service, MS. No. 722, 1974.

Birk, J. M.; Cooper, J.; and Tanney, M. F. Racial and sex-role stereotyping in career illustrations. Paper presented at the meeting of the American Psychological Association, Montreal, September, 1973.

Birk, J. M.; Cooper, J.; and Tanney, M. F. Stereotyping in occupational outlook handbook illustrations: A follow-up study. Paper presented at the meeting of the American Psychological Association, Chicago, August-September 1975.

Brandt, R. M. The accuracy of self-estimate: A measure of self-concept. *Genetic Monographs,* 1958, *58,* 55.

Broverman, I. K.; Vogel, S. R.; Broverman, D. M.; Clarkson, F. E.; and Rosenkrantz, P. S. Sex-role stereotypes: A current appraisal. *Journal of Social Issues,* 1972, *28*(2), 59–78.

Bruner, J. *Toward a theory of instruction.* Cambridge, Mass.: Belknap Press of Harvard University, 1966.

Burlin, F. D., Pearson, R. Counselor-in training response to a male and female client: An analogue study exploring sex-role stereotyping. *Counselor Education and Supervision,* 1978, *17*(3), 213–221.

Campbell, D. P. *Manual for the Strong-Campbell interest inventory.* Stanford, California: Stanford University Press, 1974.

Carnegie Commission on Higher Education. *Opportunity for women in higher education.* New York: McGraw Hill, 1973.

Casserly, P. L. An assessment of factors affecting female participation in advanced placement programs in mathematics, chemistry, and physics. Report to the National Science Foundation, July 1975, 42 pp.

Child, I. L., et al. Children's textbooks and personality development: An exploration in the social psychology of education. *Psychological Monographs,* 1946, *60,* 1–53.

Chronicle of Higher Education, February 9, 1976.

Clark, W. W. Boys and girls—Are there significant ability and achievement differences? *Phi Delta Kappan,* 1959, *41,* 73–76.

Clement, J. P. *Sex bias in school leadership.* Evanston, Ill.: Integrated Education Associates, Northwestern University, 1975.

Cole, N. S. *On measuring the vocational interests of women.* ACT Research Report No. 49. Iowa City, Iowa: The American College Testing Program, March 1972.

College Entrance Examination Board. *College handbook.* New York: College Entrance Examination Board, 1969.

Collins, A. M., and Sedlacek, W. E. Counselor ratings of male and female clients. *Journal of National Association of Women's Deans and Counselors,* Spring 1974, *37*(2), 128–132.

Crandall, V. Sex differences in expectancy of intellectual and academic reinforcement. In C. P. Smith (ed.), *Achievement related motives in children.* New York: Russell Sage Foundation, 1969.

Creager, J. A. *The American graduate student: A normative description.* Washington, D.C.: Office of Research, American Council on Education, 1971.

Crites, J. O. *Theory and research handbook, career maturity inventory.* Monterey, Calif.: CTB/McGraw-Hill, 1973.

Cross, K. P. *Beyond the open door: New students to higher education.* San Francisco: Jossey-Bass, 1971.

Cross, K. P. College women: A research description. *Journal of National Association of Women Deans and Counselors,* 1968, *32*(1), 12–21.

Cross, K. P. The woman student. In W. T. Furniss and P. A. Graham (eds.), *Women in higher education.* Washington, D.C.: American Council on Education, 1974.

Davis, J. A. *Great aspirations: Career decisions and educational plans during college.* Vol. 1, Chicago: NORC, 1963.

Diamond, E. E. (ed.). *Issues of sex bias and sex fairness in career interest measurement.* National Institute of Education Report. Washington, D.C.: U.S. Government Printing Office, 1975.

Donelson, E., and Gullahorn, J. E. *Women: A psychological perspective.* New York: John Wiley & Sons, 1977.

Donlon, T. F. Content factors in sex differences on test questions. Paper presented at the meeting of the New England Educational Research Organization, Boston, June 1971.

Donovan, V. Elementary school teachers, sex-role attitudes and classroom behavior towards girls and boys. Unpublished manuscript, June, 1973.

Doubronsky, C. What we have found. In A. G. West (ed.), *Report on sex bias in the public schools.* New York: Education Committee, National Organization for Women, 1971.

Douvan, E., and Adelson, J. *The adolescent experience.* New York: Wiley, 1966.

Dwyer, C. A. Sex differences in reading: An evaluation and critique. *Review of Educational Research,* 1973, *43,* 455–467.

Ehrlich, C. The male sociologist's burden: The place of women in marriage and family texts. *Journal of Marriage and Family,* August 1971, *33,* 421–430.

Ehrmann, W. *Premarital dating behavior.* New York: Bantam Books, 1960.

Eiden, L. J. Trends in female degree recipients. *American Education,* November 1976, Vol. 12, No. 9.

Elman, J. B.; Press, A.; and Rosenkrantz, P. S. Sex roles and self-concepts: Real and ideal. Paper presented at the meeting of the American Psychological Association, Miami, August 1970.

Engelhard, P. A.; Jones, K. O.; and Stiggins, R. J. Trends in counselor attitude about women's roles. *Journal of Counseling Pyschology,* 1976, *23*(4), 365–372.

Entwisle, D. R. Implications of language socialization for reading models and for learning to read. *Reading Research Quarterly,* 1971, *7,* 111–167.

Epstein, C. F. *Woman's place: Options and limits in professional careers.* Berkeley: University of California Press, 1970.

Ernest, J. *Mathematics and sex.* Goleta, Calif.: Triple R Press, 1976.

Estler, S. E. Women as leaders in public education. *SIGNS: Journal of Women in Culture and Society,* Winter 1975, *1*(2), 363–386.

Feminists on Children's Literature. A feminist look at children's books. *School Library Journal,* January 1971, *17,* 19–24.

Feminists on Children's Media. *Little miss muffet fights back.* New York: Feminists on Children's Media, 1971.

Fennema, E., and Sherman, J. A. Sexual stereotyping and mathematics. To appear in *The Arithmetic Teacher.*

Ferriss, A. *Indicators of trends in the status of American women.* New York: Russell Sage Foundation, 1971.

Fishel, A., and Pottker, J. Women in educational governance: A statistical portrait. *Educational Researcher,* July-August 1974, *3*(7), 4–7.

Fleming, E. S., and Anttonen, R. G. Teacher expectancy and my fair lady. *American Educational Research Journal,* March, 1971, *8,* 241–252.

Fox, L. H. Mathematically precocious: Male or female. In E. Fennema (ed.), *Mathematics learning: What research says about sex differences.* Columbus, Ohio: Ohio State University, 1975.

Fox, L. H.; Fennema, E.; and Sherman, J. *Women and mathematics: Research perspectives for change.* NIE Papers in Education and Work, Number Eight. Washington, D.C.: National Institute of Education, 1977.

Frazier, N., and Sadker, M. *Sexism in school and society.* New York: Harper and Row, 1973.

Freeman, J. Women's liberation and its impact on the campus. *Liberal Education,* December 1971, *57*(4), 474.

Gazda, G. M. *Group counseling: A developmental approach.* Boston: Allyn & Bacon, 1971.

Ginzburg, E. *Educated American women: Life styles and self-portraits.* New York: Columbia University Press, 1966.

Glueck, S., and Glueck, E. T. *One thousand juvenile delinquents.* Cambridge: Harvard University Press, 1934.

Goldman, W. J., and May, A. Males: A minority group in the classroom. *Journal of Learning Disabilities,* May, 1970, *3*(3), 276–278.

Gomberg, I., and Atelsek, F. *Composition of college and university governing boards.* Washington, D.C.: American Council on Education, 1977.

Good, T. L., and Brody, J. F. *Do boys and girls receive equal opportunity in first grade reading?* Series No. 24. Austin, Texas: Research and Development Center for Teacher Education, 1969.

Good, T. L.; Sikes, J. N.; and Brophy, J. E. Effects of teacher sex and student sex on classroom interaction. *Journal of Educational Psychology,* 1973, *65*(1), 74–87.

Grambs, J. D., and Waetjen, W. B. *Sex: Does it make a difference?* North Scituote, Mass.: Duxbury Press, 1975.

Guttentag, M., and Bray, H. *Undoing sex stereotypes: Research and resources for educators.* New York: McGraw-Hill, 1976.

Hanson, G. R.; Prediger, D. J.; and Schussel, R. H. *Development and validation of sex-balanced interest inventory scales.* ACT Research Report No. 78. Iowa City, Iowa: The American College Testing Program, March 1977.

Harmon, L. W. Sexual bias in interest testing. *Measurement and Evaluation in Guidance,* 1973, *5,* 496–501.

Harris, A. S. The second sex in academe. *American Association of University Professors Bulletin,* September 1970, *56*(3), 292.

Harvly, P. What women think men think. *Journal of Counseling Psychology,* 1971, *18*(3), 193–194.

Harway, M. Sex bias in counseling materials. *Journal of College Student Personnel,* January 1977, *18*(1), 57–64.

Haven, E. W., and Horch, D. H. *How college students finance their education.* Evanston, Ill.: College Entrance Examination Board, 1972.

Hawley, P. The state of the art of counseling high school girls. *FELS Discussion Paper No. 89.* New York: Spoons Agency, Ford Foundation, June 1975.

Heiss, A. M. *Challenges to graduate schools.* San Francisco: Jossey-Bass, 1970.

Hill, C. E.; Tanney, M. F.; Leonard, M. M.; and Reiss, J. A. Counselor reactions to female clients: Type of problem, age of client and sex of counselor. *Journal of Counseling Psychology,* 1977, *24*(1), 60–65.

Hipple, J. L. Perceptual differences in concepts of the ideal woman. *The School Counselor,* 1974, *22*(3), 180–186.

Hoffman, L. W. Fear of success in males and females: 1965 and 1971. *Journal of Consulting and Clinical Psychology,* 1974, *42*(3), 353–358.

Holmstrom, E. I., and Holmstrom, R. W. *The plight of the woman doctoral student.* Washington, D.C.: Office of Research, American Council on Education, 1973.

Horner, M. Feminity and successful achievement: A basic inconsistency. In J. Bardwick, E. M. Douvan, M. S. Horner, and D. Gutmann (eds.), *Feminine personality and conflict.* Belmont, California: Brooks-Cole, 1970.

Horner, M. *Sex differences in achievement motivation and performance in competitive and non-competitive situations.* Unpublished doctoral dissertation, University of Michigan, 1968.

Horner, M. Toward an understanding of achievement-related conflicts in women. *Journal of Social Issues,* 1972, *28,* 157–175.

Howe, F. *Seven years later: Women's studies programs in 1976.* A Report of the National Advisory Council on Women's Educational Programs, Washington, D.C., June 1977.

Hunt, D. E., and Dopyera, J. Personality variation in lower class children. *Journal of Psychology,* 1966, *62,* 47–54.

Iglitzin, L. A child's-eye view of sex roles. Paper presented at the American Political Science Association, Washington, D.C., 1972.

Jacklin, C.; Henners, M.; Mischell, H. N.; and Jacobs, C. As the twig is bent: Sex role stereotyping in early readers. Unpublished manuscript, Department of Psychology, Stanford University. 1972.

Jackson, P. W.; Getzels, J. W.; and Xydis, G. A. Psychological health and cognitive functioning in adolescence: A multivariate analysis. *Child Development,* 1960, *31,* 285–298.

Judd, C. H. *Measuring the work of the public schools.* Cleveland, Ohio: Survey Committee of the Cleveland Foundation, 1916.

Kagan, J. The childs' sex-role classification of school objects. *Child Development,* December 1964, *35*(4), 1051–1056.

Kagan, J. On the meaning of behavior: Illustrations from the infant. *Child Development,* 1969, *40,* 1121–1134.

Kagan, J. Personality and the learning process. *Daedalus,* Summer 1965, *94,* 553–563.

Karmon, F. J. *Women: Personal and environmental factors in role identification and career choice.* Unpublished doctoral dissertation, University of California, Los Angeles, 1972.

Katz, J. Evolving relationships between women and men. In *Changing roles of women in industrial societies.* Proceedings of a Bellagio Conference, March 1976. New York: Rockefeller Foundation, December 1977.

Katz, J., et al. *No time for youth.* San Francisco: Jossey-Bass, 1968.

Kemer, B. J. A study of the relationship between the sex of the student and the assignment of marks by secondary school teachers. Ph.D. Dissertation, Michigan State University, 1965.

Keniston, K. An American anachronism: The image of women and work. *Daedalus,* Summer, 1964.

Kohlberg, L. A cognitive developmental analysis of children's sex-role concepts and attitudes. In Maccoby, E. (ed.), *The development of sex differences.* Palo Alto, Calif.: Stanford University Press, 1966.

Krischner, B. F. Introducing students to women's place in society. In J. Huber (ed.), *Changing women in a changing society.* Chicago: University of Chicago Press, 1973.

Lee, D. Discrepancies in the teaching of American culture. In G. Spindler (ed.), *Education and culture.* New York: Holt, Rinehart & Winston, 1963.

Lee, P. C., and Gropper, N. B. Sex-role culture and educational practice. *Harvard Educational Review,* 1974, *44*:369–410.

Levine, A., and Crumrine, J. Women and the fear of success: A problem in replication. *American Journal of Sociology,* 1975, *80*(4), 964–974.

Levitan, T. E., and Chananie, J. D. Responses of female primary teachers to sex-typed behavior in male and female children. *Child Development,* 1972, *43,* 1309–1316.

Lewis, E. C. *Developing woman's potential.* Ames, Iowa: Iowa State University Press, 1968.

Lewis, J. (ed.). Special issue: Women and counselors. *Personnel and Guidance Journal,* 1972, *51*(2).

Maccoby, E. Woman's intellect. In S. Farber and R. Wilson (eds.), *The potential of woman.* New York: McGraw-Hill, 1963.

Maccoby, E., and Jacklin, C. N. *The psychology of sex differences.* Palo Alto, Calif.: Stanford Press, 1974.

Magarrell, J. Faculty-salary gap widens between men and women. *Chronicle of Higher Education,* September 27, 1976.

Magarrell, J. Women account for 93 pct. of enrollment gain. *Chronicle of Higher Education,* January 9, 1978, Vol. XV, No. 17.

McFarland, W. Are girls really smarter? *Elementary School Journal,* 1968, *70*(1), 14–19.

McMillin, M. R. Attitudes of college men toward career involvement of married women. *Vocational Guidance Quarterly,* 1972, *21*(4).

Mead, M. Unpublished research study. University of Maryland, College of Education, 1971.

Mednick, M. T. S.; Tangri, S. S.; and Hoffman, L. W. (eds.). *Women and achievement.* Washington, D.C.: Hemisphere Publishing Corporation for John Wiley & Sons (Halsted Press), 1975.

Mink, P. T. Introduction of the women's education act of 1972. *Congressional Record,* H 3259, April 18, 1972.

Minuchin, P. Sex differences in children: Research findings in an educational context. *National Elementary Principal,* 1966, *46*(2), 45–48.

National Education Association. *Salaries paid and salary related practices in higher education, 1971–72.* Washington, D.C., 1972.

National Education Association. *Sex-role stereotyping in the schools.* Washington, D.C.: National Education Association, 1973.

National Federation of State High School Associations. *Summary, 1977 sports participation survey.* Elgin, Ill.: National Federation of State High School Associations, December 1976.

National Institutes of Health. *Women and graduate study, report no. 13.* Washington, D.C.: Government Printing Office, 1968.

Ness, E. *Sam, bangs, and moonshine.* New York: Holt, Rinehart & Winston, 1967.

Newman, Frank (Task Force Chairman). *Report on higher education,* U.S. Office of Education. Washington, D.C.: Government Printing Office, 1971.

Nilson, A. P. Women in children's literature. In S. McAllister (ed.), *Women in english departments.* Urbana, Ill.: National Council of Teachers of English, 1971.

O'Hara, R. The roots of careers. *Elementary School Journal,* 1962, *62*(5), 277–280.

Oltman, R. Campus 170—where do women stand? *American Association of University Women Journal,* November 1970, *64*(2), 14–15.

Page, E. B. A historical step beyond Terman. In D. Keating (ed.), *Intellectual talent: Research and development.* Baltimore, Maryland: The Johns Hopkins University Press, 1976.

Palardy, J. M. What teachers believe, what children achieve. *The Elementary School Journal,* 1969, *69,* 370–374.

Palardy, M. For Johnny's reading sake. *Reading Teacher,* May 1969, *22*(8), 720–724.

Patton, F. G. *Good morning, miss dove.* New York: Dodd, Mead and Company, 1954.

Pierce, J. V. Sex differences in achievement motivation of able high school students. Cooperative research project No. 1097, University of Chicago, December 1961.

Poffenberger, T., and Norton, D. Sex differences in achievement motivation in mathematics as related to cultural change. *Journal of Genetic Psychology,* 1972, *103,* 341–350.

Preston, R. C. Reversals in reading and writing among German and American children. *Elementary School Journal,* March 1957, *57,* 333–334.

Project on Equal Education Rights. *Stalled at the start: Government action on sex bias in the schools.* Washington, D.C.: National Organization for Women's Legal Defense and Education Fund, 1978.

Project on the Status and Education of Women. Do more women doctorates = more women faculty? *On Campus with Women,* No. 17, June 1977.

Psychological Corporation. *Academic promise test manual (Grades six to nine).* New York: Psychological Corporation, 1962.

Richardson, B. *Sexism in higher education.* New York: Seabury Press, 1974.

Ricks, F., and Pyke, S. Teacher perceptions and attitudes that foster or maintain sex-role differences. *Interchange,* 1973, *4,* 26–33.

Roark, A. C. First-time college enrollment of women leaps dramatically. *Chronicle of Higher Education,* February 7, 1977, Vol. XIII, No. 21.

Robinson, L. H. *The status of academic women.* Washington, D.C.: ERIC Clearinghouse on Higher Education, 1971.

Rogers, M. A. A different look at word problems. *Mathematics Teacher,* 1974, *68*(4), 285–288.

Rosenkrantz, P. S.; Vogel, S. R.; Bee, H.; Broverman, I. K.; and Broverman, D. M. Sex-role stereotypes and self-concepts in college students. *Journal of Consulting and Clinical Psychology,* 1968, *32,* 287–295.

Rosenthal, R., and Jacobson, L. *Pygmalion in the classroom.* New York: Holt, Rinehart & Winston, 1968.

Rossi, A. S., and Calderwood, A. (eds.). *Academic women on the move.* New York: Russell Sage Foundation, 1973.

Saltz, J. W. Teacher stereotype—liability in recruiting? *The School Review,* Spring 1960, *68,* 105–111.

Sandler, B. Material presented for the record to the Committee on the Judiciary, House of Representatives, 92nd Congress, Hearings on Equal Rights for Men and Women, 31 March 1971.

Schlossberg, N. K., and Goodman, J. Imperative for change: Counselor use of the Strong vocational interest blanks. *Impact,* 1972, *2,* 25–29.

Schlossberg, N. K., and Pietrofesa, J. J. Perspectives on counseling bias: Implications for counselor education. *The Counseling Psychologist,* 1973, *4*(1), 44–54.

Schwenn, M. *Arousal of the motive to avoid success.* Unpublished junior honors thesis, Harvard University, 1970.

Sears, P., and Feldman, D. Teacher interactions with boys and girls. *National Elementary Principal,* 1966, *46*(2), 13–17.

Sells, L. W. High school mathematics as the critical filter in the job market. In *Developing Opportunities for Minorities in Graduate Education.* Proceedings of the Conference on Minority Graduate Education at the University of California, Berkeley, May, 1973.

Sells, L. W. The mathematics filter and the education of women and minorities. Paper presented at the annual meeting of the American Association for the Advancement of Science, Boston, Massachusetts, February 1976.

Serbin, L. A., and O'Leary, K. D. How nursery schools teach girls to shut up. *Psychology Today,* December 1975, *9,* 56–58.

Sexton, P. Are schools emasculating our boys? *Saturday Review,* June 1965, 57–61.

Shapiro, J. Socialization of sex roles in the counseling setting: Differential counselor behavioral and attitudinal responses to typical and atypical female sex roles. Presentation at the Annual Meeting of the American Educational Research Association, Washington, D.C., March 30-April 3, 1975.

Shertzer, B., and Stone, S. C. *Fundamentals of guidance* (2nd ed.). New York: Houghton Mifflin, 1971.

Silberman, M. Classroom rewards and intellectual courage. In M. Silberman (ed.), *The experience of schooling.* New York: Holt, Rinehart & Winston, 1971.

Smith, S. Age and sex differences in children's opinions concerning sex differences. *Journal of Genetic Psychology,* March 1939, *54,* 17–25.

Spaulding, R. Achievement, creating, and self-concept correlates of teacher-pupil transactions in elementary school. Cooperative Research Project No. 1352. Washington, D.C.: U.S. Department of Health, Education, and Welfare, Office of Education, 1963.

Stacey, J.; Bereaud, S.; and Daniels, J. (eds.). *And Jill came tumbling after: Sexism in American education.* New York: Dell, 1974.

Stafford, R. Hereditary and environmental components of quantitative reasoning. *Review of Education Research,* 1972, *42,* 183–201.

Stein, A. H.; Pohly, S. R.; and Muller, E. Sex typing of achievement areas as a determinant of children's efforts and achievement. Paper presented at Sex-Res Child Development, Santa Monica, Calif.: March 1969.

Stein, A. H., and Smithells, J. Age and sex differences in children's sex-role standards about achievement. *Developmental Psychology,* 1969, *1,* 252.

Tangri, S. *Role innovation in occupational choice.* Unpublished doctoral dissertation, University of Michigan, 1969.

Tannebaum, A. Family living in textbook town. *Progressive Education Associates,* March 1954, *31,* 133–141.

Tavis, C., and Offir, C. *The longest war: Sex differences in perspective.* New York: Harcourt Brace Jovanovich, 1977.

Thomas, A. H., and Stewart, N. R. Counselor response to female clients with deviate and conforming career goals. *Journal of Counseling Psychology,* 1971, *18*(4), 352–357.

Tittle, C. K. Women and educational testing. *Phi Delta Kappan,* October 1973, *55*(2), 118-119.

Tittle, C. K.; McCarthy, K.; and Steckler, J. F. *Women and educational testing.* Princeton, N.J.: Educational Testing Service, 1974.

Tobias, S. Towards a taxonomy of math anxiety. Paper presented at the Math = a Problem Conference, University of Wisconsin, Madison, Wisconsin, March, 1977.

Trecker, J. L. Sex stereotyping in the elementary school curriculum. *Phi Delta Kappan,* 1973, *55*(2), 110-112.

Trecker, J. L. Women in U.S. history textbooks. *Social Education,* March 1971, *35*(3), 249-261.

Trippot, L. Elementary education—A man's world. *Instructor,* November 1968, *78*(3), 50-52.

Trow, M. *Aspects of American higher education 1969-75.* Berkeley, Calif.: Carnegie Council on Policy Studies in Higher Education, 1976.

Tyler, L. *Work of the counselor* (3rd ed.). New York: Appleton-Century-Crofts, 1969.

Unkel, E. A study of the interaction of socioeconomic groups and sex factors with the discrepancy between anticipated achievement and actual achievement in elementary school mathematics. *Arithmetic Teacher,* 1966, *13,* 662-670.

U'Ren, M. B. The image of women in textbooks. In V. Gornick and B. K. Moran (eds.), *Women in sexist society.* New York: Basic Books, 1971.

U.S. Congress, House. *Hearings before special subcommittees on education of the committee on education and labor,* 91st Congress, 2nd Session, Sec. 805 of House Report. 16098, Parts 1 and 2, "Discrimination Against Women," July, 1970.

U.S. Department of Health, Education, and Welfare, National Center for Education Statistics. *Analysis of doctor's degrees awarded to men and to women, 1970-71 through 1974-75.* Washington, D.C.: U.S. Government Printing Office, 1977.

U.S. Department of Health, Education, and Welfare, Bureau of Occupational and Adult Education. *Comparative analysis of vocational education enrollment by sex and fiscal years 1972 and 1975.* Washington, D.C., undated.

U.S. Department of Health, Education, and Welfare, National Center for Education Statistics. *Earned degrees conferred: 1974-75.* Washington, D.C.: U.S. Government Printing Office, 1976.

U.S. Department of Health, Education, and Welfare, National Center for Education Statistics. *Projections of education statistics to 1985-86.* Washington, D.C.: U.S. Government Printing Office, 1977.

U.S. Department of Health, Education, and Welfare, National Center for Education Statistics. *Women's representation among recipients of doctor's and first-professional degrees, 1970-71 through 1974-75.* Washington, D.C.: U.S. Government Printing Office, 1976.

Van Alstyne, C., and Withers, J. S. *Women and minorities in higher education administration.* Washington, D.C.: College and University Personnel Association, 1977.

Vetter, L. Sex stereotyping in illustrations in career materials. Paper presented at the meeting of the American Psychological Association, Chicago, August-September 1975.

Waller, W. *The Sociology of Teaching.* New York: John Wiley & Sons, 1932.

Weisstein, N. Kinder, Kuche, Kirche as scientific law: Psychology constructs the female. In R. Morgan (ed.), *Sisterhood is powerful.* New York: Random House (Vintage), 1970.

Weitzman, L. J.; Eifler, D.; Hokada, E.; and Ross, C. Sex-role socialization in picture books for preschool children. *The American Journal of Sociology,* May 1972, *77*(61), 1125-1150.

Weitzman, L. J., and Rizzo, D. Images of males and females in elementary school textbooks in five subject areas. In *Biased textbooks*. Washington, D.C.: Resource Center on Sex Roles in Education, National Foundation for the Improvement of Education, 1974.

Weitzman, L. J., and Rizzo, D. Sex bias in textbooks. *Today's Education,* January-February 1975, 49–52.

White House Conference on Children. *Profiles of children,* Chart 124. Washington, D.C.: U.S. Government Printing Office, 1970.

Williams, J. H. *Psychology of women: Behavior in a biosocial context.* New York: W. W. Norton, 1977.

Women on Words and Images. *Dick and Jane as victims: Sex stereotyping in children's readers.* Princeton, New Jersey, 1972.

Yolen, J. *The emperor and the kite.* Cleveland, Ohio: World, 1967.

4 Sex Typing in Employment

Many of the clients counselors see—especially in school, community agency, and employment settings—have concerns about employment. "I don't know what kind of work I would be good at doing or what I would want to do." "What training and education do I need for the kind of job I want?" "How do I go about getting a job?" "What problems am I likely to encounter?" Questions and comments like these are frequent. To be effective in assisting clients in finding the answers and solutions to such concerns, counselors must be knowledgeable about the world of work. They must know the training and educational preparation required for all kinds of work and occupations. They must be able to tell their clients which types of jobs are likely to be in increasing and diminishing demand and which new ones are likely to come into being. And they must be skilled in helping their clients assess their own strengths and weaknesses and relate them to various kinds of work, set realistic goals for themselves, and plan steps which will enable them to reach their goals. Such knowledge and skills are of course basic to effective counseling with clients who have concerns and problems related to employment. But for the counselor who wishes to be nonsexist in his or her approach and avoid the possibility of responding in stereotypic ways to clients, there is much more which needs to be understood about the employment of men and women.

The purpose of this chapter is to provide counselors with an overview of the participation of men and women in the American labor force and an understanding of some of the problems workers encounter largely because of their sex. Suggestions of how counselors can use this information will not be a focus of this chapter but will be included in *section II—Counselors and Social Changes* and particularly in chapters 7 and 8: "Promoting Change in the

Portions of this chapter have been adapted from another of the author's books entitled *Locating, Recruiting and Employing Women: An Equal Opportunity Approach,* 1976.

Schools," and "Impacting the Community and Work World," respectively.

Labor Force Participation Rates

Clearly, one of the most noticeable labor force trends in America over the last several decades has been the increase in the participation of women. Presently, 40 percent of the work force are women—two out of every five workers. Table 4-1 shows the various labor force participation rates of men and women by age from 1950 through 1974. During this twenty-four-year period, the participation rate of women jumped from 33.9 percent to 45.7 percent, representing an increase of over 17 million women. The most dramatic increases occurred in the age groups over twenty-five, particularly in the twenty-five to thirty-four years of age (increased 54 percent), the forty-five to fifty-four years of age (increased 43.7 percent), and the fifty-five to sixty-four years of age (increased 50.7 percent) groups. These increases are in part a reflection of a couple of major factors. In the 1950s and early 1960s, the older women, many of whom had worked during World War II, rejoined the work force as their children entered or completed school. And, in the mid-1960s and early 1970s, many of the younger women were not dropping out of the labor force as soon as they married or had children.

Another marked change in the labor force composition during this twenty-four-year period is the declining participation rate of men, especially of those fifty-five years of age and older. This of course reflects not only the mandatory retirement age requirements in both the public and private sectors, but also social security benefits, including disability coverage, and private pension plans. After World War II, the participation rate among men fifty-five to sixty-five years of age declined from 90 percent in 1947 to 76 percent in 1975 (*Employment and Training Report of the President, 1976*).

As is shown in table 4-1, the 1974 labor force participation rate for women sixteen years of age and older was 45.7 percent and 79.4 percent for men. The projected labor force participation rates for 1985 are 45.6 percent for women and 78.3 percent for men. For 1990, the participation rates are estimated to be 45.9 percent for women and 78.4 percent for men (*Employment and Training Report of the President,* 1976). If these projections hold true, we can expect the participation of men in the labor force to continue to decline slowly in the next eight to ten years and then increase slightly or at least stabilize. For women, the projections show a stabilization and then a slight increase. It can be argued that the projections for

Table 4-1 Labor Force Participation Rates by Age and Sex: 1950, 1960, 1970, and 1974
—Noninstitutional population)

	Labor Force Participation Rates[1]				Percent change, 1950 to 1974
Sex and age	1974	1970	1960	1950	
Total, 16 Years and Over					
Women	45.7	43.4	37.8	33.9	+ 34.8
Men	79.4	80.6	84.0	86.8	− 8.5
Ratio: women/men[2]	0.58	0.54	0.45	0.39	(X)
16 to 19 Years					
Women	49.3	44.0	39.4	41.0	+ 20.2
Men	62.5	58.4	59.4	65.9	− 5.1
Ratio: wornen/men[2]	0.79	0.75	0.66	0.62	(X)
20 to 24 Years					
Women	63.2	57.8	46.2	46.1	+ 37.1
Men	87.3	86.6	90.2	89.1	− 2.0
Ratio: women/men[2]	0.72	0.67	0.51	0.52	(X)
25 to 34 Years					
Women	52.4	45.0	36.0	34.0	+ 54.1
Men	96.0	96.6	97.7	96.2	− 0.2
Ratio: women/men[2]	0.55	0.47	0.37	0.35	(X)
35 to 44 Years					
Women	54.7	51.1	43.5	39.1	+ 39.9
Men	96.1	97.0	97.7	97.6	− 1.5
Ratio: women/men[2]	0.57	0.53	0.45	0.40	(X)
45 to 54 Years					
Women	54.6	54.4	49.8	38.0	+ 43.7
Men	92.2	94.3	95.8	95.8	− 3.8
Ratio: women/men[2]	0.59	0.58	0.52	0.40	(X)
55 to 64 Years					
Women	40.7	43.0	37.2	27.0	+ 50.7
Men	77.4	83.0	86.8	86.9	− 10.9
Ratio: women/men[2]	0.53	0.52	0.43	0.31	(X)
65 Years and Over					
Women	8.2	9.7	10.8	9.7	− 15.5
Men	22.4	26.8	33.1	45.8	− 51.1
Ratio: women/men[2]	0.37	0.36	0.33	0.21	(X)

X Not applicable.
[1] Number in labor force as percent of total population in the specific group.
[2] Ratios of labor force participation rates.

Source: U.S. Department of Commerce, Bureau of the Census, *A Statistical Portrait of Women in the United States*, April 1976.

women, if not for men, are conservatively low because the impact of the changing social and economic roles of women on the labor market has not yet been fully realized. For both men and women, the greatest increases in the future labor force will be among those in the twenty-five to forty-five age bracket, and the greatest decline will be among those under twenty.

Despite their greatly increased labor force participation and the fact that they work in virtually every job listed by the Bureau of the Census, women workers are concentrated in the lower paid, traditionally female occupations such as teaching, nursing, retail sales, clerical work, and domestic service as shown in table 4-2. As table 4-2 points out, the occupational distribution of women and men has changed very little since 1958. With some exceptions, men and women are by and large holding the same kinds of jobs and doing the same kinds of work as they did ten and fifteen years ago.

In 1975, 62.9 percent of working women and 41.3 percent of the men were in white-collar jobs. The majority of the women (35.1 percent) were in clerical positions—typists, filing clerks, secretaries, and stenographers; 15.7 percent were in professional and technical positions, and only 5.2 percent held managerial/administrative positions. The majority of the male white-collar workers were in either professional and technical positions (14.6 percent) or managerial/administrative positions (14 percent).

The majority of the working men (45.3 percent) in 1975 were classified as blue-collar workers compared to 14.1 percent of the working women. A sizable proportion of the women (21.6 percent compared to 8.6 percent for men) were classified as service workers. The service occupation group consists of jobs thought to be similar to home-related activities which have traditionally been performed by women, such as preparing food, nursing sick family members, and teaching young children. Also, part-time or shift work in the service sector has been available for women who wish not to be employed on a full-time basis.

Table 4-3 provides a closer look at the representation of women and men in selected industries and gives a more complete picture of their occupational status. Some of the occupations with proportionately large numbers of women workers are registered nurses, elementary and secondary school teachers, private household workers, service workers (other than private household), social and recreation workers, and clerical workers. Some of the occupations with proportionately large numbers of male workers are accountants, engineers, lawyers and judges, physicians, dentists, religious workers, teachers, science technicians, managers and administrators, operatives, laborers, and farm workers.

Table 4-3 also provides an indication of occupational growth trends by sex. Below are lists of the occupations which experienced the largest percentage gains (if only relatively small numerical increases) in the decade from 1960 to 1970.

Women in These Occupations Increased 50 to 99 Percent

Chemists
Clerical workers
Dentists
Dietitians
Editors and reporters
Elementary and secondary
  school teachers
Judges
Lawyers
Pharmacists
Physicians
Service workers (not in home)

Women in These Occupations Increased 100 Percent or More

Accountants
Airline pilots
Architects
Biologists
College and university teachers
Craftworkers
Designers
Economists
Engineering and science
  technicians
Engineers
Health technologists and
  technicians
Nonfarm laborers
Personnel and labor relations
  workers
Public relations workers and
  publicity writers
Psychologists
Radio operators
Social workers
Therapists

Men in These Occupations Increased 50 to 99 Percent

Agricultural scientists
Airline pilots
Architects
Biologists
Designers
Dietitians
Engineering and science
  technicians
Librarians
Registered nurses
Teachers (elementary and
  secondary)
Therapists

Men in These Occupations Increased 100 Percent or More

Economists
Personnel and labor relations
  workers
Psychologists
Public relations workers and
  publicity writers
Social workers
Teachers (college and
  university)

Table 4-2 Employed Persons 16 Years and Over, by Occupation Group and Sex: Annual Averages, 1958-75[1]

Year	Total employed	White collar workers					Blue-collar workers	
		Total	Professional and technical	Managers and administrators ex. farm	Sales workers	Clerical workers	Total	Craft and kindred workers
Percent Distribution								
Male								
1958	100.0	36.5	10.4	13.6	5.7	6.9	46.8	19.4
1959	100.0	36.8	10.5	13.5	5.9	6.9	47.0	19.2
1960	100.0	37.4	10.9	13.6	5.8	7.2	46.5	19.0
1961	100.0	38.1	11.3	13.7	5.8	7.1	46.0	19.2
1962	100.0	38.5	11.7	14.2	5.5	7.1	46.1	19.1
1963	100.0	38.2	11.9	13.8	5.5	7.0	46.9	19.4
1964	100.0	38.4	12.0	13.9	5.5	7.0	47.0	19.2
1965	100.0	38.3	12.1	13.4	5.7	7.1	47.7	19.3
1966	100.0	38.6	12.4	13.3	5.7	7.1	48.0	19.9
1967	100.0	39.0	13.0	13.3	5.5	7.2	47.8	20.1
1968	100.0	39.7	13.4	13.6	5.7	7.1	47.4	20.2
1969	100.0	40.1	13.8	13.8	5.5	7.0	47.7	20.2
1970	100.0	41.0	14.0	14.2	5.6	7.1	47.0	20.1
1971	100.0	40.9	13.7	14.6	5.9	6.7	45.9	19.9
1972	100.0	39.9	13.7	13.1	6.2	6.9	47.0	20.6
1973	100.0	39.8	13.6	13.6	6.1	6.6	47.4	20.8
1974	100.0	40.3	14.0	13.9	6.0	6.4	46.8	20.9
1975	100.0	41.3	14.6	14.0	6.1	6.5	45.3	20.4
Female								
1958	100.0	55.1	12.3	5.0	7.6	30.1	17.1	1.1
1959	100.0	54.9	12.1	5.1	7.8	29.9	16.9	1.0
1960	100.0	55.3	12.4	5.0	7.7	30.3	16.6	1.0
1961	100.0	55.6	12.4	5.1	7.6	30.5	16.4	1.0
1962	100.0	56.1	12.7	5.0	7.5	30.9	16.3	1.0
1963	100.0	55.8	12.8	4.8	7.3	30.9	16.5	1.0
1964	100.0	56.1	13.0	4.6	7.3	31.2	16.7	1.0
1965	100.0	57.0	13.2	4.5	7.5	31.8	16.7	1.1
1966	100.0	57.6	13.4	4.5	7.2	32.6	17.1	1.0
1967	100.0	58.4	13.7	4.4	7.1	33.2	17.0	1.1
1968	100.0	59.1	13.9	4.5	6.9	33.8	16.9	1.1
1969	100.0	59.4	13.8	4.3	6.9	34.3	17.1	1.2
1970	100.0	60.5	14.5	4.5	7.0	34.5	16.1	1.1
1971	100.0	60.6	14.5	5.0	7.2	33.9	15.4	1.3
1972	100.0	60.9	14.5	4.5	7.2	34.7	15.3	1.2
1973	100.0	60.7	14.5	4.9	6.9	34.3	16.2	1.4
1974	100.0	61.6	14.9	4.9	6.8	34.9	15.5	1.5
1975	100.0	62.9	15.7	5.2	6.9	35.1	14.1	1.5

[1]Data are limited to 1958 forward because occupational information for only 1 month of each quarter was collected prior to 1958 and the adjustment for the exclusion of 14- and 15-year-olds was not possible for earlier years.
[2]Not available.
[3]Less than 0.05 percent.

Note: Beginning 1971, occupational data are not strictly comparable with statistics for earlier years as a result of changes in the occupational classification system for the 1970 Census of Population that were introduced into the Current Population Survey (CPS) in January 1971. Moreover, data from 1972 forward are not completely comparable with 1971 relating to major activities and duties. For further explanation, see the Note on Historic Comparability of Labor Force Statistics at the beginning of the Statistical Appendix.

Souce: U.S. Department of Labor, U.S. Department of Health, Education, and Welfare, *Employment and Training Report of the President,* 1976.

| Blue-collar workers | | | Non-farm laborers | Service workers | | | Farmworkers | | |
| Operatives | | | | | Private household workers | Other service workers | | Farmers and farm managers | Farm laborers and supervisors |
Total	Except transport	Transport equipment		Total			Total		
Percent Distribution									
Male									
19.4	(²)	(²)	8.0	6.4	0.1	6.3	10.4	7.0	3.4
19.7	(²)	(²)	8.1	6.3	.1	6.2	10.0	6.7	3.1
19.6	(²)	(²)	7.9	6.5	.1	6.4	9.6	6.1	3.9
19.2	(²)	(²)	7.5	6.7	.1	6.6	9.3	5.9	3.8
19.5	(²)	(²)	7.5	6.7	.1	6.6	8.6	5.6	3.9
20.1	(²)	(²)	7.4	6.9	.1	6.8	7.9	5.1	2.6
20.3	(²)	(²)	7.5	7.0	.1	6.9	7.6	4.8	2.1
20.7	(²)	(²)	7.7	6.9	.1	6.8	7.1	4.5	2.7
20.8	(²)	(²)	7.3	7.1	.1	7.0	6.4	4.2	2.2
20.4	(²)	(²)	7.2	7.0	.1	7.0	6.2	3.9	2.2
20.1	(²)	(²(	7.1	6.9	.1	6.8	6.0	3.8	2.1
20.2	(²)	(²)	7.2	6.7	.1	6.6	5.6	3.6	2.0
19.6	(²)	(²)	7.3	6.7	.1	6.6	5.3	3.4	1.9
18.3	(²)	(²)	7.7	8.2	.1	8.1	5.1	3.2	1.9
18.6	12.5	6.1	7.8	8.2	.1	8.1	5.0	3.1	1.9
18.8	12.8	6.0	7.7	7.9	(³)	7.9	4.8	3.0	1.8
18.3	12.3	6.0	7.7	8.0	.1	8.0	4.9	2.9	1.9
17.5	11.6	5.9	7.4	8.6	.1	8.5	4.8	2.9	1.9
Female									
15.5	(²)	(²)	0.5	23.2	9.4	13.8	4.7	0.6	4.9
15.4	(²)	(²)	.5	23.5	9.0	14.4	4.8	.6	4.1
15.2	(²)	(²)	.4	23.7	8.9	14.8	4.4	.5	3.2
15.0	(²)	(²)	.3	24.2	9.0	15.2	3.9	.6	3.9
15.0	(²)	(²)	.4	24.0	8.8	15.2	3.6	.6	3.0
15.1	(²)	(²)	.4	24.1	8.6	15.5	3.5	.6	3.0
15.3	(²)	(²)	.4	23.9	8.4	15.5	3.3	.6	2.7
15.2	(²)	(²)	.4	23.2	7.7	15.5	3.1	.5	2.5
15.7	(²)	(²)	.4	22.7	7.2	15.5	2.6	.5	2.1
15.5	(²)	(²)	.4	22.3	6.5	15.8	2.3	.4	1.9
15.3	(²)	(²(	.5	21.8	6.1	15.8	2.1	.3	1.8
15.4	(²)	(²)	.5	21.6	5.5	16.1	2.0	.3	1.7
14.5	(²)	(²)	.5	21.7	5.1	16.5	1.8	.3	1.5
13.3	(²)	(²)	.8	22.2	4.9	17.4	1.7	.3	1.4
13.3	12.8	0.4	.9	22.0	4.5	17.5	1.7	.3	1.4
13.8	13.3	.5	.9	21.6	4.1	17.5	1.6	.3	1.3
13.0	12.5	.5	1.1	21.4	3.6	17.8	1.4	.3	1.2
11.6	11.0	.5	1.1	21.6	3.4	18.2	1.4	.3	1.1

Table 4-3 Employed Persons, by Occupation and Sex, 1960 and 1970

Occupation and sex	1960	1970	Percent of employed workers		Percentage change 1960-1970
			1960	1970	
Male					
Total employed (number in thousands)	43,491.0	47,623.8	100.0§	100.0§	9.5
Professional, technical, and kindred workers ...	4,473.3	6,800.6	10.3	14.3	52.0
Accountants	392.3	520.6	0.9	1.1	32.7
Architects	29.4	54.2	0.1	0.1	84.4
Computer specialists	*	204.6	*	0.4	*
Engineers	852.0	1,187.9	2.0	2.5	39.4
Foresters and conservationists	31.3	38.2	0.1	0.1	22.0
Lawyers and judges	201.5	259.2	0.5	0.5	28.6
Mathematical specialists	20.2	23.0	0.1	0.1	13.9
Librarians	11.9	22.0	‡	0.1	84.9
Life and physical scientists	127.9	175.9	0.3	0.4	37.5
Agricultural	7.5	11.7	‡	‡	56.0
Biological	9.7	19.1	‡	‡	96.9
Chemists	74.6	95.6	0.2	0.2	28.2
Geologists	19.3	19.1	‡	‡	−1.0
Physicists and astronomers	*	21.1	*	‡	*
Other life and physical scientists	3.4†	9.3†	‡	‡	173.5†
Operations and systems researchers and analysts	*	71.8	*	0.2	*
Personnel and labor relations workers	68.7	201.4	0.2	0.4	193.2
Physicians, dentists and related practitioners	*	493.1	*	1.0	*
Chiropractors	12.6	12.6	‡	‡	0.0
Dentists	85.1	87.7	0.2	0.2	3.1
Optometrists	15.5	16.5	‡	‡	6.5
Pharmacists	84.8	96.6	0.2	0.2	13.9
Physicians (including osteopaths)	217.9	255.1	0.5	0.5	17.1
Veterinarians	14.9	18.4	‡	‡	23.5
Other health practitioners	*	6.2	*	‡	*
Registered nurses, dietitians, and therapists	32.7	53.1	0.1	0.1	62.7
Dietitians	1.8	3.2	‡	‡	77.8
Registered nurses	14.0	22.3	‡	‡	59.3
Therapists	16.9	27.6	‡	0.1	63.3
Health technologists and technicians	52.3	78.9	0.1	0.2	50.9
Religious workers	217.2	227.6	0.5	0.5	4.8
Clergymen	195.3	211.8	0.5	0.5	8.5
Other religious workers...............	21.9	15.8	0.1	‡	−27.9
Social scientists	26.8	87.7	0.1	0.2	227.2
Economists	16.0	58.6	‡	0.1	266.3
Psychologists	8.2	17.2	‡	‡	109.8
Other social scientists	2.6	11.9	‡	‡	357.7
Social and recreation workers	56.0	109.9	0.1	0.2	96.3
Social	34.5	80.8	0.1	0.2	134.2
Recreation	21.5	29.1	0.1	0.1	35.4
Teachers, college and university	138.3†	348.2†	0.3	0.7	151.8†
Teachers, except college and university	474.0†	815.7†	1.1	1.7	72.1†
Elementary and secondary school teachers	416.2†	741.0†	1.0	1.6	78.0†
Other teachers	57.8 +	74.7†	0.1	0.2	29.2†
Engineering and science technicians	451.3	715.3	1.0	1.5	58.5

*Not available or not comparable in 1960.
†Affected by reclassification. Art, dancing, and music teachers were classified under categories such as "artists and art teachers" in 1960 but were classified as teachers in 1970. This means that percentage increases in the number of college and university teachers as well as in other teacher categories between 1960 and 1970 are somewhat overstated. The increase in the number of salaried managers is also somewhat overstated because of a change in classification that occurred in 1967.
‡Less than 0.05 percent.
§In some cases, items do not add to subtotals because of rounding.

Source: *College Graduates and Jobs*, the Carnegie Commission on Higher Education, April 1973.

Table 4-3 Continued

Occupation and sex	1960	1970	Percent of employed workers 1960	1970	Percentage change 1960-1970
Male					
Technicians, except health, and engineering and science	*	137.9	*	0.3	*
Airline pilots	26.7	49.7	0.1	0.1	86.1
Radio operators	21.5	21.1	0.1	‡	− 1.9
Other technicians	51.0	67.1	0.1	0.1	31.6
Vocational and educational counselors	*	60.1	*	0.1	*
Writers, artists, and entertainers	*	526.8	*	1.1	*
Actors	6.0	5.8	‡	‡	− 3.3
Athletes and kindred workers	*	35.0	*	0.1	*
Authors	19.8	18.0	0.1	‡	− 9.1
Dancers	*	1.1	*	‡	*
Designers	53.8	83.1	0.1	0.2	54.5
Editors and reporters	63.7	87.6	0.2	0.2	37.5
Musicians and composers	*	56.3	*	0.1	*
Painters and sculptors	*	64.6	*	0.1	*
Photographers	44.9	55.8	0.1	0.1	24.3
Public relations men and publicity writers	23.3	54.4	0.1	0.1	133.5
Radio and television announcers	*	19.8	*	‡	*
Other writers, artists and entertainers	*	45.3	*	0.1	*
Research workers, not specified	*	86.0	*	0.2	*
Professional, technical and kindred workers, not elsewhere classified	548.0†	301.5†	1.3	0.6	†
Managers and administrators, except farm	4,627.8	5,315.8	10.6	11.2	14.9
Salaried	2,905.3†	4,399.3†	6.7	9.2	51.4†
Self-employed	1,722.5†	916.5†	4.0	1.9	− 46.8†
Sales workers	2,983.7	3,303.8	6.9	6.9	10.7
Clerical and kindred workers	3,027.8	3,642.4	7.0	7.7	20.3
Craftsmen and kindred workers	8,500.5	10,088.5	19.5	21.2	18.7
Operatives	8,663.8	9,309.4	19.9	19.6	7.5
Laborers, except farm	2,982.9	3,147.0	6.9	6.6	5.5
Farm workers	3,587.3	2,143.0	8.3	4.5	− 40.3
Service workers, including private household	2,660.1	3,873.3	6.1	8.1	45.6
Occupation not reported	1,983.8		4.6		
Female					
Total employed (number in thousands)	21,155.6	28,929.9	100.0§	100.0§	36.8
Professional, technical, and kindred workers	2,749.9	4,550.6	13.0	15.7	65.5
Accountants	77.8	182.9	0.4	0.6	135.1
Architects	0.6	2.0	‡	‡	233.3
Computer specialists	*	49.9	*	0.2	*
Engineers	7.5	19.6	‡	0.1	161.3
Lawyers and judges	7.1	13.2	‡	0.1	85.9
Mathematical specialists	8.5	12.0	‡	‡	41.2
Life and physical scientists	12.2	26.6	0.1	0.1	118.0
Biological	3.7	10.3	‡	‡	178.4
Chemists	6.5	12.9	‡	0.1	98.5
Other life and physical scientists	2.0	3.4	‡	‡	70.0
Operations and systems researchers and analysts	*	7.6	*	‡	*
Personnel and labor relations workers	29.6	89.3	0.1	0.3	201.7

Table 4-3 Continued

Occupation and sex	1960	1970	Percent of employed workers		Percentage change 1960-1970
			1960	1970	
Female					
Physicians, dentists and related practitioners	*	45.7	*	0.2	*
Dentists	1.8	3.1	‡	‡	72.2
Optometrists	0.7	0.7	‡	‡	0.0
Pharmacists	7.4	13.0	‡	0.1	75.7
Physicians (including osteopaths)	15.9	25.8	0.1	0.1	62.3
Other health practitioners	*	3.1	*	‡	*
Registered nurses, dietitians, and therapists	583.5	891.9	2.8	3.1	52.8
Dietitians	24.6	36.9	0.1	0.1	50.0
Registered nurses	539.3	807.4	2.6	2.8	49.7
Therapists	19.6	47.6	0.1	0.2	142.9
Health technologists and technicians	86.6	180.9	0.4	0.6	108.9
Religious workers	39.6	26.0	0.2	0.1	− 34.1
Clergymen	4.4	6.2	‡	‡	40.9
Other religious workers	35.2	19.8	0.2	0.1	− 43.8
Social scientists	7.2	20.8	‡	0.1	188.9
Economists	2.6	7.4	‡	‡	184.6
Psychologists	3.6	10.6	‡	‡	194.4
Other social scientists	1.0	2.8	‡	‡	180.0
Social and recreation workers	76.5	156.0	0.4	0.5	104.1
Social	60.6	135.8	0.3	0.5	124.1
Recreation	15.9	20.2	0.1	0.1	27.0
Teachers, college and university	38.0†	138.1†	0.2	0.5	263.4†
Teachers, except college and university	1,196.7†	1,926.2†	5.7	6.7	61.0†
Elementary and secondary school teachers	1,104.5†	1,674.4†	5.2	5.8	51.6†
Other teachers	92.2†	251.8†	0.4	0.9	173.1†
Engineering and science technicians	27.7	87.8	0.1	0.3	217.0
Technicians, except health, and engineering and science	18.9	17.6	0.1	0.1	− 6.9
Airline pilots	0.2	0.7	‡	‡	250.0
Radio operators	2.9	7.3	‡	‡	151.7
Other technicians	15.8	9.6	0.1	‡	− 39.2
Vocational and educational counselors	*	46.6	*	0.2	*
Writers, artists, and entertainers	*	227.4	*	0.8	*
Actors	3.3	3.9	‡	‡	18.2
Athletes and kindred workers	*	13.5	*	0.1	*
Authors	7.7	7.4	‡	‡	− 3.9
Dancers	*	4.9	*	‡	*
Designers	11.9	25.7	0.1	0.1	116.0
Editors and reporters	36.6	59.4	0.2	0.2	62.3
Musicians and composers	*	31.5	*	0.1	*
Painters and sculptors	*	36.3	*	0.1	*
Photographers	5.8	8.9	‡	‡	53.5
Public relations workers and publicity writers	7.3	19.4	‡	0.1	165.8
Radio and television announcers	*	1.5	*	‡	*
Other writers, artists and entertainers	*	15.0	*	0.1	*
Research workers, not specified	*	29.9	*	0.1	*
Professional, technical and kindred workers, not elsewhere classified	433.5†	352.7†	2.1	1.2	†
Managers and administrators, except farm	780.0	1,055.4	3.7	3.7	35.3
Salaried	482.6†	844.1†	2.3	2.9	74.9 −
Self-employed	297.4†	211.3†	1.4	0.7	− 29.0 −

*Not available or not comparable in 1960.
†Affected by reclassification. Art, dancing, and music teachers were classified under categories such as "artists and art teachers" in 1960 but were classified as teachers in 1970. This means that percentage increases in the number of college and university teachers as well as in other teacher categories between 1960 and 1970 are somewhat overstated. The increase in the number of salaried managers is also somewhat overstated because of a change in classification that occurred in 1967.
‡Less than 0.05 percent.

Table 4-3 Continued

Occupation and sex	1960	1970	Percent of employed workers		Percentage change 1960-1970
			1960	1970	
Female					
Sales workers	1,660.1	2,141.6	7.9	7.4	29.0
Clerical and kindred workers	6,275.5	10,105.8	29.7	34.9	61.0
Craftsmen and kindred workers	252.9	521.1	1.2	1.8	106.1
Operatives	3,256.7	4,147.1	15.4	14.3	27.3
Laborers, except farm	110.3	284.3	0.5	1.0	157.8
Farm workers	360.7	224.1	1.7	0.8	− 37.9
Service workers, except private household	2,856.0	4,790.0	13.5	16.6	67.7
Private household workers	1,655.7	1,109.9	7.8	3.8	− 33.0
Occupation not reported	1,197.8	*	5.7	*	*

Significantly, many of the fields which experienced large percentage gains of workers of one sex have been viewed as traditionally appropriate occupations for the opposite sex. Examples of this include an increase in the numbers of men entering such traditionally female occupations as library science, dietetics, nursing, and elementary education, and an increase in the numbers of women entering such traditionally male occupations as law, medicine, engineering, accounting, economics, and architecture.

This crossover of the sexes into nontraditional fields and occupations is probably due to two major factors: (1) employment opportunities, and (2) increasing awareness of expanding and changing sex roles. Of the occupations mentioned above as examples of nontraditional occupations for either men or women, the *1976–77 Occupational Outlook Handbook* lists physicians, nurses, dietitians, accountants, architects, and engineers as having a favorable outlook through 1985 with employment expected to grow faster than average. For the man or woman who selects any one of these as a nontraditional occupation for his or her sex, employment opportunities and the awareness that the occupation is appropriate for members of both sexes rather than restricted to one sex are likely to play a part in the selection decision.

But what about those occupations for which the supply of qualified persons has already exceeded or will soon exceed the demand? Such is the case with librarians, elementary school teachers, lawyers, and economists which are described in the *1976–77 Occupational Outlook Handbook* as occupations in which qualified persons will experience keen competition for the available jobs through 1985. While it is true that these occupations have a projected growth that is either on the decline or at best slower than average, because of equal employment and affirmative action laws and regulations (see chapter 5, Sex Typing, Discrimination, and the Law, for a detailed discussion) men preparing to be librarians and elementary school teachers and women preparing to be lawyers and economists will have a better chance of being employed in their respective fields than their male or female counterparts.

Educational Attainment

The level of educational attainment of the entire population has risen over the past few decades, and in general, the more education a person has, the more likely he or she will be working. This increase in educational attainment is shown in table 4-4, an illustration of the median years of school completed by the civilian labor force and those not in the labor force by sex for selected dates from 1952 through 1975.

While the median years of school completed by men in the labor force has lagged behind that of women until 1975, the proportion of working men with four or more years of college is still greater than that of working women. Table 4-5 illustrates this. In the ten-year pe-

Table 4-4 Median Years of School Completed by Labor Force Status and Sex, Selected Years, 1952-1975

Year	Civilian Labor Force		Not in Labor Force	
	Men	Women	Men	Women
1952	10.4	12.0	8.5	10.4
1962	12.0	12.2	8.7	11.2
1972	12.4	12.5	10.2	12.1
1975	12.5	12.5	10.5	12.1

Source: U.S. Department of Labor and U.S. Department of Health, Education, and Welfare, *Employment and Training Report of the President*, 1976.

Table 4-5 Educational Attainment of the Labor Force by Sex, Selected Years, 1965-75

Level of Education	Year and Percent of Distribution					
	1965		1970		1975	
	Men	Women	Men	Women	Men	Women
Total	100.0	100.0	100.0	100.0	100.0	100.0
College:						
4 or More Years	12.4	10.0	14.2	10.7	17.3	13.2
1 to 3 Years	10.5	10.4	13.5	13.2	15.5	15.3
High School:						
4 Years	32.0	41.9	35.1	45.5	36.3	44.8
1 to 3 Years	19.4	18.7	17.5	16.9	17.5	17.5
Elementary:						
8 Years or Less	25.7	19.0	19.8	13.7	13.4	9.1

Source: U.S. Department of Labor and U.S. Department of Health, Education, and Welfare, *Employment and Training Report of the President*, 1976.

riod from 1965 to 1975, the difference between the proportions of working men and women with four or more years of college has increased from 2.4 percent in 1965 to 4.1 percent in 1975.

Another meaningful way of looking at the educational attainment of men and women is by labor force participation rate over a period of time. Table 4-6 shows that at each educational level in the labor force, there is a larger percentage of the adult male population than the adult female population. However, the gains made by women (as represented by percent change), especially those with a high school education or more, in the last twenty years or so have far surpassed men. For example, in 1952 50.2 percent of the adult female population with four or more years of college were in the labor force. By 1975, this percentage increased to 64.1 percent. On the other hand, the already high adult male labor force participation rate, at the same educational level, increased only slightly from 88.0 percent in 1952 to 90.4 percent in 1975.

Table 4-6 Labor Force Participation Rates by Years of School Completed for Persons 18 Years Old and Over: 1952, 1959, 1970, and 1975 (Civilian Noninstitutional Population 18 Years Old and Over)

Sex and years of school completed	Labor Force Participation Rates				Percent change, 1952 to 1975
	1975	1970	1959[1]	1952[1]	
Not High School Graduate					
Women	31.6	33.0	31.6	31.2	+ 1.3
Men	65.2	72.6	81.2	85.3	− 23.6
Ratio: women/men[2]	0.48	0.45	0.39	0.37	(X)
High School Graduate—No College					
Women	52.5	50.3	42.8	40.7	+ 29.0
Men	87.6	90.1	92.7	93.1	− 5.9
Ratio: women/men[2]	0.60	0.56	0.46	0.44	(X)
1 to 3 Years of College					
Women	53.5	48.6	40.5	37.5	+ 42.7
Men	81.3	80.6	83.4	85.6	− 5.0
Ratio: women/men[2]	0.66	0.60	0.49	0.44	(X)
4 or More Years of College					
Women	64.1	59.7	53.3	50.2	+ 27.7
Men	90.4	90.2	92.8	88.0	+ 2.7
Ratio: women/men[2]	0.71	0.66	0.57	0.57	(X)

X Not applicable.
[1] Data exclude persons who did not report years of school completed.
[2] Ratios of labor force participation rates.

Source: U.S. Department of Commerce, Bureau of the Census, *A Statistical Portrait of Women in the United States,* April 1976.

A more extensive discussion on the education of men and women is contained in chapter 3, Sex Typing in the Schools.

Earnings Direct comparisons of men's and women's salaries are difficult to make because their occupational distributions differ markedly, their work experience and educational preparation are often not comparable, many more women than men work part-time, and men are more likely than women to work overtime. Each of these factors has considerable bearing on the earnings of men and women and will be discussed individually. However, because it is not known how much and what extent each of these factors influences employment compensation, it is somewhat useful to first take a look at some gross data comparing male and female earnings. Table 4-7 shows a comparison of the median earnings of men and women employed on a full-time, year-round basis from 1955 to 1974. According to this

Table 4-7 Comparison of Median Earnings of Year-Round Full-Time Workers, by Sex, 1955-1974
(Persons 14 years of age and over)

Year	Median earnings Women (1)	Men (2)	Earnings gap in dollars (3)	Women's earnings as a percent of men's (4)	Percent men's earnings exceeded women's (5)	Earnings gap in constant 1967 dollars (6)
1974	$6,772	$11,835	$5,063	57.2	74.8	$3,433
1973	6,335	11,186	4,851	56.6	76.6	3,649
1972	5,903	10,202	4,299	57.9	72.8	3,435
1971	5,593	9,399	3,806	59.5	68.0	3,136
1970	5,323	8,966	3,643	59.4	68.4	3,133
1969	4,977	8,227	3,250	60.5	65.3	2,961
1968	4,457	7,664	3,207	58.2	72.0	3,079
1967	4,150	7,182	3,032	57.8	73.1	3,032
1966	3,973	6,848	2,875	58.0	72.4	2,958
1965	3,823	6,375	2,552	60.0	66.8	2,700
1964	3,690	6,195	2,505	59.6	67.9	2,696
1963	3,561	5,978	2,417	59.6	67.9	2,637
1962	3,446	5,974	2,528	59.5	73.4	2,790
1961	3,351	5,644	2,293	59.4	68.4	2,559
1960	3,293	5,417	2,124	60.8	64.5	2,394
1959	3,193	5,209	2,016	61.3	63.1	2,308
1958	3,102	4,927	1,825	63.0	58.8	2,108
1957	3,008	4,713	1,705	63.8	56.7	2,023
1956	2,827	4,466	1,639	63.3	58.0	2,014
1955	2,719	4,252	1,533	63.9	56.4	1,911

Notes: For 1967-1974, data include wage and salary income and earnings from self-employment; for 1956-66, data include wage and salary income only.

Column 3 = column 2 minus column 1.
Column 4 = column 1 divided by column 2.
Column 5 = column 2 minus column 1, divided by column 1.
Column 6 = column 3 times the purchasing power of the consumer dollar (1967 = $1.00).

Source: Women's Bureau, U.S. Department of Labor, "The Earnings Gap Between Men and Women," October 1976.

data, the earnings gap between men and women was larger—in actual dollars and women's earnings as a percent of men's—in 1974 than it had been for the past nineteen years. In 1974, women earned only 57 cents for every dollar earned by men, compared to approximately 64 cents in 1975. The dollar differential between men's and women's median salaries in 1974 was $5,063.

Considering the gains women have made in employment in recent years and the federal laws and regulations (particularly the Equal Pay Act) now in effect which protect against discrimination on the basis of sex, it is shocking to think that salary equity and the concept of equal pay for equal work may be backsliding. But the factors mentioned at the beginning of this section have contributed to the widening earnings gap and can not be ignored.

One of the factors contributing to the earnings differential between men and women is their occupational distribution. Despite recent changes in the labor force and the crossing over of men and women into nontraditional occupations for their sex, women are still concentrated in the lower paying occupations and the lower status positions within higher paying occupations. This uneven distribution of women in low paying, low status jobs and men in the higher paying, high status positions makes a comparison of median earnings of all workers regardless of occupation less than useful. Table 4-8 presents information on the 1974 average earnings of men and women by occupation group. The earnings differential was largest ($7,355,

Table 4-8 Total Money Earnings of Civilian Year-Round Full-Time Workers, by Occupation Group and Sex, 1974 (Persons 14 years of age and over)

Occupation group	Women	Men	Dollar gap	Women's earnings as a percent of men's	Percent men's earnings exceeded women's
Total	$6,772	$11,835	$5,063	57.2	74.8
Professional, technical, and kindred workers	9,570	14,873	5,303	64.3	55.4
Managers and administrators	8,603	15,425	6,822	55.8	79.3
Sales workers, total	5,168	12,523	7,355	41.3	142.3
Retail trade	4,734	9,125	4,391	51.9	92.8
Other sales workers	8,452	13,983	5,531	60.4	65.4
Clerical workers	6,827	11,514	4,687	59.3	68.7
Craft and kindred workers	6,492	12,028	5,536	54.0	85.3
Operatives (including transport)	5,766	10,176	4,410	56.7	76.5
Service workers (except private household)	5,046	8,638	3,592	58.4	71.2
Farmers and farm managers	(1/)	5,459	—	—	—
Farm laborers and supervisors	(1/)	5,097	—	—	—
Nonfarm laborers	5,891	8,145	2,254	72.3	38.3
Private household workers	2,676	(1/)	—	—	—

1/ Base less than 75,000

Source: Women's Bureau, U.S. Department of Labor, "The Earnings Gap Between Men and Women," October 1976.

men's earnings exceeding women's by 142.3 percent) among sales workers, where women worked primarily in retail trade jobs while men were more likely to be in higher paying commissioned positions. The earnings gap was smallest among the nonfarm laborers where men's earnings exceeded women's by 38.3 percent.

It appears that even within occupation groups there are still large earnings differentials between men and women. To reflect accurate differentials, each broad occupation group would have to be broken down into specific occupations and job titles. When this is done, especially for highly skilled occupations, and education and work experience factors are held constant, the earnings gap narrows but does not disappear altogether.

Generally it is thought that there is a positive correlation between educational attainment and earnings for both men and women. The more education an individual has, the more money he or she is likely to be making. However, even when educational levels are identical, women earn considerably less than men, as illustrated in table 4-9. In 1974, the average income of women with a high school education was less than men who had not completed elementary school. And, men who had only completed the eighth grade had higher incomes than women with four years of college. Only at the educational attainment level of five or more years of college does the

Table 4-9 Comparison of Median Income of Year-round Full-time Workers, by Educational Attainment and Sex, 1974

Years of school completed	Median income Women (1)	Men (2)	Income gap in dollars (3)	Women's income as a percent of men's (4)	Percent men's income exceeded women's (5)	Marginal dollar value of increased educational attainment Women (6)	Men (7)
Elementary school							
Less than 8 years	$ 5,022	$ 7,912	$2,890	63.5	57.5	—	—
8 years	5,606	9,891	4,285	56.7	76.4	$ 584	$1,979
High school							
1 to 3 years	5,919	11,225	5,306	52.7	89.6	313	1,334
4 years	7,150	12,642	5,492	56.6	76.8	1,231	1,417
College							
1 to 3 years	8,072	13,718	5,646	58.8	69.9	922	1,076
4 years	9,523	16,240	6,717	58.6	70.5	1,451	2,522
5 years or more	11,790	18,214	6,424	64.7	54.5	2,267	1,974

Notes: Column 3 = column 2 minus column 1.
    Column 4 = column 1 divided by column 2.
    Column 5 = column 2 minus column 1, divided by column 1.
    Column 6 and 7 = absolute (median) dollar difference between successive years of school completed.

Source: Women's Bureau, U.S. Department of Labor, "The Earnings Gap Between Men and Women," October, 1976.

gap in absolute dollars between men's and women's incomes begin to decrease.

Average starting salaries of new college graduates are beginning to show a marked change from earlier years, when women were offered substantially lower beginning salaries than their male counterparts. For example, the average monthly starting salaries for June 1975 college graduates in selected fields were as follows (Frank, 1974):

	Women	Men
Accounting	$ 986	$ 990
Engineering	1,075	1,062
Liberal Arts	784	776
Marketing-Sales- Retailing	814	862
Business Adminis- tration—General Business	840	814
Science-Chemistry	950	992
Math-Statistics-Data Processing	885	915

Work experience plays a major part in the salary differential between men and women. The worklife expectancy, or the average number of years a person works during a lifetime, is 40.1 years for men and 22.9 years for women—a difference of 17.2 years ("The Earnings Gap between Women and Men," 1976). The discontinuous worklife pattern and the lack of career continuity of many women also have an adverse impact on their earning power. While the trend is changing slowly, women have tended to drop out of the labor market for various reasons. More women than men leave for reasons related to family responsibilities. When reentering the labor market, women often have difficulty finding a job that utilizes and builds upon their past training and experience.

Overtime work is another factor which contributes to the earnings differential between men and women, as men are far more likely to work overtime than women. For example, in May of 1975 only 13 percent of the women in the labor force worked overtime compared to 28 percent of the men. Also, the median weekly earnings of women during the same period were $138, considerably lower than the men's $215 ("The Earnings Gap between Women and Men," 1976).

While much of the earnings gap can be explained by occupational distribution, work experience, worklife pattern, and educational differences, there still remains a portion that is unexplained—a portion that is likely the result of sex discrimination.

Marital and Family Status

The increasing tendency of married women to work has been one of the major factors in the growth of the female labor market. In 1940, 30 percent of the working women were married with husbands present (*1969 Handbook on Women Workers*). In 1975, 58 percent of the women were married with husbands present ("Women Workers Today," 1976). This represents an increase of 28 percent.

The growing trend of married women to work outside the home is shown in table 4-10. In 1950, 50.5 percent of the single women of working age were in the labor force in contrast to 23.8 percent of married women with husbands present and 37.8 percent of widowed, divorced, or separated women. Twenty-five years later the participation rate of single women was 56.7 percent, an increase of only 6.2 percent; the rate for widowed, divorced, or separated women was 40.7 percent, a 2.9 percent increase; and the rate for married women with husbands present was 44.4 percent, an increase of 20.6 percent. Thus, employees can no longer assume that women will quit work when they marry nor that married women are poor employment risks.

Table 4-10 also reflects recent trends in marriage and divorce. The rate of first marriages has continued to decline while the divorce rate has increased. At the same time men and women have tended to remain single longer. For example, the median age of the first marriage was 20.3 years for women and 22.8 years for men in 1960. By 1975, the median ages had increased to 21.1 years for women and 23.5 years for men.

Table 4-10 Labor Force Participation Rates by Sex and Marital Status, Selected Years, 1950 to 1975

| | Percent of Each Group in Labor Force | | | | | |
| | Women | | | Men | | |
Year	Never Married	Married, Spouse Present	Widowed, Divorced or Separated	Never Married	Married, Spouse Present	Widowed, Divorced or Separated
1950	50.5	23.8	37.8	62.6	91.6	63.1
1955	46.4	27.7	39.6	61.2	90.7	60.7
1960	44.1	30.5	40.0	55.5	88.9	59.3
1965	40.5	34.7	38.9	50.3	87.7	55.8
1970	53.0	40.8	39.1	60.7	86.9	54.2
1975	56.7	44.4	40.7	67.1	83.1	65.2

Source: U.S. Department of Labor and U.S. Department of Health, Education and Welfare, *Employment and Training Report of the President,* 1976.

Mothers are more likely to work outside the home today than ever before. In 1950, only 9 percent of all mothers with children under eighteen years of age were working (*1969 Handbook on Women Workers*), but by 1975 the labor force participation rate of mothers increased to 47.4 percent—a gain of 38 percent. The age of the children influences the labor force participation rate of mothers. In 1975, 38.8 percent of the mothers with preschool children were working outside the home compared to 54.8 percent of those with school age children ("Women Workers Today").

One out of every eight families in 1975 was headed by a woman. Except for single working women, women heads of families are more likely to be in the labor force than any other category of women workers. More than 54 percent of the women family heads in 1975 were in the labor force—representing approximately one out of every ten women workers. About one-third of these had incomes below the 1974 low-income level. Of all families with income below the 1974 poverty level, 54 percent were headed by men and 46 percent were headed by women.

Unemployment Historically, women have had a higher unemployment rate than men, and teenagers have had a higher unemployment rate than adults (see table 4-11). Some of the reasons often given for the higher unemployment rates for women is their more intermittent labor force participation, their lack of seniority, and thus their increased likelihood of layoffs or job termination and their more frequent classification as labor force reentrants.

Studies of working age persons outside the labor force—those who are neither working nor seeking work—suggest that if all women who wished to be employed entered the labor force, unemployment of women would be even higher. Of the working age per-

Table 4-11 Unemployment Rates by Age and Sex: 1950, 1960, 1970, and 1975

Sex and Age	1950	1960	1970	1975
Total, 16 years and over				
Women	5.7	5.9	5.9	9.3
Men	5.1	5.4	4.4	7.9
16 to 19 years				
Women	11.4	13.9	15.6	19.7
Men	12.7	15.3	15.0	20.1
20 years and over				
Women	5.1	5.1	4.8	8.0
Men	4.7	4.7	3.5	6.7

Source: U.S. Department of Commerce, Bureau of Census, *A Statistical Portrait of Women in the United States*, April 1976.

sons outside the labor force in 1974, more than nine out of ten surveyed indicated that they were not looking for employment at the present. Of these, 60 percent were women who were keeping house, 15 percent were retirees, and 12 percent were students. Of the persons who indicated that they wanted to work, although they were not looking for employment, 68 percent were women. Family responsibilities was the reason these women most frequently gave for not seeking employment. Another major reason given by both men and women for not looking for employment was that they felt their job seeking efforts would be fruitless. These so-called "discouraged workers" were largely women (two-thirds of the total), male teenagers, and elderly men who: (1) had looked for a job before but did not find one, (2) thought there was no work available, (3) felt they lacked the necessary job requirements, i.e., education and skills, (4) thought they would be considered too young or too old, or (5) had some other personal handicap (*Manpower Report of the President,* 1975).

Unemployment rates were higher in 1975 than at any other period of time during the postwar era. While the labor force is expected to expand about 17 percent between 1970 and 1980 and another 11 percent between 1980 and 1990 (*Manpower Report of the President,* 1975), the numbers of persons seeking employment will also continue to increase, and the future unemployment rates are not likely to decline markedly unless there is a dramatic change in the economy.

Some Myths about Women Workers

Traditional attitudes about appropriate occupational roles for men and women have played a major role in determining employment opportunities available to each sex. Chapter 1, Sex Role Development and Socialization, is a discussion of how sex roles are developed and the stereotypes which have come about as a result of the socialization process. Some of the value traits which society has ascribed to men include aggressiveness, independence, objectiveness, lack of emotion, competitiveness, logic, unexcitable during crisis, strength, decisiveness, and self-confidence. These characteristics suggest that men are the sex best suited for positions of responsibility and high-level skill in the world of work. Young males have been encouraged to aspire to be doctors, lawyers, scientists, executives, foremen, skilled craftsmen, etc. On the other hand, value traits commonly ascribed to women include tact, supportiveness, gentleness, kindness, cooperativeness, neatness in habits and appearance, that they are dependable, and good with detail. It is not surprising that with these characteristics women have been assigned roles in teaching, nursing, clerical work, and domestic service. Generally speaking, females have been encouraged to prepare themselves first to be wives and mothers, and, if they work outside the home, to choose those occupations which are in a sense an extension of the home.

While these traditional views regarding the kinds of occupations that are "appropriate" for men and women are slowly changing, and virtually all jobs (with a few exceptions which will be discussed in chapter 5) are required by law to be open to members of both sexes, many myths still exist. Since most of the myths tend to be restrictive to women, these will be discussed here. The reader is reminded, however, that there are also myths which have tended to restrict men in their occupational choices, e.g., men aren't "nurturing" and thus would not make good nurses or preschool teachers.

Myth I: Women Quit Their Jobs More Often Than Men

This myth is a double-edged sword. If it is determined that women change jobs more often than men, their higher turnover is more costly to employers. If women are found to have longer tenure in their positions than men, they are said to be immobile and unwilling to move for advancement and new job opportunities. Actually, neither argument has any basis. Research shows that age, level of employment, length of service, and record of prior job stability are far more predictive of job retention than sex ("Facts about Women's Absenteeism and Labor Turnover," 1969).

A study conducted under the auspices of the Social Science Research Council found that among groups of men and women of the same age, marital status, length of time in the labor force, and migration patterns, women held about the same number of jobs in a given period as did men (Turner, 1964).

A Labor Department study showed that 10 percent of the men and 7 percent of the women employed in January of 1966 were working in a different occupation from the one they had held in January of 1965. The study also found that occupation changing was highest among young workers regardless of sex. By occupation group, the highest rates of turnover were among craftsmen, foremen, and kindred workers—a group with relatively few women. The highest rates of turnover for women were among the clerical workers, sales workers, and service workers. For men, the highest turnover rates were among nonfarm laborers, followed by clerical workers, operatives, service workers, craftsmen, and foremen. The least amount of occupation changing for both men and women was among professional and technical workers (Special Labor Force Report No. 84).

Actually, the public's view of turnover rates for women evolved during a time when women workers were typically single, young, and likely to leave the work force permanently for marriage. Today's typical woman worker, however, is married, in her forties, a mother, and her higher educational attainment and greater professional commitment make her a much more stable employee.

Employer practices greatly influence the turnover rate of women employees. If women are restricted to low-paying, dead-end jobs and are denied access to training and promotion opportunities, they are more likely to leave a job. Where guaranteed maternity leaves are not available, young mothers are forced to quit work, thus raising their turnover rates.

Myth II:
Women Are
Absent From
Work More
Than Men

Similar to labor turnover, absenteeism is more closely tied to job level than to sex. Men and women in higher-level professional positions take approximately the same amount of time off whether it is for illness, professional development, or pleasure. On the other hand, employees of both sexes in low-level, low-paid jobs have higher absenteeism. This myth developed in offices where low-level female employees were contrasted with males at higher levels.

Certainly frequent illness is not sex linked. A Public Health Service study of workdays lost due to illness or injury in a twelve-month period found an average of 5.6 days lost by women and 5.5 days lost by men. A U.S. Civil Service Commission study of sick leave records also showed little difference between male and female workers (Turner, 1964, p. 20).

Frequently quoted figures of workdays lost because of illness or injury are 5.6 days for women and 5.3 days for men per year, contained in a U.S. Department of Labor report. What is not usually quoted from the report, however, is that the statistics do not reflect length of time away from work as compared to frequency; thus, "since women lost more worktime because of acute conditions and men because of chronic conditions, . . . the total financial loss caused by women's absences was about the same as that caused by men's" ("Facts about Women's Absenteeism and Labor Turnover," 1969).

Myth III:
Women Do Not
Really Need
to Work

Many feel that women work to obtain luxuries, for ego self-fulfillment, or they are accused of "taking jobs away from men." This line of thinking presumes that all women are married and supported by their husbands—an assumption not in touch with reality.

It is a well-documented fact that most women in today's labor force, regardless of their marital status, work because of economic reasons. For example, in 1975, 42 percent of the women in the labor force were either single, widowed, divorced, or married with husband absent. Many of these women were not only supporting themselves but children and elderly relatives as well. Of the 58 percent with husband present, the husband's income of almost 15 percent of these women was under $7,000. In addition, 2.3 million husbands were unemployed and another 7.9 million husbands were not in the labor force ("Why Women Work," 1976).

In 1975, approximately one out of ten women workers was head of her household. Put another way, about 3.9 million families were headed by women in the labor force. Almost two-thirds of these were the only earners in their families. Just about one out of every three families which was headed by a woman, including those in and out of the labor force, had an income below the poverty level in 1974 ("Why Women Work," 1976).

Myth IV: Women Always Quit Work to Have Children

A frequently cited reason for not hiring a woman of childbearing age is that she is likely to quit within a short period of time to raise a family—wasting the time and money invested in her training. Once true for perhaps the majority of working women as they became mothers, it is no longer the common practice. Today, with improved birth control and liberalized abortion laws, women are not only choosing to have fewer children, but some are choosing not to have children. Maternity leave policies have enabled many working mothers to take a brief leave of absence from work without loss of pay or seniority. Indeed, some working mothers have been known to work right up to the day of giving birth to a child and return to work a few short weeks following.

As cited earlier in this chapter, 55 percent of women with school age children and 29 percent of women with preschool age children were working in 1975. Table 4-1 shows that women of childbearing age are staying in the work force to a much greater extent today than they were in the 1950s and 1960s.

A 1970 study conducted by the Merchants and Manufacturers Association found that not only are women somewhat less prone than men to leave jobs but that only 11.5 percent of the women who left their jobs, including all job levels, indicated they were leaving for family reasons (Bernstein, 1970).

Myth V: Women Will Not Relocate

Women have traditionally followed their husbands as better employment opportunities arose. Nonworking wives have busied themselves with the chores of setting up a new household, getting children enrolled in new schools, becoming familiar with the surrounding community, and making new friends. Working wives have had to do all of this plus look for a new job for themselves or drop out of the labor force altogether. Seldom, if ever, did a family relocate because the wife and mother was either transferred by her company or changed jobs for career advancement.

But times are changing. No longer can employers assume that female employees will not relocate; nor can they assume that a working wife will give up her job if her husband is transferred. Many working couples today are choosing a variety of alternatives to the old standard of wife always being the one to fulfill the "whither thou goest, I will go" role. One alternative, of course, is for the husband to follow the wife to a new location and then look for another job. Another is for both the husband and wife to agree to relocate simultaneously, by first determining a location or locations which would provide ample occupational opportunities for both. A growing number of couples live apart during the work week because of different job locations and maintain a "commuting marriage."

All of these alternatives presume that there will be a relocation in order to get ahead financially or professionally. Actually, some working couples may choose to make compromises between two careers and either relocate or not relocate for reasons other than monetary ones. Personal priorities are playing a more and more dominant role in the relocation decisions of employees, male or female, married or single (Jones, 1972).

Some large companies are attempting to solve some of the problems associated with relocation by hiring or relocating both the husband and wife, as pointed out in *The New York Times:* "There could be greater likelihood of retaining both than each separately" (Bender, 1971).

Employers must assume that all employees will relocate—until other information exists. Too often, employers assume women employees will not relocate to advance their careers and never even offer them an opportunity for a career-wise move (Bulwik and Elicks, 1972).

Myth VI:
Women Are Just
Not Fit for Some
Kinds of Work

Because women have traditionally been employed in "women's jobs" such as teaching, nursing, clerical work, and domestic service, some employers assume that women are not suited either by temperament or skill for other types of work. On this point, Oppenheimer (1970) comments:

> The sex-linked traits in question may not even be proven traits of one sex or the other—it is sufficient that employers believe they are, or believe that one sex has an advantage over the other in some important respect. . . . Women are supposed by many employers to have greater manual dexterity than men. This may or may not be true, but that is not particularly important. What is important is the extent to which employers believe it, and let this belief guide their hiring policies.

In actuality, there are no clear, measurable differences between the abilities of men and those of women. It has been generally believed that women are better in verbal and linguistic ability, writing-speed, finger dexterity, speed of observations, and immediate memory, and that men are better in logical deduction, numerical/mathematical ability, technical ability, and in working with spacial relationships. However, many women and men have the abilities generally attributed to the other sex, and employers must assess each applicant for employment individually. Assuming an applicant is unqualified for a particular position solely on the basis of his or her sex is not only unfair and unwise, but also illegal.

It is not yet clear whether the abilities commonly attributed to men and women are sex linked or are acquired through socialization (see chapter 1 for a more complete discussion). To the degree that such abilities are acquired, educators and counselors must provide all students, regardless of their sex, the opportunity to develop all of their abilities. Once again, not to allow learning experiences for students of either sex is not only unfair, but it is also illegal. The illegality of providing employment or educational opportunity solely on the basis of sex is discussed in chapter 5, Sex Typing, Discrimination, and the Law.

While still a minority among the overall occupational distribution of women workers, a number of women are showing up in occupations traditionally thought to be for men only. These women are proving that "women can do any type of job, given the proper training. There have been enough trail blazers in every field from auto mechanic to aquanaut to show us this" (Katzell and Byham, 1972). Being a female trail blazer in a largely male field is not easy, as women welders, truck drivers, foresters, police officers, contractors, engineers, sports reporters, veterinarians, etc., will attest. As one woman put it, being a woman in a job which has been traditionally held by men takes "the kind of courage with which not everyone—male or female—is endowed. It is not simply a matter of finding out whether you can do the job (while) being on trial in a highly visible and often publicized situation, but sometimes . . . it means being prepared to cope with an all-male work/social situation where evolved customs, language, and habits have been predicated on a one-sex grouping, and with the individual reactions (hostile, protective, derisive, ribald, gentlemanly, derogatory—rarely neutral) of the men whose group has been invaded" (Marshall, 1972).

Myth VII: Women Are Too Emotional for Positions with Heavy Responsibilities

The myth that women will "fall to pieces" if given heavy responsibility on the job is just not true. Like most men in higher-level positions, women have learned on the way up that what are thought to be typical female behaviors such as expressing too much emotion or crying are simply not acceptable on the job. In interviewing executives for her book, *The Executive Suite—Feminine Style,* Lynch (1973) found that ". . . emotionalism is no more prevalent in women than in men executives, and the use of tears is strictly *verboten.*" Women have served as governors, congresswomen, cabinet officers in public service, and as college and corporate presidents in nongovernmental organizations. There are few jobs more taxing, emotionally, than these.

Myth VIII: Women Do Not Make Good Bosses

It has often been said that women do not make good supervisors, managers, and executives and that both men and other women prefer not to work for them. This was cited in a recent study of male managers. The respondents said that women do not make good supervisors, not because of lack of ability, but because it was felt that both men and women would prefer a male supervisor (Bass et al.). Theodore Caplow (1954) explains this preference:

Women are barred from four out of every five occupational functions, not because of incapacity or technical unsuitability, but because the attitudes which govern interpersonal relationships in our culture sanction only a few working relationships between men and women, and prohibit all the others on the grounds that have nothing to do with technology.

It is Caplow's belief that our social values require women to be subordinate to men and not vice versa, and that intimate groups outside family or sexual relationships tend to be single-sexed.

Regardless of social norms or sex role stereotypes, the real effectiveness of a supervisor depends on the individual and the particular circumstances. When women are competent and fair, understand the job requirements and their staff, and give credit where credit is due, they are respected by their male and female subordinates and peers. The female supervisor who is considered "bossy" or "bitchy" may be no more so than male counterparts labeled "overbearing" or "explosive." The key to successful management is the attainment of stated objectives.

Certainly success knows no sex. There are successful and effective female and male supervisors, managers, and executives just as there are unsuccessful and ineffective persons of both sexes in these types of positions.

Myth IX:
Women Do Not
Want to be
Promoted into
Management
Positions

Like the other myths, this one has no empirical basis, but is instead an assumption that is made about women workers. So the myth goes, women do not want the additional responsibilities and extra work load that generally accompany managerial positions, because it will decrease their amount of time off and conflict with their family responsibilities. It is true that some women, just as some men, will refuse promotions for these reasons.

Many other men and women, however, are ready and willing to be promoted into more responsible positions. The idea that all women will turn down opportunities for advancement is disproved by the fact that increasing numbers of women are filing sex discrimination complaints with state and federal compliance agencies charging they have been unfairly overlooked by their employers for promotion and advancement opportunities.

Myth X:
Women Should
Not Work in
Unpleasant or
Dangerous
Surroundings

No employee, male or female, should be required to work in unnecessarily dangerous surroundings. Some jobs, such as fire fighters, police officers, and heavy construction workers necessarily involve a certain amount of danger and risk. This does not mean, however, that women who are trained, qualified, and who desire these jobs should be overlooked simply because of their sex.

This myth, oddly enough, has been supported by protective legislation for women requiring employers to meet certain hours limitations, occupational restrictions, and working condition standards. Such protective legislation has effectively discouraged the hiring of women for certain kinds of work. Women have had a difficult time being employed as bartenders, fire fighters, heavy construction workers, truck drivers, and the like.

Although the Equal Employment Opportunity Commission declared in 1969 that protective laws and regulations were in conflict with Title VII of the Civil Rights Act of 1964, by 1974 only sixteen states had either repealed such laws or changed them so that they applied to members of both sexes. The rest of the states have retained some form of protective or "restrictive" legislation (Conlin, 1974). Even though these laws are still on the books of many states, they are ignored by employers who follow more recent Federal equal employment regulations. More will be said about laws and regulations affecting employment in chapter 5.

Myth XI: Women Returning to the Labor Market Are Unskilled

Women who desire employment after having taken time off to raise a family have found it very difficult to reenter the job market at any level above the semiskilled or unskilled occupations, regardless of their prior work experiences. This assumes that women who have been home for a few years have lost all skills and knowledge and are not trainable. It argues that the only place to begin is at the bottom. This is not only unfair to women reentering the job market, but is also a waste of talent on the part of the employer.

Employers must consider prior training, work experience, length of time away from the labor force, nonpaid volunteer activities, any recent educational and professional activities, and vocational preparations made for reentry. Some women are ready to step back into a job similar to the one they left or start at an even higher level. Obviously, the more education and work experience women have prior to leaving the labor market, the more involved they remain in activities related to their profession or occupation; and the shorter their time away from work, the greater are their chances for successful reentry. Employers can help by not discounting their capacities.

While it is the individual woman's responsibility to brush up on her skills or obtain the necessary education to become updated and current in her field, employers should be willing to offer the same training opportunities to women returning to work as they offer employees of comparable ability.

All of the myths discussed in this section have been used by employers to limit the numbers of working women and the level at which they are employed. These myths are in direct conflict with many facts and federal laws and can no longer go unchallenged. Both women and the courts are demanding equal employment opportunity for all qualified persons.

Employment Outlook

Continued improvement in general economic conditions must occur if there are to be increased employment opportunities for both men and women. While the size of the future labor force is projected to increase through 1990, so is the number of persons seeking employment. The educational attainment of the labor force and the general population is expected to continue to rise along with increased educational requirements for many jobs. Thus, competition for employment will continue to accelerate, making career planning and preparation even more crucial in the future than it is today.

The Bureau of Labor Statistics projections of labor force growth through the 1980s indicate that most long-term trends in employment by major occupation groups are expected to continue, although at a much slower rate than that which occurred during the 1960s and early 1970s. Professional and technical workers will continue to be the fastest growing major occupation group despite the expected slowdown in the growth of teaching positions. The need for professional and technical workers in the natural, social, and health sciences will persist especially in areas such as health services, environmental protection, energy research and development, urban renewal, and the like.

The demand for salaried managers and administrators, especially those with technical training in automation and data processing, will grow rapidly. Some of the clerical occupations will experience growth while others will experience a slowdown because of developments in computers, communication devices, and office equipment.

The rate of increase for many sales and service workers, operatives, and laborers is expected to be somewhat slower than that projected for total employment. Employment opportunities for highly skilled craft workers are expected to rise while those for farm workers are expected to decline (*1976–77 Occupational Outlook Handbook*).

Rising levels of education and career aspirations of young women, declining birth rates, and an increased tendency for mothers to work outside the home are just a few of the factors which suggest that the future worklives of women will more and more resemble the worklives of men, both in terms of the amount of time spent in the labor force and in terms of occupational distribution. More women are preparing themselves educationally to compete in predominantly male occupations such as business, engineering, law, and medicine. And increasing numbers of men are entering such traditionally female fields as the health services, library science, and clerical work. Legislation prohibiting sex discrimination in employment will continue to enable greater diversity in work opportunities for women and men; thus, there will be less and less sex typing in the world of work.

For all individuals seeking employment in the future, as in the present, finding jobs commensurate with their abilities and expectations will not be easy. Counselors and helping professionals in all settings must be knowledgeable about the present world of work and the sex typing that exists and must keep informed of the employment trends and projections for the future if they are to be effective in assisting their clients in career and occupational planning and preparation that is based on individual abilities and interests and employment opportunities and not based on a person's sex.

References

Bass, B. M. *et al.* Male managers' attitudes toward working women. *American Behavioral Scientist,* 15, 2:221–236.

Bender, M. Executive couples: reluctance to hire husbands and wives is fading. *The New York Times,* October 29, 1971.

Bernstein, H. Women workers more stable, study claims. *Los Angeles Times,* November 1970.

Bulwick, H. C., and Elick, S. R. *Affirmative action for women: myth and reality.* Berkeley: University of California Press and Institute of Business and Economic Research, 1972.

Bureau of Labor Statistics, U.S. Department of Labor. *Special labor force report no. 84.* Washington, D.C.: U.S. Government Printing Office.

Caplow, T. *The sociology of work.* Minneapolis: University of Minnesota Press, 1954.

Conlin, R. B. Equal protection versus equal rights amendment—where are we now? *Drake Law Review,* 24, 2:259–335.

Foxley, C. H. *Locating, recruiting, and employing women: an equal opportunity approach.* Garrett Park, Md.: Garrett Park Press, 1976.

Frank, S. E. Trends in employment of college and university graduates in business and industry, 1975. *29th Annual Report,* Northwestern University, 1974.

Jones, J. A. Career wives: new factor in relocating key workers. *Los Angeles Times,* April 16, 1972

Katzell, M., and Byham, W. (eds.). *Women in the workforce.* New York: Behavioral Publications, Inc., 1972.

Lynch, E. M. *The executive suite—feminine style.* New York: AMACOM, 1973.

Marshall, P. Look who's wearing the lipstick! *Manpower,* December, 1972.

Oppenheimer, V. K. *The female labor force in the United States.* Berkeley: Institute of International Studies, University of California, 1970.

Turner, M. B. *Women and work.* Los Angeles: University of California Institute of Industrial Relations, 1964.

U.S. Department of Labor. *Occupational outlook handbook.* Washington, D.C.: U.S. Government Printing Office, 1977.

U.S. Department of Labor, and U.S. Department of Health, Education, and Welfare. *Employment and training report of the president.* Washington, D.C.: U.S. Government Printing Office, 1976.

U.S. Department of Labor, and U.S. Department of Health, Education, and Welfare. *Manpower report of the president.* Washington, D.C.: U.S. Government Printing Office, 1975.

Women's Bureau, Wage and Labor Standards Administration, U.S. Department of Labor. *The earnings gap between women and men.* Washington, D.C.: U.S. Government Printing Office, 1976.

Women's Bureau, Wage and Labor Standards Administration, U.S. Department of Labor. *Facts about women's absenteeism and labor turnover.* Washington, D.C.: U.S. Government Printing Office, 1969.

Women's Bureau, Wage and Labor Standards Administration, U.S. Department of Labor. *Handbook on women workers.* Washington, D.C.: U.S. Government Printing Office, 1969.

Women's Bureau, Wage and Labor Standards Administration, U.S. Department of Labor. *Why women work.* Washington, D.C.: U.S. Government Printing Office, 1976.

Women's Bureau, Wage and Labor Standards Administration, U.S. Department of Labor. *Women workers today.* Washington, D.C.: U.S. Government Printing Office, 1976.

5 Sex Typing, Discrimination, and the Law

Counselors and helping professionals in all types of settings—educational, employment, medical and social service, religious etc.—need to be familiar with the various laws and regulations which prohibit sex discrimination. A general knowledge of federal antidiscrimination requirements enables the counselor to assist individuals in determining whether their rights have been violated and what to do and where to go for help if such has been the case. Counselors knowledgeable about these laws can also assist institutions and organizations in ridding the environment of sexist and discriminatory elements, practices, and policies. The purpose of this chapter is to provide the counselor with a brief description of each of the major laws and regulations which prohibit discrimination based on sex. For those desiring more extensive information, I have included an annotated list of particularly helpful resource organizations and additional readings.

The Equal Pay Act

The Equal Pay Act (Public Law 88-38, June 10, 1963) is the oldest federal legislation prohibiting discrimination on the basis of sex. An amendment to the Fair Labor Standards Act of 1938, the Equal Pay Act (EPA) prohibits differential rates of pay for women and men who ". . . do equal work on jobs, the performance of which requires equal skill, effort, and responsibility, and which are performed under similar working conditions. . . ."

The provisions of the EPA also apply to overtime pay and to employer contributions to most fringe benefits. Differences in salary are permissible only where payment is based on a seniority system, a merit system, a system which measures earnings by quantity or quality of production, or a differential based on a factor other than sex. If it is determined that there exists an unfair differential in wages between male and female employees doing substantially equal work, the employer must raise the wages of the lower-paid group since wage reduction of the higher-paid group in such instances is illegal. Some explanation of the terms "equal work" and "substantially equal" work is helpful. Case law interpreting the Equal Pay Act has consistently interpreted "equal work" to mean "substantially equal." The courts have continued to stress that in prescribing "equal" work Congress did not require that the jobs be identical, only that they be "substantially equal." Any other interpretation would destroy the original purpose of the Act.

The EPA also prohibits a union or labor organization from engaging in acts which cause or attempt to cause an employer to discriminate against an employee or group of employees in violation of the equal pay provisions. Persons who have suffered pay discrimination can recover back wages of up to two years for a nonwillful violation and three years for a willful violation.

Who Is Covered by the Equal Pay Act?

Until July 1972, the Equal Pay Act covered only those employees who were also covered by the Fair Labor Standards Act, or employees who work for establishments which do a yearly business of $250,000 or more. In 1972, however, the Education Amendments of 1972 (Pub. L. 92–318, Title IX, §906 (b) (1), 86 Stat. 375) extended EPA coverage to executive, administrative, and professional employees (which includes teachers and academic administrative personnel), and outside sales employees.

Enforcement of the Equal Pay Act

The Wage and Hour Division of the U.S. Department of Labor has the authority to enforce the Equal Pay Act. Wage and hour compliance officers routinely check for equal pay violations as well as investigate specific complaints. Violations of the EPA may be brought to the attention of the Wage and Hour Division through a letter or a telephone call from the complainant to the Washington office or any one of the regional offices. Since unequal pay on the basis of sex is also prohibited by the Executive Order, Title VII and Title IX, all of which are discussed below, agrieved persons may file a complaint with each of the governmental agencies which enforce these laws and regulations.

When a violation of the Equal Pay Act has been found, the employer is requested to correct the inequity immediately. If the employer refuses to do so, the Department of Labor is authorized to take the employer to court. Most cases are settled out of court.

In order to facilitate interpretation and implementation of the EPA, the Wage and Hour division has established two sets of regulations: (1) "Equal Pay for Equal Work," 29 CFR Part 800 (1971), and (2) "Extension of Equal Pay Provisions to Formerly Exempted Employees," 29 CFR Part 541 (1973). The "Equal Pay for Equal Work" regulation deals primarily with application of the 1963 act prior to the 1972 amendments. Topics such as discriminatory "patterns" of wage payments, overtime, special assignments, vacation or holiday pay, contributions to benefit plans, commissions, and the equality standards of "skill, effort, and responsibility" are defined and discussed along with some guides for implementation. The primary purpose of the publication entitled "Extension of Equal Pay Provisions to Formerly Exempted Employees" is to clarify the terms "bona fide executive, administrative, and professional employees." Copies of these may be obtained by writing the Washington, D.C. Office of the Wage and Hour Division of the Department of Labor, Washington, D.C. 20210.

Title VII of the Civil Rights Act of 1964

Of the Federal laws and regulations dealing with employment, Title VII of the Civil Rights Act (Pub. L. No. 88–352, §701 (b) and (e), 702, 78 Stat. 253) affects the largest number of employees and includes the broadest spectrum of discriminatory practices. Title VII prohibits discrimination in employment on the basis of race, color, religion, national origin, and sex. All employment practices, terms, and conditions of employment are included, such as:

—recruitment, selection, assignment, transfer, layoff, discharge, and recall
—promotion opportunities
—in-service training and development opportunities
—wages and salaries
—sick leave time and pay
—vacation time and pay
—overtime work and pay
—medical, hospital, life, and accident insurance
—retirement plans and benefits
—other staff benefits, terms, conditions, or privileges of employment.

A considerable body of case law and legal precedent has been developed under Title VII, providing the majority of the present standards for nondiscrimination in employment.

Stereotyping of Sex Roles

Who Is Covered by Title VII? Prior to 1972, Title VII covered only private employers with twenty-five or more employees and labor unions with twenty-five or more members. Exempt from coverage were educational institutions, religious institutions, private membership clubs, Indian tribes, and government-owned corporations. The 1972 Equal Employment Opportunity Act (Pub. L. No. 92–261, 83 Stat. 103) extended Title VII coverage to state and local government agencies and public and private educational institutions. Employers which remain excluded from coverage are federal agencies (other than the federal-state employment service system), federally owned corporations, Indian tribes, and religious educational institutions and associations with respect to employment of persons of a particular religion. Also still exempt are elected officials, their personal assistants, and immediate advisers. As of March 24, 1973, employers of fifteen or more persons and labor unions with fifteen or more members were covered by Title VII.

Enforcement of Title VII Title VII is enforced by the Equal Employment Opportunity Commission (EEOC), a five-member bipartisan group appointed by the President. In addition to receiving and investigating charges and attempting to conciliate those cases in which the Commission finds "reasonable cause" to believe the charges are true, the EEOC may bring a civil suit in a federal district court for an injunction and other remedies against the charged employer, union, employment agency, or joint labor-management committee. If a case involves a state or local government, the Attorney General, rather than the Commission, is authorized to bring suit. In addition to bringing charges in individual cases, the EEOC may also bring charges in cases where it is alleged that a pattern of discrimination exists. In states which have state or local agencies for handling discrimination complaints, a complaint may be referred to such agencies for a period of sixty days. If it is not resolved at this level, the EEOC Regional Office assumes responsibility for handling the complaint.

The EEOC has issued "Guidelines on Discrimination Because of Sex" (1972) to assist employers in changing employment policies and practices where necessary. Some of the major points made in these guidelines are as follows:

—It is unlawful to label or classify jobs as "men's" and "women's" as this unnecessarily denies employment opportunities for members of both sexes.

—It is a violation of Title VII to refuse to hire an individual based on stereotyped characterizations or assumed comparative employment characteristics of the sexes, e.g., that women are less capable of aggressive salesmanship or that the turnover rate for women is higher than that for men.

—State laws which discriminate against women in employment or which discriminate on the basis of sex with regard to the employment of minors are unlawful.

—A rule which forbids or restricts the employment of married women and does not apply to married men is discriminatory.

—Private employment agencies may not deal with only the members of one sex.

—Preemployment inquiries regarding a person's sex may be made only if the inquiry is in good faith and is not used for a discriminatory purpose.

—It is unlawful for an employer to discriminate between male and female employees with regard to fringe benefits, such as insurance, retirement benefits, bonus and profit-sharing plans, and other terms, conditions, and privileges of employment.

—Written or unwritten policies which exclude applicants or employees because of pregnancy are unlawful; and disabilities arising from childbirth, pregnancy, abortion, or miscarriage must be treated like other temporary disabilities.

Executive Orders 11246 and 11375

Presidential Executive Order 11246, issued in 1965, prohibits organizations with federal contracts from discriminating against employees and applicants for employment on the basis of race, color, religion, or national origin. Executive Order 11375, which became effective in October 1968, amended the earlier order to include discrimination based on sex. In addition to prohibiting employment discrimination, the Executive Order requires the employer to take affirmative action to "remedy the effects of past discrimination." The key section reads as follows:

The contractor will not discriminate against any employee or applicant for employment because of race, color, religion, sex, or national origin. The contractor will take affirmative action to ensure that applicants are employed, and that employees are treated during employment, without regard to their race, color, religion, sex, or national origin. Such action shall include, but not be limited to, the following: employment, upgrading, demotion, or transfer; recruitment or recruitment advertising; layoff or termination; rates of pay or other forms of compensation; and selection for training, including apprenticeship (32 FR 14304, October 17, 1967).

| Who Is Covered by the Executive Orders? | The Executive Order covers all federal contractors or subcontractors and contractors who have $10,000 or more in federal construction or other contracts. In addition, those contractors with fifty or more employees and a federal contract of $50,000 or more must have a written affirmative action plan. The required contents of an affirmative action plan are discussed below. |

| Enforcement of the Executive Orders | The Department of Labor's Office of Federal Contract Compliance (OFCC) has the overall responsibility for enforcing the Executive Order. The OFCC has delegated enforcement responsibility to other federal agencies which review, award, or administer contracts. For example, in the case of colleges and universities, Labor has delegated compliance and enforcement powers to the Office of Civil Rights (OCR) in the Department of Health, Education, and Welfare (HEW). While the Executive Order is not law, the courts have continually affirmed the right of the federal government to set the terms of its contracts with its contractors. |

In January of 1970, the Department of Labor issued Order No. 4, "Affirmative Action Guidelines." Because these guidelines did not deal specifically with sex discrimination, confusion resulted as to the interpretation of the Executive Order, and it was necessary to issue the "Sex Discrimination Guidelines" in June of the same year. These sex discrimination guidelines specify the requirements for employers to be in compliance with the Executive Order and are patterned after the Title VII guidelines dealing with sex discrimination. The guidelines require employers to recruit women for positions which have been previously open only to men, specify that both sexes must have equal access to all training programs, and prohibit employers from making any distinctions based on sex in employment practices. The guidelines make it clear that it is illegal to advertise available positions in sex segregated help wanted columns, to base seniority lists on sex, to deny a person a job because of state "protective" labor laws, to make distinctions between married and unmarried persons of one sex only, to require different retirement ages for women than for men, or to penalize women because they require time off for childbearing.

Revised Order No. 4, which became effective on December 4, 1971, strengthens the earlier affirmative action guidelines, clarifies the inclusion of sex discrimination, and outlines the requirements for written affirmative action plans. The basic components of an affirmative action program as required by Revised Order No. 4 are:

1. A statement of policy forbidding discrimination.
2. A person designated to be in charge of the program.
3. A data base on all job classifications.
4. An examination of recruitment, hiring, and promotion policies and all other conditions of employment, including salaries.
5. The identification of areas where women and minority group members are underemployed, and the development of specific plans to overcome such underemployment.
6. The development of numerical goals and timetables.

Title IX of the Education Amendments of 1972

The basic provision of Title IX of the Education Amendments of 1972 is:

No person in the United States shall, on the basis of sex, be excluded from participation in, be denied the benefits of, or be subjected to discrimination under any education program or activity receiving Federal financial assistance . . . (Pub. L. No. 92–318, June 23, 1972).

The major areas included in the Title IX regulation and some corresponding examples of application are:

Admissions

Sex discrimination or differential treatment by sex in admissions to vocational, professional, graduate, and public undergraduate schools is not allowed. This includes such things as limiting the number or proportion of persons of either sex, preferring applicants of one sex, ranking applicants separately by sex, and applying different selection criteria for male and female students. Private undergraduate institutions are exempt from the admissions requirement but must treat their admitted male and female students equally.

Access to courses and other educational activities

All courses and other educational programs and activities may not be provided separately for male and female students, with the exception of sex education classes in elementary and secondary schools. A variation of this is allowed in physical education classes at all levels, where students may be grouped by sex within coeducational classes when playing contact sports—wrestling, rugby, football, ice hockey, basketball, and any other sport which involves bodily contact as a major activity.

Counseling and guidance

Educational institutions must provide counseling and guidance services which do not discriminate on the basis of sex. All programs,

Stereotyping of Sex Roles

services, tests, or other appraisal and counseling materials must be free of sex bias.

Housing and facilities

Schools may provide housing, toilets, locker rooms, and shower facilities separately for male and female students so long as they are comparable in quality and proportionate to the number of students of each sex needing the facility.

Rules and regulations

Institutions may not have different rules, regulations, and policies for male and female students, e.g., allowing one sex to live off campus, requiring different dress and appearance codes for students of each sex, etc.

Financial aid and student employment

Institutions may not, on the basis of sex, provide different types or amounts of financial aid, limit eligibility, or apply different criteria for such aid. Exceptions are athletic scholarships and single-sex scholarships established by a will or trust. It is also illegal for schools to employ students in such a way that discriminates against one sex or assists any other organization which does.

Extracurricular activities and student organizations

All programs and activities must be open to the members of both sexes, with some exceptions in athletics. Student clubs or organizations cannot have sex segregated membership unless they are voluntary youth service organizations with tax exempt status, and have always had a single-sex membership of mainly persons less than nineteen years old. The YMCA, YWCA, Boy Scouts, Girl Scouts, Campfire Girls, and social fraternities and sororities are exempt.

Athletics

Schools may have separate teams for male and female students in contact sports (see above section on courses for definition) or where selection is based on competitive skill. In noncontact sports, if a school has a team in a particular sport for one sex only and athletic opportunities have been limited for the other sex, members of both sexes must be allowed to try out for the team.

Treatment of married and/or pregnant students

Schools cannot treat female students differently from male students because they are married, or because they are parents, or because of their potential to be so. A pregnant student cannot be denied access to any class, program, or extracurricular activity just because she is pregnant, nor can she be forced to participate in a separate program designated for pregnant students.

Employment

The employment section of Title IX is very similar to Title VII (see above) in prohibiting educational institutions from sex discrimination in any aspect of the employment process, including recruitment, selections, hiring, firing, promotion, tenure, salary determination, leaves of absence, fringe benefits, and any other term, condition, or privilege of employment.

Grievance procedures

Educational institutions must establish and publish grievance procedures for prompt and equitable resolution for student and employee complaints regarding sex discrimination.

Who Is Covered by Title IX? All educational institutions which receive federal monies by way of a grant, loan, or contract (other than a contract of insurance or guaranty) are covered by Title IX. This includes public and private preschools, elementary and secondary schools, institutions of vocational education, professional education, and undergraduate and graduate higher education. Schools whose primary purpose is training for the U.S. military services or the merchant marine are exempt.

Enforcement of Title IX While the Department of Health, Education, and Welfare's Office for Civil Rights (OCR) has primary enforcement responsibility for Title IX, OCR may delegate responsibility to other federal departments and agencies which are involved in providing federal monies to educational institutions. The regulations for enforcing Title IX became effective July 21, 1975.

The Public Health Service Act Title VII (Section 799A) and Title VIII (Section 845) of the Public Health Service Act, as amended by the Comprehensive Health Manpower Act and the Nurse Training Amendments Act of 1971, prohibit institutions from discriminating on the basis of sex in admissions of students in health personnel training programs or in employment practices relating to employees working directly with applicants to or students in such programs.

Who Is Covered by the Public Health Service Act? All institutions receiving or benefiting from a grant, loan guarantee, or interest subsidy to health personnel training programs or receiving a contract under Title VII or VIII of the Public Health Service Act are covered.

The Office for Civil Rights (OCR) in the U.S. Department of
Health, Education, and Welfare has enforcement powers to conduct
reviews and investigations related to Titles VII and VIII of the
Public Health Service Act. Institutions must keep specified records
to determine whether violations have occurred. Periodic reviews of
these records may be made by OCR to determine compliance.

As an aid to the reader, the major federal laws and regulations
concerning sex discrimination discussed above are summarized in
table 5-1:

Table 5-1   Summary Table of Federal Laws Dealing with Sex Discrimination

Regulation	Coverage	Enforcement
Equal Pay Act of 1963	Discrimination in salaries (including almost all fringe benefits) on the basis of sex. Covers all employees	Wage and Hour Division of the Employment Standards Administration to the Department of Labor.
Title VII or the Civil Rights Act of 1964	Discrimination in employment (including hiring, upgrading, salaries, fringe benefits, training, and other conditions of employment) on the basis of race, color, religion, national origin, or sex. Covers all employees.	Equal Employment Opportunity Commission.
Executive Order 11246, as amended by 11375	Discrimination in employment (including hiring, upgrading, salaries, fringe benefits, training, and other conditions of employment) on the basis of race, color, religion, national origin, or sex. Covers all employees.	Office of Federal Contract Compliance (OFCC) of the Department of Labor has policy responsibility and oversees Federal agency enforcement programs. OFCC has designated HEW as the compliance agency responsible for enforcing the Executive Order for all contracts with educational institutions. HEW's Office for Civil Rights (Division of Higher Education) conducts the reviews and investigations.
Title IX of the Education Amendments of 1972	Discrimination against students or employees on the basis of sex.	Federal departments and agencies which are empowered to extend financial aid to educational programs and activites. HEW's Office for Civil Rights (Division of Higher Education) has primary enforcement powers to conduct the reviews and investigations.
Titles VII and VIII of of the Public Health Service Act	Discrimination on the basis of sex in the admission of students and against some employees.	HEW's Office for Civil Rights (Division of Higher Education)

State Legislation   Many state and local government laws prohibit sex discrimination in
employment. A recent compilation of state laws affecting equal
rights for women prepared by the Education Commission of the

States (1975) shows that a total of forty-two states have fair employment practice legislation and/or equal pay laws. The provisions of these state laws are patterned after those of Title VII of the Civil Rights Act of 1965 and are generally enforced and administered by state or local commissions in charge of fair employment practices. As already mentioned, when complaints regarding violations of Title VII are filed with the Equal Employment Opportunity Commission (EEOC), it defers them for a limited time to those state fair employment practice commissions which have comparable jurisdiction and enforcement sanctions.

While considerable progress has been made and is continuing to be made by individual states in developing fair employment practice laws and regulations, there are many states with "protective legislation" still on the books. These protective laws, which have restricted women workers from competing with male co-workers, fall into four categories: (1) minimum wage laws, (2) hours limitations, (3) occupational restrictions, and (4) working conditions. Such laws were left unchallenged until 1969 when the Equal Employment Opportunity Commission declared them to be a violation of Title VII. In abandoning its earlier position of permitting protective legislation, the EEOC (1970) issued the following statement:

The Commission believes that such laws and regulations, although originally promulgated for the purpose of protecting females, have ceased to be relevant to our technology or to the expanding role of the female worker in our economy. The Commission has found that such laws and regulations do not take into account the capacities, preferences, and abilities of individual females and tend to discriminate rather than protect. Accordingly, the Commission has concluded that such laws and regulations conflict with Title VII of the Civil Rights Act of 1964 and will not be considered a defense to an otherwise established unlawful employment practice or as a basis for application of the bona fide occupational qualification exception.

In 1971, all of the states, with the exception of Delaware, still had some form of legislation which restricted women's employment rights and opportunities. Even as late as 1974, only sixteen states had either repealed all of their protective laws or made them apply to men and women alike (Conlin, 1975). With federal laws taking precedence over state laws, such state protective laws remaining on the books are invalid.

The Equal Rights Amendment

Any discussion on laws and regulations prohibiting sex discrimination would not be complete without mention of the Equal Rights Amendment (ERA). The ERA finally passed Congress in 1972, after being introduced each session since 1923. It reads as follows:

Section 1. Equality of rights under the law shall not be denied or abridged by the United States or by any state on account of sex.

Section 2. The Congress shall have the power to enforce, by appropriate legislation, the provisions of this article.

Section 3. This amendment shall take effect two years after the date of ratification. (U.S. Const. Pro. Amend. XXVII)

At this writing, thirty-five states of the required thirty-eight states have ratified the ERA. ERA issues have been fully debated as state legislatures have ratified, denied ratification, or in at least three instances—Idaho, Nebraska, and Tennessee—attempted to rescind ratification. A total of sixteen states have equal rights provisions in their state constitutions (Women's Bureau, 1976). Most of the controversy surrounding the ERA has focused on three issues: the rights of homemakers, the draft, and public toilets.

The effect the ERA will have on protective labor laws has also been vigorously debated. It has become clear that while the protective laws were originated to prevent the exploitation of female workers, they have become barriers not only to equal employment opportunity for women but also to improved working conditions for men. Nonsupporters of the ERA contend that the equal protection clause of the Fourteenth Amendment and Title VII of the Civil Rights Act provide women equal employment opportunity rights, thus making the ERA unnecessary. But, reliance on application of the Fourteenth Amendment by the courts to counter protective legislation has been inconsistent, as many judges have ignored or abused the amendment in deciding issues of concern to women. Even the impact of Title VII, which has caused many of the protective laws to be declared invalid or to be extended to men, has been slow and uneven. Supporters of the ERA contend that the amendment is necessary if women are to achieve swift and full legal equality at a time when women are no longer patient to wait for their rights to be granted one by one.

Certainly, passage of the ERA is important for psychological and political reasons in providing a climate of opinion in which sex discrimination and its consequences are taken seriously. If the ERA is ratified, it should accelerate the present trend toward legal equality for women and men.

Women's Educational Equity Act

While the Women's Educational Equity Act (WEEA) is not an enforceable law prohibiting sex discrimination, it is important to mention here, because it declares present educational programs inequitable as they relate to women of all cultural and ethnic groups, and it provides a means of rectifying such inequities in American education.

Passed as part of the Special Projects Act of the Education Amendments of 1974 (Pub. L. 93–380), the WEEA was the result of two bills: H.R. 208, introduced by former Congresswoman Patsy T. Mink on January 3, 1973, and a companion bill S. 2518 introduced by Vice President Walter F. Mondale on October 2, 1973. The WEEA authorizes the awarding of grants for innovative approaches to the achievement of educational equity for women. Public education agencies, private nonprofit organizations, and individuals are eligible to apply for contracts and grants to carry out activities such as: the development, evaluation, and dissemination of curricula, textbooks, and other educational materials; preservice and in-service training for educational personnel, including guidance and counseling personnel; research, development, and other educational activities designed to advance educational equity; guidance and counseling activities, including the development of tests which are non-discriminatory on the basis of sex; educational activities to increase opportunities for adult women, including continuing educational activities and programs for underemployed and unemployed women; and the expansion and improvement of educational programs and activities for women in vocational education, career education, physical education, and educational administration. Males are not prohibited from participating in any activity funded under the act, thus members of both sexes benefit.

WEEA was established to achieve educational equity for women and to overcome sex bias in American education. In addition to funding such activities as listed above, Congress mandated the formation of an Advisory Council on Women's Educational Programs to help attain the goals of the act.

The Council was established to advise the assistant secretary for education and the commissioner of education with respect to broad issues of educational equity for women, as well as to advise on matters specifically relating to the Women's Educational Equity Act. The Council consists of twenty members, including seventeen public members appointed by the President, subject to Senate confirmation, for overlapping three-year terms, and three ex-officio members: the director of the Women's Action Program, U.S. Department of HEW; the director of the Women's Bureau, U.S. Department of Labor; and the chairman of the U.S. Commission on Civil Rights.

Stereotyping of Sex Roles

Selected Resources For the reader who wishes more information regarding the legal implications of sex role stereotyping and discrimination, I recommend the following books and resource organizations.

Selected Books Blaxall, Martha, and Barbara Reagan, eds. *Women and the Workplace: The Implications of Occupational Segregation.* Chicago, Ill.: University of Chicago Press, 1976.

This is a collection of articles, presentations, and comments expanded from a workshop conference on occupational segregation held in May 1975. Purposes are: to analyze occupational segregation and to consider policy changes needed to eliminate discrimination based on sex. Articles are organized under the following headings: (1) The Social Institutions of Occupational Segregation, (2) The Historical Roots of Occupational Segregation, (3) Economic Dimensions of Occupational Segregation, and (4) Combating Occupational Segregation.

Foxley, Cecelia H. *Locating, Recruiting and Employing Women: An Equal Opportunity Approach.* Garrett Park, Md.: Garrett Park Press, 1976.

This book is directed at employers—to help them provide equal opportunity for women workers. Beginning with the economic and educational status of women today, the book discusses laws, regulations, and programs which protect against sex discrimination and suggests effective ways of recruiting, employing, and working with women. A sample affirmative action plan, an extensive bibliography of materials dealing with the employment of women, and appendices containing actual texts of some of the federal laws and regulations concerning sex discrimination make this volume a useful resource for employers in all types of settings.

Ginsburg, Ruth Bader. *Text, Cases, and Materials on Constitutional Aspects of Sex-based Discrimination.* St. Paul, Minn.: West Publishing Co., 1974.

This book is intended as a guide for studying the relationship between fundamental constitutional law and gender discrimination. Court cases are presented and discussed. Four areas covered are: The Tradition, Men as Victims, The New Direction, and Equal Rights and Responsibilities for Men and Women as Constitutional Principle.

Kanowitz, Leo. *Sex Roles in Law & Society: Cases and Materials,* Albuquerque, N.M.: University of New Mexico Press, 1973.

This book is a collection of articles divided into the following topical areas: (1) Introduction, (2) The Law's Traditional View of Sex Roles: An Overview, (3) Sex Roles Without Regard to Marital Status, (4) Sex Roles and Marriage, (5) Sex Roles and Employment, (6) Sex Roles and the Constitution, (7) Sex Roles and Public Accommodations, (8) Sex Roles and Education, (9) Sex Roles and Pornography, (10) Sex Roles and the Media, (11) Sex Roles, Sex Preferences, and Appearance, (12) Sex Roles and the Military, and (13) Sex Roles and Poverty. A 1974 Supplement to this volume contains revisions, deletions, and additions to the original book.

Kanowitz, Leo. *Women and the Law: The Unfinished Revolution,* Albuquerque, N.M.: University of New Mexico Press, 1969.

In one of the first comprehensive treatments of the legal status of women, Kanowitz reviews historical and current impact of the law on women. Chapters include: Law and the Single Girl, Law and the Married Woman, Title VII of the 1964 Civil Rights Act and the Equal Pay Act of 1963, The Relationship Between the Equal Pay Act of 1963 and Title VII, and Constitutional Aspects of Sex-based Discrimination in American Law.

Larson, Arthur. *Employment Discrimination: Sex.* New York, N.Y.: Matthew Bender and Co., 1975.

This volume deals with employment discrimination based on sex and its legal implications. Topics covered are: (1) Background and History, (2) Summary and Coverage of Sex Discrimination Laws, (3) What is Sex Differentiation?, (4) The Bona Fide Occupational Qualification Exception, (5) State Protective Laws, (6) Preemployment and Employment Practices, (7) Equal Pay, (8) Benefits, Conditions, Privileges, and (9) Unions and Sex Discrimination. A 1977 Supplement to this volume contains updated information for each chapter.

Lloyd, Cynthia B. *Sex, Discrimination, and the Division of Labor.* New York, N.Y.: Columbia University Press, 1975.

This is a collection of essays dealing with areas of research concerning women in the labor force. The topics under which these are organized are: (1) Female Labor Participation, Unemployment, and Wage Differentials, (2) Discrimination and Occupational Segregation, (3) Economic Aspects of Women's Nonmarket Activities, (4) The Effect of Some Government Policies on Women's Economic Position, and (5) The Economics of Women's Liberation.

Oehmke, Thomas H. *Sex Discrimination in Employment.* Detroit, Mich.: Trends Publishing Co., 1974.

This book is written for personnel and labor relations people. It deals primarily with the application of Title VII and the Equal Pay Act. The author states his purposes as follows: to provide insights necessary to recognize discriminatory practices, to understand issues raised when sex discrimination is alleged, to begin to remedy unlawful practices, and to prevent new unlawful practices. Chapter titles are: An Overview of the Law, State Protective Legislation: Conflict of Laws; Pre-employment Issues; Compensation and Conditions of Employment; Maternity, Marital and Parental Status; and Remedies for Unlawful Employment Practices.

Pearson, William *An Overview of Federal Court Decisions Affecting Equal Rights for Women in Education.* Denver, Col.: Education Commission of the States, 1975.

This is a report of the Equal Rights for Women in Education Project. Topics include: (1) Historical Introduction—The Flowering of Romantic Paternalism, The Equal Protection Clause, Post-Civil War Civil Rights Acts, (2) The New Era: Title VII of the Civil Rights Act of 1964, (3) Sex Discrimination in Employment—Hiring, Promotion, Transfer, Recruiting, Discharge, Maternity and Pregnancy Policies, Fringe Benefits, Layoffs Pursuant to a Seniority System, and Nepotism, (4) Sex Discrimination in Educational Employment, (5) Sex Discrimination in Education, (6) Executive Order No. 11246, (7) The Equal Pay Act, (8) Title IX of the Education Amendments of 1972, and (9) Comprehensive Manpower Training Act of 1971 and Nurse Training Act of 1971. Complete appendices are included.

Raffel, Norma K., *The Enforcement of Federal Laws and Regulations Prohibiting Sex Discrimination in Education.* Washington, D.C.: Women's Equity Action League, 1975.

This is a report and set of recommendations for the U.S. National Commission on the Observance of International Women's Year. Topics include: (1) Title VII of the Civil Rights Act of 1964, As Amended, (2) Executive Order 11246, as Amended, (3) Title IX of the Education Amendments, 1972, (4) Title VII and VIII of the Public Health Service Act of 1971, and (5) The Equal Pay Act.

Stimpson, Catharine R., ed. *Discrimination Against Women: Congressional Hearings on Equal Rights in Education and Employment.* New York, N.Y.: R. R. Bowker Co., 1973.

Seven days of testimony are presented from June and July, 1970. Papers and supporting documents are organized under the following headings: Women and the American Scene, Women and Work, Women and the Law, Women and Education, Women and the Professions, Women and Government Action, and Model Remedies.

Wasserman, Elga; Arie Y. Lewin; Linda H. Bleiweis, eds. *Women in Academia: Evolving Policies Toward Equal Opportunities.* New York, N.Y.: Praeger Publishers, 1975.

This is a collection of papers presented at the symposium held at the 138th annual meeting of the American Association for the Advancement of Science, 1971. Some papers were deleted or updated, and others were added. Titles include: "Affirmative Action through Affirmative Attitudes," "Sex Discrimination, Educational Institutions, and the Law: A New Issue on Campus," "Race, Sex, and Jobs: the Drive Toward Equality," "Legal Requirements, Structures, and Strategies for Eliminating Sex Discrimination in Academe," "Developing Criteria and Measures of Equal Opportunities for Women," "Creating Opportunities for Women in Science," "Sex Discrimination at Universities: An Ombudsman's View," "A Case History of Affirmative Action," and "Affirmative Action at Stanford University."

Selected Organizations and Agencies

There are a growing number of organizations which provide information on sex roles, stereotyping, discrimination, related laws and regulations, and suggested remedies. The following list is not definitive by any means, but is a compilation of the organizations I have personally found to be most responsive and helpful.

1. Federal Women's Program, U.S. Civil Service Commission, Washington, D.C. 20415.

Primarily responsible for equal employment opportunity within the federal government, the Civil Service Commission sponsors a wide variety of training programs and resource materials on affirmative action programs and equal employment opportunities for women which can be used in many employment settings.

2. Project on Equal Education Rights (PEER), 1029 Vermont Ave., N.W., Suite 800, Washington, D.C. 20005.

PEER is a project of the NOW Legal Defense and Education Fund which is funded by the Ford Foundation to monitor enforcement progress under federal law forbidding sex discrimination. By merely requesting to be placed on PEER's mailing list, individuals can receive a host of free or low cost materials including the very informative newsletter, "Peer Perspective," a periodically updated and annotated list of "Resources for Ending Sex Bias in the Schools," and an information packet entitled "Cracking the Glass Slipper: PEER's Guide to Ending Sex Bias In Your Schools." The information packet was prepared for use by school personnel, parents, students, and other interested individuals to help make Title IX work. In a very effective manner, the packet explains the law, tells what to look at, what questions to ask, and whom to ask in your own educational system. Helpful ways to work for constructive change are suggested.

3. Project on the Status and Education of Women, Association of American Colleges, 1818 R Street, N.W., Washington, D.C. 20009.

Funded by the Carnegie Corporation, the Project on the Status and Education of Women was one of the first organizations to function as a clearinghouse of information concerning women in education, and works with institutions, government agencies, and other associations and programs affecting women in higher education. Like PEER, a request to be placed on the mailing list of the Project on the Status and Education of Women enables interested persons to receive numerous free materials such as the up-to-date newsletter "On Campus with Women," an information sheet entitled "Recruiting Women for Traditionally 'Male' Careers: Programs and Resources for getting Women Into the Men's World," a pamphlet entitled "Sex Discrimination Against Students: Implications of Title IX of the Education Amendments of 1972," and many other very helpful publications.

4. Resource Center on Sex Roles in Education, National Foundation for the Improvement of Education, 1201 16th St. NW, Suite 701, Washington, D.C. 20036.

The Resource Center contracts with other agencies and organizations to prepare materials for broad distribution and to conduct training programs on regional and national levels. Examples are: the Title IX Equity Workshops Project for the Council of Chief State School Officers (regional workshops were held for school personnel of all educational levels), and publications distributed by the U.S. Office of Education such as "A Student Guide to Title IX," "Selecting Professionals in Higher Education: A Title IX Perspective," "Title IX and Physical Education: A Compliance Overview," and "Title IX Grievance Procedures: An Introductory Manual."

5. Women's Bureau, Employment Standards Administration, U.S. Department of Labor, 200 Constitution Avenue, NW, Washington, D.C. 20210.

Established by an act of Congress in 1920, the Women's Bureau was originally created to formulate standards and policies to promote the welfare of wage earning women. The Women's Bureau does not enforce laws nor provide funds for projects, but works toward the goal of improving the status of women in the workforce and in the nation's economy by: (1) providing information about laws safeguarding women's rights, (2) initiating projects and model programs to benefit women workers, and (3) conducting research and gathering data on the status of women workers. Some of the publications which may be ordered free of charge from the Women's Bureau are: "Women Workers Today," "Minority Women Workers: A Statistical Overview," "Get Credit for What You Know," "Why Not Be an Apprentice?," "A Working Woman's Guide to Her Job Rights," "Working Mothers and Their Children," and "The Earnings Gap between Women and Men."

6. Women's Equity Action League (WEAL) Educational and Legal Defense Fund, 805 15th Street, NW, Suite 822, Washington, D.C. 20005.

The WEAL Fund publishes a variety of materials for purchase at minimum fees. The "WEAL Washington Report" is published six times a year and provides a report on issues of concern to women including current legislation, Supreme Court rulings and executive branch actions. Other materials and publications include: "How to Prepare a Resume," "The Equal Rights Amendment for Equal Rights under the Law," "Sex Discrimination in Insurance—A Guide for Women," "Women and Health," "Marriage: Focus on Change," "School Self-evaluation under Title IX," and "Facts about Women in Higher Education."

7. U.S. Department of Health, Education, and Welfare's Office for Civil Rights, Washington, D.C. 20201.

In addition to its function as a compliance agency, HEW's Office for Civil Rights (OCR) assists employers with affirmative action program development and the identification of recruitment resources. Individuals and organizations are given assistance in assessing whether or not they have been victims of sex discrimination, and if so, they are advised on what steps should be taken for redress. Ten regional offices are located throughout the country to make the OCR more accessible.

8. U.S. Equal Employment Opportunity Commission, 1800 G Street, NW, Washington, D.C. 20506.

As discussed in an earlier section on Title VII, the Equal Employment Opportunity Commission (EEOC) was established to enforce Title VII. In addition to enforcement functions, the EEOC is useful as an information service to applicants for employment, employees, and employers. The EEOC, through its Office of Voluntary Programs, maintains a talent bank of women with qualifications for professional-level jobs. The EEOC also publishes helpful affirmative action and equal employment opportunity materials and like HEW's Office for Civil Rights has regional offices located throughout the United States.

Conclusion Counselors and other helping professionals are in a much better position to assist their individual clients and client organizations in recognizing discrimination based on sex and working to rectify the situation if they are knowledgeable about the legal aspects—the laws dealing with sex discrimination, what they cover, how persons can seek redress and overcome the effects of discriminatory treatment, and how organizations can rid themselves of sexist elements. This chapter provides an overview of the various laws and regulations which prohibit sex discrimination and suggests supplemental resources the reader can go to for additional information. Suggestions as to how counselors and helping professionals can work toward equality for women and men in a variety of settings are included in sections II and III of this book.

References Blaxall, Martha, and Barbara Reagan, eds. *Women and the Workplace: The Implications of Occupational Segregation.* Chicago, Ill.: University of Chicago Press, 1976.

Conlin, Roxanne B. Equal protection versus Equal Rights Amendment—where are we now? *Drake Law Review, 1975, 24,* 2:59-335.

Education Commission of the States, *Equal Rights for Women in Education: A Handbook of State Laws and Policies Affecting Equal Rights for Women in Education,* December 1975.

Foxley, Cecllia H. *Locating, Recruiting and Employing Women: An Equal Opportunity Approach.* Garrett Park, Md.: Garrett Park Press, 1976.

Ginsburg, Ruth Bader. *Text, Cases, and Materials on Constitutional Aspects of Sex-based Discrimination.* St. Paul, Minn.: West Publishing Co., 1974.

Kanowitz, Leo. *Sex Roles in Law & Society: Cases and Materials,* Albuquerque, N.M.: University of New Mexico Press, 1973.

Kanowitz, Leo. *Women and the Law: The Unfinished Revolution.* Albuquerque, N.M.: University of New Mexico Press, 1969.

Larson, Arthur. *Employment Discrimination: Sex.* New York, N.Y.: Matthew Bender and Co., 1975.

Lloyd, Cynthia B. *Sex, Discrimination, and the Division of Labor.* New York, N.Y.: Columbia University Press, 1975.

Oehmke, Thomas H. *Sex Discrimination in Employment.* Detroit, Mich.: Trends Publishing Co., 1974.

Pearson, William *An Overview of Federal Court Decisions Affecting Equal Rights for Women in Education.* Denver, Col.: Education Commission of the States, 1975.

Raffel, Norma K., *The Enforcement of Federal Laws and Regulations Prohibiting Sex Discrimination in Education.* Washington, D.C.: Women's Equity Action League, 1975.

Stimpson, Catharine R., ed. *Discrimination Against Women: Congressional Hearings on Equal Rights in Education and Employment.* New York, N.Y.: R. R. Bowker Co., 1973.

United States Department of Labor, Wage and Labor Standards Administration, Women's Bureau. *State Equal Rights Amendments,* December 1976.

United States Equal Employment Opportunity Commission. Statement on protective legislation, 29 CFR §1604.1 (b) (2), 1970.

Wasserman, Elga; Arie Y. Lewin; Linda H. Bleiweis; eds. *Women in Academia: Evolving Policies Toward Equal Opportunities.* New York, N.Y.: Praeger Publishers, 1975.

Counselors and Social Change

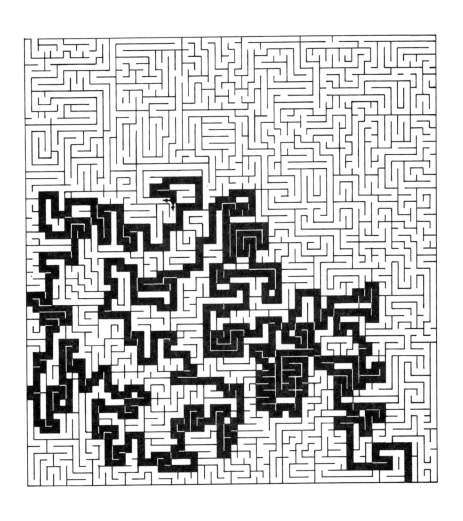

6 Counseling for Psychological Androgyny

The term "androgynous" which literally means both female and male in one, or hermaphroditic, was popularized by Rossi (1964), although she defines it more broadly as a "socially androgynous conception of the roles of men and women, in which they are equal and similar in such spheres as intellectual, artistic, political, and occupational interests and participation, complementary only in those spheres dictated by physiological differences between the sexes."

The idea that a single person embodies both femininity and masculinity has been expressed by others. Jung (1953) described the anima and animus which he believed to be present in everyone. Bakan (1966) argues that individual and societal viability depend on the successful integration of both communion (a concern for the relationship between oneself and others) and agency (a concern for oneself as an individual). In defining Bakan's terms Block (1973) says agency "manifests itself in self-protection, self-assertion, and self-expansion," while communion "manifests itself in being at one with other organisms." More recently, psychologists have advocated psychological androgyny as a more practical and human standard of psychological health (Bem, 1974, 1975, 1977; Berzins and Welling, 1974; Block, 1973; Marecek, 1977; Pleck, 1975; Singer, 1976; Rawlings and Carter, 1977; Spence and Helmreich, 1978; Spence, Helmreich, and Stapp, 1975).

A psychologically androgynous person is "both masculine and feminine, both instrumental and expressive, both agentic and communal, depending upon the situational appropriateness of these various modalities; and [can] . . . blend these complementary modalities in a single act, being able, for example, to fire an employee if the circumstances warrant it, but to do so with sensitivity for the human emotion that such an act inevitably produces" (Bem, 1977). Psychological androgyny does not refer to a person's gender identity, i.e., a secure sense of one's femaleness or maleness, or sexual preference for members of the same or opposite sex. Fears that nonsexist child-rearing to facilitate psychological androgyny will lead to identity problems, sexual confusion, and gray, affectless "neuter" children (Landman, 1974) are unfounded. Children raised in a nonsexist fashion still have a strong sense of gender identity but are encouraged to develop interests, abilities, and behaviors that are not restricted by culturally imposed definitions of femininity and masculinity. As Bem (1977) puts it, ". . . behavior should have no gender." Thus, psychologically androgynous individuals behave appropriately for a given situation or circumstance rather than appropriately for their sex as defined by traditional sex roles. "An androgynous personality would thus represent the very best of what masculinity and femininity have each come to represent, and the more negative exaggerations of masculinity and femininity would tend to be cancelled out" (Bem, 1977). Heilbrun (1973) speaks of androgyny as a "condition under which the characteristics of the sexes, and the human impulses expressed by men and women are not rigidly assigned." To her, androgyny presages a world "in which individual roles and the modes of personal behavior can be freely chosen."

Because the concept of androgyny presupposes that the concepts of masculinity and femininity have distinct, substantive, and dyadic content, it has been viewed by some as not providing a completely desirable alternative to traditional sex roles (Bernard, 1975; Gelpi, 1974; Harris, 1974; Rebecca, Hefner, and Oleshansky, 1976; Secor, 1974). Hefner, Nordin, Rebecca, and Oleshansky (1974) prefer the term "sex-role transcendence" rather than androgyny because: "The popular use [of the term androgyny] puts too much emphasis on polarity *combined* instead of polarity *transcended*." They define sex role transcendence as individual behavioral and emotional choice, based on the full range of possible human characteristics, which are appropriate and adaptive for the particular individual in the specific situation and are not determined by adherence to sex role stereotyped conceptions of appropriateness. Their model of sex role transcendence asserts that sex role development proceeds through three stages: (1) a stage in which there is an undifferentiated conception of sex roles, (2) a stage in which there is an over-differentiated or polarized conception of sex roles, and (3) a stage in which there is a flexible, dynamic approach to human roles that transcends sex role constraints. According to Hefner and associates, an individual need not necessarily to through the second stage before she or he can transcend it. Rather, "there may be different tracks leading to a transcendent view of sex roles. . . . It may not be necessary for an individual to pass through a stage in which she firmly (or at all) accepted the stereotypes. The fact that children appear to do this overdifferentiating may be the result of the milieu only and not a step required for transcendence." While Hefner and associates believe that the movement from the first stage to the second stage is gradual, they think the individual takes a "quantum leap," which becomes "the resolution of a crisis which produces both a lack of fit with stage two conceptions and the awareness of stage three that leaves behind the defensive need to cling to the pole to which one has been assigned." Another term used to describe this quantum leap from the second stage to the third stage is O'Reilly's (1972) "click"—the sudden perception of "the basic disorder in what has been believed to be the natural order of things."

Whatever one wishes to call it—psychological androgyny or sex role transcendence—it appears that individuals who possess a high degree of both masculine and feminine characteristics may be better adjusted than those who do not. While research in the area is too new and sparse to be in any way definitive, Spence and Helmreich (1978) found such androgynous individuals to display more self-esteem, social competence, and achievement motivation than nonandrogynous persons. In a series of studies, Bem (1977) found androgynous men and women to function effectively in both the instrumental and expressive domains, e.g., stand firm in opinions when necessary, show affection and warmth toward kittens and babies, and listen sympathetically to someone in distress. In contrast, masculine individuals of both sexes were found to be high in independence but low in nurturance, and feminine individuals of both sexes were high in nurturance but low in independence.

Greater maturity as measured by Kolhberg's Moral Judgement Test was "accompanied by more androgynous, less sex typed definitions of self" for both sexes; and women who scored high levels of ego maturity using the Loevinger Sentence Completion method were found to have a better balance of agentic and communion concerns (Block, 1973). And, according to several studies (Dellas and Gaier, 1970; Donelson, 1973; Hammer, 1964; Helson, 1966), greater creativity in both sexes depends on a balance of feminine and masculine traits. Also, greater intellectual development has been correlated with cross sex typing, i.e., with femininity in boys and masculinity in girls (Maccoby, 1966).

Other studies have shown that a high level of sex typing may be detrimental. Deutsch and Gilbert (1976) found sex typing in college girls (i.e., high femininity scores on the Bem Sex Role Inventory) to be associated with poor adjustment (as measured by the revised Bell Adjustment Inventory). Gump (1972) found ego strength negatively related to the adoption of the traditional female sex role, and suggests that "purposiveness, resourcefulness, and self-direction may be inconsistent with adoption of a role limited to the traditional, other-oriented goals and satisfactions." Others (Cosentino and Heilbrun, 1964; Gall, 1969; Gray, 1957; Sears, 1970; Webb, 1963) have found that high femininity in females is correlated with high anxiety, low self-esteem, and low social acceptance. Although Mussen (1961) found high masculinity in adolescent males to be related to better psychological adjustment, he also found that high masculinity in male adults correlated with high anxiety, high neuroticism, and low self-acceptance (Mussen, 1962). Hartford and associates (1967) found similar results with adult males. Regarding intelligence and cognitive functioning, Maccoby (1966) found that girls and boys who are more sex typed have lower overall intelligence, lower spatial ability, and lower creativity.

Marecek (1977) summarizes the unhealthy result when both masculine and feminine sex types are carried to the extreme without cross-sex balance: "The 'feminine' triad of passivity, dependency, and docility, when carried to an extreme, resembles the clinical syndromes of depression or passive personality disorders. The ego-centered, impulsive, aggressive masculine stereotype resembles the psychopath or sociopath."

Compatibility of Psychological Androgyny with Rogerian and Maslowian Theories

While the term psychological androgyny can not be found in the writings of Rogers and Maslow, there are many similarities between an androgynous individual, Roger's flexible individual, and Maslow's self-actualizing individual.

Maslow's (1954) self-actualized person is one who has succeeded in developing his or her basic, healthy inner natures to their fullest expression. In order to determine what characteristics distinguish self-actualizing persons from others, he undertook a series of studies involving subjects from all sectors of life: historical figures such as Thoreau, Whitman, Lincoln, Jane Addams, Eleanor Roosevelt, and Harriet Tubman. Among the distinguishing features he found common to all actualized persons he studied are these:

—Realistic orientation, accepting themselves, others, and the natural world for what they are.
—Democratic values, identifying readily with all kinds of people.
—Fresh rather than stereotyped appreciation of people and things.
—Problem-centered rather than self-centered.
—Creative, resisting conformity to the culture by transcending it.
—Emotionally self-sufficient, striving for autonomy.
—Enjoy privacy and solitude.
—Fair and unexploitative with others, never confusing means with ends.
—Spontaneous, open, and relatively free of neurotic defenses.
—Develop and maintain a few deep relationships with certain important others.
—Sense of humor which is philosophical rather than hostile.

The above concept of the healthy, self-actualizing personality which Maslow found in both men and women is independent of sexual identity. It is not biased toward femininity nor masculinity but is a combination of traits one would expect an androgynous person to have.

One of Maslow's (1942) early studies suggests how an androgynous model of personality might be manifested in healthy women. Women who were high in self-esteem were also found to be assertive, decisive, ambitious, self-reliant, independent, and tolerant of others. They also eschewed the double standard of sexual behavior, permitting themselves a wider range of sexual experience. These characteristics do not describe the stereotyped traits related to the traditional female sex role discussed in chapter 1 nor the "healthy woman" as perceived by clinicians in chapter 2.

Rogers' (1951) self theory provides a framework for understanding the influence of sex role stereotypes on mental health. According to self theory, the accurate perception and subsequent integration of social expectations with personal values are essential to adaptive behavior. Sex role stereotypes are social expectations for sex appropriate behavior and are thus potential sources of conflict with personal values. For example, if the sex role stereotype of female nurturance and desire to have children does not correspond with a woman's view of herself, what she ideally would like to be, or with what she thinks others want her to be, then according to Rogerian theory, she would experience psychological conflict. Another example would be a young man who desires to raise the children while his wife works to support the family. The stereotype of men as providers for their families and the expectations of the young man's associates that he fulfill this male role could be the source of real psychological conflict for him.

According to Rogers, the persons who are least likely to experience conflicts between personal goals and social norms are flexible individuals who can find a variety of ways to integrate personal needs and social demands. The androgynous person described at the beginning of this chapter has the necessary flexibility to do so. As more and more people are psychologically androgynous, social norms related to sex role stereotypes will diminish, and a new norm of variance and humanism will emerge, thus lessening the likelihood of individuals experiencing psychological conflict because their personal goals are incompatible with social norms.

Do Counselors Have a Social Responsibility to Facilitate Psychological Androgyny? Some theorists argue that counselors and therapists should avoid social and political issues and keep the counseling process completely neutral and value-free. But in practice, it does not work that way. Counselors, whether consciously or unconsciously, bring their own set of values and beliefs into the counseling process; and these help determine what actions counselors take with clients (see chap. 7 for a fuller discussion of this issue). I would argue further that counselors can not ignore the clients' environment in working towards a solution to personal problems. Basic to mental health is that an individual can function effectively in his or her social environment. And the social environment regarding sex roles today is very different than it has been at any other time in American history. While a sex typed view of men's and women's roles and their mental health may have worked for earlier times, it is not appropriate today.

Marecek (1977) effectively outlines the current shifts in life expectancy, marriage and family structures, and the work patterns of women which require individuals to be flexible, situationally adaptable, and non-sex typed. She argues strongly that androgynous individuals will adapt to contemporary life style changes more successfully than sex typed individuals. Some of the life situations she feels androgynous women would adapt to more easily than sex typed women are the "empty nest"—the time when offspring have left the household, divorce, and widowhood. For men and women, the more androgynous, the better the adjustment to retirement. Each of these situations merits comment here, and I will do so expanding Marecek's ideas to include my own thinking regarding both sexes, rather than just women, when it comes to divorce and widowhood.

(1) Divorce. That the divorce rate has increased rapidly in America in recent years is a well known fact. In 1964, there was 1 divorce for every 4 new marriages; this changed to a ratio of 1 divorce to 2.3 marriages in 1974. Bernard (1972) predicts that the divorce trend will continue, and it won't be long before half of the marriages in the United States will end in divorce. Sex typed men and women are not as prepared for independent, single status living which results after a divorce. They have learned to rely on each other for very sex role stereotypic kinds of things—she on him for financial support and business matters and he on her for emotional support and domestic matters. Following a divorce, the sex typed woman is not ready to support herself financially, and the sex typed man is at a loss when it comes to taking care of his domestic needs. When there are children involved, the problems are much more severe. The single parent, like it or not, is thrust into an androgynous role of managing a household while at the same time bearing the burden of financial support for the family. Presently, more women than men are single parents due to traditional expectations and child custody laws. However, both the laws and expectations are changing, and more men are finding themselves in the role of single parent. Androgynous men and women do not experience role incompatibility when divorce occurs because of their flexibility and sharing of roles prior to the divorce. "The individual who is androgynous will have a better basis for meeting the demands of both masculine and feminine roles than will the individual who is sex typed. Although it may always require a balancing act to juggle the many demands of the single-parent role, the balancing act will be more successful if the actor has the personal capacity to play each of the roles involved without engendering anxiety, excessive self-doubt, or discomfort" (Marecek, 1977).

(2) Widowhood. Due to differences in average life expectancy for men and women and the typical pattern of men marrying women younger than themselves, there are more widows than there are widowers. But whether the survivor is male or female, there are more than personal stresses of bereavement experienced by the sex typed individual. Similar to divorced individuals, survivors whose life roles were completely complementary to their spouses in the traditional stereotypic sense, " . . . find the loss of their spouses difficult to cope with on pragmatic as well as emotional levels. Women [and men] who are inhibited in performing nonstereotypic behaviors will have to break down those inhibitions before they can function adequately as single persons. On the other hand, women

[and men] with androgynous sex-role orientations may accommodate to the role of widow [widower] with greater ease" (Marecek, 1977).

(3) The "Empty Nest." The feminine sex role which focuses almost exclusively on homemaking and child rearing is too narrow, particularly in a time of smaller families, for women who will have twenty to thirty more years to live after their children leave home. In her studies of women suffering from depressive disorders, Bart (1971) found that women who have singlemindedly pursued a life centered around home and children risk feelings of worthlessness and inadequacy, apathy, and depression when their children move into adulthood. Androgynous parents not only would share the child rearing function equally, but would also share the sense of emptiness when the children left to be on their own. Thus, providing each other support and understanding and lessening the likelihood of one person (the mother) losing her central role in life. The androgynous woman would have the flexibility to be involved in other meaningful activity during the child rearing years and/or to make the transition from a life style centered on the home to one centered on outside interests, such as paid employment. "Her value orientation would allow her occupational involvement to be meaningful and self-satisfying. The departure of her children would not signify the loss of her own raison d'etre" (Marecek, 1977).

(4) Retirement. With increased longevity of the American population comes greater numbers of people experiencing and approaching retirement. Financing a disproportionately large segment of a population is not the only concern of social scientists and government officials. Increasing attention is being focused on the need for older persons to retain their feelings of usefulness and sense of worth. Retirees often report difficulties in switching from a life style of competition, contribution, and pressure centered around their jobs to one of relaxation and free time. While there is no empirical evidence that androgynous persons face retirement with greater equanimity than sex typed persons, ". . . androgynous men who are more open to the pleasures of such 'feminine' interests as caring for grandchildren, participating in culture and the arts, and enjoying close personal relationships in addition to more conventionally 'masculine' activities may find retirement more stimulating than stereotypically 'masculine' men. Similarly, if androgynous women enjoy such 'masculine' activities as competitive athletics in addition to their 'feminine' interests, they may spend their retirement years in a more diversified and stimulating way than sex typed women do" (Marecek, 1977).

(5) Working wives and mothers. I have listed this one last because it has been alluded to or mentioned directly in each of the situations discussed above, and it is, in my mind, the single most important factor contributing to the development of a psychologically androgynous society. The dramatic increase of women in the labor force has been discussed in chapter 4 and will not be repeated here except to say that is will not be long before the majority of wives and mothers will be working outside the home. When a woman works outside the home, domestic responsibilities need to be shared by other members of the family, thus engendering shifts away from traditional sex role conceptions. These shifts are made more easily by androgynous individuals. Sex typed couples have a more difficult time sharing child care and housework responsibilities, oftentimes leaving women with two full-time jobs—their outside paid position as well as their home duties. But there are indications that this is changing as women and men recognize the unfairness of such an arrangement. "When both wife and husband participate in paid work and home responsibilities, the polarities on which traditional sex-role conceptions rest are minimized. In addition, power in the marriage tends to be distributed more equally, with husbands relinquishing some control and primacy within the home and wives gaining some. Finally, the very fact of a woman's paid employment challenges the traditional sex-role dichotomy. The view of husbands as protectors and providers of the household loses credence when wives share in providing income and support for their families. The traditional view of wives is belied by the working wife who has non-family commitments, has her own schedules, and draws personal gratification from her work as well as her family" (Marecek, 1977). Not only do adults become androgynous in such an environment, but the children participate in both cross-sex and same-sex activities and responsibilities and learn from their parents' role models how to live more fully and humanely as androgynous individuals.

While psychological androgyny for children may be modeled and encouraged in the home, it is necessary that other institutions in our society, e.g., schools, employment settings, community organizations, etc., sustain psychological androgyny by encouraging the full development of abilities and interests of individuals without regard to "sex-role appropriateness" and by providing equal opportunities to girls and boys, women and men alike—without unfair discrimination on the basis of sex.

The counselor or therapist who ignores the potential of psychological androgyny in promoting a more healthy and fair society is not keeping her or his professional work "value-free," but has instead selected the "value" of viewing men and women in sex role stereotypic ways which is not in keeping with today's rapidly changing society and is thus doing clients a disservice. At the very least, as Lerner (1978) points out, "It is hoped that mental health professionals will continue to reexamine and clarify their thinking regarding sex-role stereotypes and bipolar concepts of masculinity and femininity. . . . [As] There is unquestionably a powerful trend in this country away from dichotomous concepts of masculinity and femininity. . . ." At the most, counselors and therapists could assume social responsibilities, become actual agents of change, and "use their power and expertise to make society aware of the social etiology of personal problems and to participate in social and political action to create a society which promotes the growth of women and other minority groups" (Rawlings and Carter, 1977).

Counseling Women and Men for Psychological Androgyny: Two Illustrations

Mental health and illness of women and men was the topic of chapter 2. Men and women tend to be more prone to different kinds of mental illness. "All statistical (as well as observational studies) agree that women fall ill of depression and hysteria more often than men. The evidence shows that men fall ill of alcoholism, addictions, sexual perversions, obsessional neurosis, and schizophrenia more often than women" (Lewis, 1976). While biological imbalances and deficiencies may be related to some of these mental illnesses, there is no evidence that they are sex linked. However, as Lewis (1976) observes, there may be sociological reasons for the sex differences in mental health: ". . . a genuine trend for either sex to be ahead in frequency of mental illness must not be interpreted as a deficiency in the member of that sex so much as a reflection of a difference in the way society injures both sexes." Earlier in this chapter, I reviewed the research which shows that highly sex typed individuals are not as well-balanced or mentally healthy as androgynous persons. Carried to extremes, high femininity or masculinity blocks or inhibits the full development of a healthy human being. Counselors and therapists often see clients whose problems are related to their sex role socialization. For women, some common problems are: dependency, passivity, fear of achievement and success, difficulty in expressing anger, the "empty nest" syndrome, lack of self-fulfillment, sexuality, aging, and dual role conflicts. For men, frequent problems have to do with pressures to succeed and achieve, inexpressiveness, sexual inadequacy, aging, and new role conflicts and ambiguities. For many women and men these sex role related problems are interrelated, causing an intensity and severity that require professional help over a period of time.

Two common problems—dependency in women and inexpressiveness in men—will be discussed here as illustrations of how a counselor may, using psychological androgyny as a model of mental health, "resocialize" individuals to overcome their problems related to traditional sex roles.

The Inexpressive Man

Masculinity in American society is expressed largely through physical courage, toughness, competitiveness, and aggressiveness, while femininity is expressed through gentleness, expressiveness, and responsiveness. Young boys are taught by their parents that "big boys don't cry" and by their peers that "only sissies and girls cry." Not wanting to be like girls in any way, boys quickly learn to hide their emotions. They learn not to cry at sad movies, funerals, and other occasions where they are expected to be the strong, silent comforters of women. While women are expected to share their innermost thoughts with others, men are expected to keep their private thoughts and feelings to themselves. Research (Jourard, 1961; Jourard and Lasakow, 1958; Jourard and Richman, 1963) has shown that this expectation is born out; men typically reveal less personal information about themselves to others than women. Komarovsky (1962) has suggested that "the ideal of masculinity into which . . . (men are) . . . socialized inhibits expressiveness both directly, with its emphasis on reserve, and indirectly, by identifying personal interchange with the feminine role." Balswick (1970) found that males are less capable than females of expressing or receiving companionship support from their spouses.

This masculine inexpressiveness and control of emotions helps men fulfill their major role as provider, but does not enhance the role of husband and father. Sociologists (Parsons, 1959) and psychologists (Keniston, 1965) alike have contrasted the rational mentality of the work world with the more expressive style of the family. The incompatibility of values and expectations that surround familial and occupational roles is expressed by Keniston (1965):

To be very successful in occupational pursuits requires a fairly active acceptance of the modes of interpersonal interaction predominant in the occupational world. To be successful, one has to be competitive and aggressive; others have to be judged with some degree of rationality and calculation. The family, obviously, defines the modes of interpersonal relationship differently; individuals should mildly and cheerfully cooperate with others in the family group; family members are to be loved, to be treated as ends—and not as means.

As a result of this incompatibility of work and family roles, many men excel in the role for which they have been socialized and in which they feel comfortable—the provider role—and fail in the role of family member, remaining emotionally detached, disappointed, and even embittered. Keniston (1965) quotes sons of such men who describe their fathers as "very difficult to talk to" or "finds it hard to show emotions, no matter how deeply felt" or "inability to be relaxed and affectionate in our company." Keniston (1965) summarizes the main themes in the descriptions these sons give of their fathers as "related terms like 'unable to express himself,' 'withdrawn,' 'cold'—and yet at the same time these subjects sense (or perhaps wishfully imagine) some lost part of their fathers which wants to express itself." In short, these men were so well specialized (and socialized) for the occupational world that they could hardly function in any other.

Jourard (1971) relates the inexpressiveness (or lack of self-disclosure) of men to their health and psychotherapy:

Men keep their selves to themselves and impose thereby an added burden of stress beyond that imposed by the exigencies of everyday life. The experience of psychosomatic physicians who undertake psychotherapy with male patients suffering peptic ulcers, essential hypertension, and kindred disorders seems to support this contention. Psychotherapy is the art of promoting self-disclosure and authentic being in patients who withhold their real selves from expression, and clinical experience shows that, when psychotherapy has been effective with psychosomatic patients, the latter change their role-definitions, their self-structures, and their behavior in the direction of greater spontaneity and openness with salutory consequences to their bodies. The time is not far off when it will be possible to demonstrate with adequately controlled experiments the nature and degree of correlation between levels and amounts of self-disclosure and proneness to illness and/or an early death age.

How does the counselor promote and encourage expressiveness and self-disclosure from a client who has been socialized to believe that to be expressive and show emotion is not "manly"? Recognizing that the client is likely to avoid or minimize expressiveness and self-disclosure, the counselor draws attention to any beginnings in that direction, encouraging the client to a full examination of his feelings. If such efforts reach a dead end, a tool such as Jourard's (1971) self-disclosure questionnaire provides some structure and direction. The questionnaire has six subject areas with ten corresponding statements each to which the client can react: (1) Attitudes and Opinions, e.g., "My personal views on sexual morality," (2) Tastes and Interests, e.g., "My favorite ways of spending spare time," (3) Work (or Studies), e.g., "What I find to be the most boring and unenjoyable aspects of my work," (4) Money, e.g., "How I budget my money," (5) Personality, e.g., "The kinds of things that make me just furious," and (6) Body, e.g., "My feelings about different parts of my body." In talking through the questionnaire items with the client, the counselor begins with the items which are easy for the client to discuss and works up to the more difficult ones. The counselor can then ask which of these items the client has shared with others (e.g., wife or companion, parents, friends, children, etc.), and if not what have been the reasons for not sharing. Contracts or agreements for the client to discuss certain topics with appropriate persons will give the client practice in expressive behavior outside the counseling sessions. Behavioral rehearsal or role-play may help prepare the client for experimentation with others.

Another approach to help the client more fully understand the problem of inexpressiveness and unemotionality in men is bibliotherapy. Popularly, bibliotherapy consists of providing fictional characters and situations with which people can identify and thus experience catharsis. The bibliotherapy suggested here, however, is cognitive in nature and provides the client with nonfictional readings to help him understand his personal circumstance—to help him understand and become aware of how he was socialized into being inexpressive, the unhappy experiences of others who have also been socialized to be inexpressive, the advantages of becoming more expressive, and some ways in which others have become more expressive. In addition to the references already cited in this section, I would suggest the following three readings as effective bibliotherapy selections: Bernard's (1975) chapter "The Bitter Fruits of Extreme Sex-role Specialization," Balswick and Peck's (1971) article "The Inexpressive Male: A Tragedy of American Society," and Pleck's (1976) article "The Male Sex Role: Definitions, Problems, and Sources of Change."

Another approach in working with the inexpressive male client is the involvement of others in some of the counseling sessions. Involving the wife or companion in couples counseling can be very effective as can the involvement of children in family counseling, giving the inexpressive man an opportunity to try out some new behaviors with those closest to him. Group counseling sessions with other men experiencing similar problems because of their inexpressiveness is also very helpful. Another group experience men have found very helpful in becoming aware of the restrictiveness of the male sex role is consciousness-raising (C.R.) groups. See chapter 7 for a discussion of C.R. groups.

The Dependent Woman

In each of our discussions regarding the female sex role throughout this volume (particularly in chapters 1 and 2) the dependency of women stands out. Women are socialized to be dependent on first their parents and then later on their husbands for support and direction. Goldberg and Lewis (1969) report a significantly greater reliance on parents in girls as early as one year of age, and Bardwick and Douvan (1971) found that after the age of two boys gradually lose their dependency upon parents while girls do not. Upon reaching school age, male dependency drops off sharply, but this is not true for girls (Oakley, 1972), as teachers reinforce dependent behaviors in girls to a much greater extent than in boys (Serbin et al., 1973).

Kagan and Moss (1961) found that whatever women's predispositions are as children, they tend to develop into dependent adults. This female dependency is manifested in a variety of ways; some of the more common are a reliance on others for acceptance, approval, and guidance; and a lack of faith in one's own judgment and abilities. Dependent persons often base their self-esteem on the reactions of others (Bardwick, 1971), and rely on external rather than internal controls (Douvan, 1960). Carried to an extreme, the dependent person does not determine what she does with her own life but relies on others to decide what she will do, when, and how. When left without this external support, as are many widows and divorcees (see discussion earlier in this chapter), dependent persons are at a loss to know what to do and fail to function.

The extremely dependent person is the antithesis of an emotionally healthy one, as defined by (Jakubowski, 1977):

Emotionally healthy, fully functioning people believe that they can make an effective impact on the people in their environment. They do not feel that they are helpless victims of life's events or of other people's demands. Instead they feel in charge of themselves because they believe that they can engage in direct behavior which will affect other people in constructive ways.

The dependent woman as a client presents the counselor with a particularly delicate situation since the counselor represents an authority figure, and the client will want the counselor to make her decisions for her. Thus, the counselor should be alert to any signs of the client looking to others for approval (including the counselor) and referring to others' opinions when describing herself. Soliciting the expression of the client's own opinions, first regarding non-threatening topics and then topics regarding her self-concept will help her begin to "hear" herself formulate ideas without relying on others. Since self-reliance and independence are the goals of the counseling process for the dependent person, the client must be urged to reach her own conclusions regarding actions she should take, with the counselor merely assisting in the weighing of alternatives rather than providing answers or solutions.

Since the dependent woman has never learned to make decisions for herself, some instruction in the decision-making process (see chap. 7) may be useful. Practice in using the decision-making model can begin with small, less significant decisions like "how can I spend the rest of this day most beneficially" and progress to the major ones like "what do I want to do with my life and how can I make it happen." Behavioral contracts for progress steps and activities to develop independence based on the decisions made by the client is a logical extension of the decision-making process.

Another effective technique used with dependent women is assertion training (see discussion in chap. 7). Dependent women are generally nonassertive, failing to stand up for their own rights, failing to express honest thoughts and feelings in a straightforward manner, for fear of appearing aggressive—a characteristic "appropriate" for the male sex role but not the female sex role. Assertion training helps participants learn how to be strong and effective in dealing with others, while still remaining sensitive and empathic. In the process of becoming assertive, a sense of their own identity and self-esteem is allowed to emerge. While increasing numbers of useful assertion training manuals are now available, Jakubowski's (1977) writings are particularly useful in that they provide the counselor with assertion training theory and techniques for a wide variety of clinical problems of women. Two volumes which both client and counselor will find informative are Alberti and Emmons' (1974) *Your Perfect Right: A Guide to Assertive Behavior* and Bloom, Coburn, and Pearlman's (1975) *The New Assertive Woman.*

As suggested for the inexpressive man, bibliotherapy can also be a useful tool in helping the dependent woman understand her sex role socialization and its detriments. An annotated bibliography to be used in feminist bibliotherapy has been compiled by Sanders and Stewart (1977). A consciousness-raising group experience can also enable the dependent woman to become aware that she is not alone, that many other women share her problems; and she can see how others are overcoming their dependency. Couples counseling and family counseling are also very useful in helping the client establish new behaviors with her family—a necessary step to independence.

Conclusion   Psychologically androgynous individuals are "both masculine and feminine, both instrumental and expressive, both agentic and communal, depending upon the situational appropriateness of these various modalities" (Bem, 1977). Studies have shown that androgynous individuals are better adjusted, have more self-esteem and social competence, and can function in both instrumental and expressive domains more effectively than highly sex typed persons. A high level of sex typing has been found to be detrimental. For example, high femininity in women is highly correlated with poor adjustment, high anxiety, low self-esteem, and low social acceptance. Similarly, high masculinity in males is associated with high anxiety, low self-acceptance, and high neuroticism. In addition, highly sex typed children of both sexes have lower overall intelligence, spatial ability, and creativity than children with both cross-sex and same-sex traits.

Psychological androgyny as an approach to mental health is consistent with Rogers' flexible person and Maslow's self-actualizing individual and is more compatible with contemporary American life than traditional sex roles. Counselors and other helping professionals have a social responsibility and a professional responsibility to their clients to help them overcome dysfunctional aspects of sex typing in order to live more gratifying, contributing, and humane lives. Two examples of problems due to sex typing—dependency in women and inexpressiveness in men—are discussed with suggestions for treatment.

References   Alberti, R. E., and Emmons, M. L. *Your perfect right: A guide to assertive behavior,* 2nd ed. San Luis Obispo: Impact, 1974.

Bakan, D. *The duality of human existence.* Chicago: Rand McNally, 1966.

Balswick, J. O. The effect of spouse companionship support on employment success. *Journal of Marriage and the Family,* 1970, *32,* 212–215.

Balswick, J. O., and Peek, C. W. The inexpressive male: A tragedy of American society. *The Family Coordinator,* October 1971, 363–368.

Bardwick, J. *The psychology of women: A study of biocultural conflicts.* New York: Harper and Row, 1971.

Bardwick, J., and Douvan, E. Ambivalence: The socialization of women. In V. Gornick and B. Moran (eds.), *Woman in sexist society.* New York: Basic Books, 1971.

Bart, P. B. Depression in middle-aged women. In V. Gornick and B. K. Moran (eds.), *Woman in sexist society.* New York: Basic Books, 1971.

Bem, S. L. Beyond androgyny: Some presumptuous prescriptions for a liberated sexual identity. In C. G. Carney and S. L. McMahon (eds.), *Exploring contemporary male/female roles.* La Jolla, Calif.: University Associates, 1977.

Bem, S. L. Sex-role adaptability: One consequence of psychological androgyny. *Journal of Personality and Social Psychology,* 1975, *31*(4), 634–643.

Bem, S. L. The measurement of psychological androgyny. *Journal of Consulting and Clinical Psychology,* 1974, *42,* 155–162.

Bernard, J. *The future of marriage.* New York: World, 1972.

Bernard, J. *Women, wives, mothers: Values and options.* Chicago: Aldine, 1975.

Berzins, J. I., and Welling, M. A. The PRF ANDRO scale: A measure of psychological androgyny derived from the personality research form. Unpublished manuscript, University of Kentucky, 1974.

Block, J. H. Conceptions of sex role: Some cross-cultural and longitudinal perspectives. *American Psychologist,* 1973, *28,* 512–526.

Bloom, L. Z.; Coburn, K.; and Pearlman, J. *The new assertive woman.* New York: Delacorte Press, 1975.

Cosentino, F., and Heilbrun, A. B. Anxiety correlates of sex-role identity in college students. *Psychological Reports,* 1964, *14,* 729–730.

Dellas, M., and Gaier, E. L. Identification of creativity: The individual. *Psychological Bulletin,* 1970, *73,* 55–73.

Deutsch, C. J., and Gilbert, L. A. Sex-role stereotypes: Effect on perceptions of self and others and on personal adjustment. *Journal of Counseling Psychology,* 1976,*23*(4), 373–379.

Donelson, E. *Personality: A scientific approach.* New York: Appleton-Century-Crofts and Goodyear Publishing Co., 1973.

Douvan, E. Sex differences in adolescent character processes. *Merrill-Palmer Quarterly,* 1960, *6,* 203–211.

Gall, M. D. The relationship between masculinity-femininity and manifest anxiety. *Journal of Clinical Psychology,* 1969, *25,* 294–295.

Gelpi, B. The politics of androgyny. *Women's Studies,* 1974, *2,* 151–160.

Goldberg, S., and Lewis, M. Play behavior in the year old infant: Early sex differences. *Child Development,* 1969, *40,* 21–31.

Gray, S. W. Masculinity-femininity in relation to anxiety and social acceptance. *Child Development,* 1957, *28,* 203–214.

Gump, J. P. Sex-role attitudes and psychological well-being. *Journal of Social Issues,* 1972, *28*(2), 79–92.

Hammer, E. Creativity and feminine ingredients in young male artists. *Perceptual and Motor Skills,* 1964, *19,* 414.

Harris, D. Androgyny: The sexist myth in disguise. *Women's Studies,* 1974, *2,* 171–184.

Hartford, T. C.; Willis, C. H.; and Deabler, H. L. Personality correlates of masculinity-femininity. *Psychological Reports,* 1967, *21,* 881–884.

Hefner, R.; Nordin, V.; Rebecca, M.; and Oleshansky, B. Sex-role transcendence: Role polarity and sex discrimination in education. University of Michigan. Technical proposal to National Institute of Education, Contract No. NIE-C-74-0144, May, 1974.

Heilbrun, C. *Toward a recognition of androgyny.* New York: Knopf, 1973.

Helson, R. Personality of women with imaginative and artistic interests; the role of masculinity, originality, and other characteristics in their creativity. *Journal of Personality,* 1966,*34,* 1.

Jakubowski, P. A. Assertive behavior and clinical problems of women and self-assertion training procedures on women. In E. I. Rawlings and D. K. Carter (eds.), *Psychotherapy for women: Treatment toward equality.* Springfield, Ill.: Charles C. Thomas, 1977.

Jourard, S. M. Age and self-disclosure, *Merrill-Palmer Quarterly of Behavioral Development,* 1961, *7,* 191-197.

Jourard, S. M. *The transparent self.* New York: D. Van Nostrand, 1971.

Jourard, S. M., and Lasakow, P. Some factors in self-disclosure. *Journal of Abnormal and Social Psychology,* 1958, *56,* 91–98.

Jourard, S. M., and Richman, P. Disclosure output and input in college students. *Merrill-Palmer Quarterly of Behavioral Development,* 1963, *9,* 141–148.

Jung, C. G. Anima and animus. In *Two essays on analytical psychology: Collected works of C. G. Jung.* Vol. 7. Bollinger Foundation, 1953.

Kagan, J., and Moss, H. *Birth to maturity.* New York: John Wiley, 1961.

Keniston, K. *The uncommitted.* New York: Delta, 1965.

Komarovsky, M. *Blue-collar marriage*. New York: Random House, 1962.

Landman, L. Recent trends toward unisex: A panel. *American Journal of Psychoanalysis*, 1974, *34*, 27–31.

Lerner, H. E. Adaptive and pathogenic aspects of sex-role stereotypes: Implications for parenting and psychotherapy. *American Journal of Psychiatry*, January 1978, *135*(1), 48–52.

Lewis, H. B. *Psychic war in men and women*. New York: New York University Press, 1976.

Maccoby, E. E. Sex differences in intellectual functioning. In E. E. Maccoby (ed.), *The development of sex differences*. Stanford, Calif.: Stanford University Press, 1966.

Marecek, J. Psychological androgyny and positive mental health: A biosocial perspective. In C. G. Carney and S. L. McMahon (eds.), *Exploring contemporary male/female roles*. La Jolla, Calif.: University Associates, 1977.

Maslow, A. *Motivation and personality*. New York: Harper & Row, 1954.

Maslow, A. Self-esteem (dominance feeling) and sexuality in women. *Journal of Social Psychology*, 1942, *16*, 259–294.

Mussen, P. H. Long-term consequents of masculinity and interests in adolescence. *Journal of Consulting Psychology*, 1962, *26*, 435–440.

Mussen, P. H. Some antecedents and consequents of masculine sex typing in adolescent boys. *Psychological Monographs*, 1961, *75*, 506.

Oakley, A. *Sex, gender and society*. New York: Harper and Row, 1972.

O'Reilly, J. The housewife's moment of truth. *Ms*, Spring 1972, 55–59.

Parsons, T. The social structure of the family. In R. N. Anshen (ed.), *The family: Its function and destiny*. New York: Harper, 1959.

Pleck, J. H. The male sex role: Definitions, problems, and sources of change. *Journal of Social Issues*, 1976, *32*(3), 155–164.

Pleck, J. H. Masculinity-femininity: Current and alternative paradigms. *Sex Roles*, 1975, *1*, 161–178.

Rawlings, E. I., and Carter, D. K. (eds.). *Psychotherapy for women: Treatment toward equality*. Springfield, Ill.: Charles C. Thomas, 1977.

Rebecca, M.; Hefner, R.; and Oleshansky, B. A model of sex-role transcendence. *Journal of Social Issues*, 1976, *32*(3), 197–206.

Rogers, C. R. *Client-centered therapy*. Boston: Houghton Mifflin, 1951.

Rossi, A. S. Equality between the sexes: An immodest proposal. In R. J. Lifton (ed.), *The women in America*. Boston: Houghton Mifflin, 1964.

Sanders, C. J., and Stewart, D. C. Feminist bibliotherapy—prescription for change: A selected and annotated bibliography. In E. I. Rawlings and D. K. Carter (eds.), *Psychotherapy for women: Treatment toward equality*. Springfield, Ill.: Charles C. Thomas, 1977.

Sears, R. R. Relation of early socialization experiences to self-concepts and gender role in middle childhood. *Child Development*, 1970, *41*, 267–289.

Secor, C. Androgyny: An early reappraisal. *Woman's Studies*, 1974, *2*, 161–169.

Serbin, L.; O'Leary, D.; Kent, R.; and Tonick, L. A comparison of teacher responses to the pre-academic and problem behavior of boys and girls. *Child Development*, 1973, *44*, 796–804.

Singer, J. *Androgyny: Toward a new theory of sexuality*. New York: Anchor Press/Doubleday, 1976.

Spence, J. T., and Helmreich, R. L. *Masculinity and femininity: Their psychological dimensions, correlates, and antecedents*. Austin: University of Texas Press, 1978.

Spence, J. T.; Helmreich, R.; and Stapp, J. Ratings of self and peers on sex-role attributes and their relation to self-esteem and conceptions of masculinity and femininity. *Journal of Personality and Social Psychology*, 1975, *32*, 29–39.

Webb, A. P. Sex-role preferences and adjustment in early adolescents. *Child Development*, 1963, *34*, 609–618.

7 Promoting Change in the Schools

Schools are an important socializing agency for our multicultural nation. Our educational system reflects and reinforces the attitudes and values of our society. Attitudes, values, and behaviors which are reinforced by the schools have lifelong effects in encouraging or limiting motivation and achievement in adulthood. Present education-socialization processes do not encourage nor facilitate the development of the full range of skills and knowledge required by young women and men if they are to fully realize their potential and contribute as much to this society and their own lives as they possibly can. Too often the kinds of educational opportunities and assistance available to students is determined by—or at least greatly influenced by—the student's sex. Chapter 3 describes the sex stereotyping and discrimination that still exist in our schools today despite federal laws prohibiting discriminatory treatment on the basis of sex.

School counselors at all levels have contributed to the sex role stereotyping of students. In helping students to identify and develop their abilities and interests, counselors have encouraged young women and men to develop those traits ascribed to them by society. They have encouraged young boys and men to be aggressive, independent, objective, unemotional, competitive, logical, unexcitable during crises, strong, decisive, self-confident, and to aspire to become doctors, lawyers, scientists, businessmen, and skilled craftsmen. They have encouraged young girls and women to be sensitive to others, supportive, tactful, gentle, cooperative, dependable, neat in habits and appearance, and to aspire to become nurses, teachers, social workers, secretaries—occupations which are compatible with the role of being a wife and mother and are in a sense an extension of the home. This kind of counseling has been limiting to the members of both sexes—but especially to women.

What can counselors do not only to alter their own approach and eliminate sex typing in counseling students but to promote the necessary changes in the schools to help free the student's environment of sex role stereotyping elements? The focus of this chapter is to explore some plausible answers to this complex question.

The Proactive/ Change Agent* Role of the Counselor

The need for dramatic change on many fronts in American education is overwhelmingly apparent. The difficulties in providing equal educational opportunity to all Americans in all regions of our country is a problem of increasing concern. The removal of sex role stereotyping elements in the schools must be a major thrust if all students, female and male alike, are to be provided equal educational opportunity.

Effective change in any system rarely just happens without skilled direction and planning. The suggestion that counselors assume the proactive role of change agent or social reconstructionist in the schools is not new. Fifteen years ago Shoben (1962) issued the following challenge to counselors:

> . . . willy-nilly, the school represents a society-in-little. The challenge before it is whether it can transform itself into a developmentally productive one on an articulate and informal basis and, by a regular and planful process of self-appraisal, maintain itself as a true growth-enhancing community. In such an effort to sharpen the impact of the school and to give it greater cogency for individual students, guidance workers can play a key role, forging in the course of it, a genuine new profession for themselves.

The concept of the role of the school counselor or psychological specialist in the school has moved from one of centering on the individual to one of including the individual's environment as another focus for change (Wrenn, 1962; Shoben, 1962; McCully, 1965; Danskin, Kennedy, & Friesen, 1965; Stewart and Warnath, 1965; Blocher, 1966; Bardon, 1968; Alderson, 1971; Lewis and Lewis, 1977). This role change necessitates an active involvement on the part of the counselor in assisting the individual in determining goals for personal change and in improving the environment where necessary in an effort to further facilitate the development of the individual. Lewis and Lewis (1977) explain this active involvement of counselor and client as a mutual exploration for the answers to four basic questions:

1. To what extent is the individual capable of resolving the issue through personal change?
2. What resources in the environment are available to help the individual grow?

*Note: "Proactive Counselor" and "Change Agent Counselor" will be used in combination and interchangeably in this chapter.

3. To what extent does the solution really rest in the environment instead of in the individual?
4. How can the counselor and/or the counselee act to bring about the necessary changes in the environment?

A paraphrasing of these four general questions is easily done to make them specifically tailored to the problem of sex role stereotyping in the schools and the counselor's proactive role of social change agent or reconstructionist.

1. To what extent is the student capable of resolving conflicts and problems resulting from sex role stereotyping through personal change?
2. What resources in the school are available to help the student grow and overcome traditional sex role restrictions?
3. To what extent does the solution really rest in the school environment instead of in the individual student?
4. How can the counselor and/or the student act to bring about the necessary changes in order to free the school environment from sex role stereotyping elements?

It is clear that in working through these questions with the student, the traditional role of the counselor must change—both in working individually with the client and in impacting the environment. The following is a discussion of some of the ways the traditional role of the counselor must change if the counselor is to be effective as an agent of change or social reconstructionist in the schools.

Assuming Increased Responsibility One obvious change in the traditional counseling role is in the amount of responsibility the counselor has been willing to assume. In order for proactive/change agent counseling to make a difference, the counselor assumes much more responsibility than some writers in the field have proposed. In insisting that counselors demonstrate conclusively that counseling can make a difference, Krumboltz (1967) has written, "Counseling goals need to be stated as those overt behavior changes desired by the client and agreed to by his counselor. The counselor has an obligation to share in the determination of the client goals and would not be expected to work goals which were outside his interests, competencies or ethical standards." Effecting change in the behavioral patterns of individuals is, in a sense, social reconstruction in microcosm and assists greater social or institutional reform.

| Articulating Values | Along with assuming more responsibility for what transpires in counseling sessions with students, Krumboltz (1967) is stressing that the goals which the counselor is helping the student determine should be consistent with the counselor's own interests, competencies, and ethical standards. For our purposes in discussing the change agent counselor and sex role stereotyping, I would expand this to include the counselor's values and attitudes regarding sexism and the value or belief that change concerning this issue is necessary in our society. In doing so, I have identified another change in the traditional role of the counselor if the counselor is to be an effective change agent— moving from the once acclaimed professional ideal of complete objectivity, impartiality, and moral neutrality to that of being up front with one's own values and beliefs in the counseling relationship. Like it or not, the values of the counselor consciously or unconsciously permeate the entire counseling process. This point is made by Williamson (1958) as he describes the intrusion of values into counseling: |

> If we agree that value judgments are implicit in every action we take, we should also agree that counselors cannot fully escape introducing their own value systems into the counseling interview. While the counselor's moral and ethical standards may not be made clear to clients or even to the counselor himself, they are influential in his reactions to the client's story, his emphases, his choice of objectives and counseling method, and in the techniques he uses to carry out the chosen method of interviewing.

For the proactive/change agent counselors working with individual students around sex role stereotyping issues and endeavoring to rid the school system of sexist and discriminatory elements, clarifying and articulating their own values regarding the need for such change is a necessary part of the process. This can be done without violating the freedom of others to select their own values.

| Providing Role Models | While the concept of the counselor as role model is not new, the *extent* to which counselor modeling of nonsexist behavior facilitates both individual client change and school environment change can be great. |

It has been demonstrated that vicarious learning through observation of social models can have a powerful effect on human growth and learning (Bandura, 1971). Research has also shown us that certain factors or conditions in social relationships can significantly affect learning (Rogers, 1967; Truax & Mitchell, 1971). These conditions are usually described by such terms as "congruence," "accurate empathy," and "unconditional positive regard." Truax and

Carkhuff (1967) reached the following conclusion about the personal qualities of the counselor, their effect on the counseling relationship, and the modeling that can occur:

That the therapist, within the relationship, be himself integrated, genuine, and authentic seems most basic to therapeutic outcome. Without such genuineness, a trusting relationship could scarcely exist. The counselor or therapist must be a real person in the encounter, presenting himself without defensive phoniness, without hiding behind the facade of the professional role. The current conceptualization of genuineness (or authenticity or congruence) requires the therapist's personal involvement; he is not simply "doing his job" as a technician. The therapist's capacity for openness and personal freedom in the therapeutic encounter offers, in part, a model for the client to follow in moving toward openness and freedom to be oneself.

This modeling can be carried a step further. The counselor's capacity for genuineness and openness in examining his or her own attitudes regarding sexism in the presence of the client can provide the client with a model or example to do likewise. Since, as chapter 1 points out, we have all been socialized to think and feel and behave in certain ways because of our sex, the counselor and client are likely to have had some similar experiences to share with each other and learn from. For example, few individuals cannot recall vividly a time in their lives when they were told they should or should not take some course of action because "only little girls do that" or "its only appropriate for men." Sharing such experiences and trying to understand their impact on the shaping of our present attitudes and behaviors can be a very beneficial process for both client and counselor.

Intervening With the Environment

Perhaps the most dramatic difference between the traditional counselor and the proactive/change agent counselor in the schools is that the latter must be a behavioral-social scientist in the best sense of the combined terms. Drawing from such fields as anthropology, sociology, economics, political science, and social psychology, the change agent counselor must possess effective intervention and consultation skills. Since consultation and intervention often have been loosely defined in the literature, the following definitions are useful. According to Argyris (1970), "To intervene is to enter into an ongoing system of relationship, to come between or among persons, groups or objects for the purpose of helping them." The proactive counselor intervenes with the school environment—school personnel, students, curriculum, policies, practices, etc.—for the purpose of eliminating sex role stereotypic elements. Lippitt (1959) defines consultation as "a voluntary relationship between a professional helper (consultant) and a help-needing system (client) in which the consultant is attempting to give help to the client in the solving of current or potential problems and the relationship is perceived as temporary by both parties. Also, the consultant is an outsider, that is, he is not part of the hierarchical power system in which the client is located." Caplan's (1970) view of consultation, while in many ways similar to Lippitt's, puts more stress on the professional role of both the consultant and the client. To Caplan, consultation, is "a process of interaction between two professional persons—the consultant who is a specialist, and the consultee, who invokes the consultant's help in regard to a current work problem with which he is having some difficulty and which he has decided is within the other's area of specialized competence." In an effort to make the consultation process more applicable to educational settings, Lanning (1974) broadens the more traditional view of consultation to include more than a process dealing with "problems" and "professionals" with the helper coming from outside the system. Thus, for Lanning, "consultation is the activity or process in which one person engages with another person, group, or agency in order to identify the needs and/or capabilities of that person, group, or agency and then to plan, initiate, implement, and evaluate action designed to meet and/or develop those needs and/or capabilities." For our purposes, the proactive/change agent counselor becomes a consultant with individuals and groups in the school environment, jointly identifies sexist elements in need of change, and assists in planning, implementing, and evaluating agreed upon changes.

While the many definitions of intervention and consultation may vary somewhat in specific details, there are some characteristics which can be identified as common to all and which are useful for the proactive/change agent counselor to keep in mind:

1. Participation is voluntary, both on the part of the consultant and those receiving assistance.
2. The relationship involves, and is usually initiated by, an individual, group, or organization asking for assistance from an individual or individuals perceived as having the ability to give the needed assistance. The proactive counselor can facilitate this "asking for assistance" by carefully pointing out some of the areas needing change and suggesting some alternatives, thus increasing the awareness of others and at the same time demonstrating ability to provide help.

3. The consultant does not have power over the actions of those he or she assists. The working relationship is one of cooperation not coercion, with the person(s) who asked for help choosing what action they will take. This is oftentimes the most difficult aspect of the consultation process for the proactive counselor trying to rid the schools of sexist elements. What may seem like an easy step to the committed, enthusiastic proactive counselor may be viewed as too radical a change for other individuals.
4. The process of consultation is educational. While the initial request for consultation may be based on a specific concern or need, the skills and information learned through the consultation process can be applied to future concerns or needs.
5. The relationship is temporary. The consultation process is not a permanent working relationship but is terminated when the individual, group, or organization has received the assistance requested. The proactive counselor may have a series of such "temporary" relationships as various segments of the school environment are identified as needing assistance in changing sexist attitudes, behaviors, practices, etc.

A consultation process using many of the assumptions described above is utilized in a project developed by Hansen and associates (see Hansen and Keierleber, 1978) and supported by a grant awarded under the Women's Educational Equity Act, U.S. Office of Education. Entitled "BORN FREE," the project attempts to reduce career-related sex role stereotyping in schools at all levels—elementary and secondary through college—by combining models of consultation, change process, and career development.

Knowledge and Skills of Proactive/Change Agent Counselor   Given the above description of the consultation process and the desire to assist individuals, groups, and organizations in eliminating sex role stereotyping elements from the schools, what special areas of knowledge and skills should a proactive/change agent counselor have in order to be effective? The following, while not a definitive list, includes some of the special areas of knowledge and skills believed by this author to be extremely helpful to the proactive/change agent counselor. Some of these are highlighted in the literature (Lanning, 1974; Argyris, 1970; Miles & Solmick, 1971; Bennis, 1966; Bennis, Benne & Chin, 1962; Lippitt, 1959; Lippitt,

Watson & Westley, 1958; Lewin, 1947) and others are added by this author because of their importance to the focus of this chapter.

1. Interpersonal competence. This includes awareness of self and others, effective communication skills, ability to work with others, ability to manage conflict, flexibility, openness, and the like. Of particular importance here is:
   a. self-examination and the awareness of one's own and others' attitudes and values regarding sexism, and
   b. identification of one's own sexist behaviors in counseling and consulting relationships. (See chap. 11, Self-education for Awareness, Change, and Growth.) The proactive counselor's ability to recognize his or her own sexist attitudes and behaviors and willingness to change is especially important as a role model for others.

2. Knowledge of intervention, consultation, change theories, and methods. Understand these theories and methods and be able to apply and adapt appropriate strategies to particular situations. Eliminating sexism from the schools requires change. Proactive counselors with knowledge and skills in promoting change through intervention and consultation will have a much easier time working within schools to eliminate sexism.

3. Diagnostic, planning, and evaluation skills. While these skills are actually part of item 2 above, they are included here for emphasis. The knowledge and skills to diagnose the present state of affairs, plan and implement strategies for change—including goal-setting, problem-solving, decision-making, etc.—and evaluate the results are central to the functions of the change agent counselor.

4. Understanding of sex role stereotyping and its detrimental effects. Self-awareness of sexist attitudes and behaviors and the ability to perceive these in others is included under interpersonal competence and will not be repeated here. Other areas included here are:
   a. Knowledge of how sex roles are developed and the concomitant socialization processes (see chap. 1).
   b. Knowledge of common sex typing in clinical judgments of mental health (see chap. 2) and familiarity with biased and unbiased instruments and materials used in counseling students (see chap. 3).
   c. Understanding of educational barriers and opportunities which exist for students largely because of their sex (see chap. 3).

d. Familiarity with the world of work and employment opportunities and problems that exist for both women and men (see chap. 4).

e. Knowledge of laws and regulations which prohibit discrimination or differential treatment on the basis of sex (see chap. 5).

The sensitive and aware proactive counselor with the knowledge and skills discussed above can act as an agent of change in his or her school to help remove those sex role stereotyping elements which are keeping students—male and female—from receiving an education which allows the fullest possible range of choices and opportunities for growth and development. While not an easy task, planned change can occur with the stimulation and direction of a skilled and patient change agent. The remainder of this chapter discusses ways in which counselors in the schools—elementary, secondary, and postsecondary—can facilitate change in the area of traditional sex role stereotyping.

The Proactive/ Change Agent Counselor in the Elementary School

Due to the nature of elementary schools and the age of the students, change agent counselors wishing to remove sex role stereotyping elements will work more with parents, teachers, and other school personnel than directly with the students themselves. This is not to say that individual and group counseling are not included as ways of helping students—particularly in the fourth, fifth, and sixth grades—question and challenge traditional sex roles as they develop their own self-concepts. Generally speaking, however, individual and group counseling around such issues are more effective with students at the junior high, high school, and college levels, and thus will be included in the sections of this chapter dealing with those educational levels. Most of the work counselors do with elementary students to help them overcome already established stereotypic attitudes and beliefs will be done in the classroom context in conjunction with or at the invitation of the teacher.

Working With Teachers

As presently structured, the elementary education of most students occurs in a self-contained classroom with a teacher or team of teachers determining and controlling what the students are exposed to and how concepts and ideas are introduced. Because over 90 percent of the students' school day is spent in the presence of the teacher, including supervision during recess and lunch time, the teacher's attitudes and behaviors regarding traditional and changing sex roles becomes a central focus for the change agent counselor. Most teachers want to be better teachers and thus will respond to and oftentimes seek assistance to help them improve their teaching approach and/or methods. This is particularly true if a teacher is having some difficulty, i.e., working with a student who has a learning disability or has difficulty making friends, adjusting to the classroom setting, and the like. In working first informally with the more receptive teachers, initially around their presenting problems and then later easing into sex role stereotyping issues, the effective change agent counselor will gradually be sought out by other teachers to assist them in a variety of ways. Some of the more fruitful ways a change agent counselor can assist elementary school teachers are discussed here.

Behavioral Consultant   Many teachers are unaware of their classroom behaviors, and those of the students, which stereotype people on the basis of their sex. Unconsciously, a teacher will request a "strong boy" to help her move some piece of equipment or furniture when a "strong student" would reach the same objective in getting the job done. The teacher and the students themselves oftentimes view the outspoken, active boy as the one needing corrective attention and the quiet, withdrawn girl as the cooperative, exemplary student, when in actuality they both may need encouragement and guidance in developing alternative behaviors which would be more growth producing. The quiet, withdrawn boy who prefers to stay inside and read during recess rather than participate in sports is likely to be considered a "sissy" by his peers, while a girl doing the same thing may go unnoticed. In observing the classroom, the change agent counselor can assist both the teacher and the students in recognizing their own sex stereotyping behaviors and choosing more appropriate alternative behaviors. The teacher may request private sessions with the counselor to further explore, confront, and plan steps to eliminate his or her sexist attitudes and behaviors. This self-exploration often has more impact if done with a small group of teachers sharing common experiences and offering new ideas. Some group activities to help such self-exploration can be found in Carney and McMahon's (1977) *Exploring Contemporary Male/Female Roles: A Facilitator's Guide* and Verheyden-Hilliard's (1976) *Handbook for Workshops on Sex Equality in Education.* Chapter 10 presents some specific training programs and activities that may be used.

The change agent counselor can also assist the teacher as a behavioral consultant in working with parents, helping them to realize the impact on their children of their own attitudes and behaviors regarding sex roles. (More will be said about this in a later section.)

Curriculum Consultant The change agent counselor can be very helpful in suggesting ways in which teachers can revise and update what they are teaching in an effort to eliminate traditional sex typing. Some helpful suggestions might be:

a. Review all texts and teaching materials for sex stereotyping images of girls and boy/men and women. Some publishers and educational groups have developed guidelines which can greatly assist the teacher with this task. Some examples are Scott, Foresman and Company's (1972) *Guidelines for Improving the Image of Women in Textbooks* and *Biased Textbooks: A Research Perspective,* prepared by the National Foundation for the Improvement of Education's Resource Center on Sex Roles in Education (1974). *A Consumer's Guide to Sex, Race and Career Bias in Public School Textbooks* (Britton and Lumpkin 1977). Such reviews of texts and teaching materials might be more efficiently carried out by teachers working together in teams or small groups, assigning portions of the task to each member.

A helpful booklet on the evaluation of educational materials used in elementary and secondary classrooms in the form of tapes, films, filmstrips, records, filmloops, and transparencies is *A Feminist Looks at Educational Software Materials* (Hart, 1973). The educational materials produced by eleven companies are evaluated according to five criteria: women in biographical form, roles as presented in "Community Helpers" units for primary children, jobs presented in vocational guidance sections, the historical presentation of the women's movement, and roles as portrayed in "Family Life" series.

Where budgetary constraints make it impossible for unsatisfactory texts and teaching materials to be replaced, plans can be made for developing supplemental materials showing males and females in nontraditional roles and using the old materials as examples of traditional stereotyping which can be harmful and limiting to the members of both sexes.

b. Include sex role content and discussions in the teaching of other subjects. History and literature are naturals as the teacher can point out the typical omissions of great women who were instrumental in the early development of our country, noted women authors, the stereotyping of fictional characters, etc. Other particularly good vehicles for learning about sex typing and its impact on the students themselves are instruction programs in career education, value clarification, and human relations.

For example, career education programs which bring boys and girls into contact with not only typical but atypical role models like male nurses, secretaries, preschool and elementary teachers, and female doctors, lawyers, executives, fire fighters, mechanics, and the like can be very helpful in broadening students' perceptions of what men and women can do and can have considerable impact on their own aspirations. Introduction to such atypical role models can be done in a variety of ways: inviting guest speakers to the class, visiting selected persons in their work settings, packaged materials, "on hands" experiences, films, special bulletin boards, just to name a few.

In value clarification, human relations, and human development instruction, children can be encouraged to identify their own values and attitudes regarding sex roles and the ways in which they relate to individuals of the opposite and same sex. This can be done most effectively with young children if pictures and words are used to describe the way they feel about something or someone. Stories, films, filmstrips, and discussions of TV programs and commercials, and magazine advertisements can also be useful in stimulating thought and discussion of what is important to the students themselves. A delightful instructional package consisting of stories, poems, songs, games, filmstrips, and records is *Free to Be . . . You and Me,* a project by the Free to Be Foundation, Inc. published by McGraw-Hill Films (1975). Designed to expand children's personal horizons so they can invent their own futures without limitation, the package contains some selections which dispel such myths as "big boys don't cry," "all mothers stay in the kitchen," and "pretty equals good." Other selections redefine fairy tales so that Sleeping Beauty can stay awake and view her life with her eyes open, and the prince can relax and enjoy his life without always having to prove his manhood.

Magic Circles is an example of adapting an elementary level human development program to include learning about contemporary sex roles. The program can be used in expanding one's own concept of what men and women and girls and boys can do and thus removing limitations on what the individual (male or female) can do.

Magic Circles are a major learning vehicle of the Human Development Program, developed in San Diego by child psychiatrist, Harold Bessel (1972 and 1974). The program, consisting of a two-year sequence of lesson plans to improve a primary school child's self-confidence and awareness, is based on Karen Horney's (1950) theory of personality development. Horney emphasizes that the basic drives in personality development are to achieve mastery and to gain approval. Substantial early success in fulfilling these basic drives leads to a healthy self-concept, and that self-concept serves as a learning plateau from which the child gains both confidence and motivation to seek further development.

Essentially, Magic Circles are modified encounter-group or T-groups, in which ten or so students experience a variety of simulated games or structured learning designs that highlight socio-emotional factors. Basically, the Magic Circle helps dispel the notion that because a child may be different from others he or she consequently is inferior to them. The approach is not moralistic but existential, based on what the children see and feel. Thus, the children see and feel that they and others have similar fears and concerns, as they experience a variety of learning designs that are challenging but on which success is also probable. Each success is reinforced positively by approval from the teacher or counselor and often from the other children. Those designs focus on acceptance by the children of both their negative and positive feelings, as well as developing the identification, compassion, and empathy that all people need to function in effective ways. The atmosphere in the Magic Circles is open and free. The goal is the development of a sense of mastery and a healthy self-concept. What better environment is there in which to explore and learn about new, expanding sex roles while dispelling limiting stereotypes and myths? The following is an outline of six Human Development Program units adapted to deal with sex role subject matter at the early elementary level.

Human Development Program Unit	Suggested Sex Role Subject Matter
1. Awareness of self and others. (positive feelings, thoughts, behavior)	1. What do you like about being a girl/boy? What do boys/girls do that you would like to do?
2. Mastery. (language concepts)	2. Words: girl, boy, woman, man, male, female. How do you describe each of these?

Human Development Program Unit	Suggested Sex Role Subject Matter
3. Social interaction. (recognizing kind and unkind behavior; learning to ask for and give kind behavior)	3. How would you feel if someone called you a sissy, bully, tomboy, etc.? What playground equipment can girls/boys use?
4. Awareness. (positive and negative feelings, thoughts, and behaviors)	4. Simulate a situation where each student, on the basis of their sex, experiences being included and left out of some activity. Discuss positive and negative feelings, thoughts, and behaviors that resulted.
5. Mastery. (repetition of mastery unit at a more sophisticated level)	5. Assign "male," "female," or "both" to the following: secretary, teacher, dentist, bus driver, lawyer, telephone operator, doctor, mail carrier, engineer, firefighter, nurse, astronaut, etc.
6. Social interaction. (repetition of social interaction unit at a more sophisticated level)	6. Do you like to play with girls/boys best? Why?

The Human Development Program is a combination of education and psychology, a curriculum based on a model of personality development which seeks early in life to sensitize to common varieties of defensiveness and maladaptive behavior. The goal is to reduce the degree to which defensiveness and maladaptive behavior complicate learning processes, and to do so very early in a person's life. Such is also the goal of developing new, expanded sex roles for both girls and boys, men and women.

c. Develop and present a special unit or educational program on sex role stereotyping. *Non-sexist Education for Young Children: A Practical Guide* (Sprung, 1975) contains many suggestions on early educational programs that focus on nonsexist child development.

An example of what can be done at the elementary, intermediate, and high school levels has been developed by the National Foundation for the Improvement of Education's Resource Center on Sex Roles in Education (*Today's Changing Roles: An Approach to Non-sexist Teaching,* 1974). For each educational level, an introduction and three lessons cover the following: becoming aware of role stereotypes, exploring sex role stereotypes, clarifying and understanding the meaning of sex role stereotypes, and applying the learnings to one's own life and future. Behavioral objectives, major concepts, and instructional materials are outlined for each lesson. For example, the behavioral objectives, major concepts, and instructional materials outlined for the introduction to the elementary lessons are as follows:

Behavioral Objectives	Concepts	Materials
Students will— 1. match objects which they perceive as desirable to people of different ages and sexes.	1. We select gifts for different people for different reasons.	"Gift List"
2. identify reasons for choices.	2. We select gifts on the basis of what people ought to want rather than on what they really want.	
	3. Our perceptions and concepts of what is right for boys and for girls influences our selections of gifts.	

Another rich resource to assist the counselor and teacher in developing special units, programs, and activities on sex roles and sex role stereotyping is *Undoing Sex Stereotypes: Research and Resources for Educator* (Guttentag and Bray, 1976). The book describes a systematic effort to "modify the rigidity of children's sex role stereotypes." The Nonsexist Intervention Project carried out in three school systems in the Boston area is described in such detail that it can be replicated in other settings. Research design, measurements, curriculum materials, teacher-training, and data analysis are all included. Of particular use to the counselor assisting the classroom teacher in developing learning experiences and units are chapter 3, 4, and 5 which outline specific objectives and curricula for early childhood classes, the middle grades, and the junior high level. Also very useful is chapter 6, "Resources for Teachers," which contains a collection of poignant articles and annotated bibliographies.

Because the training and background of counselors is likely to make them better prepared than teachers to help students explore, identify, and express attitudes, values, and feelings, the teacher may request the counselor to assist in the actual instruction and/or participate as a resource person with such learning activities as those described in the preceding paragraphs. Whatever involvement is requested of the counselor, it is time well spent. Since so much of the elementary student's time is spent with the teacher, the change agent counselor who can impact the instructional staff and gain their active involvement has made one of the first major and necessary steps in eliminating sex role stereotyping elements in the educational process.

Working With Librarians

Elementary students rely a great deal on school librarians to help them locate and select nonclassroom text reading materials, whether the additional reading materials are for a class assignment or for pleasure reading. Thus, the librarian's awareness of and attitude toward sexist and nonsexist reading material for young students is very important. In working with the librarian, the change agent counselor can:

1. Suggest that the librarian begin to collect the many annotated lists of nonsexist readers for children which are being compiled by educational and women's rights groups and to make these lists available to teachers, students, and parents. Two examples of nonstereotypic reading lists are *Little Miss Muffet Fights Back* by the Feminists on Children's Media (1974) and *A Guide to Non-sexist Children's Books* by Adele and Klein (1976).

   Little Miss Muffet Fights Back contains an annotated list of over 200 children's books grouped into four categories: picture books, fiction, biography, and history and women's rights. The books were chosen for this bibliography "because they show girls and women as vital human beings—active, assertive, clever, adventurous, brave, creative—or because they show some understanding of the social conditions that encourage meaningful choices toward self-fulfillment, or that prevent women from being all they might be." A special section at the back of the booklet gives instructions on how to order books, how to work for change in children's book publishing, and where to find articles and reports on sexism in children's books.

A Guide to Non-sexist Children's Books includes a selected list of books that "are the kind that treat boys and girls as people who have the same kinds of frailties and strengths." The books are divided into four age categories, each containing a fiction and nonfiction subdivision: preschool through third grade, third grade through seventh grade, seventh grade through twelfth grade, and all ages.

2. Suggest ways in which the librarian can cooperate with and assist the teachers in reviewing present texts, teaching, and library materials for sex role stereotyping and in selecting new nonstereotypic materials.

3. Suggest ideas for library displays and bulletin boards using materials which depict girls and boys/men and women in atypical roles.

Working with School Policy Makers
While it is considered somewhat of a "natural" for counselors to act as consultants to teachers, librarians, and auxillary school personnel, it is not generally expected that counselors develop a consultative relationship with school policy makers—principals, superintendents, and school boards. And yet, if students are receiving differential treatment on the basis of sex because of school policies or traditional practices, impact and change must occur at the level where school policy is determined.

Counselors with the knowledge and skills of the change agent, as described at the beginning of this chapter, are able to work with school policy makers in such a way that their expertise will be recognized, and they will be requested to assist in an overall review of school policies, practices, and programs in an effort to omit or change discriminating or unfair elements. The change agent counselor who is knowledgeable about Title IX requirements (see chap. 5) to eliminate sex discrimination in educational programs will be particularly welcome by administrators who do not have the time or staff to carry out the required institutional self-evaluation.

One area the change agent counselor might study and make recommendations in is hiring and staffing patterns. Since most elementary school teachers are women and most administrators are men, a recommendation that more male teachers—particularly at the lower grades—and more female administrators be hired to bring a balance to the staff and provide role models for the children.

In discussing the elementary school setting and the counselor's ability to effect change, Aubrey (1972) says:

> The desires and aspirations of many elementary school counselors are constantly thwarted by many nonnegotiable factors within the educational system. These non-negotiable factors are institutional constraints that have been ingrained and longestablished by custom and tradition, e.g., the ultimate authority of the principal in instructional and noninstructional matters, the inviolate sovereignty of the teacher in his classroom, the rigid time schedule in schools, the inflexible methods in the grouping of children . . ., the premium placed on docility and conformity, and so on. In the course of time, they become sanctioned and therefore present themselves to counselors as routine procedures, structional patterns, organizational practices, hierarchical processes, and conventional observances. Collectively, these school heirlooms represent tremendous impediments to counselors wishing to innovate programs and practices for children. Without power, a viable means of influencing the school policy makers, counselors have little or no chance of effecting changes for children.

Aubrey suggests that the logical power bases of the counselor are among parents and teachers. We have already discussed how counselors can work with teachers to bring about teacher awareness and involvement in changing sex role stereotypic elements in the elementary schools and will discuss later on how counselors can involve parents in the same process. In working with both groups—teachers and parents—and in bringing them together to discuss changes needed in the school, the counselor increases pressure on school policy makers to implement change. The development of such power bases, along with the legal requirements for nondiscrimination on the basis of sex, greatly assist the counselor in initiating and implementing change at the policy-making level.

Working with Parents

As is discussed in chapter 1, parents play a primary role in the sex role development of their children. Thus, many writers contend that any attempts to alter cultural role definition must be focused on the family system. In working to provide students with a school environment that is free of stereotypic elements, the change agent counselor cannot ignore the student's home environment. Parents have the right to know what efforts the school is making to provide equel educational opportunity for their children, and counselors should work with parents to gain their understanding and support and hopefully their active participation. Just as most teachers desire to become better teachers, most parents want to be better parents. In addition to working with individual parents, with students alone, and with their parents (family counseling), counselors can offer special parent and family programs. A few possible programs are mentioned here as examples.

1. Parent-staff meetings to discuss subjects related to sex-role stereotypes. One way of generating interest and getting such meetings started is to begin with topics of general interest such as educational goals, physical and emotional development, the impact of television, the meaning of play, working mothers, etc. Any such topics can lead to a full discussion of sex role stereotyping. A description of successful parent-staff meetings conducted in the New York metropolitan area is found in chapter 3 of *Non-sexist Education for Children* (Sprung, 1975). The goals of working with parents through such meetings were as follows:

   —To help parents become aware of sexism in our society.
   —To help parents become aware that sexist attitudes affect the way we handle children from birth on.
   —To help parents become aware that sexist attitudes and behavior deprive children, both girls and boys, of the opportunity to develop to their fullest potential.
   —To help parents become aware of everyday influences, such as language, television advertising, and packaging, and how these perpetuate sexism in ourselves and our children.
   —To help parents become aware of what they can do to combat sexism in general and in the lives of their children in particular.
   —To mobilize parents to conduct letter writing campaigns against sexist advertising, packaging, and programming on television.
   —To mobilize parents to raise the issue of sexism in their local public schools.

2. Parent education programs which focus on effective parenting, e.g., P.E.T. (Parent Effectiveness Training, Gordon, 1971), and which also emphasize the effects of traditional sex roles of family members and assist participants in reshaping and expanding their own roles within the family.

3. Parent awareness/consciousness-raising programs which focus on individual awareness and growth of participants as they examine their own and other's sexist attitudes and behaviors.

4. Joint parent-child awareness and development groups which

have primarily the same focus as item 3 above, but with parent's and children participating together. For obvious reasons this kind of program is more appropriate for students in the higher grades and into high school.

Two helpful resources which contain ideas and suggestions for designing and conducting any of the above activities with parents are *A Handbook for Workshops on Sex Equality in Education* (Verheyden-Hilliard, 1976) and *Exploring Contemporary Male/Female Roles: A Facilitator's Guide* (Carney and McMahon, 1977). In addition to giving instructions for planning a workshop, the *Handbook* provides background information for workshop leaders on topics like the socialization of girls and boys, curriculum problems, athletics in educational settings, semantics, and the law. An annotated list of useful resources is also included. *The Facilitator's Guide* contains twenty-four structured experiences, four instruments—including the Bem Sex Role Inventory (BSRI) and the Attitudes Toward Women Scale (AWS), and ten short readings dealing with sex stereotyping.

5. Parent Projects. As an outcome of one of the above programs involving parents or as an initial activity involving parents, action projects which investigate various issues related to sex role stereotyping and/or plan and implement strategies for change can be enlightening as well as productive. Such an action project is described in *Sex Discrimination in an Elementary Reading Program* (Michigan Women's Commission, 1974), which is a report of the work of a group of parents and others in the Kalamazoo public schools.

Working with Other Psychological Specialists

It is important that all psychological specialists in the schools (e.g., guidance counselors, school psychologists, social workers, etc.) understand the detrimental effects of sex role stereotyping and become aware of their own sexist attitudes and behaviors in working with students, parents, and other members of the school community. The change agent counselor can assist his or her colleagues informally on a one-to-one or group basis as well as formally through providing some in-service training and education programs (see chapter 10). These other psychological specialists in the schools provide a rich resource for the change agent counselor to expand his or her consulting and change efforts through building a team of change agents and thus helping to speed up the change process.

In summary, elementary school change agent counselors with the objective of ridding the school environment of sex role stereotypic and discriminatory elements need to work primarily with other school personnel and parents in promoting and implementing change. While there is of course some individual and group counseling with students around sex role attitudes and behaviors as the need arises, the counselor's role is one of child/youth advocacy in working with the significant adults in the lives of the students.

The Proactive/ Change Agent Counselor in the Secondary School

A major focus of the proactive/change agent counselor in the junior high and high school is of course the students themselves, working directly with individual students and groups of students. Because of the students' developmental and maturation processes during these years, a questioning of traditional sex roles and a realization of expanded and changed roles for men and women are particularly helpful as the students begin to really grapple with their identity, seeking answers to the questions: Who am I? What do I want to do with my life?

Working with Students

The development of the adolescent from essentially that of a child to that of an adult is significant and complex. In search for identity and independence, the adolescent has a variety of concerns—personal, academic, and vocational—all interrelated. In helping the adolescent student identify, articulate, understand, and deal with these concerns, the proactive/change agent counselor can also help the student assess the impact traditional sex role stereotyping has had on his or her self-concept and aspirations and strive to overcome the limitations placed on them because of society's expectations for the members of their sex. In doing so, there are several frameworks which the proactive counselor can use. Three which are particularly appropriate will be discussed here: (1) value clarification, (2) decision making and problem solving, and (3) interpersonal effectiveness training.

Value Clarification Raths, Harmin, and Simon (1966) have identified seven criteria which constitute the definition of a value:

Choosing:
1. freely
2. from alternatives
3. after thoughtful consideration of the consequences of each alternative

Prizing:
4. cherishing, being happy with the choice
5. willing to affirm the choice publicly

Acting:
6. doing something with the choice
7. repeatedly, in some pattern of life.

The first three criteria rely on the student's cognitive abilities; the second two criteria emphasize emotions or feelings; and the last two criteria are concerned with behavior. In using the value clarification process with students, the counselor can be especially helpful in expanding the alternatives at the choosing stage. For example, the young woman or man whose career or occupational interests tend to follow only the traditional ones for their sex can be introduced to nontraditional ones for which they may have the ability but have just not considered. The girl at the top of her class in mathematics and science who thinks she might like to become a high school math teacher as well as a wife and mother can be encouraged to also consider atypical alternatives such as engineering and medicine, both of which can be compatible with her other values regarding marriage and family life. For these atypical alternatives to become real alternatives, however, the proactive counselor does more than just mention them in passing. The proactive counselor makes special efforts to: (a) provide the student with helpful information about the occupations and the educational and training requirements necessary, (b) put the student in touch with atypical role models, and (c) provide the student with experiences which will enable her to test out her interests and abilities. Such special efforts on the part of the counselor will assist the student in working through the prizing and acting stages of the value clarification process. A similar approach could be used with a young man whose abilities and interests are considered atypical for his sex. Sadker's (1978) instructional manual for teachers, *Being a Man: A Unit of Instructional Activities on Male Role Stereotyping,* provides many suggestions.

Decision Making and Problem Solving Along with assisting students in clarifying their values, counselors can provide assistance to junior high and high school students in an ongoing process of identifying and examining their abilities, interests, needs, and drives and using this knowledge in making some real decisions that will affect their futures. So that students don't make these decisions hastily and without much thought, instruction in the decision-making/problem-solving process is very valuable. Basically, the process consists of five steps:

1. Defining the problem to be solved or the decision to be made.
2. Diagnosing the causes of the problem or the need for the decision.
3. Identifying and formulating alternatives.
4. Selecting and implementing the best alternative.
5. Evaluating the outcome or results of the decision.

As with the value clarification process, the proactive/change agent counselor wishing to assist students in breaking out of traditional sex roles and expanding their options can be most helpful. At steps one and two, the counselor can assist the student in asking and finding answers to questions such as: To what extent is my problem due to my sex and what I, my parents, or society in general, feels is appropriate? At step three, the most valuable assistance a counselor can give is to broaden the alternatives by asking such questions as: If you were a member of the opposite sex, what other alternatives would you have? At steps four and five, the counselor can give the student assistance and support in choosing the best alternative for the individual regardless of his or her sex, and in evaluating the decision as it relates to the student's long-range goals. If the student's decision is considered atypical for his or her sex, the counselor can be helpful in providing support and assisting the student in acting on the decision. This may mean working with the parents of the student and the school environment to enable the student to follow through on his or her decision.

Throughout the decision-making/problem-solving process, the student is provided with as much information as possible. If the decision is career related, for example, educational and training requirements are pointed out along with a plan for achieving them. Job market prospects are discussed. And, again, if the career decision is atypical for the student's sex, the advantages, disadvantages, potential discrimination problems, and the like are frankly discussed.

Hansen (1974) describes a career development curriculum to be used by counselors and teachers in implementing career education programs. A special portion of the career development curriculum is concerned primarily with women's development; a parallel portion could easily be developed to deal with special concerns of men as well. While the curriculum model is designed for all educational levels, from kindergarten through grade twelve, only the objectives of grades ten through twelve are presented here to show how the decision-making process is an integral part of the curriculum.

Objectives for Career Development
Relating to Emerging Life Patterns of Women
(Senior High Years, 10–12)

1. *Reality Testing of a Self-Concept*
   Describes the social roles and social demands one must fulfill for successful performance in preferred occupation(s).
   > Describes the multiple roles one may fill and ways in which they affect and may be affected by occupational preferences.

2. *Awareness of Preferred Life Style*
   Makes explicit one's own life style needs and priorities at this point in time.
   > Identifies several life patterns which might be followed by women.

   > Discusses the significance of each in regard to the personal development and family life of a woman.

   > Identifies from a variety of life styles those which seem most compatible with personal characteristics and needs.

   > Projects consequences of preferred life style on family, leisure, significant others.

3. *Reformulation of Tentative Career Goals*
   Studies and projects a career plan that will enable one to pursue an occupation which will fulfill the personal needs and values one considers most important.
   > Describes power and authority relationships characteristic of preferred work setting and occupation.

   > Identifies three work environments compatible with his or her needs.

4. *Increasing Knowledge of and Experience in Work Settings and Occupations*
   Describes work as a principal instrument for coping with and changing one's own environment.
   > Cites examples of change within the modern work society which have affected the traditional division of labor by sex.

   > Identifies discriminatory practices in the work environment which one might help to change.

   > Describes women's changing roles in the labor force.

Lists five career-family or life style patterns open to men and women.

Examines labor force data on women and men in different occupations.

Describes how the work contribution of woman is as socially significant as that of man.

Participates in and observes situations in which women are found in roles other than traditional ones.

Gathers information concerning vocational opportunities for women in various areas of work.

5. *Clarification of the Decision-making Process as Related to Self*
Describes the factors which may influence one's career decisions.

Identifies alternatives and possible outcomes of each.

Projects the potential satisfactions of preferred occupations in relation to priority values and needs.

Identifies alternate occupations if first preferences do not work out.

6. *Commitment with Tentativeness within a Changing World*
Identifies the possible sources of the attitudes toward women held by the individual and the society in which he or she lives.

Reads and discusses relevant literature dealing with women, their traditional roles, and their place in the world of work.

Discovers elements within our culture which have contributed to the continuance of the traditional view of women.

Investigates the opinions that contemporary women hold of themselves and their place in the world of work.

Identifies the changing meanings of work over time and between cultures.

Examines different career patterns of women and men and their potential effect on family patterns and life styles.

Compares work ethic at the turn of the century with contemporary work ethic(s).

Identifies the changing meanings of work in one's life in relation to other values.

Examines the extent to which one accepts the work values and career patterns of the predominant culture.

Describes the ways in which changing work and leisure values may bring about career shifts in adults.

Interpersonal Effectiveness   The junior high and high school years are especially important for individual students in learning about themselves and the way they relate to and are perceived by others. The peer group is particularly important to the individual during adolescence, and most students strive to be accepted by their peers—first by those of the same sex and then later on by those of the opposite sex. In helping students answer the questions, Who am I? How do I view myself? How do others view me? How can I be more effective in communicating with and relating to others?, the proactive/change agent counselor can help young people challenge traditional sex role stereotypes and begin to explore new ways of relating to members of the same and opposite sex. While the author believes that such learning can occur more effectively in groups (see discussion below), counselors can work individually with students to help them communicate more effectively (e.g., developing listening, attending, and self-exploration skills) with others and to develop self-awareness of others that is nonstereotypic of traditional sex roles. The counselor can help the student work through such questions as: Would your attitudes or behaviors be different if you were a member of the opposite sex? What sex role stereotypic behaviors facilitate or inhibit effective communication and human relations? Do you make assumptions about people based on their sex? Do you respond to members of the opposite sex differently than you do to those of your same sex?

Working With Groups of Students   Much of what a proactive/change agent counselor does to assist students in developing an awareness of sex role stereotyping and expanding or redefining traditional sex roles for themselves can be more effectively done with groups of students than with individuals. In addition to the efficiency factor of reaching more students in the same amount of time, the group provides some dynamics which are not possible in a one-to-one helping relationship. In a group setting, students realize that they are not the only one with a given problem or concern. They feel support in knowing others are experiencing the same things. In addition, the group provides a setting in which to experiment and try out new behaviors. And the group provides a rich resource of varying opinions, attitudes, and suggestions.

The use of "strength groups" or "growth groups," as they are sometimes called, in which students are given assistance in focusing on their potentials and developing action plans for becoming the person they would like to be, can be very potent experiences for students as they become aware of their own and others' sexist attitudes. Such consciousness-raising, growth-producing groups can be either single-sex or coed, depending on the age of the students and the central focus or purpose of the group training. Generally, students are more comfortable starting out in a single-sex group and then perhaps later moving into a coeducational group. The proactive counselor will need to carefully assess the readiness of the students to deal with particular issues and problems and determine the sex makeup of the group in order to provide the optimum environment for learning and growth.

Working more directly with the students in the secondary schools than with elementary students around sex role stereotyping and the changing roles of men and women does not mean that the proactive/change agent counselor in the junior high and high school works any less with teachers, parents, administrators, and other school personnel to promote change in the school environment.

Working with School Personnel   What has been discussed previously regarding the role of the elementary school change agent counselor in working with teachers, librarians, school policy makers, parents, and other counselors also applies to the proactive/change agent counselor in the junior high and high school and thus will not be repeated here. (The reader is referred to the section of this chapter which discusses the proactive/change agent counselor in the elementary school.) However, there are some additional activities and change efforts particularly applicable to secondary schools which deserve attention.

Curriculum Consultant Because of flexible scheduling in many secondary schools, the counselor's role as curriculum consultant is of special import in not only helping weed out sexist elements such as discriminating content in existing courses and teaching materials, and single-sex home economics and industrial arts courses, but in assisting the development of new courses and educational programs. Some new courses and programs which could be especially beneficial are in the area of women's studies. While women's studies courses were first developed on college and university campuses, (also see discussion of women's studies and men's studies courses and programs in the section of this chapter dealing with colleges and universities), many junior high and high schools are offering women's studies courses in an effort to compensate for the omission of women from the curriculum and bring some balance to what has been viewed by many as a male-centered and male-biased curriculum. Other related goals of such women's studies courses are to recover the lost or neglected history and culture of women of all classes, nationalities, and race and to raise the consciousness of students about the sexist curriculum and sexism in the larger society. A book containing syllabi and outlines of several such courses is *High School Feminist Studies* (Ahlum and Fralley, 1976). The courses are grouped into three categories: history, literature, and interdisciplinary. "The history courses illustrate new directions among scholars in women's history: the need to reperiodize history (beyond wars and revolutions); the use of autobiography as an important source, especially for the lives of women; and the inclusion of class and race as additional key factors in describing the history of women. Similarly, the literature courses include a variety of women writers not ordinarily to be found on high school reading lists: Zora Neale Hurston, Edith Wharton, Alice Childress, Charlotte Perkins Gilman, Margaret Walker, Kate Chopin, Agnes Smedley, Susan Glaspell, Sylvia Plath, Doris Lessing, just to name a few." The interdisciplinary courses resemble college courses on the sociology of women and sex roles. It might be said that all the women's studies courses are interdisciplinary by their very nature since they "must begin by convincing students of their *raison d'etre.*" For example, a history or literature course may begin with a consciousness-raising unit on women's roles or status, or lesson on the nature of prejudice, or an analysis of sex bias in textbooks. Some of the course titles included in the collection are "Women in American History," "History or Herstory: Changing Roles of the American Woman," "Woman and Man in Literature," "Woman and Work," "Female-Male Roles: Interdisciplinary Social Studies Course."

Other new courses and programs counselors can assist teachers in developing are in the areas of career and vocational exploration and development, personal decision making and problem solving, contemporary values and life styles, and human relations and interpersonal skills. Such courses and programs would be designed to assist the student in exploring who they are, what they want their lives to be like, and how they can get there—all in the context of expanding and changing roles for both men and women in an effort to remove limitations and constraints based on traditional sex roles.

A number of packaged materials, audio-visual aids, and teaching guides are available for counselors and teachers wishing to design and offer such programs and courses. Those that do not address sex role issues directly can be easily adjusted to do so. Particularly useful for the junior high level are the College Entrance Examination Board units entitled *Deciding* (Varenhorst, Gelatt, & Carey, 1972) and the Life Career Game (Varenhorst, 1969). The filmstrip "Jobs and Gender" (Guidance Associates, Inc., 1971) is useful in stimulating class discussions on careers for men and women. Lesson outlines on the subject of the changing roles of men and women are provided in *Today's Changing Roles: An Approach to Nonsexist Teaching* (Resource Center on Sex Roles in Education, the National Foundation for the Improvement of Education, 1974) and *Undoing Sex Stereotypes* (Guttentag and Bray, 1976). Many decision-making, problem-solving, human relations, and interpersonal behavior activities and simulation games for all age groups are in Johnson's (1972) *Reaching Out,* Johnson & Johnson's (1975) *Joining Together* and Pfeiffer and Jones' (1972–1977) *Annual Handbook for Group Facilitators.* Value clarification exercises, workshops, and classes are outlined in Kirschenbaum's (1977) *Advanced Value Clarification,* Smith's (1976) *A Practical Guide to Value Clarification,* and Simon and Clark's (1975) *More Values Clarification.* Structured group experiences dealing with sex roles are provided in *Exploring Contemporary Male/Female Roles: A Facilitator's Guide* (Carney and McMahon, 1977).

In addition to such special courses and programs, the change agent counselor works with teachers and administrators to ensure that the curriculum has the necessary flexibility to allow apprenticeship experiences for students to try out tentative occupational and career preferences with on-the-job role models. Where students' expressed vocational and career interests are nontraditional for their sex, e.g., a male student interested in nursing or a female student interested in engineering, special effort is made to match these students with role models of their same sex.

Behavioral/Organizational Consultant Just as the elementary school change agent counselor assists teachers and other school personnel in becoming aware of the general issue of sex role stereotyping and its detrimental effects and recognizing their own stereotypic attitudes and behaviors, so does the change agent counselor in the secondary schools. (To avoid repetition here, see earlier sections on the counselor in the elementary school, much of which is equally applicable to the junior high and high school settings.) Observing behavior in the classroom, during faculty and staff meetings, and during informal get togethers can provide the proactive counselor with enough information to know where to begin his or her change efforts. For example, a sexist comment by a teacher that "Sally, like most girls, is having difficulty with algebra,'' provides an opening for the counselor to not only approach the teacher about Sally's academic performance but to begin an exploration with the teacher of his or her attitudes regarding female students. On a school-wide basis, a topic of concern for counselors, teachers, administrators, students, and parents might be the large discrepancy between the numbers of males and females who take the full range of math courses. The proactive counselor can help others become aware of the need for concern with this discrepancy by pointing out that young women who avoid math in high school limit their choice of career not only in science and technology, but also in business, banking, and accounting. In addition, in contemporary American society the lack of training in basic computation and the use of numbers and symbols can adversely affect one's self-image and self-esteem. Since anxieties regarding math may be causing girls' (and some boys') disinterest in mathematics courses and hampering their development of mathematical ability, the proactive counselor can work with teachers to develop programs to reduce these anxieties. Such a program has been developed by Tobias (1977). Entitled the "Mathematics Anxiety Clinic," the program employs techniques of desensitization, immersion, and psychological support. Counselors can also work with teachers to make math instruction more comprehensible and more closely related to the specific tasks performed in occupations requiring math.

Another example of an opportunity for a proactive/change agent counselor to intervene: learning that another counselor still uses the Women's Form of the Strong Vocational Interest Blank for all female students provides an opportunity for the proactive counselor to inquire if the counselor is aware of the new neuter form of the Strong and offer to share materials and information. Needless to say, to be successful such an approach must be made very carefully and tactfully, keeping in mind the sensitivities of the other professional. The change agent counselor must remember, after all, that the acceptance of consultative assistance must be voluntary.

Organizationally, secondary schools are in a way a microcosm of the stereotyping that exists in the larger society and in the world of work. That is, generally speaking, men dominate the decision-making positions (administrators); women dominate the support services (secretaries, cooks, etc.); and the instructional staff consists of both men and women but in fields that are historically traditional for their sex (e.g., women teaching home economics, girls physical education, and literature, and men teaching science, mathematics, and industrial arts). Thus, more often than not, the schools provide students with only traditional stereotypic role models. In addition, male and female students and staff may be treated differently on the basis of sex either because of school policy or traditional practice (see chap. 3). As an organizational/environmental agent of change, the counselor can be especially effective in working with the school policy makers to implement Title IX of the Educational Amendments of 1972 (see chap. 5 and the discussion on institutional self-evaluation in the section below on colleges and universities.) In doing so, however, a great deal of groundwork needs to be done with the counselor's power bases (as mentioned earlier in connection with Aubrey's ideas)—teachers and parents. Added to these two power bases are the students, a power base in the secondary schools. Each of these groups needs to be educated about the detrimental effects of sex role stereotyping and the requirements of Title IX, and dialogues begun between the groups. This is the job of the change agent counselor, while simultaneously working with the administration to establish a procedure to review all school policies, practices, and programs related to both education and employment and make recommendations for change. Representatives from all major interest groups in the school community—teachers, parents, students, administrators—should be involved in this review and recommendation process. Generally speaking, the greater the involvement of those persons affected, the greater their acceptance of change.

Working with Parents

The need for school counselors to work with parents as they assist the growth and development of students does not lessen at the secondary level, although the involvement of the parents is different than it was at the elementary level. This difference is marked by the increasing responsibility on the part of the student for determining her/his own future, with the support and assistance of the adults around him/her.

As at the elementary level (see earlier discussion) the proactive change agent counselor at the secondary level works with parents in a variety of ways, e.g., special parent education programs, information sessions to gain their collective support for changes in school policies, practices, and programs, and the like. Of prime importance is the work the proactive counselor does with parents and students together—as a form of family counseling seeing that the student has the necessary support and understanding at home to assist him or her in making the best decisions and plans for the future—decisions and plans based on the student's abilities and interests, not on his or her sex.

The academic and nonacademic components of the educational process in colleges and universities have traditionally been even more separate and distinct than at the elementary and secondary levels. College counselors on most campuses are organizationally and physically isolated from the teaching faculty and the institutional policy makers. And yet the personal and academic development of students cannot be viewed and assisted separately because the two are so interrelated. Thus, it is imperative that the college and university environment facilitate the development of the whole person, and the efforts of those involved in the shaping of the environment must be orchestrated. Change agent counselors with the knowledge and skills discussed at the beginning of this chapter are the logical ones to orchestrate such efforts. The proactive/change agent counselor wishing to rid the college environment of sexism and differential treatment of students on the basis of sex must assume such a responsibility if any impact is to be made beyond what occurs in the individual counselor's office. The proactive counselor who assumes such responsibility would be consistent with three relatively new frameworks or approaches to the college counselor working with the environment to implement change: milieu management, community counseling, and the student development approach.

The first of these, milieu management, is explained by Crookston (1975) as:

> . . . the systematic coordination and integration of the total campus environment—the organizations, the structures, the space, the function, the people, and the relationships of each to all the others and to the whole—toward growth and development as a democratic community. In furtherance of human development theory, the relationship of the whole milieu with all its parts and vice versa must be symbiotic, or mutually enhancing or growth producing. Thus, as the individual and the group contribute to the total community they give the community the capacity to create the conditions that contribute to the enhancement of the individual and the group. This symbiotic relationship of the individual to the community is the classical definition of democracy.

Obviously, the proactive counselor who is not also employed in an administrative capacity does not have managerial responsibilities as part of his/her ordinary job functions, but this does not keep the proactive counselor from endeavoring to impact the administrative structure by working with students, faculty members, administrators, and others in the institutional community and developing cooperative efforts to promote change.

The community counseling concept (Lewis & Lewis, 1977) also stresses the involvement of the counselor with the client's environment. The five basic assumptions which guide the work of community counselors are:

1. In the Community Can Be Found the Keys to Both Cause and Cure.

   Community counselors recognize that individuals constantly interact with their surroundings. This interaction can be helpful *or* harmful. As individuals grow and develop, they use the environment as a source of learning and as a source of support. Their personal and physical needs are met through their interactions with others. But the environment can also serve as a negative force, stunting growth and limiting development.

2. A Multifaceted Approach is More Efficient than a Single Service Approach.

   A multifaceted approach to helping is one that has many sides. The community counselor uses a number of different methods to deliver services to people, and never relies on just one type of approach.

   Traditionally, many helpers have depended on direct, one-to-one relationships for helping individuals. More and more, this model is being called into question.

3. A Developmental or Preventive Approach is More Efficient than a Remedial Approach.

   Prevention aims to eliminate a specific problem or group of problems, or at least to keep a difficulty from becoming prevalent. "The intent is to anticipate future problems and move to prevent them by providing individuals or groups with needed skills or by creating changes in the environment so as to prevent the development of problems" (Morrill et al., 1974).

   Developmental programs help healthy individuals to be even more effective in their everyday lives. "Development has the primary focus of promoting positive growth for all, not only for those identified as having or about to have problems" (Morrill et al., 1974, p. 357).

4. The Community Counseling Approach is Applicable to any Institutional or Agency Setting.

   Any person offering psychological, social, educational, or vocational services to individuals or groups has a responsibility to some community. This fact is obvious to a worker in a community mental health center, who deals with a geographically defined "catchment area" and who has a clear mandate to identify community needs. It is less obvious in situations where "community involvement" is not a required aspect of the job, or where the nature of the community is not well defined. Counselors in educational settings, for instance, can be "community counselors" if their orientation is toward a recognition of the interplay between the individual and the environment.

5. Human Service Needs to Override the Traditional Boundaries Between Professions.

Community members cannot receive all of the services that they need if helpers limit their practices to the programs and skills that have traditionally formed their professional identities. There will always be gaps in service delivery if the helping professions continue to perpetuate accustomed roles and functions at the expense of new programs to meet emerging community needs.

Many of the principles or assumptions which are central to the milieu management and community counseling concepts also form the basis of the student development approach. Miller and Prince (1976) outline the principles which provide the foundation for the student development approach:

—Human development is a continuous and cumulative process of physical, psychological, and social growth which can be divided into an orderly series of life stages. Each stage is characterized by certain developmental tasks that require the human to alter his or her present behavior and master new learning.

—Development is most likely to occur in an environment where change is anticipated, where individuals and groups work together to actively influence the future rather than just reacting to it after the fact.

—Systematic integration of cognitive, affective, and psychomotor experiences produces the most effective development.

—Several abilities and skills that facilitate growth in others have been identified; these can be learned, used, and taught by student development educators.

—The individual's development can be advanced by exposure to an organized problem-solving process that enables him or her to complete increasingly complex developmental tasks.

—Development is enhanced when students, faculty members, and student affairs practitioners work collaboratively to promote the continuous development of all.

Milieu management, community counseling, and the student development approach all focus on the development of the whole student as a task of the entire college community through cooperative and integrative efforts of all persons involved. Operating from one or a combination of all three of these frameworks is useful to the proactive/change agent counselor focusing on eliminating sexist elements from the college or university environment. Below are some suggested change agent activities for the proactive college counselor whose actions are consistent with the philosophy espoused by milieu management, community counseling, and the student development approach.

Impacting Institutional Policies, Practices, and Programs

Institutional Self-Evaluation Every educational institution or agency that receives federal funds must comply with Title IX of the Education Amendments of 1972 and prohibit discrimination on the basis of sex in all programs and activities including student admissions and recruitment, student programs, and employment (see chap. 5 for a detailed discussion). One of the first requirements of Title IX is an institutional self-evaluation to assess institutional policies and practices for compliance with regulation requirements and to modify them where necessary to ensure equity. The proactive/change agent counselor, knowledgeable about Title IX, will want to be involved in the institutional self-evaluation in some capacity, including one or more of the following activities:

1. Volunteer to serve on the institutional self-evaluation task force committee if your college or university has one.
2. Provide the persons responsible for the institutional self-evaluation with helpful information regarding examples of sexism and equality that you know exist on campus. At minimum would be information about the counseling students receive—instruments and materials used, programs and services offered, awareness and attitudes of counselors regarding sex role stereotyping, etc. Also appropriate would be the sharing of information the counselor has learned through others, e.g., students, faculty members, other colleagues, while keeping the source of the information confidential. Such information might include examples of sexist attitudes and behaviors of faculty members in the classroom, sexist texts and teaching materials presently being used, unequal access to educational (both curricular and noncurricular) programs and activities, unfair treatment in employment matters, and the like.

3. If an institutional self-evaluation has already been completed, ask to review it and offer suggested changes and additions which you feel would be appropriate. If an institutional self-evaluation has not been completed and is not planned for the future, suggest to the appropriate administrator, e.g., president, vice president, or affirmative action/equal employment opportunity officer, that one be started immediately. Offer to give whatever assistance you can.

In addition to being involved with an institution's Title IX self-evaluation, the proactive counselor can work on other fronts for institutional change regarding sexism. Some of these are:

1. Become a voting member of major governing bodies of the college or university. Once a member, work for changes of institutional policies, practices, and programs which contribute to differential treatment of men and women. Examples: special recruitment program for attracting male and female students into atypical fields of study for their sex, e.g., men into nursing, women into engineering; fair child care and maternity/paternity benefits for students and staff, treating maternity leave as any other sick or disability leave, and allowing fathers, as well as mothers, the flexibility in their work and study schedules to participate in the child rearing process.

2. Serve on advisory committees and grievance procedure panels dealing with human rights. Most colleges and universities have human rights committees, councils on the status of women, and grievance panels which are concerned with equality of treatment for all individuals within the university or college community. Recommendations given and actions taken by these bodies can have considerable influence on institutional policies and practices. If your institution does not have such bodies, suggest that they be formed, and offer assistance.

3. Offer to serve in a consultant capacity to individual or groups of faculty members and administrators in assessing classroom behaviors, educational programs, and administrative policies, practices, and procedures for sexist and nonsexist elements. As has been said in earlier sections of this chapter, this type of activity requires unusual sensitivity and skill. The persons and/or groups most needing assistance in recognizing and eliminating sexist attitudes and behaviors are generally the ones least likely to ask for it. Therefore, it is important for the change agent

counselor to start with a few willing participants, slowly gaining their respect, and establishing a reputation of a competent helper in this area. If effective and successful, the change agent counselor will gradually be sought out to consult with departments, programs, and offices throughout the institution.

4. Design and implement special workshops and programs for faculty and administrators (see chap. 10, In-Service Training Programs That Work). Workshops and programs on topics such as the following are particularly appropriate: (a) the limiting effects of sex stereotyping, (b) sex discrimination in higher education, (c) sex discrimination and the law, and (d) changes an institution can make to provide equal opportunity. Backup information for such programs and workshops is provided in Section I of this book. A helpful guide in planning such activities is *A Handbook for Workshops on Sex Equality in Education* (Verheyden-Hilliard, 1976). The handbook contains information, resources, models, and activities used by the American Personnel and Guidance Association's Sex Equality in Guidance Opportunities (SEGO) Project staff in the designing, organizing, and running over 300 workshops throughout the nation on sex equality in education. Specific steps for planning a workshop and suggested time frames for each activity are also provided.

5. Encourage and support through active involvement and contribution those institution-wide programs which have as a major focus (a) the study of traditional and changing sex roles and the implications for the individual, the institution, and society, and/or (b) the active involvement in efforts to change the status quo in order that both women and men may have a broader range of opportunities and choices. Three such institution-wide programs are discussed below. With the exception of some women's centers, men are welcome as full participants with the recognition that as the woman's role changes so must the man's.

Women's Studies Programs   Sometimes called the "educational arm of the women's movement," women's studies is but one of several names for a national effort to develop interdisciplinary approaches to study the history, culture, and status of women. Other titles include feminist studies, female studies, sex role studies, gender studies, and studies in masculinity and feminity. But whatever the title of the program, women's studies courses, as part of the Feminist

Movement, have two major functions: (1) to discover and provide new information on the history, culture, and accomplishments of women, and (2) to help women and men examine alternative ways of looking at their roles in society and the assumptions of our culture (Howard, 1975). Compatible with these functions are three tasks which Howe (1975) feels women's studies should accomplish: (1) the development of courses and teaching strategies aimed at adding new knowledge and changing the consciousness of women and men, (2) the addition of new areas of knowledge and new research developments in such fields as sex role socialization and gender identity, and (3) to change the male-centered college curriculum.

The growth of women's studies courses has been remarkable during the last eight to nine years—from approximately 50 in late 1969 to over 15,000 today. Initially, about 10 percent of the students and faculty were male. While there is no current estimate on the numbers of male teachers, approximately 20 percent of the students are now male. Courses have developed in almost every area of study with the bulk of them in literature, history, and sociology or interdisciplinary combinations of these. From the beginning instructors of women's studies courses have shared their syllabi and bibliographies through a unique series of monographs entitled *Female Studies,* published first by KNOW, Inc. and more recently by the Feminist Press (Howe, 1970; Ahlum and Howe, 1971, 1972; Miller, et al., 1973; Rosenfelt, 1973). These course descriptions and materials are very useful to individuals developing women's studies courses and workshops. For a full description of women's studies courses and programs, see Howe and Ahlum's (1973) "Women's Studies and Social Change," and Howe's (1977) *Seven Years Later: Women's Studies Programs in 1976.*

Another indicator of the growth of women's studies is the birth of new journals to accommodate the rapid growth of scholarship. Such journals include *Feminist Studies, Women's Studies: An Interdisciplinary Journal, Signs: Journal of Women in Culture and Society, Sex Roles: A Journal of Research, The Psychology of Women Quarterly,* and the University of Michigan *Papers in Women's Studies.* In addition, *Women Studies Abstracts* provides annotated bibliography four times a year.

Feminists who teach women's studies courses are concerned not only with curriculum but with pedagogy. Student participation and student responsibility—for reports, project presentations, and the like—are stressed. Even in large classes where some lectures are necessary, the students are divided into small groups for discussions, sometimes deliberately designed for consciousness-raising experiences. The trend is to substitute, wherever possible, group processes and cooperative projects for authoritarian techniques and individual competition which are so often a part of academe. "None of this is surprising, given the emphasis in the women's movement on sisterhood, antielitism, leaderless consciousness-raising groups, and the power of collective decision-making activity. What is surprising is the speed with which the movement's priorities and principles have been extended into the classroom" (Howe and Ahlum, 1973).

Of particular concern to the proactive counselor looking for ways to impact the entire educational process and interrupt the perpetuation of sex role stereotyping in the schools would be the inclusion of women's studies courses in the educational and preparational programs of school personnel. Suggestions for curricular changes in graduate counselor education programs are contained in chapter 9. A useful handbook of women's studies course materials for teacher educators is Howard's (1975) *Liberating Our Children, Ourselves*. Provided in this one small volume are a course outline, objectives, syllabi, readings, and suggested learning projects for a women's studies course in teacher education programs.

Women's Centers   Women's centers, like women's studies programs, have become increasingly common on campuses throughout the nation. Also like women's studies programs, the degree of diversity among the centers is striking as each center strives to meet the needs of women at a particular campus and/or community setting. Some centers are highly academic with close ties to a women's studies program; others are more concerned with political or social change. Some focus on serving older students, faculty, staff, or community women, while the primary target for others is the typical eighteen-twenty-two-year-old undergraduate woman. Women's center activities vary from individual and group counseling, to women's studies and continuing education classes, to child care centers, to temporary half-way houses, to information centers, to centers of political action. The common link among all women's centers is that each is attempting in some way to provide services specifically for women. The Project on the Status and Education of Women (1975) of the Association of American Colleges keeps an updated listing of all women's centers and their addresses.

Men's Studies Programs and Men's Centers   While not as widely spread or accepted as women's studies courses and programs, men's studies courses are appearing on some campuses. The focus of men's studies courses is generally the American male stereotype which can be just as confining as the female stereotype. Other common topics include men's responses to the changing role and consciousness of women, liberated sexual identity, the male and parenting, and the like. A listing of reading materials often used in these courses is in the *Men's Studies Bibliography* (1977) made available through the Human Studies Collection, MIT Humanities Library. The bibliography contains approximately 1,100 citations. Also included is a list of books providing an overview of the current research in men's studies.

Like men's studies programs, men's centers are beginning to be organized on a few college and university campuses. Most of these centers serve as information centers and a place where men wishing to explore nontraditional roles can form support groups and consciousness-raising groups.

Adult and Continuing Education Programs   While continuing education programs have been a part of the educational offerings of institutions of higher education for many years, they have been characterized by a recent surge of growth—particularly in programs for women. While there is no recent up-to-date count, in 1971 there were over 450 colleges and universities with some type of special programming for women (Women's Bureau, 1974).

Some of the special features of continuing education programs which have been particularly attractive to mature women students are: part-time enrollment, removal of age or other admissions restrictions, limited residence requirements, relaxation of time requirements for degrees, liberal acceptance of course credits, credit by examination, credit for volunteer experience, flexible course hours, short-term courses, refresher and reorientation courses, curricula geared to adult experiences, counseling services for the mature student, child care facilities, and job placement assistance.

Tailored to the special needs and interests of the adult students—of which 55 to 60 percent are women—the particular focus of these programs varies from campus to campus. Many of them, however, offer courses or learning experiences which deal with contemporary issues related to work, education, family, marriage, and community relationships. An increasing number of the programs are offering courses in the psychology and sociology of women and special training experiences which reflect local and national labor market demands.

As part of or in addition to continuing education programs, many institutions of higher education are offering nontraditional educational opportunities such as "external degrees," "university without walls," or "the open university." These relatively new approaches to education include few if any conventional on-campus courses and instead utilize such teaching innovations as television, newspaper and correspondence courses, learning centers located throughout the community, apprenticeships and supervised work experiences, and development of study "contracts" between institution and student (Freeman, 1971). These more flexible methods of learning can extend educational opportunities to many women and men who cannot, for a variety of reasons, conform to rigid classroom or residential requirements.

The involvement of the proactive/change agent counselor in campus-wide programs such as women's studies and continuing education can take a variety of forms from actually teaching courses and counseling students, to acting as a consultant and making suggestions for program content and administrative concerns dealing with matters such as program access, support services, and the like.

Nonsexist Counseling for College Students

Sexist counselor behavior is defined by Randolph and Zimmerman (1974) as "any behavior on the part of the counselor which only encourages the expression of feelings, thoughts, attitudes, and behavior on the part of the client in line with traditional sex role stereotypes and actively discourages non-sex role feelings, thoughts, attitudes, and behaviors. Sexist counselor behavior may be overt or covert—that is, outright verbal behavior which indicates approval or disapproval or non-verbal bodily cues which give the same message." Sexist counseling also includes the use of sex biased instruments and materials, without pointing out the biases and shortcomings to the client and suggesting nonbiased alternatives. Nonsexist counseling, on the other hand, involves helping individuals strive toward the full development of their potential, not simply adjustment to societal norms. It involves using standards of psychological health that are equal for men and women (see chap. 6). In counseling women, counselors are supportive of achievement, intelligence, strength, and assertiveness as well as tenderness, sensitivity, and the expression of emotions. In counseling men, counselors are supportive of the expression of feelings and emotions, sensitivity to others, tenderness, and the like, as well as strength, assertiveness, achievement, and intelligence. Women are helped to view themselves as important in their own right rather than simply their part in a male-female relationship. They are encouraged to develop their abilities and talents and to use them for further self-development and satisfaction as well as a contribution to others, to society. Men are helped to view the women in their lives as equals and to be supportive of their efforts of self-development and achievement. Both men and women are encouraged to select a life style that is appropriate for them, one that will allow them to maximize their potential. Marriage and children are not expected goals of women any more than they are of men. Rather both men and women are allowed to choose freely from many options—remain single and work; marry and work and not have children; marry and work and have children; marry and have children and not work; marry and have children and then return to work; or live with "significant other" with or without children and work or not work. Both men and women are helped to realize that sexual enjoyment and choice is as much the right of women as it is of men.

In working with male and female clients to dispel sex role stereotypes and to facilitate the full development of each individual, the nonsexist counselor will often work with groups. This is not to say that one-to-one counseling is not done with clients who prefer it or who have a problem, such as severe emotional disturbance, which may be more effectively handled in individual counseling. However, one-to-one counseling clients may also benefit by participating in specially selected and structured groups, either following or concurrent with their individual counseling. Group counseling can be significantly more beneficial than individual counseling in meeting counseling goals, especially those related to sex role stereotypes. When the problem being worked on is shared, group members serve as models, reinforcing each other, and facilitating the problem-solving process (Krumboltz and Thoresen, 1969). Many clients of the nonsexist change agent counselor on the college or university campus share common problems and concerns. Some of these common problems and concerns center around personal effectiveness and the ability to establish meaningful relationships with members of the opposite and same sex, educational and career plans and goals, personal life style including such things as sexuality, work and leisure, role conflicts, and the like.

Working with groups of students who share a common problem or concern has some advantages over one-to-one counseling. An obvious advantage of course is that far more students can receive assistance—not a minor point in this age of accountability and diminishing funds. Another advantage is that the group participants learn from each other; they find they are not the only ones with a particular problem, and some group members' solutions may serve as models for others as they learn new attitudes, information, and skills.

The change agent counselor wishing to help others rid themselves of traditional stereotypic attitudes and behaviors and redefine their own roles—developing their potential to the fullest and expanding their opportunities—will select the participants for such group activities very carefully. Almost always the initial groups will be more effective if they are single sex. Since the "other sex" is oftentimes perceived as the problem, it is necessary for the group members to experience the support and commonalities of their own sex before confronting and relating to members of the opposite sex in the group setting. But too many group counseling programs end here. Sex roles cannot undergo effective change if women and men continue to work on the problem separately. Eventually, it is necessary that the sexes work together for mutual liberation and expansion of roles. Thus, well-designed groups that are first single sex and then coeducational, with flexibility to regroup or subgroup again when the need arises, can be most beneficial. In addition to considering the sex of the participants, counselors can design group experiences tailored for special groups such as single, divorced, widowed, married, typical college age (eighteen–twenty-two years old), older, and reentry students. The commonalities shared by each of these groups provide rich resources for mutual helping and learning.

While it is not my intent to list or outline all the various types of groups and group activities which the change agent counselor can use in helping individuals redefine and expand their roles, a few will be discussed here because of their centrality to our topic, their broad applicability, and their usefulness. More research is needed to determine their success—whether or not they actually change behavior of the participants. The types of groups and group activities discussed here can be categorized into two umbrella terms: (1) personal effectiveness and (2) decision making.

Personal Effectiveness Groups Some of the personal effectiveness groups frequently used on college campuses today are laboratory training, or "T" groups or sensitivity training groups as they are more commonly known (where participants develop interaction skills, giving each other feedback in the "here-and-now" and trying out new behaviors); encounter groups (where participants are assisted in experiencing themselves and others wholly); developmental group counseling (which assists participants in dealing with independence and maturity tasks and issues); human potential groups (which use structured exercises to increase empathy toward others, self-assurance, and self-motivation); contract groups (where individual participants and the group as a whole set specific objectives for behavioral learning); leaderless groups (which generally follow structured exercises to increase interpersonal effectiveness); consciousness-raising groups, sometimes called support or strength groups, (where individuals are encouraged to share the facts of their own lives and to challenge the societal norms that helped form them); and assertive training groups (where individuals learn to stand up for their legitimate rights without violating the rights of others). This list is not offered as a definitive one, as there are new types of personal effectiveness groups being developed all the time, nor should the types of groups be viewed as mutually exclusive since they all are meant to provide individuals with growth-producing experiences in personal and interpersonal skills and in doing so may employ similar techniques and methodologies.

Two of these personal effectiveness groups—consciousness-raising and assertive training—merit special mention because of their frequent use in assisting individuals in challenging and changing sex role stereotypic attitudes and behaviors.

1. Consciousness-raising groups

According to Mitchell (1971), "The concept of 'consciousness-raising' is the reinterpretation of a Chinese revolutionary practice of 'speaking bitterness' . . . Like Chinese peasants who took a step out of thinking their fate was natural by describing the conditions of their lives to each other, middle class women in the U.S. brought the facts of their own lives to the surface . . . The first symptoms of oppression is the repression of words; the state of suffering is so total and so assumed that it is not known to be there." "Speaking bitterness" or unhappy truths brings the barely conscious to consciousness. When the process occurs in a small group, "one person's realization of an injustice brings to mind other injustices for the whole group." Once a basic teaching tool of the women's movement used to facilitate women learning not only about the sexual politics of their own lives but about the potential power of "sisterhood," consciousness-raising groups can be used by a skilled change agent counselor to bring about the participants' awareness of the detriments and stifling nature of traditional sex role stereotyping. Few "rules" govern a consciousness-raising group, but a basic one is an atmosphere of supportive acceptance of all group members, regardless of their problems, experiences, ideas, or values. Thus, direct criticisms of another member's statement, dependence on outside authorities, and deference to or domination of the group or any of its members is not sanctioned. Once awareness or consciousness of harmful effects of sex stereotyping is achieved, the group can then be guided into any of the personal effectiveness groups mentioned above. For example, the group members may wish to form a contract group in which each member sets a specific personal objective (e.g., developing independence, assertive behavior, confrontation or empathy skills) and also a collective group objective on the types of assistance the group participants will try to provide each other.

Consciousness-raising groups are not just for women. As Farrell (1974) states:

Men's involvement in breaking out of the strait jacket of sex roles is essential because of the way it confines men at the same time as it confines women. As soon as men define themselves as the only ones capable of handling certain situations, of being aggressive, of earning the most money, then a woman who is equally capable in these areas becomes a threat to his very self-definition. He defines himself as *having* to earn the most money, and that definition still further defines him as a person who cannot afford too much time with his attache, housework, his children or their routine discipline.

Men's consciousness-raising groups combine supportiveness, through the understanding of common problems in socialization, with challenging the group members to change. According to Farrell:

Men's consciousness-raising groups combine supportiveness (through understanding common problems in socialization) with challenging each other to change. They support other men not only by highlighting the expectations of men, but by understanding how these expectations become pressures, how pressures become anxieties, how anxieties give us feelings of powerlessness and *how anxieties about powerlessness, combined with expectations for power, make us fight to be in control.* Men support each other in understanding how our hang-ups about masculinity affect our relationships with other women and men. They both support and challenge each other to change by the use of "follow-through hours" at the beginning of new meetings as a way of showing the concern for the changes each man has experienced during the week.

Once individuals have experienced single-sex consciousness-raising groups, it can be very beneficial (especially in couples counseling) for the group members to participate in a joint consciousness-raising group, involving both men and women. In joint groups, distortions about who is doing what to whom can be checked and kept at a minimum, and the mixed group provides a laboratory where such behaviors as condescension, dominance, and automatic sex role assumptions can be focused on while they are actually happening. Joint groups are generally not very effective, however, if the members haven't first experienced the support of their "sisters" or "brothers" in a single-sex group and become aware of what traditional sex role stereotyping has done to their own lives and the lives of others.

2. Assertive training groups

While there has been increasing interest in assertive training in recent years it is not a new concept. Wolpe (1958, 1969; Wolpe & Lazarus, 1966) developed the assertive training procedure fifteen years ago. Assertive behavior can be described as interpersonal behavior in which a person stands up for her or his legitimate rights in a way that does not violate the rights of others, in contrast to aggressive behavior in which the rights of others are violated. According to Jakubowski-Spector (1973) assertive training has four goals: "(a) to help participants identify their interpersonal rights, (b) to develop and refine assertive behaviors through active practice methods, (c) to identify emotional blocks which prevent the participants from acting assertively, and (d) to reduce these emotional blocks." Many counseling and group techniques (e.g., role-play and behavioral rehearsal, anxiety reduction, etc.) can be used to achieve these goals. A useful instructional tool is the film, *Assertive Training for Women* (Jakubowski-Spector, Pearlman & Coburn, 1973, distributed by the American Personnel and Guidance Association). Particularly helpful are empathy skill training (Carkhuff, 1969, 1972; Truax & Carkhuff, 1967) and confrontation skill training (Carkhuff & Berenson, 1967) techniques integrated into assertion training programs.

As with consciousness-raising, assertion training is not only for women. Although nonassertive women have tended to seek out such training much more than men, the training is valuable for aggressive or nonassertive men as well.

Decision-Making Groups   "Generally, the basic purpose of counseling is the facilitation of good choices, decisions, plans . . . The morality of the future may rest at least partly on the training in choice-making that counseling provides. . . . Counseling aimed at producing good choices and improving the ability to make good choices in the future involves doing one or more of the following things: (a) canvassing the whole range of possibilities; (b) facilitating decision-making through consideration of the probable consequences of alternative courses of action; (c) identifying and removing obstacles to the individual's development; (d) creating new possibilities through planned learning experiences'' (Tyler, 1972). While, both men and women need to learn decision-making skills, different approaches may be needed in teaching and counseling many women to make decisions than are used with men. Due to their socialization, many women have been taught or conditioned to ''let things happen'' and then act accordingly rather than decide, plan for, and take steps to determine their futures. Because of this, more prodding and encouragement may be needed in working with some—not all—women.

Decision-making skills are presently taught separately and as part of other group counseling and training programs on college campuses throughout the country, such as career development counseling, study skill development groups, life-span planning groups, and the like. The various stages and components of making decisions and solving problems were discussed earlier in the section dealing with secondary schools and will not be repeated here. Instead, some effective decision-making programs used in career counseling programs will be discussed. To do so, the basic career counseling and career development tasks are outlined. The first stage is exploration, including dreaming and pretending and assessing personal values, interests, aptitudes, needs, as well as training opportunities, and occupational opportunities. The next step involves contrasting and comparing all information. Then comes the planning stage where a career is chosen, obstacles are identified, and plans are made. The last or implementation stage involves learning necessary skills, overcoming obstacles, and obtaining a job (Farmer, 1975). Effective decision making is crucial to all stages of career development. Following are some specialized programs which integrate decision-making skill learning with career development.

Katz (1966) has developed a decision-making curriculum especially for community college students and adults, adapted for the computer-assisted counseling procedure entitled SIGI (System of Interactive Guidance Information) developed by the Educational Testing Service (Harris, 1974; Jepsen and Dilley, 1974).

Another decision-making procedure for career counseling is Farmer's (1975) "Guided Inquiry Career Counseling," which is designed for adults and is based on the assumption that a person's freedom to choose is enhanced by a broad range of information on personal strengths and weaknesses and on environmental opportunities and obstacles.

The Effective Problem Solving program developed by Magoon (1969) is a self-instructional model which leads participants through a series of steps beginning with the examination of their own interests, abilities and tentative career goals, then gathering and evaluating occupational information, and finally developing alternate plans of action.

Figler (Drum and Figler, 1973) developed PATH for use with college students to help them assess their environment and themselves in terms of self-evaluation, decision making, personal priorities related to work, and evaluation of job markets. The steps used in this program can be used again by the group participants whenever they face a future decision point.

The career development needs of women generally differ from men's, and the change agent counselor is aware of the differences and acts accordingly if women are to receive effective career and decision-making guidance. For example, women who have dropped out of school or work for family or other personal reasons may need to spend more time than their male counterparts at the initial stage of career development, dreaming and fantasizing what they would like to be if there were no restrictions before they begin reality testing their tentative career choice. Some women, e.g., those recently divorced or widowed, may need considerable help in working through economic, security, and emotional concerns before they are ready to fully participate in career counseling (Harmon, 1975). More time may need to be spent in helping women learn job-search skills such as writing resumes and participating in job interviews. The list of differences between the career development needs of women and men could go on and on, and the effective counselor must identify these needs and work with the clients to satisfy them.

Throughout the decision-making career development counseling groups, it is the counselor's responsibility to see that nonbiased information and instruments are used. For example, the neuter Strong-Campbell Interest Inventory is an improvement over the male and female forms of the Strong Vocational Interest Blank. Accurate occupational and work world information (such as provided in chap. 4) should illustrate that men and women can do and are employed in all types of work, including many atypical occupations.

In addition to offering individual and group counseling programs designed to dispel sex role stereotypes and assist women and men in redefining and broadening their roles, change agent counselors can give impetus to—by suggesting, helping plan, sponsoring, and/or participating in—a wide variety of special workshops and conferences around such topics as: new roles for men and women, alternate life styles, human sexuality, assertive training, life-long planning, nontraditional occupations for women and men, and applying for that first job. Group work, and one-to-one counseling can be either integrated into these workshops and conferences or offered as follow-up activities.

As mentioned earlier, two very good resources for developing such workshops and conferences are *A Handbook for Workshops on Sex Equality in Education* (Verheyden-Hilliard, 1976) and *Exploring Contemporary Male/Female Roles: A Facilitator's Guide* (Carney and McMahon, 1977). Some other useful materials not included in previous sections, although they may be used in a variety of settings and with several age groups, are listed here. *How to Decide: A Guide for Women* (Scholz, Prince, and Miller, 1975) is a workbook designed to meet the changing needs of women by increasing their decision-making ability in planning their own lives in a world of broadening opportunities and different expectations. The workbook is appropriate for women from college age through retirement and can be used effectively with individuals and groups.

Women as Winners: Transactional Analysis for Personal Growth (Jongeward and Scott, 1976) applies TA specifically to women and includes awareness exercises. *Womanpower: A Manual for Workshops in Personal Effectiveness* (Manis, 1977) contains worksheets and exercises on such topics as men-women relationships, values clarification, setting goals and decision making, planning for contingencies of the future, assertiveness training, improving communication in interpersonal relationships, and leadership training. *Assert Yourself! How to Be Your Own Person* (Galassi, 1974) is a manual designed to help educators develop assertion training programs. It can also be used on an individual basis as a self-help manual. *New Career Options for Women* (Farmer and Becker, 1977) is a three-part series containing "A Counselor's Sourcebook," "A Woman's Guide," and "A Selected Annotated Bibliography." The Sourcebook contains listings of books, films, organizations, and other resources valuable to the career counselor, as well as a discussion of the current labor market and suggestions about changing stereotyped attitudes and implementing sex role changes. The Guide is a summary of the major topics covered in the

Sourcebook and may be used independently or as a part of individual or group counseling.

Special programs, workshops, and conferences on such topics as those mentioned above have the potential of reaching large numbers of students and nonstudents, especially if they are offered as outreach programs and held in high traffic locations like the dormitories, classroom buildings, recreation centers, and certain off-campus locations.

Conclusion As has been discussed here, the proactive/change agent counselor works on a variety of fronts in the schools to eliminate sexist elements in the environment which limit the full growth and development of their clients—women and men—and to assist individuals in broadening and changing their own roles in order to take advantage of a greater range of opportunities and life styles. Because there is so much to be done in this area, and all of it cannot be done at once, the change agent counselor will have to make some choices and begin with those efforts which can make the most impact. This of course will vary for individual counselors and their particular settings. For some, the greatest impact can be made by working as a consultant with teachers, administrators, and other school personnel to change sexist school policies and practices. For others, working directly with the students in one-to-one or group counseling which focuses on changing stereotypic attitudes and behaviors may be more productive. In deciding what efforts to make and what steps to take, the change agent counselor must assess her or his own attitudes, skills, and abilities, and the readiness or receptivity of those he or she is trying to help. Remembering that successful consultation and counseling involves a willing client or client system and that major change generally does not occur quickly, the change agent counselor in the schools must not give up if things do not improve overnight, but must be persistent and patient and carefully and strategically plan each step, each effort in working towards change.

References Adell, J., and Klein, H. D. *A Guide to Non-sexist Children's Books.* Chicago: Academy Press Limited, 1976.

Alderson, J. J. The challenge for change in school social work. *Social Casework,* 1971, *52*(1), 3–10.

Ahlum, C., and Fralley, J.*High School Feminist Studies.* Old Westbury, NY: Feminist Press, 1976.

Ahlum, C., and Howe, F. *The New Guide to Female Studies,* No. 1. Pittsburg: KNOW, Inc., 1971.

Ahlum, C., and Howe, F.*The New Guide to Female Studies,* No. 2. Old Westbury, NY: The Feminist Press, 1972.

Argyris, C. *Intervention Theory and Method: A Behavioral Science View,* Reading, Mass.: Addisen—Wesley, 1970.

Aubrey, R. Power Bases: The consultant's vehicle for change. *Elementary School Guidance and Counseling, December, 1972, 7*(2), 90-97.

Bandura, A. Psychotherapy based upon modeling principles. In A. E. Bergin and S. L. Garfield (eds.), *The Handbook of Psychotherapy and Behavior Change.* NY: Wiley, 1971.

Bardon, J. I. School psychology and school psychologists: an approach to an old problem. *American Psychologist,* 1968, *23*(3), 187-194.

Bennis, W. G.; Benne, K. D.; and Chin, R. *The Planning of Change: Readings in the Applied Behavioral Sciences.* New York: Holt, Rinehart & Winston, 1962.

Bennis, W. G. *Changing Organizations.* New York: McGraw-Hill, 1966.

Bessel, H., and Ball, G. *Human Development Program.* La Mesa, Calif.: Human Development Training Institute, 1972 and 1974.

Blocher, D. N. Can the counselor function as an effective agent of change? *The School Counselor,* 1966, *13,* 202-206.

Britton, G., and Lumpkin, M. *A Consumer's Guide to Sex, Race and Career Bias in Public School Textbooks.* Corvallis, Oregon, Britton and Associates, 1977.

Caplan, G. *The Theory and Practice of Mental Health Consultation.* New York: Basic Books, Inc., 1970.

Carkhuff, R. R., and Berenson, B. G. *Beyond Counseling and Therapy.* New York: Holt, Rinehart & Winston, 1967.

Carkhuff, R. R.*Helping and Human Relations.* Vols. I and II. New York: Holt, Rinehart & Winston, 1969.

Carkhuff, R. R. *The Art of Helping.* Amhurst, Mass.: Human Resource Development Press, 1972.

Carney, C. G., and McMahon, S. L. *Exploring Contemporary Male/Female Roles: A Facilitator's Guide.* La Jolla, Calif.: University Associates, 1977.

Crookston, B. B. Milien management: An emerging key role of the principal student affairs officer. Paper presented at the Fifty-seventh Annual Conference of the National Association of Student Personnel Administrators, San Francisco, March 1975.

Danskin, D.; Kennedy, C. E.; and Friesen, W. S. Guidance—the ecology of students. *Personnel and Guidance Journal,* 1965, *44*(2), 130-135.

Drum, D., and Figler, H. *Outreach in Counseling.* New York: Intext, 1973.

Farmer, H. S. Career counseling. In C. Rose, *Meeting Women's New Educational Needs.* San Francisco: Jossey—Bass Inc., 1975.

Farmer, H. S. *Guided Inquiry Group Career Counseling.* Unpublished manuscript, 1975. (Available from the author at the College of Education, University of Illinois, Urbana, IL 61801.)

Farmer, H. S., and Backer, T. *New Career Options for Women.* NY: Human Science Press, 1977.

Farrell, W. *The Liberated Man.* New York: Bantam Books, 1974.

Feminists on Children's Media. *Little Miss Muffet Fights Back.* New York: Feminists on Children's Media, 1974.

Free to Be . . . You and Me. NY: Free to Be Foundation, Inc. And McGraw-Hill Films, 1975.

Furniss, W. T. Degrees for nontraditional students: an approach to new models. American Council on Education, Special Report, April 9, 1971.

Galassi, M. D., and Galassi, J. P. *Assert Yourself! How to Be Your Own Person.* NY: Human Science Press, 1977.

Gordon, T. *A New Model for Humanizing Families and Schools.* Pasadena: Effectiveness Training Associates, 1971.

Guttentag, M., and Bray, H. *Undoing Sex Stereotypes: Research and Resources for Educators.* NY: McGraw-Hill, 1976.

Hansen, L. S. A career development curriculum framework for counselors to promote female growth. In *Women and ACES: Perspective and Issues,* M. A. J. Guttman, and P. A. Donn (eds.). Washington, D.C.: Commission for Women, Association for Counselor Education and Supervision, 1974.

Hansen, L. S. and Keierleber, D. L. BORN FREE: A Collaborative Consultation Model for Career Development and Sex-role Stereotyping. *Personnel and Guidance Journal,* 1978, 56, 7, 395–399.

Harmon, L. Career counseling for women. In D. Carter and E. Rawhigs (eds.), *Psychotherapy for Women: Treatments Toward Equality.* Illinois: Charles C. Thomas and Sons, 1975.

Harris, J. The computer: guidance tool of the future. *Journal of Counseling Psychology,* 1974, *21,* 331-339.

Hart, L. B. *A Feminist Looks at Educational Software Materials.* Amhurst: Continuing Education Press, University of Massachusetts, 1973.

Horney, K. *Neurosis and Human Growth: The Struggle Toward Self-realization.* NY: Norton, 1950.

Howard, S. *Liberating Our Children, Ourselves.* Washington, D.C.: American Association of University of Women, 1975.

Howe, F. *Female Studies II.* Pittsburg: KNOW, Inc., 1970.

Howe, F. *Seven Years Later: Women's Studies Programs in 1976.* Washington D.C.: National Advisory Council on Women's Educational Programs, June 1977.

Howe, F. (ed.) *Women and the Power to Change.* NY: McGraw-Hill, 1975.

Howe, F., and Ahlum, C. *Female Studies III.* Pittsburg: KNOW, Inc., 1971.

Howe, F., and Ahlum, C. Women's studies and social change. In *Academic Women on the Move,* A. R. Rossi and A. Calderwood (eds.). New York: Russel Sage Foundation, 1973.

Jakubowski-Spector, P. *An Introduction to Assertive Training Procedures for Women,* Washington, D.C.: American Personnel and Guidance Association, 1973.

Jepsen, D., and Dilley, J. Vocational Decision-making models: a review and comparative analysis. *Review of Educational Research,* 1974,44(3), 331-349.

Johnson, D. W. *Reaching Out: Interpersonal Effectiveness and Self-actualization.* Englewood Cliffs, NJ: Prentice-Hall, 1972.

Johnson, D. W., and Johnson, F. P. *Joining Together: Group Theory and Group Skills.* Englewood Cliffs, NJ: Prentice-Hall, 1975.

Jongeward, D., and Scott, D. *Women as Winners! Transactional Analysis for Personal Growth.* NY: Addisen-Wesley, 1976.

Katz, M. A model of guidance for career decision-making. *Vocational Guidance Quarterly,* 1966, *14,* 2–10.

Kirschenbaum, H. *Advanced Value Clarification.* La Jolla, CA: University Associates, Inc., 1976.

Krumboltz, J. D. Changing the behavior of behavior changers. In A. C. Riccio & G. R. Walz (eds.) *Forces for Change in Counselor Education.* Washington, D.C.: Association for Counselor Education and Supervision, 1967.

Krumboltz, J. and Thoresen, C. *Behavioral Counseling.* New York: Holt, Rinehart & Winston, 1969.

Lanning, W. An expanded view of consultation for college and university counseling centers. *Journal of College Student Personnel,* 1974, *15,* 171–176.

Lewin, K. Frontiers in group dynamics. *Human Ralations,* 1947, *1,*5–41.

Lewis, J., and Lewis, M. D. *Community Counseling: A Human Services Approach.* New York: John Wiley & Sons, 1977.

Lippitt, R.; Watson, J.; and Westley, B. *Dynamics of Planned Change.* New York: Harcourt, Brace & Co., 1958.

Lippitt, R. Dimensions of the consultant's job. *Journal of Social Issues,* 1959, *15*(2), 5-13.

Magoon, T. Developing skills for educational and vocational problems. In J. Krumboltz and C. Noresen (eds.), *Behavioral Counseling: Cases and Techniques.* New York: Holt, Rinehart, & Winston, 1969.

Mavis, L. G. *Womanpower: A Manual for Workshops in Personal Effectiveness.* Cranston, RI: Carroll Press, 1977.

McCully, H. The counselor: instrument of change. *Teachers College Record,* 1965, *66*(5), 405-412.

Men's Studies Bibliography. Cambridge: Human Studies Collection, MIT Humanities Library, 1977.

Michigan Women's Commission. *Sex Discrimination in an Elementary Reading Program.* Lansing: Michigan Women's Commission, 1974.

Miles, M. B. and Solmick, R. A. *Organization Development in Schools.* Palo Alto, CA: National Press Books, 1971.

Miller, J.; Filzmaurice, M.; Berkowitz; and Ahlum, C. *The New Guide to Female Studies,* No. 3. Old Westbury,.NY: The Feminist Press, 1973.

Mitchell, J. *Women's Estate.* New York: Pantheon Books, 1971.

Morrill, W. H., Oetting, E. R.; and Hurst, J. C. Dimensions of counselor functioning. *Personnel and Guidance Journal,* 1974, 52(6), 354-359

Pfeiffer, J. W., and Jones, J. E. *Annual Handbook for Group Facilities.* La Jolla, CA: University Associates, Inc., 1972-1977.

The Project on the Status and Education of Women. *Women's Centers: Where Are They?* Washington, D.C.: Association of American Colleges, 1975.

Randolph, C., and Zimmerman, J. A counselor's role in helping women. In M. A. J. Guttman and P. A. Donn (eds.), *Woman and ACES: Perspective and Issues.* Washington, D.C.: Commission for Women, Association for Counselor Education and Supervision, 1974.

Raths, L. E.; Harmin, M.; and Simon, S. *Values and Teaching.* Columbus, OH: Charles E. Merrill, 1966.

Resource Center on Sex Roles in Education. *Biased Textbooks: A Research Perspective.* Washington: The National Foundation for the Improvement of Education, 1974.

Resource Center on Sex Roles in Education. *Today's Changing Roles: An Approach to Non-sexist Teaching.* Washington: The National Foundation for the Improvement of Education, 1974.

Rogers, C. R. The interpersonal relationship in the facilitation of learning. In R. Leeper (ed.), *Humanizing Education.* Washington, D.C.: ASCD, NEA, 1967.

Rosenfelt, D. S. *Female Studies VII: Going Strong.* Old Westbury, NY: The Feminist Press, 1973.

Sadker, D. *Being a Man: A Unit of Instructional Activities on Male Role Stereotyping.* Washington D.C.: U.S. Office of Education, 1978.

Scholz, N. T.; Prince, J. S.; and Miller, G. P. *How to Decide: A Guide for Women.* NY: College Entrance Examination Board, 1975.

Scott, Foresman and Company's Sexism in Textbooks Committee. *Guidelines for Improving the Image of Women in Textbooks.* Glenview, IL: Scott, Foresman and Company, 1972.

Shoben, E. J., Jr. Guidance: remedial function or social reconstruction? *Harvard Educational Review, Guidance—An Examination* (a special issue), 1962, *32*(4), 442.

Simon, S. B., and Clark, J. *More Values Clarification.* San Diego: Pennant Press, 1975.

Smith, M. *A Practical Guide to Value Clarification.* La Jolla, CA: University Associates, Inc., 1977.

Sprung, B. *Non-sexist Education for Young Children: A Practical Guide.* NY: Citation Press, 1975.

Stewart, L. H., and Warnath, C. J. *The Counselor and Society.* Boston: Houghton Mifflin, 1965.

Tobias, S. Towards a taxonomy of math anxiety. *Math = A Problem.* Proceedings of a conference held at the University of Wisconsin, Madison, Wisconsin, March 1977.

Truax, C. B., and Carkhuff, R. R. *Toward Effective Counseling and Psychotherapy.* Chicago: Aldine, 1967.

Truax, C. B., and Mitchell, K. M. Research on certain therapist interpersonal skills. In A. E. Bergin and S. L. Garfield (eds.), *The Handbook of Psychotherapy and Behavior Change.* NY: Wileys, 1971.

Tyler, L. E. Counseling girls and women in the year 2000. In E. A. Whitfield and A. Gustan (eds.), *Counseling Girls and Women Over the Life Span.* Washington, D.C.: The National Vocational Guidance Association, 1972.

Varenhorst, B. Learning the consequences of life's decisions. In J. Krumboltz and C. Thoresen (eds.), *Behavioral Counseling.* New York: Holt, Rinehart & Winston, 1969.

Varenhorst, B.; Gelatt, H. B.; and Carey, R. *Deciding: A Program in Decision Making for Grades 7-8-9.* New York: College Entrance Examination Board, 1972.

Verheyden-Hilliard, M. E. *A Handbook for Workshops on Sex Equality in Education.* Washington, D.C.: American Personnel and Guidance Association, 1976.

Williamson, E. G. Value-orientation in counseling. *Personnel and Guidance Journal,* 1958, *36,* 520–528.

Wolpe, J. *Psychotherapy by Reciprocal Inhibition.* Stanford, CA: Stanford University Press, 1958.

Wolpe, J., and Lazarus, A. A. *Behavior Therapy Techniques.* New York: Pergamon Press, 1966.

Wolpe, J. *The Practice of Behavior Therapy.* New York: Pergamon Press, 1969.

Women's Bureau. Continuing education for women: current development. Washington, D.C.: U.S. Department of Labor, 1974.

Wrenn, C. G. *The Counselor in a Changing World.* Washington, D.C.: American Personnel and Guidance Association, 1962.

8 Impacting the Community and Work World

In the preceding chapter, the counselor's role as change agent and internal consultant in the schools was discussed. Just as proactive counselors in the schools work toward eliminating sexist elements which affect their students and colleagues, so can proactive counselors and helping professionals in a variety of community and work settings endeavor to create a nonsexist environment for their clients and co-workers. This chapter takes a look at some of the community and work settings where counselors and other helping professionals can, as a regular part of their job functions, assess their environment for sexist and stereotypic practices and attitudes and take steps to facilitate change.

The Nonsexist Counselor's Impact on Employment

There is no doubt that sex typing occurs in employment (see chap. 4), to the extent that occupations in the American work force are practically sex segregated. Such segregation, on the basis of sex along occupational lines, operates to the detriment of women. By and large, men are employed in the higher status, higher paying positions, while women occupy the lower paying, lower status jobs. And the myths about women workers discussed in chapter 4, e.g., women do not make good bosses, women do not really need to work, women are just not fit for some kinds of work, etc., are still believed by many employers and employees. Such beliefs about women workers cause employers to treat women employees and applicants for employment differently than they treat men. Oftentimes this different treatment is discriminatory. Men have also experienced discriminatory treatment when seeking training and employment in traditionally female occupations, such as nursing, early childhood education, and secretarial and clerical positions. And as the job market tightens and employers are trying to hire more women and minority group members to comply with affirmative action and equal employment opportunity regulations (see chap. 5), men (and particularly Caucasian men) are experiencing a type of reverse discrimination. What can be done to alleviate this situation? What can employment counselors do to issue fair employment practices and equal employment opportunity for all qualified persons seeking employment? Some suggestions are presented here for employment counselors in three settings— (1) job placement services at colleges and universities, (2) employment agencies, and (3) company personnel offices.

College and University Job Placement Services

Colleges and universities are required by law (see chap. 5) to not discriminate on the basis of sex in any employment practices, including assisting other employers in hiring students. Thus, career planning and placement counselors have an obligation to inform employers of their nondiscriminatory policy and to insure that employers using the placement services provide equal employment opportunity for both women and men. Employers may not be allowed to post advertisements for available positions indicating they want the best "man" for the job, nor are they allowed to interview only the members of one sex, or in any way treat male and female applicants for employment differently.

In addition to the legal obligations of college placement services, there are some steps placement counselors can take to assist the students using the service in becoming informed applicants for employment. Some of these steps are as follows:

1. Provide nonsexist programs and packaged materials on careers and occupations.
2. Encourage students to apply for all jobs for which they are qualified regardless of the sex role stereotyping of some jobs.
3. Advise and counsel students on legal and illegal actions of job interviewers and employers—e.g., an interviewer may not ask different questions of male and female applicants regarding their marital and family status and plans, and only job-related information is to be used in assessing a person's qualifications for a position.
4. Provide information, demonstration, and practice sessions for students on appropriate behavior and dress for job interviews.

Employment Agencies

State and private employment agencies and services have the same legal obligations to insure fair employment practices as do college and university placement services and employers themselves.

Employment counselors working in such agencies can do their part in facilitating nonsexist practices by:

1. Checking their own attitudes and the attitudes of their co-workers regarding women workers and "appropriate" work for women and men.
2. Reviewing all application forms, tests, and other screening and selection procedures for sexist and discriminatory elements.
3. Keeping employers honest and legal by reviewing their employment practices for sexist elements and by reminding them of their responsibilities in providing equal employment opportunities to women and men alike.
4. Suggesting nontraditional work alternatives to job applicants who have the interest and necessary abilities, e.g., clerical work for men and blue collar crafts for women.
5. Preparing applicants for job interviews with prospective employers, i.e., providing as much information as possible about the specific position, the employer, and the employment setting, and making suggestions for appropriate interview behavior and dress.
6. Indicating the strengths of nontraditional applicants to employers who are hesitant to employ a man or woman in a job which is atypical for their sex.
7. Assisting applicants for employment in filing complaints if federal or state sex discrimination laws have been violated.

Employers Counselors in company personnel offices are in a particularly good position to know whether or not the organization is following fair employment practices and to act as an internal consultant in promoting change where change is needed. In "watchdogging" an organization to insure equal opportunity, equity, and legality in employment practices, and helping to provide for the best possible utilization of "personpower," employment counselors can be most effective if they do the following:

1. Familiarize themselves with the antidiscrimination laws and regulations and with the particular problems employees, especially women employees, encounter related to these laws and regulations.
2. Become aware of their own attitudes and the attitudes of their co-workers regarding "appropriate" work for men and women.

Are there some jobs members of the organization feel women (or men) cannot handle effectively?

3. Review all employment policies and practices for sexist elements. Do application forms ask for information which is not job-related? Are employment interviewers instructed to not ask inappropriate and perhaps discriminatory questions of applicants?

Company policies and practices may appear on paper to provide equality for men and women when in practice such is not the case. Old traditions and ways of doing things are comfortable for employers and employees alike, and special efforts must be made if employees, and particularly women employees, are provided real equality in the world of work. Some special efforts employment counselors can help the organization make are suggested here.

(1) Motivate employees for nontraditional jobs. Motivating women to consider jobs which have been traditionally viewed as men's jobs and men to consider traditionally women's jobs is not an easy task. Employers must do more than just let the employees and applicants for employment know that such positions exist. They must demonstrate that the atypical jobs are indeed available and appropriate for members of the sex not usually found in such positions. How this is best done varies from organization to organization. Employment counselors can oftentimes convince individuals to consider nontraditional positions by pointing out the abilities the individual has which are required for the job and the aspects of the job the person may enjoy. Some employers hold special sessions where workers can obtain information and ask questions about nontraditional jobs. Others have programs which provide workers a chance to actually observe a job of interest for a day, participating in some of the job functions.

The Polaroid Corporation has developed another approach to encourage women to consider nontraditional jobs (Ells, 1973). It has developed two traveling road shows. One is a twenty-minute slide and tape presentation showing women mechanics, machine operators, drafters, and security guards on the job. The women employees describe the pros and cons of their positions, tell why they chose these new fields, and give advice to other women who might want to join their ranks. This show is presented to women employees currently concentrated in lower-paying hand-assembly jobs throughout the corporation. It assumes that once these employees see other women performing nontraditional, higher-paying jobs, their interest in entering "men's ranks" will increase. The other road show is similar to the first one only geared for a different audience—women in upper-level technical and clerical jobs—and focused on introducing entry-level professional jobs, such as production supervisor, buyer, production planner, computer programmer, and sales representative. In addition to being used as road shows, the films are useful tools in management awareness sessions—making it easier for managers to realize that women can and must be encouraged to enter these traditionally male job areas.

(2) Help plan and implement special training and development programs. Employee training programs are not new to organizations. Management training programs in large companies have existed for some time. Much less common are internal training programs which prepare women for nontraditional positions—in all areas and types of jobs where they do not now exist or where they exist in small numbers. Here are some suggested steps in developing company-sponsored training programs for women:

—identify women employees who demonstrate the ability and potential to be advanced to more responsible positions.
—analyze the requirements of the nontraditional jobs to see what knowledge and skills are needed.
—design special training programs which focus on required skills and knowledge which the women do not presently have.
—involve representative women employees in the planning and implementation of the training programs.
—give women employees a chance to apply newly learned skills and knowledge in a "dry run" practice situation.
—see that women who successfully complete these programs are placed in responsbile positions which enable them to utilize their newly acquired training.

The above steps are general guides for the development of any training program. Buchanan (1968), offers more specific suggestions on creating programs to develop women's managerial potential:

(a) Open up the entire program for managerial training and development to women.

—Extend management training programs now geared to recent college graduates to the mature, college-educated women now starting a full-time career.

—Expect the mature woman's training to advance more rapidly and accelerate here progress accordingly.
—Open to qualified women the higher levels of in-service training, within their related job rotation and cross-functional assignments.
—Grant her objective performance evaluation, with straightforward, constructive criticism, without soft-pedaling from fear of imagined sensitivity.
—Expect satisfactory performance and reward it with commensurate pay, promotion, status, and privileges.
—Open the training ladder at more position levels, so that a mature woman with relevant experience may be added in at the most appropriate rung.
—Broaden the training program by including interim jobs that provide equivalent development experiences that are not now seen as part of executive development sequences.
—Rethink distributed experience within the company. Is it really essential for each candidate for a vice-presidency to have had a stint in managing the factory at Podunk?

(b) Use work-sharing, split-shift techniques for management positions so that opportunities to sharpen problem-attacking tools and develop responsible, decision-making skills are more widely extended to competent, motivated, younger married women.

—Develop modified, full-time positions, with lighter initial loads, to recruit, develop, and screen the younger women before their families and domestic demands have released them for full-time work.
—Redesign appropriate positions into a series of one-shot, single-problem assignments that are full-time but temporary, and can be handled by a woman on a reduced-load basis similar to the method of farming out assignments to consulting or legal firms.
—Develop promising women candidates, who are not yet available for full-time management, through assignment of overflow management problems that presently overburden the full-time staff but are not sufficiently accummulated to necessitate a new, full-time position.

(3) Provide special support services for employees in positions which are atypical for their sex. For example, prepare the men with

whom a woman will be working prior to her first day on the job. Don't surprise them with a new female co-worker. This is especially important for the skilled trade areas which to date have not had many women workers. Inform the men that a woman will be joining their ranks. Give them a chance to voice their concerns and offer suggestions to handling problems they feel might arise. Place the first few women managerial employees with working associates who are most likely to accept them. Survey the attitudes of employees to determine which ones are the least resistant to working for and with women. This is less crucial as more and more women are placed and employees adjust to the idea of having female working associates. The first few placements, however, are likely to set the trend for subsequent placements, and it is important that they are successful. Take the same precautions in placing the first male clerical worker in an office of all female clerical workers.

Provide more than a normal amount of support for both the newly placed atypical employees and their co-workers to help them work out differences and solve problems which may arise. This may be in the form of individual counseling, group sessions with other women/men experiencing similar problems, awareness/sensitivity sessions for male/female co-workers, "coping training" to assist women in becoming more assertive in personal style and expectations, or a variety of other support programs.

(4) Encourage the establishment of flexible work schedules, thus giving women and men greater autonomy in scheduling of their work hours to better fit the sharing of home and family responsibilities. The most common departures from the regular five-day, forty-hour workweek include compressed or compact schedules (e.g., four-day, forty-hour workweek); flexible schedules or "flexitime" which requires employees to be at work during a core period but allows for flexibility of starting and finishing times; and staggered schedules. Studies trying to assess the impact of revised work schedules show mixed results (Glickman and Brown, 1973, Goldberg, 1975; U.S. Department of Labor, 1975). While some employees liked revised work schedules, others complained of fatigue or conflict with hours worked by other family members. In some organizations, productivity increased; in others it remained the same or decreased. While no turnover reduction was found, there appeared to be reductions in absenteeism. Progress in recruitment of employees was reported, although it was not certain that revised work schedules contributed to the progress. Such mixed results are not surprising since revised work schedules are still relatively new in

America, unlike western Europe, and they have not been implemented widely enough to make a thorough assessment. However, they do have the potential of fitting the changing work and domestic patterns of women and men better than the typical five-day, forty-hour workweek.

(5) Encourage the establishment of superior child care facilities. Inadequate child care arrangements make it difficult or impossible for women to work. Child care facilities near the work site coupled with flexible work schedules enable both men and women to more equally share the responsibilities of financially supporting the family and participating in the rearing of children. The Day Care and Child Development Council of America (1977) has compiled an extensive list of resources for the development and implementation of child care centers. Included in the list are resources in areas such as starting and evaluating programs, establishing a curriculum, staff development and training, and nonsexist and nonracist literature.

The Nonsexist Counselor Making A Difference in Community Agencies

Counselors of various educational backgrounds and training are employed in a wide range of community agencies and organizations which provide services for thousands of people of all ages. A representative sample of some of these agencies and organizations is listed here.

1. Regional Counseling Centers
2. Mental Health Centers
3. Psychiatric Clinics and Hospitals
4. Area Social Service Departments
5. Drug and Alcohol Centers
6. Crises Intervention Centers
7. Rehabilitation Education and Services
8. Child and Family Services
   a. Adoption and Foster Care Agencies
   b. Family Planning and Counseling
9. Youth Services
   a. YMCA, YWCA
   b. Emergency Shelters
10. Correctional Services
   a. Penal Institutions
   b. Juvenile Homes
   c. Half-way Houses
   d. Probation Departments

11. Women's Resource Centers and Health Clinics
12. Services for the Elderly
13. Church-related Counseling Services

In each of these settings, and others not listed, counselors and other helping professionals deal with clients who in addition to other problems and concerns have been limited in their personal development because of society's sex role stereotyping. We have already discussed in chapters 2 and 3 how counselors have perpetuated sex role stereotypes and in some cases exacerbated the problems of their clients rather than facilitated solutions. Counselors aware of sex typing and aware of their own sexist attitudes are in a much better position to work with a client toward a solution to his or her problem than those counselors without such awareness. For example, such an aware counselor working with a forty-year-old woman alcoholic is more likely to understand some of the sex role related problems the woman has experienced and work out a treatment plan that recognizes these factors. As another illustration, in a youth services setting, an aware YWCA/YMCA counselor will recognize the needs of young women and men to participate in developmental and recreational activities that are nontraditional for their sex and thus will develop a balanced program to fit the needs of all participants regardless of their sex. A family planning counselor who is aware of the changing expectations of some young mothers and fathers to share child rearing and financial support functions equally is better able to deal with the frustrations of a client whose partner doesn't share the same values. The list of examples could go on and on.

While it is not possible to discuss each of the above types of community agencies and organizations, the differential treatment that clients receive because of their sex, and recommend strategies for change, I have selected one—penal institutions—to use as an example, and will then make some general recommendations for counselors and helping professionals working in any of the community agencies or organizations.

Example: Differential Treatment of Men and Women in Penal Institutions

The percentage of crimes committed by women and their arrest rate are increasing. The tables 8-1/8-2 illustrate this increase in the crime rate for women from 1950 to 1970.

Einsele (quoted in Howard and Howard, 1974) suggests that this increase in crime rate for women is a reflection of the effects of

Table 8-1 Arrest Rates in the U.S.A. for Some Crimes, by Sex, for 1952 and 1970

Crime and Year	Number per 100,000 of same sex in the reporting population*		Arrests for this offense as a percent of total arrested		Percent of those arrested for this offense who are	
	Women	Men	Women	Men	Women	Men
Total						
1952	1022	8549	100%	100%	11%	89%
1970	1217	7622	100%	100%	14%	86%
Murder						
1952	2.07	9.02	.20%	.11%	19%	81%
1970	2.54	14.71	.21%	.19%	15%	85%
Aggravated Assault						
1952	17.47	84.82	1.71%	.99%	17%	83%
1970	20.45	149.16	1.68%	1.95%	13%	87%
Larceny-theft						
1952	47.17	296.26	4.62%	3.46%	14%	86%
1970	221.27	601.62	18.18%	7.89%	28%	72%
Drunkenness						
1952	322.73	4039.80	31.60%	47.30%	7%	93%
1970	137.53	1905.02	11.31%	24.90%	7%	93%
Narcotic drug laws						
1952	3.96	22.77	.40%	.27%	15%	85%
1970	69.58	396.11	5.72%	5.19%	16%	84%
Stolen Property; buying, receiving, possessing						
1953	1.26	13.97	.12%	.16%	8%	92%
1970	7.38	75.58	.60%	.99%	9%	91%

*Reporting population: 1952—23,334,035; 1970—151,604,000.

Source: Howard, E. M. and Howard, J. L. Women in Institutions: Treatment in Prisons and Mental Hospitals. In V. Franks and V. Burtle (Eds.), *Women in therapy.* New York: Brunner/Mazel, 1974.

Table 8-2 Persons in Correctional Institutions in the U.S.A., by Sex, for 1950 and 1970*

Year	Number**		Number per 100,000 of same sex in the population of the U.S.		Percent of those in prison who are	
	Women	Men	Women	Men	Women	Men
1950	12,995	251,562	17.13	336.09	4.9%	95.1%
1970	19,052	293,620	18.27	322.92	6.1%	93.9%

*Excludes Alaska and Hawaii. Data for 1950 are presented rather than for 1952 as in Tables 1 and 2 since available prison data for 1952 did not include the city and county institution information. Data presented include these institutions for 1950 and 1970 and hence may be compared to overall arrest rates which include persons who might be sentenced to all institutions.
**Excludes 20,252 persons in institutions in 1970 where no breakdown by sex was reported.

Source: Howard, E. M. and Howard, J. L. Women in Institutions: Treatment in Prisons and Mental Hospitals. In V. Franks and V. Burtle (Eds.), *Women in Therapy.* New York: Brunner/Mazel, 1974.

Counselors and Social Change

ongoing societal changes in social behavior in general and that of women in particular. Sutherland and Cressey (1970) feel that the increase may be related to the changes in sex differentiated roles in our society, and they hypothesize that as girls and women are less closely supervised there will be a decrease in sex differences in crime. According to Howard and Howard (1974), "It is not clear whether these data reflect a trend toward equalizing the social treatment afforded the two sexes, or whether women are assimilating the societal norms of the dominant male group." Whatever the reasons, the fact remains—women's crime rate is on the increase.

While women's crime rate is increasing, the numbers of women offenders compared to men is still relatively small and little attention has been paid to their treatment. "It was not until 1926 that a separate chapter on women's reformatories appeared in a general work on penology, and Lekkerkerker's (1931) was perhaps the first comprehensive study in this area" (Howard and Howard, 1974). While it has been recommended that institutions for women should be separate from those for men and should be headed by women (Eymon, 1971; Lekkerkerker, 1931; Monahan, 1941), the 1971 Directory of Correctional Institutions and Agencies lists only thirty-seven institutions (thirty-one headed by women and six headed by men) for women. Because there are so few prisons for women, women are more likely to be placed in institutions far away from family and friends, and felons and serious offenders are much more likely to be placed with less serious offenders in female prisons. Due to their small size, women's institutions have fewer medical, religious, recreational, industrial, vocational and educational programs, and facilities than men's institutions.

In summarizing many studies on female criminality, Pollak (1950) asked the following questions and provided an answer: "(1) Are crimes in which women participate exclusively or to a considerable extent offenses which are known to be greatly underreported? (2) Are women offenders generally less often detected than are men offenders? (3) Do women if apprehended meet with more leniency than do men? It seems that each of these questions will have to be answered in the affirmative and that the long discussion which has centered around the apparent sex differential in crime may have been based on a statistical deception." Pollak (1950) asserts that lenient attitudes toward women offenders prevail at all levels of the criminal justice system because "men hate to accuse women and thus indirectly send them to their punishment, police officers dislike to arrest them, judges and juries to find them guilty, and so on." Howard and Howard (1974) found twenty years later that while the degree of implied chivalry of Pollak's statement has changed considerably, there still "continues to be differential treatment from the very beginning of the process, with women appearing to be treated preferentially." In their review of other studies and their own interviews with offenders, ex-offenders and staff members of prisons and postprison systems, Howard and Howard (1974) found that of persons arrested proportionately fewer women than men are incarcerated, but their preferential treatment ends with the entry phase into the prison system, and during the remainder of the correctional process they receive worse treatment than male offenders. Their findings regarding the differential treatment of women and men during the remainder of the correctional process are summarized below:

1. Intake. Classification systems have been developed for male offenders in order to provide the type of security arrangements deemed necessary to protect society and to take in consideration the personal characteristics of the individual for rehabilitation and skills training. No separate classification systems have been developed for women. If any classification system is used, it is an adaptation of one used for men. And, "since most states have, at best, only one institution for women, all convicted women, hardened felons as well as fledging misdemeanants sentenced for over one year, are sent to the same facility."

2. Education and Skills Training. Educational programs available to women usually consist of classes such as remedial English and preparation for high school equivalency examinations, whereas men's institutions have a wider variety of academic subjects and some college-level courses. Most vocational training programs for both men and women are based on their practical contribution to the ongoing operation of the institution rather than an assessment of the labor market or the potential employee; however, the programs for men usually include a wider variety of choices which are more likely to be helpful in finding employment upon release from prison.

3. Work Release. Work release programs for women have only recently been started, since they had to first be proven successful in men's institutions. Because of the poor education and skills training programs for women, few are able to participate in work release programs. And to compound the problem, such programs for women are not adapted to their particular needs.

4. Psychotherapy. The use of psychotherapeutic methods in attempting to reorient offenders in new and more socially acceptable ways of responding to life situations are introduced into women's institutions only after success has been demonstrated in men's institutions.

5. General Conditions. Women offenders usually experience psychological and physical harassment (e.g., given frequent physical examinations and used as sex objects by staff), while men tend to experience more physical abuse. Conjugal visits are viewed as male privileges and are rarely extended to women.

6. Release. While proportionately more women are released from prison, they are usually required to have reasonable assurance of employment and approved living accommodations; men on the other hand are released with significantly less restriction as to living arrangements. Also, more assistance is given to the male ex-offenders in preparing for their release and finding employment. Halfway houses or community centers to assist ex-offenders focus almost exclusively on the needs of men.

What can counselors working at the various levels of the criminal justice system do to rid the system of this differential treatment for the men and women offenders? The following are a few suggestions.

1. Observe and begin to keep documentation of any differences in the treatment men and women offenders receive.

2. Make co-workers aware of these differences, and try to obtain their understanding and support for implementing change.

3. Cooperatively plan tentative programs and strategies to equalize the treatment of women and men offenders.

4. Present documentation of differential treatment and tentative plans for equalizing treatment of men and women offenders to system officials.

5. Work with volunteer groups and community resources which are interested in helping offenders.

6. Ask offenders what kinds of programs they think would be useful.

7. Involve appropriate unions and employers as consultants to insure that training and educational programs are appropriate for skills needed in the labor market and are not restricted to members of one sex.

8. Help provide in-service training programs for correctional educators, counselors, parole officers, administrators, etc., on sex typing and stereotypic attitudes toward women and men offenders.

Two recent publications of the Women's Bureau, U.S. Department of Labor, provide useful information on the establishment of special programs for women offenders. The first publication, *Women Offenders: Must We Bar Them from Employment?* (Women's Bureau, 1977b), explains the bureau's offender program and how it led to consultations in various communities and to the formulation of task forces to bring about needed change. It tells what the program does, how it works, why it is important, and what citizens and community organizations can do and lists Women's Bureau regional offices where technical assistance can be obtained. The second publication entitled *Employment Needs of Women Offenders: A Program Model* (Women's Bureau, 1977a) includes a "how-to" section for organizations who want to replicate the bureau's offender program as well as a resource directory for developing or carrying out a program for women offenders.

While the criminal justice system is the focus of the above recommended actions to remove differential treatment of men and women, similar recommendations can be made in the form of general steps to take in working with any community agency or organization. While several intermediate steps and actions may need to be taken due to organizational and personnel differences, some general steps to facilitate the elimination of sexism are these:

Step 1: Assess the situation. Collect information on how girls and boys, men and women are perceived and treated differently.

Step 2: Bring the differential treatment information to the attention of others within the organization.

Step 3: Work cooperatively with staff, clients, and other interested groups to develop programs and strategies for change.

Step 4: Help provide in-service training programs on sexism and discrimination for staff members (see chap. 10). Note: This step may need to precede step 3.

Step 5: Evaluate the outcomes and impact of programs in step 3 and step 4.

Conclusion As part of their regular job functions, nonsexist counselors in employment settings and community agencies and organizations can help eliminate differential treatment of boys and girls, women and men. In utilizing consultation and change agent skills described at the beginning of chapter 7, counselors and other helping professionals in a variety of settings can: collect information on how males and females are treated differently, bring this to the attention of others within the organization, develop programs and strategies to eliminate sexist elements, provide in-service training programs on the subject for their co-workers, and evaluate such programs and strategies.

References

Buchanan, E. The growing opportunities for women in management. *Colorado Business Review*, 1968,*57*(9), 60–65.

Day Care and Child Development Council of America *Resources for child care*. Washington, D.C.: Day Care and Child Development Council of America, Inc., 1977.

Directory of correctional institutions and agencies, 1971. College Park, Md.: American Correctional Association, 1972.

Ells, S. C. How Polaroid gave women the kind of affirmative action program they wanted. *Mangement Review,* November 1973, *62*(11), 11–15.

Eymon, J. *Prisons for women*. Springfield, Ill.: Charles C. Thomas, 1971.

Foxley, C. H.*Locating, recruiting, and employing women: An equal opportunity approach*. Garrett Park, Md.: Garrett Park Press, 1976.

Glickman, A. S., and Brown, Z. H. *Changing schedules of work: Patterns and implications*. Silver Spring, Md.: American Institutes for Research, 1973.

Goldberg, H. *A comparison of three alternative work schedules: Flexible work hours, compact work week and staggered work hours*. Ph.D. dissertation, University of Pennsylvania, 1975.

Howard, E. M., and Howard, J. L. Women in institutions: Treatment in prisons and mental hospitals. In V. Franks and V. Burtle (eds.), *Women in therapy*. New York: Brunner/Mazel, 1974.

Lekkerkerker, E. *Reformatories for women in the U.S.* The Hague: Walters, 1931.

Monahan, F. *Women in crime*. New York: Ives Washburn, 1941.

Pollak, O. *The criminality of women*. Philadelphia: University of Pennsylvania Press, 1950.

Sutherland, E., and Cressey, D.*Criminology*. New York: Lippincott, 1970.

U.S. Department of Labor, Bureau of Labor Statistics. *The revised workweek: Results of a pilot study of 16 firms*. Washington, D.C.: U.S. Department of Labor, 1975.

Women's Bureau, U.S. Department of Labor. *Employment needs of women offenders: A program model*. Washington, D.C.: U.S. Department of Labor, 1977a.

Women's Bureau, U.S. Department of Labor. *Women offenders: Must we bar them from employment?* Washington, D.C.: U.S. Department of Labor, 1977b.

Training for Nonsexist Counseling

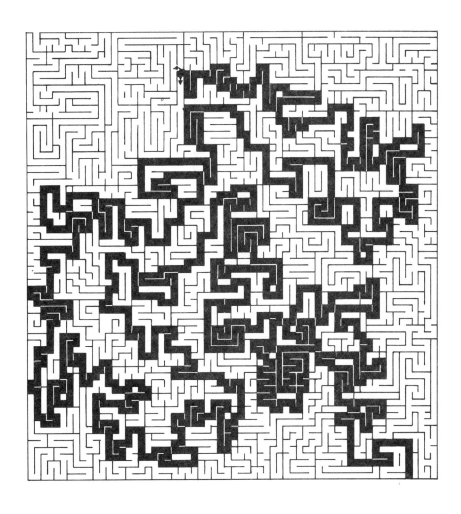

9 A New Curriculum for Counselor Education Programs

That counselors have done their share in perpetuating sex-role stereotypes has been demonstrated (see chaps. 2 and 3). One of the logical places to begin changing couneelors' sexist attitudes and behaviors is in the counselor education and training curriculum—as counselor trainees are in the process of forming their own theories, techniques, and styles of counseling that they will some day use as full-fledged practitioners. Several authors (Guttman, 1974; Hansen, 1974; Lewis and Lewis, 1974; and Leonard, Hansen, and Knefelkamp, 1974; Schlossberg and Pietrofesa, 1973; Westervelt, 1963) have pointed to the need for changes in counselor education programs if indeed we are to begin training nonsexist counselors. This chapter suggests some curricular changes which can be made in order to provide counselor trainees with necessary knowledge and skills to be nonsexist in their counseling. Some suggested efforts to change sexist attitudes and behaviors of counselor educators are included in chapters 7 and 10.

Most counselor education programs espouse the concept of interdisciplinary training which provides the counselor trainee with the necessary knowledge and skills to treat the "whole person"—the functioning individual interacting with the environment. What does this interdisciplinary training consist of? The counselor training process set forth by Wrenn (1962) in *The Counselor in a Changing World* is "multidisciplinary" in order to prepare the counselor trainee adequately. His multidisciplinary training program includes a broad knowledge of psychology and sociology, understanding of educational philosophy and curriculum, applied counseling skills and techniques, supervised practica, introduction to research, and exposure to professional ethics and legal issues. In stressing that counselor trainees be given an opportunity to learn about themselves in relation to what they have learned about counseling, Kemp (1962) states that the trainee ". . . must understand his [her] own personality dynamics since his [her] counseling, if genuine, will be in agreement with his [her] inner attitudes. . . . Sufficient experience should be provided in simulated 'cases' to aid the counselor-in-training not only to improve in technique, but to discover to a greater degree his [her] genotypical attitudes—the form of responses which coincide with his [her] approach to life." Van Hoose (1970), noting a shift in counselor trainee orientation, from primarily cognitive to combined affective-cognitive behavior, explained the shift as an effort to produce counselors who "feel" as well as "think." As stated by Island (1972), "Counselor education must provide the conditions in which students can see social, educational, political, psychological, and economical contradictions in the environment."

Few counselor educators would argue with any of these statements regarding counselor education and training, since most counselor education programs have made concerted efforts to include courses, practica, and other learning experiences which reflect a "multidisciplinary" approach to both cognitive and affective learning about human behavior, understanding of self and others, and helping and consultation theories and skills—in one-to-one, group, and environmental contexts. And yet, few counselor education programs offer their students, as part of the regular curriculum, any instruction regarding sex role stereotyping—a phenomenon that has set limitations on the development of both women and men and one that has been upheld by practicing counselors (see chap. 2). Is not such instruction compatible with—even called for—in the counselor education and training programs described by the above writers? Certainly a "multi-disciplinary" approach includes the study of sex roles. Being able to see the "social, educational, political, psychological, and economical contradictions in the environment" would include being able to see the contradictions and detrimental effects of sex role stereotyping. And, recognizing and understanding one's "genotypical attitudes"—including sexist and nonsexist attitudes—is the first step the counselor trainee takes in becoming a nonsexist counselor. Taken in combination, these aspects of counselor education and training dealing with sex bias and sex role stereotyping can bring about both cognitive and affective understandings of sexism and the extent to which it can interfere with effective counseling.

It has been fifteen years since Westervelt (1963) called for a change in the preparation of counselors for girls and women. The same call for change could be made today, for not only the benefit of female clients, but male clients as well. While there have been some changes, they have not been major nor have they come quickly enough. Too many of the concerns she expressed then are still all too evident in the training of counselors today:

. . .counselors who express the conviction that women's primary and socially essential roles are domestic and maternal and take place in the home may be reflecting a covert need to keep them there.

Girls and women in the lower socioeconomic brackets who particularly need counseling help to recognize and plan for paid employment will get little assistance from such counselors. Nor, of course, will these counselors help intellectually and educationally privileged girls to use their gifts and training to best advantage.

. . .No formal, university-sponsored, graduate-level, degree-awarding program in counselor education requires even a one-semester course in social and psychological sex differences which affect development or provides focus on sex differences in a practicum or internship in counseling. . . .

Trends toward the integration into counselor education, at basic levels, of more subject matter from social psychology, anthropology, sociology, and economics would also provide more exposure to materials on psycho-social sex differences and changing sex roles. Again, however, the effect of such exposure will depend on the student's initial sympathetic interest, since the material will be only a small part of a much larger whole.

The implications for counselor training, and particularly counseling practica, are clear when she says:

Counselors, guidance workers, and student personnel workers . . . should have as many opportunities as possible to counsel with females—and, ideally, with females of all ages, in order than, no matter what the age level with which they eventually work, they get an opportunity to observe first hand the patterns of continuity and discontinuity in feminine development. Counseling experience should not, however, be limited to working with females; opportunity to counsel with boys and men is most important, both because it will provide insights into psycho-social sex differences and because it will provide a chance to explore useful variations in approaches to counseling the two sexes. All counselors-in-training should be helped to identify, understand and work with sex differences in their counseling practicum or internship. . . .

One way of including sex role issues and material in the counselor education curriculum is to integrate discussions of sex bias into already existing courses on counseling-oriented subject matter. For example, sexual biases of tests and other instruments are assessed in a regular appraisal course. Counseling theory courses become more meaningful when generalizations regarding the male as the prototype of humanity are examined. Research courses are broadened with questions regarding the sexist contamination of scientific inquiry, where female subjects have often been ignored or placed into inappropriate categories. Environmental information courses are made more pertinent when resources are looked at in terms of their being nondiscriminatory or discriminatory. Counseling practica are made more impactful when counselor trainees are provided the opportunity to examine their own sexist attitudes and behaviors in working with clients of both sexes. If such content were included in all facets of a counselor education and training program, there would be little need for additional courses, practica, and learning experiences dealing with sexism and sex role issues. But the fact is we're just not there yet. Not all counselor educators recognize sex role stereotyping as a problem. Indeed, a mere suggestion that such content be included in their teaching may be viewed as an infringement upon academic freedom. Until there is broader awareness among counselor educators that sexism does exist and is detrimental to the members of both sexes, probably the most effective way of providing counselor trainees with the necessary information and training that will enable them to be nonsexist practitioners is to add special courses, practica, and other learning experiences to the curriculum.

Before going into some specific courses, practica, and other learning experiences which can be added to the counselor education curriculum, let me first say a few words about who should be teaching such course offerings and supervising the practica and other learning experiences. Faculty most effective in teaching courses and supervising practica dealing with sexism and sex role issues are those who are not only aware and knowledgeable of the many facets of sexism, sex role stereotyping, sex discrimination, and the like, and are cognizant of the need for individual and societal change, but who have also undergone self-examination and assessment of stereotypic and sexist attitudes and behaviors, both in and out of the counselor-client relationship. In short, the person is a feminist, one who believes in the equality of women and men. This is not to say that anyone having a less than clean slate regarding sexist attitudes and behaviors is "unfit" for such a teaching responsibility, since we all are victims of our own upbringing and educational training—most of which was based on the presumption that traditional sex roles were the only appropriate models of behavior. But being aware of one's own sexist attitudes and behaviors, understanding where they came from, and working to change them are necessary for counselor educators endeavoring to teach others to do the same. In addition, a faculty member's teaching style may either facilitate or inhibit effective instruction in such courses and learning experiences. Those who prefer the lecture format and are uncomfortable with informal discussion groups and structured and unstructured learning experiences in which basic beliefs, attitudes and opinions can be shared and challenged will not be as effective as those who are comfortable with and competent in using a variety of teaching-learning formats such as those mentioned here. More will be said later about the use of small groups for awareness training and consciousness-raising both in the special courses as a vehicle for increased class participation and learning and in practica and other out-of-class learning activities.

New Courses to Be Added to the Curriculum

The four courses outlined here are presented as examples of special courses which could be added to the counselor education curriculum as part of an effort to train nonsexist counselors: (1) Psychological Aspects of Men's and Women's Roles, (2) Sex Role Stereotyping and Socialization in Education, (3) Human Sexuality, and (4) Nonsexist Counseling for Men and Women.

There are of course other courses which could be designed, using segments of these courses or entirely different topics. It might also be argued that in an already full curriculum, adding four new courses is not feasible, but one or two new additions might be possible. And, too, there may be less resistance from faculty and administrators who are not convinced of the value of such courses if a single course is first added to the curriculum and others are added gradually at a later time. The courses presented here could easily be redesigned into one major survey course dealing with sex role stereotyping and the counselor's past and future roles, with topical seminars on subjects such as human sexuality. Another approach would be to offer two main courses, one course combining the basic content of "Psychological Aspects of Men's and Women's Roles" with the major topics of "Sex Role Stereotyping and Socialization in Education," and the other course merging subject matter from "Nonsexist Counseling for Men and Women" and "Human Sexuality." Obviously with such combinations and mergers, some subject matter will be slighted or not covered at all. In designing such courses and selecting the areas to be given emphasis, a helpful question to keep in mind is, "What is necessary for the counselor trainee to know in order to become a completely nonsexist practicing professional?" In answering that question, some obvious major areas are: (1) thorough understanding of what sex role stereotyping and sexism are and their many resulting detrimental effects, (2) knowledge of the part counselors have played in perpetuating sex role stereotypes in the past and what they can do to facilitate nonstereotypic development of girls and boys, men and women in the future, and (3) recognition of one's own sexist attitudes and behaviors and establishment of a personalized plan for changing such attitudes and behaviors.

Two of the courses outlined below—Sex Role Stereotyping and Socialization in Education'' and "Human Sexuality"—are presently being offered by the Division of Counselor Education at the University of Iowa. The author has taken the liberty of expanding and changing the courses in order to tailor them to fit the objectives of this chapter. "Sex Role Stereotyping and Socialization in Education," originally developed in 1971 by the author and Gail T. McLure, was the first course specifically dealing with sex roles and sex role stereotyping to be offered at the University of Iowa. The course entitled "Human Sexuality" was originally designed by Lauralee Rockwell.

While the other two courses—"Psychological Aspects of Men's and Women's Roles" and "Nonsexist Counseling for Men and Women"—were developed by the author for the purposes of this chapter, ideas for the courses stemmed from two related courses also offered by the University of Iowa's Division of Counselor Education—"Psychological Aspects of Women's Roles" and "Issues and Applications in Counseling Women," respectively. Both courses deal with only women's roles and counseling women and were originally developed by Dianne K. Carter, with Kathleen Staley and Marlin Schmidt contributing to the refining of the first course. Considerations are presently underway to make the content of both courses include men's roles as well.

Some feminists would argue that courses dealing with sexism and sex role stereotyping should focus entirely on women as women have suffered the most negative consequences from such phenomena and that special counseling courses should focus entirely on feminist therapy as an approach to helping women overcome the detrimental effects of sexism and sex role stereotyping. While the author is a feminist who agrees that this may very well be where we must start, it should only be viewed as a starting point. In order for women's roles to make drastic changes, men's roles—which have also resulted from stereotyping—must change too, and while there need to be different approaches in helping women and men change and expand their roles, the male half of the population should not be ignored. Depending on the needs of a particular counselor education program and the expertise and interests of its faculty, issues regarding counseling women and men for expanding and changing roles may be handled in separate courses or in combined courses.

It should be pointed out that the four courses below are listed in a sequential order, according to how the author views the relationship of the subject matter in each course with the other courses and the building effect from starting with the most basic material and progressing to more complex or applied material. This is not to say that one course could not be offered singly without the others nor that there is no overlap in subject matter. Indeed, as the reader will observe, each course is designed to stand alone as a complete course offering, thus the need for some slight overlap in content. The major focus of each course is, however, distinctly different from the others.

It should also be pointed out that while such courses may and perhaps should utilize extensive reading lists, only twenty or so selected readings for each course are presented here because of space limitations. Instructional aids, such as the use of small groups, films, resource organizations, and possible assignments and projects, are presented in a section following the course outlines.

Psychological Aspects of Men's and Women's Roles

Course Description

The course provides an introduction to women's and men's roles as they have been traditionally defined by society and as they are changing and developing in America today. The development of sex role identity, sex role acquisition, and societal and institutional reinforcement of sex roles are analyzed and alternative approaches and strategies for change are discussed.

Course Objectives

—To become familiar with sex role development and socialization processes.
—To become familiar with the differences and similarities between the sexes.
—To become aware of sex role stereotyping, how it develops, and its many detrimental effects.
—To provide an opportunity for students to discuss their knowledge and attitudes regarding sex role stereotyping and the changing roles of men and women.

Discussion Topics

Sex Role Development and Sex Role Acquisition
Stereotyped Male and Female Characteristics

Overview of Sex Differences

Biological Perspectives

Sources of Socialization: Family, Schools, Media, etc.

Some Consequences of Socialization: Self-esteem vs. Self-dislike, the Achievement Motive, Power vs. Powerlessness, Occupational Choices and Workforce Status, Marriage and Family Roles, etc.

Clincal Judgements of Mental Health—Female and Male

Male and Female Sexuality

Cultural and Ethnic Variations in Men's and Women's Roles: Blacks, Asian Americans, Native Americans, Mexican Americans, the Soviet Union, the People's Republic of China, Sweden, and the Israeli Kibbutz

Legal Rights of Men and Women—Equal Opportunity Laws and Regulations

Changing Roles—Means Toward Human Liberation, Psychological Androgyny

Selected Readings

Bardwick, J. M. *Psychology of women: A study of biocultural conflicts.* New York: Harper & Row, 1971.

Bernard, J. Sex differences: An overview. *MSS Modular Publications,* 26, 1974.

Bird, C. *Born female.* New York: David McKay, 1968.

Broverman, I. K.; Broverman, D. M.; Clarkson, F. E.; Rosenkrantz, P. S.; and Vogel, S. R. Sex-role stereotypes and clinical judgements of mental health. *Journal of Consulting and Clinical Psychology,* 1970, *34,* 1–7.

Chafetz, J. S. *Masculine/Feminine or human?: An overview of the Sociology of sex roles.* Itasca, Illinois: F. E. Peacock Publishers, 1974.

Cox, S. (ed.). *Female psychology: The emerging self.* Chicago: Science Research Associates, 1976.

David, D. S., Brannon, R. (eds.). *The forty-nine percent majority: The male sex role.* Reading, Mass.: Addison-Wesley Publishing Co., 1976.

Donelson, E., and Gullahorn, J. E. *Women: A psychological perspective.* New York: John Wiley & Sons, 1977.

Farrell, W. *The liberated man: Beyond masculinity; freeing men and their relationships with women.* New York: Random House, 1974.

Foxley, C. H. *Locating, recruiting, and employing women: An equal opportunity approach.* Garrett Park, Maryland: Garrett Park Press, 1976.

Foxley, C. H. "Stereotyping of Sex Roles," Section I of this book.

Goldberg, H. *The hazards of being male: Surviving the myth of masculine privilege.* New York: Nash, 1976.

Kanowitz, L. *Women and the law.* Albuquerque: University of New Mexico, 1969.

Kaplan, A. G., and Bean, J. P. *Beyond sex-role stereotypes: Readings toward a psychology of androgyny.* Boston: Little, Brown & Company, 1976.

Levine, J. A. *Who will care for the children? New options for fathers (and mothers).* Lippincott, 1975.

Maccoby, E. (ed.). *The development of sex differences.* Stanford: University Press, 1966.

Maccoby, E. E., and Jacklin, C. N. *The psychology of sex differences.* Stanford, Cal.: Stanford University Press, 1974.

Mead, M. *Male and female: A study of the sexes in a changing world.* New York: Dell, 1968.

Mednick, M. T. S.; Tangri, S. S.; and Hoffman, L. W. (eds.). *Women and achievement: Social and motivational analyses.* Washington, D.C.: Hemisphere Publishing Corporation, 1975.

Mussen, P. H. Early sex-role development. In D. A. Goslin (ed.), *Handbook of socialization theory and research.* Chicago: Rand McNally College Publishing Company, 1969.

Nichols, J. *Men's liberation: A new definition of masculinity.* New York: Penguin Books, 1975.

Tavis, C., and Offir, C. *The longest war: Sex differences in perspective.* New York: Harcourt Brace Jovanovich, 1977.

Unger, R. K., and Denmark, F. L. *Women: Dependent or independent variable.* New York: Psychological Dimensions, Inc., 1975.

Wesley, F., and Wesley, C. *Sex-role psychology.* New York: Human Sciences Press, 1977.

Yorburg, B. *Sexual identity: Sex roles and social change.* New York: John Wiley & Sons, 1974.

Sex Role Stereotyping and Socialization in Education

Course Description

The primary focus of the course is a consideration of the part education plays in the socialization of the sexes. The school's reinforcement of sex role stereotyping is analyzed, and alternative educational approaches and strategies for change are discussed.

Course Objectives

—To facilitate identification, exploration, study and research of concerns and problems related to sex role stereotyping in education.

—To provide an opportunity for student discussion of knowledge and attitudes regarding the topic.

—To explore various steps school personnel—particularly counselors—can take in eliminating sex role stereotypic elements in the schools.

Discussion Topics

Overview of Sex Role Development

Sex Role Stereotyped Characteristics Attributed to Students at the Various Educational Levels

Sex Differences in Learning Ability, Academic Performance, and Educational and Vocational Aspirations

Student, Teacher, and Counselor Perceptions of Appropriate Sex Role Behaviors

Sexist Elements in the Curriculum

Sex Role Stereotyping in Textbooks and Instructional Materials

Sex Bias in Measurement

Sex Bias in Occupational/Vocational/Educational Materials Used by Counselors

Sexist Elements in Extracurricular Activities

Role Models in the Schools—Staffing Profiles

Differential Treatment of Men and Women in Colleges and Universities

Title IX of the Education Amendments of 1972—Legislation for Sex Equality in Education

Steps to Removing Sex Role Stereotypic and Discriminatory Elements in the Schools

Counselors as Agents for Change

Selected Readings

Diamond, E. E. (ed.). *Issues of sex bias and sex fairness in career interest measurement.* Washington, D.C.: U.S. Department of Health, Education and Welfare, 1975.

Filene, P. G. *Him/Her/Self: Sex roles in modern America.* New York: Harcourt, Brace, Jovanovich, 1975.

Fitzpatrick, B. E. *Women's inferior education: An economic analysis.* New York: Praeger Publishers, 1976.

Foxley, C. H. "Sex Typing in the Schools," "Sex Typing, Discrimination, and the Law," and "Promoting Change in the Schools," Chapters 3, 5, and 7 of this book.

Frazier, N., and Sadker, M. *Sexism in school and society.* New York: Harper & Row, 1973.

Furniss, W. T., and Graham, P. A. (eds.). *Women in higher education.* Washington, D.C.: American Council on Education, 1974.

Grambs, J. D., and Waetjen, W. B. *Sex: Does it make a difference?* North Scituate, Massachusetts: Duxbury Press, 1975.

Guttentag, M., and Bray, H. *Undoing sex stereotypes: Research and resources for educators.* New York: McGraw-Hill, 1976.

Hansen, L. S. A career development curriculum framework for counselors to promote female growth. In M. A. J. Guttman and P. A. Donn (eds.), *Women and aces: Perspectives and issues.* Washington, D.C.: Commission for Women, Association for Counselor Education and Supervision, 1974.

Harway, M. Sex bias in counseling materials. *Journal of College Student Personnel,* January 1977, *18*(1), 57–64.

Horner, M. Toward an understanding of achievement related conflicts in women. *Journal of Social Issues, 28*(2), 1972.

Humanist Educator. Special issue, Implementing sex equality: Humanist prescription for education, June, 1976.

Jones, B. C. Male pupils vs. sexist educators. *Educational Forum,* March 1974, *38*(3), 315–320.

Maccoby, E. E. (ed.). *The development of sex differences.* Stanford, California: Stanford University Press, 1966.

Matthews, E. E., *et al. Counseling girls and women over the life span.* Washington, D.C.: National Vocational Guidance Association, 1972.

Personnel and Guidance Journal. Special issue on Women and Counselors, October, 1972.

Phi Delta Kappan. Special issue on Education and the Feminist Movement, October, 1973.

Richardson, B. *Sexism in higher education.* New York: Seabury Press, 1974

Rossi, A. S., and Calderwood, A. (eds.). *Academic women on the move.* New York: Russell Sage Foundation, 1973.

Schlossberg, N. K., and Pietrafesa, J. Perspectives on counseling bias: Implications for counselor education. *Counseling Psychologist,* 4:1, 1973.

Sprung, B. *Non-sexist education for young children: A practical guide.* New York: Citation Press, 1975.

Stacey, J.; Bereaud, S.; and Daniels, J. *And Jill came tumbling after: Sexism in American education.* New York: Dell Publishing Co., 1974. *Title IX of the education amendments of 1972—a summary of the implementing regulation.* Washington, D.C.: Resource Center on Sex Roles in Education, National Foundation for the Improvement of Education, 1976.

Wesley, F., and Wesley, C. *Sex-role psychology.* New York: Human Sciences Press, 1977.

Women on campus. New York: *Change Magazine,* 1975.

Women on words and images. *Help wanted: Sexism in career education materials.* Princeton, N.J.: National Organization for Women, 1975.

Human Sexuality

Course Description

This course provides an exploration of the physiological and psychological aspects of human sexuality. Effects of sex role stereotyping on the sexuality of men and women, trends in sexual behavior, and attitudes toward sexuality are discussed.

Course Objectives:

—To become more comfortable and accepting on one's own and of other's sexuality.

—To increase awareness of the wide variation of human sexual response.

—To become aware of the sex role stereotyping of male and female sexuality.

—To discuss the various points of view in controversial sexual issues.

—To gain information about sexual dysfunctioning and treatment.

—To discuss trends in sexual behavior and attitudes toward sexuality.

Discussion Topics:

Physiology of Sexuality
Psychosexual Development
Cross-cultural Comparisons of Attitudes about Sexuality
Contraception
Pregnancy

Venereal Disease

Expressions of Human Sexuality

Varieties of Expression: Oral-Genital, Masturbation, Orgasm, Fore-Play, etc.

Homosexuality and Bisexuality

Transvestites and Transsexuals

Sex and Aging

Legal Aspects of Sexuality

Pornography

Sexual Dysfunctioning and Treatment

Sex Role Stereotyping and Male and Female Sexuality

The Counselor as Sex Educator and Therapist

Selected Readings

Butler, R. H., and Lewis, M. I. *Sex after sixty.* New York: Harper & Row, 1976.

Denmark, F. L. Some aspects of female sexual behavior: An overview. In R. K. Unger and F. L. Denmark (eds.), *Woman: Dependent or independent variable?* New York: Psychological Dimensions, Inc., 1975.

Dodson, B. *Liberating masturbation.* New York: Bodysex Designs, 1974.

Ellis, A. *Sex and the liberated man.* Secaucus, N.J.: Lyle Stuart, Inc., 1976.

Feinbloom, D. H. *Transvestites and transsexuals: Mixed views.* New York: Delacorte Press, 1976.

Graber, G. K. and Graber, B. *Women's orgasm.* Indianapolis: Bobbs-Merrill Co., 1975.

Hammer, S. (ed.). *Women: Body and culture: Essays on the sexuality of women in a changing culture.* New York: Perennial Library, 1975.

Hite, S. *The hite report: A nationwide study of female sexuality.* New York: Dell Publishing Co., 1976.

Katchadurian, H. A., and Lunde, D. T. *Fundamentals of human sexuality.* Chicago: Holt, Rinehart & Winston, 1975.

Kelly, G. F. *The guidance counselor as sex educator.* New York: Behavioral Publications, 1976.

Kinsey, A.; Pomeroy, W.; and Martin, C. *Sexual behavior in the human male.* Philadelphia: W. B. Saunders Co., 1948.

Kinsey, A.; Pomeroy, W.; Martin, C.; and Gebhard, P. *Sexual behavior in the human female.* Philadelphia: W. B. Saunders Co., 1953.

Lieberman, B.(ed.). *Human sexual behavior: A book of readings.* New York: John Wiley & Sons, 1971.

Masters, W., and Johnson, V. *Human sexual inadequacy.* Boston: Little, Brown, 1970.

Masters, W., and Johnson, V. *Human sexual response.* Boston: Little, Brown, 1966.

McCary, J. L. *Sexual myths and fallacies.* New York: Schocken Books, 1975.

National Institute of Mental Health Task Force on Homosexuality. *Final report and background papers.* U.S. Department of Health, Education, and Welfare Publication Number ADM 76-357, 1972.

Petras, J. W. *Sex/Male—gender/masculine: Readings in male sexuality.* New York: Alfred, 1975.

Pietrofesa, J J., and Carlson, J. Human sexuality and the school counselor. *Counseling and Values,* 1973, 17, 228-234.

Sherfey, M. J. *The nature and evolution of female sexuality.*

Singer, J. *Androgyny: Toward a new theory of sexuality.* New York: Anchor Press/Doubleday, 1976.

Tyler, L. *The psychology of human differences.* New York: Apleton-Century-Crofts, 1965.

Nonsexist Counseling for Men and Women

Course Description

The course begins with a look at sex stereotyping and judgments of mental health and moves to a study of various nonsexist approaches and techniques used in counseling women and men.

Course Objectives

—To review the detrimental effects of sexism and sex role stereotyping.

—To examine the extent to which sex role stereotyping has influenced clinical judgments of mental health.

—To recognize one's own sexist attitudes and behaviors in counseling men and women and develop a personal plan for change.

—To gain information about nonsexist approaches and techniques in counseling men and women with a variety of problems and concerns.

Discussion Topics

Sex Bias and Sex Role Stereotyping in Counseling and Psychotherapy

Sex Bias in Counseling Instruments and Materials

The Double Standard of Mental Health

The Female Role and Psychological Disturbances—Depressions, Frigidity, Neurosis, Schizophrenia, Paranoia, etc.

The Male Role and "Male Illnesses"—Alcoholism, High Blood Pressure, Heart Disease, Gastric Ulcer, Personality Disorders, etc.

Patients in Psychiatric Facilities—Sex, Class, Race, and Marital Status

Sex Roles, Marital Status, and Mental Illness

Counseling Women for Psychological Androgyny—Some Selected Foci: Aggression and Anger vs. Assertion; Dependency vs. Independence; Fear of Achievement vs. Success; Sexuality, Aging, and Dual Role Conflicts

Counseling Men for Psychological Androgyny—Some Selected Foci: Stoicism vs. Expressiveness and Emotionality; Superiority vs. Equality; Pressure to Succeed and Achieve; Sexuality, Aging, and Conflicts with Nontraditional Sex Roles

Single-sex and Combined-sex Group Counseling for Shared Problems: Consciousness Raising; Assertion Training; Career, Vocational, and Life Planning; Sexuality and Personal Relationships; Divorce; etc.
Recognizing and Dealing with One's Own Sex Bias as a Counselor

Selected Readings

Bardwick, J. M.; Douvan, E.; Horner, M. S.; and Gutmann, D. *Feminine personality and conflict.* Belmont, Calif.: Brooks/Cole, 1970.

Blum, H. P. *Female psychology: Contemporary psychoanalytic views.* New York: International Universities Press, Inc., 1977.

Brim, O. G., Jr. Theories of the male mid-life crisis. *Counseling Psychologist,* 1976, 6(1), 2–9.

Brodsky, A.; Holroyd, J.; Sherman, J.; Payton, C.; Rosenkrantz, P.; Rubenstein, E.; and Zell, F. *Report of the task force on sex bias and sex-role stereotyping in therapeutic practice.* American Psychological Association, 1975.

Chesler, P. *Women and madness.* New York: Doubleday, 1972.

De Rosis, H. A., and Pellegrino. V. Y. *The book of hope and how women can overcome depression* New York: Macmillan, 1976.

Farrell, W. *The liberated man; beyond masculinity: Freeing men and their relationships with women.* New York: Random House, 1974.

Foxley, C. H. "Sex Typing and Judgments of Mental Health" and "Counseling for Psychological Androgyny," chapters 2 and 6 of this book.

Franks, V., and Burtle, V. (eds.). *Women in therapy: New psychotherapies for a changing society.* New York: Brunner/Mazel Publishers, 1974.

Goldberg, H. Men in therapy. In Goldberg, H., *The hazards of being male.* New York: Nash, 1976.

Green, R. *Human sexuality: A health practitioner's text.* Baltimore: Williams & Williams Co., 1975.

Groups for the Advancement of Psychiatry. *Assessment of sexual function: A guide to interviewing,* November, 1973, 8, 88.

Grove, W. R. Relationship between sex roles, marital status, and mental illness. In A. G. Kaplan and J. P. Bean (eds.), *Beyond sex-role stereotypes: Readings toward a psychology of androgyny.* Boston: Little Brown, 1976.

Horney, K. *Feminine psychology.* New York: W. W. Norton, 1967.

Jourard, S. M., Some lethal aspects of the male role. In Journard, S. M. *The transparent self.* New York: Van Nostrand, 1964.

Kaplan, A. B. Androgyny as a model of mental health for women: From theory to therapy. In A. G. Kaplan and J. P. Bean (eds.), *Beyond sex-role stereotypes: readings toward a psychology of androgyny.* Boston: Little, Brown, 1976.

Kaye, H. E. *Male survival: Masculinity without myth.* New York: Grosset & Dunlap, 1974.

Meyer, J. K. (ed.). *Clinical management of sexual disorders.* Baltimore: Williams & Wilkins Co., 1976.

Miller, J. B. (ed.). *Psychoanalysis and women.* New York: Brunner/Mazel, 1973.

Rawlings, E. I., and Carter, D. K. *Psychotherapy for women: Treatment toward equality.* Springfield, Ill.: Charles C. Thomas, 1977.

Ruitenbeek, H. M. (ed.). *Psychoanalysis and male sexuality.* New Haven, Conn.: College and University Press, 1966.

Tiger, L. *Men in groups.* New York: Random House, 1969.

Unger, R. K., and Denmark, F. L. (eds.). Section II. How the therapist looks at women. In R. K. Unger and F. L. Denmark (eds.), *Woman: Dependent or independent variable?* New York: Psychological Dimensions, 1975.

Vaillant, G. E. Natural history of male psychological health. *Archives of General Psychiatry,* July 1974, 31, 15–22.

Some Instructional Aids

Due to the similarity, and in some instances overlap, in subject content and learning objectives of the four courses described above, many of the instructional aids discussed and listed below could be used effectively in any one or all of the courses, with perhaps a slight variation in emphasis, theme, or major focus. The counselor educator teaching any of the above courses, courses similar to these, or a special unit dealing with sexism and sex role stereotypes in a traditional counseling course will find the following instructional aids helpful. With a little imagination, innovative counselor educators can design and implement their own instructional aids and learning experiences, tailored to meet the specific needs of a particular group of counselor trainees and emphasizing certain desired content.

Small Groups

Dividing a large group of students into smaller groups for the purpose of discussion is not a new teaching-learning format. In courses dealing with sexism and sex role stereotyping, the small group approach is particularly effective in facilitating not only the assimilation of course subject matter, but perhaps more importantly, the opportunity of counselor trainees to share personal attitudes, beliefs, and experiences, and try out new behaviors. Small group activities can be integrated into regular class sessions, conducted at regularly scheduled times outside of class, or a combination of the two, depending on the type of group activity and learning objectives. The groups will be most productive if the size is kept to from five to eight members, the membership is kept constant, and basic principles of small group dynamics are adhered to (e.g., equal opportunity to speak and participate, openness, confidentiality, tolerance, support, etc.). The sex makeup of the small groups will depend upon the nature of the learning objectives and the needs and desires of the participants, although it is generally agreed that at least initially the groups should be same-sex.

Two of the most helpful types of small group activities in courses on sex roles are awareness exercises and consciousness-raising. Consciousness-raising (C-R) groups can be potent learning experiences offered as part of a course dealing with sex role stereotyping. (See discussion on C-R in chap. 7.) Such groups are probably most effective if they are not given time constraints by trying to work them into a regular class session with lectures and class discussion. A better format would be to have C-R groups meet on alternate class sessions or to schedule meeting times for C-R groups in addition to the regular class sessions. Since the nature of C-R groups is discussed in more detail below, such discussion will not be repeated here.

Awareness exercises can be easily integrated into a course to demonstrate specific points and enable counselor trainees to learn through structured and semistructured experiences with others what sex role stereotyping is and its detrimental effects. A couple examples of such exercises, with optional variations, are presented here.

Exercise in Identifying Sex Role Stereotypes Divide class into same-sex groups of approximately five members each. Ask each group to identify and agree among themselves on the five most common assumptions men make about women and the five most common assumptions women make about men. Have a representative from each group write their assumptions on the board. Discuss with the class such questions as: Which ones appear to be obvious stereotypes? How widely accepted do you feel these assumptions are? What are their origins? How do such assumptions tend to limit aspirations of men and women? How can these assumptions be challenged and changed—in personal relationships, in the home, school, workforce, and society at large?

Variations:

1. Use mixed-sex groups instead of same-sex for above exercise.
2. Have the groups (either same-sex or mixed-sex) identify and agree upon any of the following:
   a. Assumptions male/female counselors make about male/female clients.
   b. Assumptions teachers (specify level, i.e., elementary, secondary, college) make about male/female students.
   c. Assumptions employers make about male/female applicants for employment.
   d. What I like/dislike about my sex.
   e. What I like/dislike about the opposite sex.

Career-line Exercise for Counseling Trainees Instruct counselor trainees to individually draw their career lines on a blank sheet of paper, identifying the types of professional positions they would like to have following completion of their education and the approximate number of years they would like to serve in each position. Ask them to project their career lines up to and including retirement. Then have them make two lists: (1) those factors which they think might facilitate their careers developing as they have drawn them on the career line, and (2) those factors which might keep them from reaching their career goals. Divide the students into small mixed-sex groups of six or seven members and ask them to share their career lines with their group. Ask each group to discuss the following: What are the similarities and dissimilarities between the male and female career lines? Do male and female counselor trainees tend to select different work settings or positions with different functions and responsibilities? Do males and females project different time-tables to reach their career objectives? Are there differences and similarities between the male and female lists of factors which they think may either facilitate or keep them from reaching their career goals?

Variations:

1. Use same-sex groups instead of mixed-sex groups for the above exercise.
2. Working in same-sex or mixed-sex groups, instruct half of the class to construct (by group consensus) a career line for the "typical male counselor" and the other half to construct a career line for the "typical female counselor." Bring the groups together for a reporting, sharing, and discussion of similarities and differences.

Such awareness exercises as these and others involving simulation, role-playing and other demonstration/learning techniques can be developed by instructors and students. Ideas for developing one's own awareness exercises as well as a wealth of tried and tested exercises can be found in *Exploring Contemporary Male/Female Roles: A Facilitator's Guide* (Carney and McMahon, 1977), *A Handbook for Workshops on Sex Equality in Education* (Verheyden-Hilliard, 1976), Russell (1977), and Moberg (1972).

Selected Audio-visual Teaching Aids
General films and filmstrips on the market do an excellent job of raising the viewer's consciousness about sex role stereotyping, its detrimental effects and positive alternatives, and provide focal points for class discussion on related topics. The following is a list of audio-visual instruction aids which I have found to be especially effective.

Anything You Want to Be, 1971. Eccentric Circle. P.O. Box 4085, Greenwich, Conn. 06830. A short, eight-minute film that portrays the way in which role expectations are fostered in young women by school personnel, parents, and peers.

A Chance to Choose. Project on Sex Equality in Guidance Opportunities, American Personnel and Guidance Association, 1607 New Hampshire Avenue, N.W., Washington, D.C. 20009. Filmstrip on counseling included in Multi-media Kit developed by the SEGO Project.

Fable of He and She, 1974. Learning Corporation of America, 1350 Ave. of the Americas, New York, N.Y. 10019. Presents the animated fable by Eliot Noyes Jr. Challenges stereotyped and sexist thinking and celebrates the joys of individual self-expression. A color, eleven- minute film.

Growing Up Female, 1971 and *Men's Lives,* n.d. New Day Films, P.O. Box 315, Franklin Lakes, N.J. 07417. Both films are approximately fifty minutes long and picture the pressures on young women and men respectively as they mature and move into young adulthood.

A Male Condition, 1974. Antioch Documentary Films, Antioch College, Yellow Springs, Ohio 45387. Film describes the male condition as stereotyped and limiting.

Masculine or Feminine—Your Role in Society, 1969. Coronet Instructional Films, 65 E. South Water Street, Chicago, Ill. 60601. An in-depth study of today's changing attitudes. What is the man's role in the home? What about the woman in business? Conflicting viewpoints on many levels and on various aspects of male-female identification are expressed in this powerful film, which leaves viewers to reach their own conclusions. Color, nineteen minutes.

Masculinity, 1974. Schloat Productions, 150 White Plains Rd., Tarrytown, N.Y. A four-part filmstrip series on masculinity and the male role.

Sex and the Professional, 1976. Texture Films, 1600 Broadway, New York, N.Y. 10019. In order to understand the diverse sexual needs and patterns of patients and students, professionals in the health and service fields must first recognize and accept their own sexual feelings and impulses. Draws on actual experiences with the humor, confusion, warmth, anxiety, and other attendant feelings which are involved. Provides a rich context for discussion in training programs and seminars. Restricted to use by professionals in the fields of health science, social work, and education. Color, twenty-five minutes.

Sex Role Development, 1974. CRM/McGraw-Hill Films, Del Mar, Cal. 92014. Color, twenty-three-minute film examining some of the sex-role stereotypes and traces their transmission to children via the socialization process. Also explores alternative approaches to socialization. Concludes with scenes at Pacific Oaks School to demonstrate methods of elimination stereotypes through education.

Sugar and Spice, 1974. Odeon Films, 1619 Broadway, New York, N.Y. 10019. A thirty-two-minute film which describes the efforts made by a preschool and private elementary school to offer a nonsexist educational environment.

Take This Woman, 1971. National Broadcasting Company/Films, Incorporated, 30 Rockefeller Plaza, New York, N.Y. 10020. A study of equal employment in relation to women which cites several cases to show that women have been denied promotional, career, and educational opportunities. Judge Joan Dempsey Klein; Aileen Hernandex of the National Organization for Women (NOW); Congresswomen Yvonne Brathwaite; and Chancellor Charles E. Young of UCLA express their views. The effect of the landmark Rosenfield decision on female employment also is examined. Color, twenty-five minutes.

Title IX: The Regulation that Prohibits Sex Discrimination in Public Education, 1976. Don Cain, Marketing/Audio Visual Library Service, 3300 University Ave. S.E., Minneapolis, Minn. 55414. A slide/tape presentation which introduces the Title IX regulation and reviews who must comply and what the requirements are for compliance.

We Are Woman, 1975. Motivational Media, 8271 Melrose, Los Angeles, Calif. 90069. Traces the historic, social, and economic restraints which have affected the equality of men and women throughout the ages. Deals with the conditioning for women's roles; the affect it has on men's health and life span, and the reasons why so many women now have jobs outside the home. Makes a strong case for individual rights of women, at the same time making an equally strong case for the rights of the individual regardless of sex. Narrated by Helen Reddy. Color, twenty-nine minutes.

Woman's Place, A, 1974. Xerox Films, 245 Long Hill Road, Middletown, Ct. 06457. Narrated by Bess Myerson, the film studies the role of women and how it is changing in American society today. Shows how children's books and playthings, advertisements and movies influence the child's concepts of male and female roles. Color, fifty-two minutes.

Women: The Hand that Cradles the Rock, 1973. Document Associates, Inc., 43 Britain Street, Toronto 285, Ontario Canada. Women's liberation from traditional social roles and why some women desire this liberation are discussed. These views are contrasted with a wife and mother of four who likes things as they are. Color, twenty-two minutes

Women in Management—Threat or Opportunity, 1975. CRM/McGraw-Hill Films, Del Mar, Calif. 92014. Color, twenty-nine-minute film explaining how men acquire stereotyped views toward women in management, and women's attitudes toward these prejudices. Discusses the ways in which women will affect social and organizational improvement through their new positions.

Women's Film, The, 1971. New Day Films, P.O. Box 315, Franklin Lakes, N.J. 07417. Depicts women's liberation in the truest and most far-reaching sense of the word. Five women are interviewed and talk about their problems. They express what they feel is wrong with the system and how women are victimized by class, racial, and sexual inequality. They realize that they play a supportive role to men, and that their needs as human beings and women are not recognized. Black/white, thirty-five minutes.

Women's Rights in the U.S.—An Informal History, 1973. Altana Films, 340 E. 34th Street, New YorkKN.Y. 10016. Provides an historical setting for women's rights movement. Pictures, cartoons, and illustrations from colonial days to the present reveal underlying attitudes toward women and women's roles. Conditions which brought about changes in women's status—frontier, Civil War, industrialism, etc., are examined as well as attitudes toward marriage, employment, fashion, and education. Dialogue between feminists and antifeminists based on actual speaches, diaries, and newspaper reports provides a spirited commentary. Color, twenty-seven minutes.

Because of space limitations only selected films and filmstrips could be mentioned here. In searching for additional audio-visual teaching aids, the reader is referred to the following film catalogues:

Clinical Human Sexuality Films. Focus International, Inc., 505 West End Avenue, New York, N.Y. 10024.

Films on the Women's Movement. GSA Federal Women's Program, Washington, D.C. 20405.

Women and Film: A Resource Handbook. Project on the Status and Education of Women, Association of American Colleges, 1818 R Street, N.W., Washington, D.C. 20009.

Sex Role Stereotyping in Schools Series. University of California, Extension Media Center, 2223 Fulton Street, Berkeley, Calif. 94720.

Women's Film Coop Catalog. Women's Film Cooperative, Valley Women's Center, 200 Main Street, Northampton, Mass. 01060.

Resource Organizations

A growing number of associations and organizations have staff, films, books, and other resources which are available to the counselor educator developing courses dealing with sex role stereotypes such as the four described in this chapter. Many of these organizations provide minimal cost or free materials which the instructor can order. In addition to the organizations listed here, the reader is encouraged to contact campus Women Studies Program Offices and Women's Centers (and Men's Studies Programs and Centers, where they are available) to see what assistance can be given in building bibliographies and collecting teaching materials on topics related to sex role stereotyping.

The following list is not intended to be extensive nor all-inclusive, since that would be impossible to compile. Rather it is a list of organizations and associations the author has found to be particularly responsive to requests for information and assistance.

American Association of Sex Educators, Counselors, and Therapists (AASECT), 5010 Wisconsin Avenue, N.W., Suite 304, Washington, D.C. 20016.

American Association of University Women, Office of Higher Education, 2401 Virginia Ave. N.W., Washington, D.C. 20037.

American Council on Education, Office of Women in Higher Education, 1 Dupont Circle N.W., Washington, D.C. 20036.

American Federation of Teachers, Women's Rights Committee, 1012 14th St., Washington, D.C. 20005. Write for their list of pamphlets and education materials.

Clearinghouse on Women's Studies, Feminist Press, College at Old Westbury, Box 334, Old Westbury, N.Y. 11568. Clearinghouse for information on nonsexist educational curriculum materials for elementary, secondary, and college levels. Publishes feminist biographies, women's studies course outlines and syllabi, noneexist children's books, and reprints of various works by women. Write for free catalogue.

Education Commission of the States, Task Force on Equal Rights for Women in Education, 300 Lincoln Tower, 1860 Lincoln St., Denver, Col. 80203.

KNOW, Inc., P.O. Box 86031, Pittsburg, Penn. 15221. Packet of articles on men's liberation.

Masculine Mystique Task Force of NOW, 5 South Wabash St., Suite 1615, Chicago, Ill. 60603. Packet of literature, bibliography, and information on starting men's groups.

MIT Humanities Library, Human Studies Collection, Cambridge, Mass. 02139, will provide free of charge a *Men's Studies Bibliography* containing over 1,100 citations.

National Education Association, Teacher Rights, 1201 16th St. N.W., Washington, D.C. 20036.

Project on Equal Education Rights (PEER), 1029 Vermont Ave., N.W., Suite 800, Washington, D.C. 20005.

Project on Sex Equality in Guidance Opportunities, American Personnel and Guidance Association, 1607 New Hampshire Avenue, N.W., Washington, D.C. 20009. Project holds workshops and disseminates information on sex equality in education. Copies of *Resources for Counselors, Teachers and Ad-*

ministrators and *Handbook for Workshops on Sex Equality in Education* available from the Project.

Project on the Status and Education of Women, Association of American Colleges, 1818 R Street, N.W., Washington, D.C. 20009. Project complies materials on the status and education of women in higher education.

Resource Center on Sex Roles in Education, The National Foundation for the Improvement of Education, 1201 16th Street, N.W., Washington, D.C. 20036. The center is funded to assist school systems and state departments of education in combating sexism.

Sex Information and Education Council of the United States (SIECUS). 137–155 N. Franklin, Hempstead, N.Y. 11550.

Women's Action Alliance, 370 Lexington Avenue, New York, N.Y. 10017. Alliance provides organizing assistance and information packets on the women's movement; is developing a nonsexist early childhood education program. Available for 25¢.

Women's Bureau, U.S. Department of Labor, Washington, D.C. 20210. Write for their publication list. Over seventy-five listings of excellent resource material. Useful in the classroom. Price list included although much of the material is free.

Possible Assignments and Projects

The following assignments and projects are examples that have worked for the author in teaching courses, seminars, and workshops on sex role stereotyping and related topics. They are presented here as idea stimulators for the reader in developing his or her own instructions and guidelines for student projects and assignments tailored for specific courses.

Journal All students keep a journal or log of their reactions to what they are learning in class and related out-of-class experiences and observations. Their own thoughts, attitudes, and feelings demonstrating both cognitive and affective learning of the subject matter are recorded. Students are instructed to make entries in their journals on a regular basis for each class session and as soon as possible following the occurrence of an event, idea, reaction, or experience so that their thoughts and feelings are fresh and can be recorded accurately. Students may or may not wish to share certain journal entries with the class. When students are willing to share some of the contents of their journal with other members of the class—their small group, for example—impactful learning and increased awareness can result. Journals are read by the instructor and the contents kept confidential if the student so wishes. It is common to see significant attitude change expressed in these journals over a period of a semester. And the rereading of what one has written over such a period of time can be an awareness experience in and of itself for the student.

Research or Grant Proposal Students take an idea they have for a study or an experiment related to sex roles, sex differences, etc., and write it up in the form of a research or grant proposal. A survey of the literature and what has been done by other researchers is included as well as an experimental design for testing the hypothesis. The proposal is presented orally to the class and critiqued. Especially promising proposals may be written up in the form of a grant proposal—including an estimated budget, projected timetable of activities, and a listing of individuals who would carry out the activities if the proposal were funded—and submitted to appropriate funding agencies.

Review of the Literature Students conduct a thorough review of the literature on some aspect of sex differences, sex role stereotyping, or differential treatment on the basis of sex. The review is written up in form of a term paper and may or may not be shared with other members of the class.

Empirical or Experimental Research A small piece of empirical or experimental research is carried out by an individual or team of students. The focus of the research is to explore or test some aspect of sex differences among a selected and defined group of children, young people, or adults. The results of the research are written up and reported to the class. Outstanding pieces of research which add to the field of knowledge in some way, may be developed into an article and submitted to an appropriate professional journal or magazine for publication.

Survey Students identify an area of educational practice in which the two sexes appear to be treated differentially and design and construct inventories and/or observational techniques to collect data. Results are written up in the form of a report, including relevant theory and research. Again, as with empirical studies, publishable papers may result from this kind of activity.

Biographical or Autobiographical Reports Students reconstruct their own or someone else's educational and vocational development and analyze the possible effects of sex role stereotyping. When shared with other members of the class, this project can be the basis of an effective awareness exercise, as students learn that many of their experiences also occurred to others.

Action Plan/Project Students prepare a plan for instituting and evaluating an innovative educational practice that would promote nonstereotypic development of individuals. The action plan may also be implemented as part of the assignment or at some time in the future. The stress on this assignment is its actual practicality and usefulness to the students in their own work or educational settings. Such action projects might include: (1) The development of a special course, unit, or training workshop for a specified group, e.g., teachers, counselors, or students at a particular school, their own peers, etc. (2) The development of a set of guidelines for teachers, counselors, or others to use in enhancing the nonstereotypic development of young people. (3) The development of a plan for implementing Title IX of the Educational Amendments of 1972 in a particular educational institution.

Case Study Skeleton case studies of actual unidentified counselees are presented to the students. As counselor trainees, the students are requested to add any data they think is missing so that they can then develop treatment plans for helping the counselees overcome their problems which resulted from their sex role stereotypic upbringing. This can be either an individual or group project.

Annotated Bibliography In an effort to keep abreast of the most recent literature dealing with sex role issues, the students and instructor join together in a planned effort to abstract as many new books, articles, etc., as possible. Abstracts are placed on file cards for easy organization and reference. Such activity not only assists the student in building a file on a selected topic of their own interest, but also assists the instructor in keeping class reading lists current.

Practica and Other Learning Experiences Special courses which provide counselor trainees with information on sexism and sex role stereotyping as applied to counseling and helping relationships provide a good knowledge base for special counseling practica dealing with the same issues. Even though counselor trainees have a chance to explore their own attitudes and feelings in the small groups which are often a part of such courses, they need an opportunity in a practicum setting for further self-exploration and a chance to try out some newly learned behaviors and techniques. Also helpful at this stage of their training is an opportunity to work with both female and male feminist role models (see earlier discussion in this chapter regarding who should teach and supervise such courses and practica). Too often supervision of these practica is carried out solely by women faculty members, leaving the male counselor trainees without a same-sex role model and perhaps causing some doubt in the minds of the trainees as to the appropriateness of the specialty area to male counselors. Certainly teaching and training regarding sex role stereotyping and nonsexist counseling should not be viewed as the responsibility of only the women faculty—thus starting a new stereotype of "women's work."

In practica which involve working directly with clients, counselor trainees will learn more about how effective they are in helping both women and men develop in nonsexist ways if they are assigned clients of both sexes. Too often counselor trainees are assigned the kinds of clients with whom they are "most comfortable" or can "relate to most effectively." It is not uncommon for such preferred clients to tend to be all one sex, thus not providing the counselor trainee experience and supervised training in counseling the members of both sexes. In observing counselor trainees working with their first real clients, supervisors are on the lookout for comments like "fields that are compatible with marriage," or "boys don't usually," or "girls usually" and nonverbal responses which tend to be stereotypic. Feedback regarding such sexist statements and responses is given as soon as possible to the counselor trainee along with some suggested alternate responses which promote sex equality and individual growth.

To become exposed to the broadest array of issues and problems related to sexism and sex role stereotyping, counselor trainees are placed in settings such as women's centers, men's centers, crises centers, and the like, where many of the clients' presenting problems are sex role related, e.g., rape, sexual relationships, family problems, etc.

In preparation for working directly with clients, counselor trainees first work with role-model-supervisors in a variety of activities designed to increase the awareness of the counselor trainee's own sexist attitudes and behaviors and develop their techniques and approaches in working with clients. While such learning can be achieved through a variety of methods, two—role-playing and consciousness-raising—will be discussed here.

Role-playing   Role-playing in which counselor trainees enact the parts of both clients and counselors in various situations can be a very effective tool in learning about one's own biased attitudes, practicing to change them, and learning various ways of helping others overcome

   Training for Nonsexist Counseling

the negative effects of sexism and develop according to their own interests and abilities rather than those ascribed to them by society because of their sex. Some suggested role-playing situations which facilitate such learning are listed below. Counselor trainees take turns playing both the role of the client and the role of the counselor trying to help the client.

1. A female high school student wanting to go to college against her parents' wishes.
2. A male college student trying to decide whether to accept a football scholarship or a teaching assistantship in an early childhood education center.
3. A couple trying to decide how to share child care responsibilities.
4. A middle-aged, divorced mother of teen-aged children exploring possible ways of preparing for a career and supporting her family.
5. A professional couple trying to determine how best to go about seeking/changing employment when a move to a different state is involved.
6. A male college student trying to decide between majoring in nursing and physiology.
7. A female college student trying to decide between majoring in engineering and home economics.
8. A young couple desiring sexual equality in their relationship.

Feedback from the practicum supervisor and the other counselor trainees regarding each person's enactment of such roles can provide insightful learning for all participants. Video taping segments of such role-playing exercises can provide impactful feedback to counselor trainees regarding their verbal and nonverbal behavior.

Concurrently with role-playing of the counselor helping out clients in situations such as those listed above, a discussion and instruction in special approaches in working with female and male clients—both individually and in groups—around topics like decision making, educational, vocational, and career choice, interpersonal relationships, etc., is appropriate and timely (see chaps. 6 and 7 for some suggestions).

Consciousness-raising   Another valuable method for increasing counselor trainees' awareness of sex role stereotyping and their own sexist attitudes and behaviors is consciousness-raising. The origin and background as well as a brief description of consciousness-raising groups are presented in chapter 7 and will not be repeated here. Rather, some of the differences between consciousness-raising groups (or "C-R" groups as they are popularly referred to) and therapy groups will be discussed since many people tend to confuse the two.

C-R groups are topic-oriented, identifying problems that individuals (initially women) face in a society in need of social reform. As participants share concerns and experiences, they learn that the same feelings and problems are experienced by many others as a result of cultural and societal sex role stereotyping and resultant inequitable treatment. The focus is on an awareness of the need for change in society, rather than personal change. However, it is not uncommon for participants to make changes in their personal lives and behavior following an increase in their awareness of what factors have caused them to be the way they are, and support from the C-R group assists them to take such action. Although actual action steps or projects to promote change in the environment may also be an outcome from a C-R group's experience, it is not viewed as a goal of C-R groups. The supervisor should be prepared, however, to deal with the students' desire to promote change in their own educational environment—e.g., sexist attitudes of other faculty, policies which treat males and females differently, etc.—as a result of their increased awareness. Such student pressure for change can be helpful to the proactive change agent counselor discussed in chapter 7.

Therapy groups, on the other hand, are person-oriented and are designed to be personally corrective experiences for the participants. As Brodsky (1977) states, "Perhaps the greatest distinction between C-R and therapy lies in the intensity of the need of the individual and the response that results from that experience; while techniques from C-R groups can be adapted to therapy with women, women who need intensive therapy cannot be served exclusively through the C-R experience. . . . Some candidates may be deemed inappropriate for a C-R group if they appear too defensive about or too vulnerable to the issues, or if their position is so deviant from the group's values that alienation and lack of support might be an issue."

As has been stated in chapter 7, C-R groups are not for women only. Men, too, need to heighten their awareness of what societal sex role stereotyping has done to women as a group and to men—keeping both sexes, but especially women, from equal opportunity and full development. Such learning is most effectively done first in single-sex or same-sex groups, however. Only through separation do individuals seem willing and free to openly examine their own sexism. In mixed C-R groups, women and men tend to react to the expectations of members of the opposite sex and traditional patterns of interaction are perpetual and reinforced.

Following experience in same-sex C-R groups, counselor trainees, when ready, are assigned to a mixed C-R group to learn how "the other half" feels and to try out recently-learned behaviors. These mixed groups provide an excellent environment for trial and error experimentation before counselor trainees try out new behaviors and approaches with clients and others.

Such experience with same-sex and mixed C-R groups not only facilitates a great deal of learning about one's self, but also enables the counselor trainee to learn how to structure C-R groups for future clients. It is not unusual for counselor trainees to request further training in specialty areas such as assertion training (see discussion in chap. 7) following their C-R experiences in an effort to strengthen their own skills and learn additional techniques to use with others. Lewis and Lewis (1974) have suggested that C-R experiences also be offered to the spouses of trainees, since results of such experiences are likely to cause some changes and/or strain in personal relationships at home.

Conclusion   There is no doubt that counselors have perpetual and reinforced traditional sex role stereotypes ascribed by society to girls and boys, men and women. The need for counselors to recognize their sexist approach in the helping relationship and develop a nonsexist approach to facilitating equality and the full growth and development of all of their clients is great. One of the most logical places to begin helping counselors overcome their own sex biases and stereotypic behaviors is during the time of their training—in their counselor education programs in universities throughout the country.

This chapter has suggested some curricular changes to be made in counselor education programs in an effort to provide counselor trainees with the necessary knowledge and learning experiences which will enable them to develop into nonsexist, unbiased practitioners. Four new courses have been outlined, with selected reading lists and suggested instructional aids, and ideas for special practica have been presented—all with the hope of stimulating and encouraging counselor educators to review their own training programs and develop and implement whatever courses/practica/learning components are necessary.

Suggestions concerning how counselor educators can increase their colleagues' awareness of sexism and equality and help promote change in their attitudes and behaviors are presented in chapter 10. Ways in which counselor educators can increase their own awareness and knowledge and take steps for planned, personal change are presented in chapter 11.

References

Bardwick, J. M. *Psychology of women: A study of biocultural conflicts.* New York: Harper & Row, 1971.

Bardwick, J. M.; Douvan, E.; Horner, M. S.; and Gutmann, D. *Feminine personality and conflict.* Belmont, Calif.: Brooks/Cole, 1970.

Bernard, J. Sex differences: An overview. *MSS Modular Publications,* 26, 1974.

Bird, C. *Born female.* New York: David McKay, 1968.

Blum, H. P. *Female psychology: Contemporary psychoanalytic views.* New York: International Universities Press, Inc., 1977.

Brim, O. G., Jr. Theories of the male mid-life crisis. *Counseling Psychologist,* 1976, *6*(1), 2–9.

Brodsky, A. M. Therapeutic aspects of consciousness-raising groups. In E. I. Rawlings and D. K. Carter (eds.), *Psychotherapy for women: Treatment toward equality.* Springfield, Ill.: Charles C. Thomas, 1977.

Brodsky, A.; Holroyd, J.; Sherman, J.; Payton, C.; Rosenkrantz, P.; Rubenstein, E.; and Zell, F. *Report of the task force on sex bias and sex role stereotyping in therapeutic practice.* American Psychological Association, 1975.

Broverman, I. K.; Broverman, D. M.; Clarkson, F. E.; Rosenkrantz, P. S.; and Vogel, S. R. Sex-role stereotypes and clinical judgements of mental health. *Journal of Consulting and Clinical Psychology,* 1970, *34*, 1–7.

Butler, R. H., and Lewis, M. I. *Sex after sixty.* New York: Harper & Row, 1976.

Carney, C. G., and McMahon, S. L. (eds.). *Exploring contemporary male/female roles: A facilitator's guide.* La Jolla, Calif.: University Associates, 1977.

Chafetz, J. S. *Masculine/Feminine or human?: An overview of the sociology of sex roles.* Itasca, Illinois: F. E. Peacock Publishers, 1974.

Chesler, P. *Women and madness.* New York: Doubleday, 1972.

Cox, S. (ed.). *Female psychology: The emerging self.* Chicago: Science Research Associates, 1976.

David, D. S., and Brannon, R. (eds.). *The forty-nine percent majority: The male sex role.* Reading, Mass.: Addison-Wesley Publishing Co., 1976.

Denmark, F. L. Some aspects of female sexual behavior: An overview. In R. K. Unger and F. L. Denmark (eds.), *Woman: Dependent or independent variable?* New York: Psychological Dimensions, Inc., 1975.

De Rosis, H. A., and Pellegrino, V. Y. *The book of hope and how women can overcome depression.* New York: Macmillan, 1976.

Diamond, E. E. (ed.). *Issues of sex bias and sex fairness in career interest measurement.* Washington, D.C.: U.S. Department of Health, Education and Welfare, 1975.

Dodson, B. *Liberating masturbation.* New York: Bodysex Designs, 1974.

Donelson, E., and Gullahorn, J. E. *Women: A psychological perspective.* New York: John Wiley & Sons, 1977.

Ellis, A. *Sex and the liberated man.* Secaucus, N.J.: Lyle Stuart, Inc., 1976.

Farrell, W. *The liberated man: Beyond masculinity; freeing men and their relationships with women.* New York: Random House, 1974.

Feinbloom, D. H. *Transvestites and transsexuals: Mixed views*. New York: Delacorte Press, 1976.

Filene, P. G. *Him/Her/Self: Sex roles in modern America*. New York: Harcourt, Brace, Jovanovich, 1975.

Fitzpatrick, B. E. *Women's inferior education: An economic analysis*. New York: Praeger Publishers, 1976.

Foxley, C. H. *Locating, recruiting, and employing women: An equal opportunity approach*. Garrett Park, Maryland: Garrett Park Press, 1976.

Franks, V., and Burtle, V. (eds.).*Women in therapy: New psychotherapies for a changing society*. New York: Brunner/Nazel Publishers, 1974.

Frazier, N., and Sadker, M. *Sexism in school and society*. New York: Harper & Row, 1973.

Furniss, W. T., and Graham, P. A. (eds.). *Women in higher education*. Washington, D.C.: American Council on Education, 1974.

Goldberg, H. *The hazards of being male: Surviving the myth of masculine privilege*. New York: Nash, 1976.

Goldberg, H. Men in therapy. In Goldberg, H., *The hazards of being male*. New York: Nash, 1976.

Graber, G. K., and Graber, B. *Women's orgasm*. Indianapolis: Bobbs-Merril Co., 1975.

Grams, J. D., and Waetjen, W. B. *Sex: Does it make a difference?* North Scituate, Mass.: Duxbury Press, 1975.

Green, R. *Human sexuality: A health practitioner's text*. Baltimore: Williams & Williams Co., 1975.

Group for the Advancement of Psychiatry. *Assessment of sexual function: A guide to interviewing*, November, 1973, 8, 88.

Grove, W. R. Relationship between sex roles, marital status, and mental illness. In A. G. Kaplan and J. P. Bean (eds.), *Beyond sex-role stereotypes: Readings toward a psychology of androgyny*. Boston: Little, Brown, 1976.

Guttentag, M., and Bray, H. *Undoing sex stereotypes: Research and resources for educators*. New York: McGraw-Hill, 1976.

Guttman, M. A. J. Counselor biases and practices in counseling females: Implications for training the nonsexist counselor. In M. A. J. Guttman and P. A. Donn (eds.), *Women and ACES: Perspective and issues*. Washington, D.C.: Commission for Women, Association for Counselor Education and Supervision, 1974.

Hammer, S. (ed.). *Women: Body and culture: Essays on the sexuality of women in a changing culture*. New York: Perennial Library, 1975.

Hansen, L. S. A career development curriculum framework for counselors to promote female growth. In M. A. J. Guttman and P. A. Donn (eds.), *Women and ACES: Perspectives and issues*. Washington, D.C.: Commission for Women, Association for Counselor Education and Supervision, 1974.

Harway, M. Sex bias in counseling materials. *Journal of College Student Personnel*, January 1977, *18*(1), 57–64.

Hite, S. *The hite report: A nationwide study of female sexuality*. New York: Dell Publishing Co., 1976.

Horner, M. Toward an understanding of achievement related conflicts in women. *Journal of Social Issues, 28*(2), 1972.

Horney, K. *Feminine psychology*. New York: W. W. Norton, 1967.

Humanist Educator. Special issue, Implementing sex equality: Humanist prescription for education, June, 1976.

Island, D. An alternative for counselor education. *Personnel and Guidance Journal,* 1972, 50, 762–766.

Jones, B. C. Male pupil vs. sexist educators. *Educational Forum,* March 1974, *38*(3), 315–320.

Jourard, S. M. Some lethal aspects of the male role. In S. M. Jourard, *The transparent self.* New York: Van Nostrand, 1964.

Kanowitz, L. *Women and the law.* Albuquerque: University of New Mexico, 1969.

Kaplan, A. B. Androgyny as a model of mental health for women: From theory to therapy. In A. G. Kaplan and J. P. Bean (eds.), *Beyond sex-role stereotypes: Readings toward a psychology of androgyny.* Boston: Little, Brown, 1976.

Kaplan, A. G., and Bean, J. P. *Beyond sex-role stereotypes: Readings toward a psychology of androgyny.* Boston: Little, Brown, 1976.

Katchadurian, H. A., and Lunde, D. T. *Fundamentals of human sexuality.* Chicago: Holt, Rinehart & Winston, 1975.

Kaye, H. E. *Male survival: Masculinity without myth.* New York: Grosset & Dunlap, 1974.

Kelly, G. F. *The guidance counselor as sex educator.* New York: Behavioral Publications, 1976.

Kemp, G. C. Influence of dogmatism on the training of counselors. *Journal of Counseling Psychology,* 1962, 9, 155–157.

Kinsey, A.; Pomeroy, W.; and Martin, C. *Sexual behavior in the human male.* Philadelphia: W. B. Saunders Co., 1948.

Kinsey, A.; Pomeroy, W.; Martin, C.; and Gebhard, P. *Sexual behavior in the human female.* Philadelphia: W. B. Saunders Co., 1953.

Leonard, M.; Hansen, L. S.; and Knefelkamp, L. A process model for changing counselor education departments. In M. A. J. Guttman and P. A. Donn (eds.), *Women and ACES: Perspective and issues.* Washington, D.C.: Commission for Women, Association for Counselor Education and Supervision, 1974.

Levine, J. A. *Who will care for the children? New options for fathers (and mothers).* Lippincott, 1975.

Lewis, J. A., and Lewis, G. J. Attacking institutional sexism: Raising counselor consciousness. In M. A. J. Guttman and P. A. Donn (eds.), *Women and ACES: Perspective and issues.* Washington, D.C.: Commission for Women, Association for Counselor Education and Supervision, 1974.

Lieberman, B. (ed.). *Human sexual behavior: A book of readings.* New York: John Wiley & Sons, 1971.

Maccoby, E. (ed.). *The development of sex differences.* Stanford: University Press, 1966.

Maccoby, E. E., and Jacklin, C. N. *The psychology of sex differences.* Stanford, Cal.: Stanford University Press, 1974.

Masters, W., and Johnson, V. *Human sexual inadequacy.* Boston: Little, Brown, 1970.

Masters, W., and Johnson, V. *Human sexual response.* Boston: Little, Brown, 1966.

Matthews, E. E., et al. *Counseling girls and women over the life span.* Washington, D.C.: National Vocational Guidance Association, 1972.

McCary, J. L. *Sexual myths and fallacies.* New York: Schocken Books, 1975.

Mead, M. *Male and female: A study of the sexes in a changing world.* New York: Dell, 1968.

Mednick, M. T. S.; Tangri, S. S.; and Hoffman, L. W. (eds.). *Women and achievement: Social and motivational analyses.* Washington, D.C.: Hemisphere Publishing Corporation, 1975.

Meyer, J. K. (ed.). *Clinical management of sexual disorders.* Baltimore: Williams & Wilkins Co., 1976.

Miller, J. B. (ed.). *Psychoanalysis and women.* New York: Brunner/Mazel, 1973.

Moberg, V. *Consciousness razors.* New York: Feminist Press, 1972.

Mussen, P. H. Early sex-role development. In D. A. Goslin (ed.), *Handbook of socialization theory and research.* Chicago: Rand McNally College Publishing Company, 1969.

National Institute of Mental Health Task Force on Homosexuality. *Final report and background papers.* U.S. Department of Health, Education, and Welfare Publication Number ADM 76–357, 1972.

Nichols, J. *Men's liberation: A new definition of masculinity.* New York: Penguin Books, 1975.

Personnel and Guidance Journal. Special issue on Women and Counselors, October, 1972.

Petras, J. W. *Sex/Male—gender/masculine: Readings in male sexuality.* New York: Alfred, 1975.

Phi Delta Kappan. Special issue on Education and the Feminist Movement, October, 1973.

Pietrofesa, J. J., and Carlson, J. Human sexuality and the school counselor. *Counseling and Values,* 1973, 17, 228–234.

Rawlings, E. I., and Carter, D. K. *Psychotherapy for women: Treatment toward equality.* Springfield, Ill.: Charles C. Thomas, 1977.

Richardson, B. *Sexism in higher education.* New York: Seabury Press, 1974.

Rossi, A. S., and Calderwood, A. (eds.). *Academic women on the move.* New York: Russell Sage Foundation, 1973.

Ruitenbeek, H. M. (ed.). *Psychoanalysis and male sexuality.* New Haven, Conn.: College and University Press, 1966.

Russell, D. S. Teaching about sexism: A challenge for teacher educators. *Integrated Education,* 1977, 15(3), 6–8.

Schlossberg, N. K., and Petrofesa, J. Perspectives on counseling bias: Implications for counselor education. *Counseling Psychologist,* 4:1, 1973.

Sherfey, M. J. *The nature and evolution of female sexuality.*

Singer, J. *Androgyny: Toward a new theory of sexuality.* New York: Anchor Press/Doubleday, 1976.

Sprung, B. *Non-sexist education for young children: A practical guide.* New York: Citation Press, 1975.

Stacey, J.; Bereaud, S.; and Daniels, J. *And Jill came tumbling after: Sexism in American education.* New York: Dell Publishing Co., 1974.

Tavis, C., and Offir, C. *The longest war: Sex differences in perspective.* New York: Harcourt Brace Jovanovich, 1977.

Tiger, L. *Men in groups.* New York: Random House, 1969.

Title IX of the education amendments of 1972—a summary of the implementing regulation. Washington, D.C.: Resource Center on Sex Roles in Education, National Foundation for the Improvement of Education, 1976.

Tyler, L. *The psychology of human differences.* New York: Appleton-Century-Crofts, 1965.

Unger, R. K., and Denmark, F. L. *Women: Dependent of independent variable.* New York: Psychological Dimensions, Inc., 1975.

Vaillant, G. E. Natural history of male psychological health. *Archives of General Psychiatry,* July 1974, 31, 15–22.

Van Hoose, W. H. Conflicts in counselor preparation and professional practice: An analysis. *Counselor Education and Supervision.*

Verheyden-Milliard, M. E. *A handbook for workshops on sex equality in education.* Washington, D.C.: American Personnel and Guidance Association, 1976.

Wesley, F., and Wesley, C. *Sex role psychology.* New York: Human Sciences Press, 1977.

Westervelt, E. The recruitment and training of educational/vocational counselors for girls and women. Background paper for Sub-committee on Counseling, President's Commission on the Status of Women, 1963.

Women on campus. New York: *Change Magazine,* 1975.

Women on words and images. *Help wanted: Sexism in career education materials.* Princeton, N.J.: National Organization for Women, 1975.

Wrenn, C. G. *The counselor in a changing world.* Washington, D.C.: American Personnel and Guidance Association, 1962.

Yorburg, B. *Sexual identity: Sex roles and social change.* New York: John Wiley & Sons, 1974.

10 In-service Training Programs That Work

The need for in-service education and professional development programs focusing on sex typing for practitioners in the helping professions is obvious. In previous chapters I have discussed the sex role stereotyped views of men and women, girls and boys, held by counselors and other helping professionals. Counselors, like others, reflect their own experiences and upbringing in a sexist society. As Schlossberg and Pietrofesa (1973) have pointed out, ". . . counselors are like people-in-general—no better, no worse. We all share one thing; we make judgments about appropriate behaviors for different groups of people. Such prejudgments may be important in influencing the behavior of others." Counselors need to be aware of their own sex biases and the degree to which these biases influence their work with clients. While practicing counselors may be aware of the concerns expressed about sexism in the media and in the professional literature, there is no indication that their attitudes and behaviors toward their clients have changed because of this awareness. For all but a few counselors now graduating from degree programs which provide specialized nonsexist training, the training and preparation of practicing professionals did not prepare them for today's changing views regarding sex roles, much less prepare them to facilitate the development of psychological androgyny in their clients (see chap. 6). As Gardner (1971) states,

Right now, in our excessively sexist society, it is unlikely that anyone without special training in feminism can create conditions which would encourage females to "exercise their right to select goals of the counselor." The goals of counselors trained in traditional programs can hardly be expected to do other than reflect the sexist values. . . .

Thus, the need for in-service training and education programs. Professional associations such as the American Psychological Association and the American Personnel and Guidance Association have recognized this need and offer special self renewal and in-service continuing professional development workshops as a part of their annual conventions. For example, five of the forty-one preconvention workshops sponsored by the American Personnel and Guidance Association in 1978 dealt with topics related to sex typing and overcoming sexism. Some of the workshop titles: "For Women and Men: Sex Equality in Counselor Education and Supervision," "Women and Careers: Success Determinants and Deterrents," and "Women and Power." These preconvention workshops are part of APGA's program of continuing professional development designed to focus on problems and issues of concern to the profession. The workshop format is a practical means of resolving and sharing solutions to these problems with a wide segment of the professional membership. Continuing Education Units (CEU's) and a Certificate of Participation are awarded each participant who successfully completes one or more of the workshops.

Such professional development programs would be included, along with many other types of in-service training programs, in Swansburg's (1968) list of in-service education programs:

—Supplementary education to keep up-to-date with the "knowledge explosion" and new skills.
—Education for better practice.
—Education for professional development.
—Education for personal development.
—Education for today: On-the-job orientation and training.
—Education for tomorrow: To institute and effect changes in practice.

In-service education and training regarding sex typing fits into each of these areas, potentially benefitting the individual staff members professionally and personally as well as improving the services of the organization.

Objectives of In-service Training and Education

In-service training and education programs regarding sexism and sex role stereotyping may take a variety of forms ranging from periodic seminars of one to two hours in length to week-long conferences and workshops. Some organizations include college courses and externally sponsored institutes in their in-service training and education programs. But whatever the form, such programs focusing on sexism have some common general objectives and purposes:

1. To increase staff members' understanding and awareness of sex typing and sex bias and the detrimental effects on both women and men.
2. To increase staff members' awareness of their own sexist attitudes and behaviors with clients.
3. To improve service to clients, by removing sexist elements from the counseling/helping process in particular and the helping organization in general.

Participants   Who should be involved in the in-service training program? To this point, the focus has been on practicing counselors and other helping professionals. But the paraprofessionals and support personnel who have contact with clients should also be included in such training programs. Indeed, they are frequently the ones who provide clients with information regarding services offered by the organization and who make referrals or suggestions to the clients as to which services might benefit them most. Sexist attitudes and behaviors on the part of support personnel and paraprofessionals can cause serious limitations for clients. The receptionist who views women and men in sex role stereotypic ways may not consider the full range of services provided by the organization as appropriate for both sexes, and thus may provide clients and potential clients with only partial information. The paraprofessional staff member who believes that only certain activities are "appropriate" for girls and others are "appropriate" for boys may not provide clients of both sexes with all the possible solutions to a problem. Thus, it is necessary that all personnel participate in in-service training programs regarding sexism and sex typing. Whether support and paraprofessional personnel are involved in the same types of programs as the professional staff depends on the nature of the organization, the working relationships of the various levels of staff, and the personnel involved. Generally speaking, personnel whose job functions are similar and/or interface with each other will benefit by participating in the same in-service training programs. This facilitates application of concepts learned in training to actual on-the-job situations. And too, many times a side product of such training will be improved working relationships even though that is not the focus of the training.

As has already been mentioned, in-service training and education can take many forms. Asking staff members to read an article or chapter on sex typing and discussing it at a staff meeting is one approach which takes minimal effort. Viewing an insightful film together and relating it to professional practice is another. More extensive approaches provide theory and background information and also utilize techniques such as role-play, simulation games, and on-the-job application and practice. Such approaches may be in a seminar, workshop, or conference format, taking anywhere from a couple hours to a couple weeks. It is not possible to outline here in-service training and education programs for all of the various settings in which counselors and other helping professionals work. Even if it could be done for each setting, the differences in organizational structures and personnel require that programs be tailored to meet specialized needs in order to be effective. Therefore, general suggestions will be given here which the author and others have found helpful in planning and implementing such programs.

Planning
Programs

First some comments about planning in-service education and training programs.

1. A planning committee consisting of representatives from the participating groups and the training staff will not only help insure that the program meets the interests and needs of the participants but also gives them a feeling of involvement and ownership which enhances commitment to making the program succeed.

2. Surveying the participants, or a representative sample if the number is too large, to get their ideas on what they think needs to be covered in the program and how it can be done most effectively, not only provides suggestions for program content but also helps set the stage for the program and primes the participants.

3. Getting the backing and support of the administration or management for the program should go without saying; however, too many well-planned programs without such endorsement have difficulty in the implementation and follow-through stages.

4. Establishing short-range and long-range goals and methods for assessing whether or not they have been met provide direction for the planning process and enable necessary evaluation of the program.

5. Attention to detail during the planning phase can help insure a smooth-running, effective program. Some of the details to be concerned with are:

Training for Nonsexist Counseling

—Schedule the program at a time that is best for the participants, avoiding peak work load periods, and times whe staff members are likely to be overly tired.

—Arrange the logistics, i.e., location, date, and time of program.

—Prepare publicity materials and notices to participants well ahead of time so that calendars can be cleared. Careful wording of such notices can help generate enthusiasm for the program.

—Plan a program format that has flexibility and variety, i.e., alternate presentations and information-giving activities with participant involvement activities; and be prepared with backup activities for on the spot changes (e.g., a speaker doesn't show, or a question is raised that adds an important dimension to the program).

—Arrange for resource persons, e.g., speakers, panelists, group discussion leaders, etc.

—Arrange for resource materials, e.g., reading materials, audio-visual materials, and machines.

Program Content and Format

As has been stated earlier, it is not practical to outline here specific in-service programs on sex typing for specific settings, as organizational structures and purposes and needs of individual participants must be taken into consideration in order for the program to be effective. Therefore, suggestions as to content and format which may be altered and adapted by a program planning committee is the focus of this section.

In an attempt to study three different methods of training dealing with sexism (and racism), Sedlacek, Troy, and Chapman (1976) found that each of the three different methods was "successful," but the criterion for success was different for each method. If the criterion for success is how good the participants felt about the training experience, then the simulation game "Starpower" (a bargaining and trading game resulting in a three-tiered society, where one group receives preferential treatment and is allowed to alter the rules of the game) was the most successful. If the success criterion is planning to do something about sexism or racism, then the movie workshop (involving three films showing the various aspects of sexism and racism followed by an unstructured question and answer discussion) seemed to motivate the most participants. If the criterion of success is the amount of knowledge gained, the "model workshop" was best. The model workshop was a six-stage structured discussion involving a small number of students seated in a circle and a discussion leader. The topics of the six stages of the discussion were: (1) "Cultural, racial, and sexual differences," (2) "How sexism/racism operates," (3) "Examining racial/sexist attitudes"—facilitated through the use of the Situational Attitude Scale (SAS), which shows negative attitudes by whites towards blacks, and the SAS-W, which shows that men tend to have negative attitudes toward women in nontraditional roles, (4) "Sources of racial/sexist attitudes," (5) "Changing behavior"—setting short-term and long-term goals, and (6) Principles of change and strategies for accomplishing goals. Since the three training methods appear to achieve different ends, it appears that the best approach would be to incorporate elements of all three methods into an in-service training program. Also, by combining elements of all three, a nice variety of activities results. Cognitive material regarding sexism is presented through lectures and films; an experiential component is provided in the Starpower simulation; and an opportunity to set goals and plan strategies for change is the focus of the model workshop.

A somewhat similar training model is suggested by Schlossberg and Pietrofesa (1973), although they carry the model a step further to include skill development and follow-up tutorial projects. Their four major components of a training program "to enable counselors and teachers to participate with their constituency in an unbiased fashion" are:

1. Expanding the cognitive understanding of participants regarding the role of women through lectures and readings.
2. Raising the consciousness of participants regarding sexual bias through group techniques.
3. Promoting the acquisition of nonbiased helping skills among participants through audio-video taping and role-playing.
4. Fostering skill development in program planning and implementation among participants through tutorial projects.

One group technique used by Schlossberg and Pietrofesa in the second component is the inner circle—outer circle or "fishbowl technique," in which participants observe each other discussing an assigned reading on sex roles and then provide feedback on their behaviors and attitudes. The third component provides the participants with the opportunity to learn specific skills by role-playing situations which may elicit sex-biased behaviors. Each participant plays the role of both the "helpee" and the "helper." Video and audio taping of the role-playing sessions, as well as actual counseling sessions, are critiqued with special attention given to situations where counselor biases are likely to influence the counseling process and the client's decision-making. The fourth component of the program assists the participants in developing programs to be implemented in their own work settings. Follow-up activities allow participants to return four months after the training program to report on the results of their own programs.

Each of three training methods used by Sedlacek and associates was designed for a two-hour workshop. Combined, they would provide enough material for a full day training session. The Schlossberg and Pietrofesa training model provides fifty-six hours of training, and they recommend an intensive period of one week followed by sixteen hours of follow-up sessions.

A workshop which is more extensive than Sedlacek and his associates' methods and yet not as extensive as the Schlossberg and Pietrofesa model can be easily formulated from *A Handbook for Workshops on Sex Equality in Education* (Verheyden-Hilliard, 1976). The handbook presents background information, training models and activities, and resources used by fifty-one State Trainers in the Sex Equality in Guidance Opportunities (SEGO) Project to conduct over 300 workshops on sex equality in education in every state in the nation. The SEGO Project was sponsored by the American Personnel and Guidance Association under a contract from the U.S. Office of Education. The following is the workshop outline provided in the handbook. An expanded outline with specific instructions and suggested activities is also included in the handbook.

SEGO Workshop Outline

8:30 A.M.	Registration and Gathering Time
9:00	Welcome
9:05	Opening Activity
9:20	Overview of Sex Equality in Education
9:45	Group Activity
10:00	Media Presentation
10:30	Break
10:45	Title IX
11:15	Group Activity
11:30	Display of Print Material

12:00 P.M.	Lunch
1:00	Short Media Presentation or a Time for Questions
1:30	Strategies for Change
2:30	Closing Remarks
2:50	Evaluation Sheets

Another nationwide effort in providing training workshops regarding sexism and sex equality for educators and educational administrators at all levels is the Title IX Equity Workshops Project sponsored by the Council of Chief State School Officers. Detailed workshop manuals, prepared by the Resource Center on Sex Roles in Education (1977) of the National Foundation for the Improvement of Education provide workshop outlines with specified time requirements for each activity, stated purposes and objectives, a list of needed materials, procedural instructions and background information, and participants worksheets. The following is a sample program outline.

Title IX and Achieving Sex Equity: The Conditions for Change
Time Required: 60 minutes

A. Lecturette—"Title IX and Achieving Sex Equity: The Conditions for Change" (10 minutes)
B. Questions and answers (5 minutes)
C. Individual activity—"Implementing Title IX and Achieving Sex Equity: Assessing Conditions for Change" (15 minutes)
D. Small group discussions (15 minutes)
E. Total group processing (15 minutes)

Purpose of the Activity:
The purposes of this activity are:
- to provide participants with an overview of the conditions necessary for organizational change related to Title IX implementation and the attainment of sex equity
- to provide participants with a framework for assessing organizational change needs as they relate to Title IX implementation and the attainment of sex equity
- to involve participants in an analysis of the organizational changes necessary for Title IX implementation and attainment of sex equity in their own colleges and universities

- to involve participants in the identification of interventions and actions which may be used to assist Title IX implementation and the attainment of sex equity in their own institutions

Materials needed:
For participant use:
- "Assessing Conditions for Change" (included in participant notebook—Participant Worksheet 17)

For facilitator use: None

Facilitator preparation required:
The facilitator(s) should:
- thoroughly review this total session outline and all participant materials
- review suggested lecturette and adapt it to accommodate unique group needs or facilitator style

Procedure:

A.	Lecturette—"Implementing Title IX and Attaining Sex Equity: Conditions for Change" [Suggested text is supplied.]	(15 minutes)
B.	Questions and answers	(5 minutes)
C.	Individual activity—"Assessing Conditions for Change" [Instructions and participant worksheet provided.]	(15 minutes)
D.	Small group discussions [Directions provided.]	(15 minutes)
E.	Total group processing [Directions and questions provided.]	(10 minutes)

Packaged materials for in-service education and training regarding sexism and sex equality are becoming available at reasonable costs. An example is Stebbins, Ames, and Rhodes' (1978) *Sex Fairness in Career Guidance: A Learning Kit.* The kit contains a four-chapter text manual plus a variety of supplementary materials for use by counselors and their clients, including spirit masters for use with client groups, scenario cards for role-plays, transcripts of counselor-client interactions, and a tape cassette of four simulated counseling segments, each with two versions—a sex biased and a sex fair approach to the same client in the same situation. Chapter 1 of the text manual introduces the dual role system which limits career and other life choices for both men and women in our society, discussing traditional family and work roles for both sexes as well as current challenges to this system. Chapter 2 proposes a comprehensive sex fair guidance program, providing perspectives on sex-fairness in the counseling process and recommending activities for such a program. Chapter 3 trains counselors to identify sex bias in career interest inventories and provides remedial measures to minimize bias in administering, reporting, and interpreting vocational inventories. Chapter 4 is a comprehensive resource guide to supplementary reading and audiovisual materials, containing annotated listings of general information sources on sex stereotyping and sex fair counseling, activities for counselors and educators, and names and addresses of helpful organizations and agencies.

An impactful in-service program on sexism and sex equality, designed specifically for counselors and other helping professionals, and the paraprofessional and support staffs with whom they work, is possible with a little ingenuity. Considerable resources are now available so that the program can effectively instruct and facilitate the learning of the participants. Some of the resources which I have used in various combinations, depending on the length of the program and the needs of the participants, are:

1. Selected readings
2. Guest speakers and panelists
3. Films
4. Group techniques, exercises and simulations
5. Audio-video taping equipment
6. Attitude measures regarding sex roles and sexism
7. Projects planned and presented by the participants themselves
8. Contracting to change behaviors, develop future projects/ programs, or take other action steps.

I will comment on each of these resources to give the reader an idea of why and how I use them. By assigning a few selected readings to the participants prior to the in-service program, two things are achieved: (1) the participants come to the program prepared with a common knowledge base, and (2) more program time can then be spent on application of ideas rather than presentation of information; thus, allowing the program to be highly participative and experiential. The readings should be short enough to increase the likelihood that they will in fact be read. An entire book is likely to be set aside and at best skimmed. A few articles or chapters have a better chance of being read. Some of the chapters in this volume, particularly in section I, would be appropriate as would several of the articles and chapters appearing in the list of references.

Outside speakers and panelists bring different perspectives to the topic of sexism. Both sexes should be included so that program participants are not given the idea that sexism is a woman's problem or a man's problem, but a joint problem which needs to be solved jointly.

Several outstanding films on the effects of sex typing are available. An annotated list of some I have used is provided in chapter 9. Films are particularly good program starters. They can effectively set the stage and provide a focus for discussion.

Group techniques, exercises, and simulation games can provide unlimited awareness and learning if timed and administered skillfully. They can be used as "ice breakers" to get a program started and at strategic times throughout the program to provide participants with common experiences from which they learn about their own and others' sexist attitudes and behaviors and can experiment with new behaviors. Simple ones can be designed on the spot as the program evolves and the facilitator assesses the need to bring out certain points through an experiential approach. Breaking into diads or small groups to role-play biased and unbiased attitudes and behaviors, "fishbowling" a discussion and then giving feedback to inner-circle participants, and small group brainstorming for solutions to a problem of a hypothetical client are examples. Others are more complex and need prior planning and preparation. The simulation Starpower has already been mentioned as one which can be effective in allowing participants to experience how it feels to be a member of advantaged and disadvantaged groups. Many such exercises and simulation games are described in Sargent's (1977) *Beyond Sex Roles,* Carney and McMahon's (1977) *Exploring Contemporary Male/Female Roles: A Facilitator's Guide,* Jongeward and Scott's (1976) *Women as Winners: Transactional Analysis for Personal Growth,* and Drum and Knott's (1977) *Structured Groups for Facilitating Development.* Others can be specially designed by the program facilitator to bring out certain aspects of sexism.

Audio-visual taping equipment takes feedback provided to the individual participants through group techniques one step farther—the participant can see and hear herself/himself as other participants give their perspective. Changes in behavior are visible, thus facilitating the acquisition of new behaviors and skills. The use of such equipment is particularly effective when the size of the group is small enough and the length of the program allows for individual treatment in developing new nonsexist helping/counseling skills.

Attitude measures regarding sex roles and sexism are useful tools which assist participants in assessing their attitudes toward sex roles and their own "masculinity," "femininity," and "androgyny." Some of the instruments I have used as part of in-service training programs are listed below and described briefly.

The Attitudes Toward Women Scale (AWS)   Developed by Spence and Helmreich (1977), the AWS is an instrument to survey attitudes people have about the proper roles of women. The scale contains fifty-five items, each consisting of a declarative statement (e.g., "Women should worry less about their rights and more about becoming good wives and mothers;" "The intellectual equality of woman with man is perfectly obvious.") for which there are four response alternatives: Agree Strongly, Agree Mildly, Disagree Mildly, and Disagree Strongly. Each item is given a score from 0 to 3, with 0 representing the most traditional, conservative attitude and 3 representing the most liberal, profeminist attitude. Each person's score is obtained by summing the values for the individual items. The range of possible scores goes from 0 to 165. The instrument is easy to administer (may be read aloud) and score with large groups.

The Bem Sex-Role Inventory (BSRI)   Developed by Sandra Bem (1977), the BSRI is an instrument that treats masculinity and femininity as two independent dimensions rather than as opposite ends of a single dimension, thus allowing an individual to say she or he is both masculine and feminine (high masculine-high feminine would indicate an androgynous view of oneself). The BSRI presents sixty personality characteristics (e.g., self-reliant, tender, assertive, compassionate, etc.) and asks the individual to indicate on a scale from 1 to 7 (with 1 representing "Never or Almost Never True" and 7 representing "Always or Almost Always True") how true the various characteristics are for him or her. The masculinity and femininity scores are simply the means of the ratings of the masculine and feminine adjectives on the BSRI. The BSRI can be either hand scored or computer scored.

The Personal Attribute Questionnaire (PAQ)   Developed from the Rosenkrantz et al. (1968) Sex-Role Stereotype Questionnaire (SRSQ) by Spence, Helmreich and Stapp (1974), the PAQ contains fifty-five psychological characteristics (e.g., timid, aggressive, emotional, dominant, etc.) and instructs the individual to use a five-point scale to: (1) rate himself/herself on each characteristic, and (2) compare the "typical male" and "typical female" on each characteristic. Thus, a measure of one's own masculinity-femininity may be obtained as well as one's view of sex roles for men and women in general.

The Women's Liberation Scale (WLS) The WLS, developed by Carlos Goldberg (1976), is a fourteen-item, Likert-type scale designed to measure attitudes toward positions advocated by women's groups. Examples of the items: "Women, whether married or single, should receive the same salary as men for doing the same job;" "Men and women should share equally the responsibilities for making a living, running the home, and bringing up children." The scores for each item range from 1 to 4, representing "Strongly Disagree" to "Strongly Agree." The WLS has been found to correlate with the AWS (see above).

New instruments to measure attitudes toward sex roles are in the process of being developed. For example, Project DELTA at Wichita State University, funded by the Women's Educational Equity Act (WEEA) Program (see chap. 5) and directed by Konek (1977), is developing a battery of bias-free leadership and decision-making instruments. The instruments will be self-assessment tools for measuring leadership style, decision-making strategies, sex role values and role satisfaction. Another WEEA funded effort in progress is the compilation of a sourcebook of instruments which measure attitudes toward sex roles and sexism, equity in counseling, sex stereotyping behaviors, career interests and plans, leadership opportunities and abilities, changes in self-concept, and institutional change (American Institutes for Research, 1978). Such a sourcebook should be very valuable for use in in-service training programs on sexism and sex fairness in counseling and other helping professions.

Special projects planned and presented by the program participants themselves during the in-service training program can be a valuable experience for individuals and can contribute greatly to the overall program. An example would be to develop and demonstrate a similation to be used in training new counselors to be nonsexist. Another example would be to develop and present an action plan for change (either personal or organizational) regarding nonsexist treatment of clients. By developing such projects and presenting them during the in-service training program, individuals have an opportunity to get a kind of a "dry run" before trying their projects out in the real life setting and can benefit from the suggestions and comments from the other participants. Needless to say, such projects can not be incorporated into a short in-service training seminar because of the time required to develop, present, and critique.

Related to the special projects idea above is the technique of contracting with program participants to change behaviors, develop future projects/programs, or take other action steps. Contracting enables participants to plan for extending their learning of nonsexist behavior outside of the training program and helps promote other programs on the topic. Contracts or agreements are made in writing before the end of the in-service training program and a follow-up session is held at an appropriate later date to enable reporting and sharing of results. Some suggested steps in developing such contracts or agreements are:

1. Select a behavior, project, or program you want to work on.
2. Describe the behavior so it can be observed and counted. (For a project or program, describe it in as much detail as possible indicating measures for success and/or completion.)
3. Identify rewards that will help provide the motivation to complete contract.
4. Identify people who are in a position to observe the behavior and perhaps supply some of the rewards. (For projects and programs, identify individuals who will be involved in all phases.)
5. Establish a timetable for completion of contract.

Conclusion In-service training and education programs to promote nonsexist counseling help fill a void in the professional education and preparation of most practicing counselors and other helping professionals, since only recently have a few degree programs recognized the need to include in the curriculum material regarding sex bias. The objectives of such in-service education and training programs are: (1) to increase participants' understanding and awareness of sex typing and sex bias and the detrimental effects on both women and men, (2) to increase participants' awareness of their own sexist attitudes and behaviors with clients, and (3) to improve service to clients, by removing sexist elements from the counseling/helping process and the helping organization.

In-service training and education programs on sex typing and sexism are for paraprofessionals and support staff as well as counselors, since these personnel have contact with clients and may influence how the clients view the helping organization and the services and programs available.

Suggestions for planning in-service programs are given and various approaches to program content and format are discussed.

References   American Institutes for Research. Search for evaluation instruments that measure aspects of educational equity for women. *Association for Measurement and Evaluation in Guidance Newsletter,* Winter, 1978.

American Personnel and Guidance Association. *APGA annual preconvention workshops,* Washington, D.C., March 17–19, 1978.

Bem, S. L. Bem Sex-Role Inventory (BSRI) In C. G. Carney and S. L. McMahon (eds.) *Exploring contemporary male/female roles: A facilitator's guide.* La Jolla, Calif.: University Associates, 1977.

Carney, C. G., and McMahon, S. L. (eds.) *Exploring contemporary male/female roles: A facilitator's guide.* La Jolla, Calif.: University Associates, 1977.

Drum, D. J., and Knott, J. E. *Structured groups for facilitating development.* New York: Human Sciences Press, 1977.

Goldberg, C. Women's liberation scale (WLS): A measure of attitude toward positions advocated by women's groups, MS. No. 1187. Washington, D.C.: Journal Supplement Abstract Service, American Psychological Association, 1976.

Jongeward, D., and Scott, D. *Women as winners: Transactional analysis for personal growth.* New York: Addison-Wesley, 1976.

Konek, C. Personal Communication, December 13, 1977.

Resource Center on Sex Roles in Education, National Foundation for the Improvement of Education. *Implementing title IX and attaining sex equity: Planning for change.* Washington, D.C.: Council of Chief State School Officers, September 1977.

Rosenkrantz, P. S.; Vogel, S. R.; Bee, H.; Broverman, I. K.; and Broverman, D. Sex-role stereotypes and self-concepts in college students. *Journal of Consulting and Clinical Psychology,* 1968, 32, 287–295.

Sargent, A. G. (ed.) *Beyond sex roles.* New York: West Publishing Co., 1977.

Schlossberg, N. K., and Pietrofesa, J. J. Perspectives on counseling bias: Implications for counselor education. *Counseling Psychologist,* 1973, 4, *1,* 44–54.

Sedlacek, W. E.; Troy, W.; and Chapman, T. An evaluation of three methods of racism-sexism training. *Personnel and Guidance Journal,* 1976, 55, *4,* 196–198.

Spence, J. T., and Helmreich, R. The attitude toward women scale (AWS). In C. G. Carney and S. L. McMahon (eds.). *Exploring contemporary male/female roles: A facilitator's guide.* La Jolla, Calif.: University Associates, 1977.

Spence, J. T.; Helmreich, R.; and Stapp, J. The personal attributes questionnaire: A measure of sexx role stereotypes and masculinity-femininity. MS. No. 617. Washington, D.C.: Journal Supplement Abstract Service, American Psychological Association, 1974.

Stebbins, L. B.; Ames, N. L.; and Rhodes, I. *Sex fairness in career guidance: A learning kit.* Cambridge, Mass.: Abt Publications, 1978.

Swansburg, R. C. *In-service education.* New York: G. P. Putnam's Sons, 1968.

Verheyden-Hilliard, M. E. *A handbook for workshops on sex equality in education.* Washington, D.C.: American Personnel and Guidance Association, 1976.

11 Self-education for Awareness, Change, and Growth

The reduction of sexism must be a conscious priority. It will not just happen because we wish it. The leadership in omitting sexism should come from counselors and other helping professionals whose goal is to facilitate the psychological health of others. It has been shown that highly sex typed individuals are not as psychologically healthy as androgynous individuals (see chaps. 2 and 6). In order to help others overcome the detrimental effects on sex role stereotyping and become fully aware, functioning, and humane persons, we as helping professionals must first be able to recognize our own biases and work to change them—for our own benefit as well as that of our clients.

There are many ways to begin this self-assessment regarding sex bias. Some suggested activities and exercises are presented here.

Awareness and Assessment Activities

Listed below are sex role stereotypic characteristics which have generally been attributed to men and women, girls and boys. Read through the lists carefully.

Activity A

Characteristics Generally Attributed to Men/Boys	Characteristics Generally Attributed to Women/Girls
1. aggressive	1. passive
2. independent	2. dependent
3. dominant	3. talkative
4. good at math and science	4. emotional
5. mechanical ability	5. considerate
6. good at sports	6. easily influenced
7. competitive	7. excitable in crises
8. skilled in business	8. tactful
9. worldly	9. gentle
10. adventurous	10. helpful to others
11. outspoken	11. home oriented

Characteristics Generally Attributed to Men/Boys	Characteristics Generally Attributed to Women/Girls
12. interested in sex	12. sensitive
13. decisive	13. religious
14. demonstrates leadership	14. neat in habits
15. intellectual	15. indecisive
16. self-confident	16. supportive
17. ambitious	17. submissive
18. autonomous	18. devoted to others
19. strong	19. conforming
20. unemotional	20. concerned about appearance

Do you agree with the categorizing of these characteristics for men and women in general?

Do you see yourself as having more of the stereotypic traits of your sex than those of the opposite sex?

Do you view your spouse and/or other members of your family (parents, siblings, children, other relatives) as having the characteristics generally attributed to their sex rather than those of the opposite sex?

Do you view your friends and colleagues as having the sex role stereotypic characteristics?

Do you view your clients as having the sex role stereotypic characteristics?

Activity B Write down all the ways you think your life would be different if you were the opposite sex. How would your personal life be affected? How would your professional life be affected? What would the advantages and disadvantages be?

Activity C Keep a diary for one week of all the sexist and nonsexist behaviors and attitudes you observe around you: at home (family and friends, TV, newspaper, recreational/pleasure activities, home duties, etc.), in the office (colleagues, clients, etc.), and in public places (stores, restaurants, buses, etc.).

Activity D Visit a public school (if it is not your work setting) for a day and observe the sex role stereotypic behaviors of students, teachers, counselors, and other school personnel.

Activity E   Ask trusted friends and colleagues how they view your attitudes toward and treatment of women and men, boys and girls. Are there differences based on sex? If so, what do you think are the reasons for this differential behavior?

Activity F   Video tape one of your counseling sessions with a male client and one with a female client with similar problems. Do you respond differently to the two clients? Do you follow different treatment plans for the two clients because of their sex?

Activity G   What is your knowledge of differential (and oftentimes discriminatory) treatment of men and women, girls and boys, in various settings? List five-ten examples of unequal treatment on the basis of sex which are common in the following settings:

Homes:

Schools:

Employment Settings:

Churches:

Medical Settings:

Other Community Settings:

Activity H   What is your knowledge of the various federal laws and regulations which prohibit discrimination on the basis of sex? Describe what actions are prohibited, who is protected, and what institutions/organizations are covered by the following:

Equal Pay Act of 1963

Training for Nonsexist Counseling

Executive Order 11246 as Amended by 11375

Title VII of the Civil Rights Acts of 1964

Title IX of the Education Amendments of 1972

Title VII and Title VIII of the Public Health Service Act

If you had difficulty with this exercise, review the discussion of these laws and regulations in chapter 5.

Activity I The checklist below was prepared by McCune and Matthews (1975), of the Resource Center on Sex Roles in Education, for use by faculty members in institutions of higher education. How many of these actions have you and your institution undertaken? (Substitute "clients" for "students" and "colleagues/staff members" for 'faculty'' if your work setting is not an educational institution.)

Your Individual Actions—Have You:

1. examined your personal sex-role socialization experiences and their impact upon your present beliefs, attitudes, and values?   Yes _____ No _____
2. examined the effects of your sex-role attitudes upon your behavior or expectations for male and female students?   Yes _____ No _____
3. read three articles on the nature of sex-role socialization, sex-role stereotyping, and its relationship to education?   Yes _____ No _____
4. obtained and reviewed information regarding federal laws prohibiting sex discrimination?   Yes _____ No _____
5. read at least three professional books concerning the issues of sexism and education?   Yes _____ No _____
6. engaged in or designed a personal reading and research program to gain an in-depth understanding of the sex-role

issues most closely affecting your special academic interests or responsibilities? Yes _____ No _____

7. reviewed materials used in your courses for sex bias or stereotyping in either content or omissions? Yes _____ No _____

8. incorporated content, discussion, and activities regarding sex roles, sex stereotyping, and sex discrimination in education into those courses or programs for which you have responsibility? Yes _____ No _____

9. designed or conducted research or development efforts which address or incorporate considerations of sexism in education: Yes _____ No _____

10. discussed issues of sexism in education with other faculty or administrators? Yes _____ No _____

11. designed a workshop or training program to assist others in understanding sexism in education? Yes _____ No _____

12. reviewed policies or practices of your department or program to identify possible sources of sex bias or discrimination?
   _____ affecting employers? Yes _____ No_____
   _____ students? Yes _____ No _____

13. contacted your professional association with regard to activities, programs, or publications related to sex bias or sex discrimination? Yes _____ No _____

14. developed a program for systematic correction of the sources of bias or discrimination you have identified? Yes _____ No _____

Actions in Your Institution

1. Has a systematic institutional self-evaluation been undertaken to investigate sources of sex bias and sex discrimination in:
   • employment practices and policies, including—
   —recruitment Yes _____ No _____
   —hiring and assignment Yes _____ No _____
   —promotion Yes _____ No _____

—provisions for staff development	Yes ____	No ____
—tenure	Yes ____	No ____
—salary	Yes ____	No ____
• practices and policies pertaining to students—		
—recruitment	Yes ____	No ____
—admissions	Yes ____	No ____
—treatment	Yes ____	No ____
—employment opportunities	Yes ____	No ____
• curriculum content	Yes ____	No ____
• research and development programs	Yes ____	No ____

2. Has a policy of nondiscrimination on the basis of sex been formally adopted by the institution and distributed to all students and employees?   Yes ____   No ____

3. Has a procedure for handling faculty and student grievances regarding discrimination been developed?   Yes ____   No ____

4. Have opportunities for training regarding sex-bias and sex discrimination in education and related federal legislation been provided to all staff?   Yes ____   No ____

5. Has an outreach program been developed to assist local education agencies with change efforts related to sexism?   Yes ____   No ____

6. Are women represented on faculty and government committees in proportion to their representation on the faculty?   Yes ____   No ____

7. Has a plan for continuing systematic investigation of sex-bias and the remediation of its effects been developed—
   • for employment policies and practices?   Yes ____   No ____
   • for student programs?   Yes ____   No ____

8. Has a program been developed which would assist women and minorities to gain training and experience for positions in educational administration?   Yes ____   No ____

The above activities will help you identify your own sex biased attitudes and behaviors and become more aware of the sexist elements in your home and work environments. The next step is to do something—take some action to eliminate sexism in yourself, as an individual and as a practicing professional, and facilitate the elimination of sex bias and unfair treatment of women and men, boys and girls in your work setting.

Setting Goals for Personal Growth

The first step in setting goals for personal growth related to sex equality is to identify the behavior needing change. Once this is done, ways in which the behavior can be changed can be listed, and the best one(s) selected.

Sexist behavior to be changed: _____

_____

Ways in which behavior can be changed: _____

_____

_____

_____

_____

Then identifying the barriers or constraints and supports or positive influences for change will enable you to visualize the kinds of assistance and difficulty you can expect in trying to reach your goal—change your behavior.

Barriers/Constraints:	Sources of Support/ Assistance:
_____	_____
_____	_____
_____	_____
_____	_____

Once the positive and negative influences for reaching your goal have been delineated, ask yourself the following questions:

Can the barriers and constraints be overcome?
Are the sources of support and assistance adequate?
Am I motivated to change?
    (What are my motivations?)
Is the behavior change possible?
Is the behavior change observable and/or measureable?
    (How will I know when behavior change has occurred?)
Do I really want to change this behavior?
What is an appropriate timetable for reaching my goal?

If your answers to the above questions demonstrate that you desire to go ahead with changing your sexist behavior for personal and professional growth, outlining the action steps to be taken and the appropriate time you hope to have each step completed provides a useful guide in reaching your goal.

Action Steps:	Completion Date:
1. _____	1. _____
2. _____	2. _____
3. _____	3. _____
4. _____	4. _____
5. _____	5. _____

Once the goal of changing a sexist behavior has been reached, other behaviors may be identified as needing change for personal and professional growth, as self-change and self-growth is a continual process requiring conscious effort.

Setting Goals for Environmental Change
Environmental change to eliminate sexist elements is the focus of section II of this volume. The role of counselors and other helping professionals in facilitating environmental change and suggested actions will not be repeated here, but I do want to point out that the same goal setting process suggested above for individual behavior change is also effective in setting goals and planning for en-

vironmental change. Since environmental change usually involves large groups of individuals and sometimes entire systems, the process is generally more complex and time consuming.

Conclusion Maintaining a perspective free of bias and behavior free of oppression is not easy in a sexist society. Counselors were reared and educated in sex role stereotypic ways just like everyone else. But counselors and other helping professionals have a professional obligation to assist their clients and their client organizations (in the case of an organizational change agent role) in ridding themselves of sexist restrictions to allow the full development of men and women, girls and boys, alike. This professional obligation begins with an awareness and assessment of one's own sexist attitudes and behaviors and knowledge of the detrimental effects of sex role stereotyping. Suggested in this chapter are various ways in which counselors and others can begin to make this self-assessment and establish goals for changing sexist behaviors.

Removing restrictions and discriminatory treatment based on outmoded sex role stereotypes from society is an abstract and distant goal. This goal may be obtained only when we as individuals take actions to affirm our own values of equality and fairness and also work with others to achieve the collective objective of equal opportunity for all individuals—regardless of their sex.

Reference McCune, S., and Matthews, M. *Rate yourself and your institution—a checklist.* Washington, D.C.: Resource Center on Sex Roles in Education, National Foundation for the Improvement of Education, 1975.

Index

301

Project DELTA, 289
Project on Equal Education Rights (PEER), 40,
    147-149, 264
Project on Sex Equality in Guidance
    Opportunities, 264
Project on the Status and Education of Women,
    88, 148, 211, 265
Protective laws, 127-128, 142
Provenzano, F., 13
Psychoanalysis, 21-22
Psychological Aspects of Men's and Women's
    Roles (course), 249, 250, 251-253
Psychological Corporation, 53
Psychology textbooks, 59-60, 72
Psychoneuroses, defined, 31
Psychophysiological disorders, defined, 31-32
Psychosis, functional, 31
Psychosomatic disorders, defined, 31-32
Psychotherapy in penal institutions, 239
Public Health Service, 122
Public Health Service Act, 140-141
Pyke, S., 49

Quantum leap, 157

Rabban, M., 7
Race and sex typing, 7
Raffel, Norma K., 146
Randolph, C., 213
Raths, L. E., 193
Rawlings, E. I., 155, 164, 258
Reading in schools, 41, 42, 57
Reagan, Barbara, 145
Rebecca, M., 156
Rebelsky, F., 15
Reeves, N., 7
Reinforcement, learning, 9-10
Relocating and job, 124
Research projects by counseling students, 266
Resource Center on Sex Roles in Education, 148,
    183, 187, 201, 265, 284, 295
Retirement, 162
Rheingold, Joseph, 22
Rhodes, I., 285
Richardson, B., 39, 255
Richman, P., 165
Ricks, F., 49
Rizzo, D., 55, 57
Roark, A. C., 85, 86
Robinson, L. H., 70
Roche Report, 21
Rockwell, Lauralee, 250
Rogers, C. R., 158, 159-160, 176
Rogers, M. A., 60
Roipke, A., 21
Role-playing, 268-269, 282-283
Rosenfelt, D. S., 210
Rosenkrantz, P. S., 29, 79, 80, 252, 258, 288
Rosenthal, R., 51
Ross, D., 10
Ross, S. A., 10
Rossi, A. S., 39, 155, 255
Rubenstein, E., 258
Rubin, J., 13
Ruitenbeek, H. M., 258
Russell, D. S., 261

Sadker, D., 194
Sadker, M., 39, 254
Salaries, See Earnings
Saltz, J. W., 65
Sanders, C. J., 169
Sandler, Bernice, 68
Sargent, A. G., 287
Schachter, S., 14
Schlossberg, N. K., 61, 63, 75, 245, 255, 277,
    282-283
Scholastic Aptitude Test-Mathematics (SAT-M),
    43, 53
Scholz, N. T., 221
Schools, 39-91, 173-222. See also Training
    programs
    college-level, 44, 61-62, 64-65, 67-91, 204-222,
        228
    elementary, 40-43, 47-48, 57, 181-193
    laws affecting, 39, 67, 133, 138-140, 143-144,
        179, 189, 203, 207-208, 289
    secondary, 43-46, 47, 48, 57-60, 61-65,
        193-203
Schwenn, M., 82
Science, 43
    textbooks in, 60
Scott, 89
Scott, D., 221, 287
Scott, Foresman and Company, 183
Sears, P., 50
Sears, R. R., 6, 9, 10, 158
Secondary schools, 43-46, 47, 48, 57-60, 61-65,
    193-203
Secor, C., 156
Sedlacek, W. E., 74, 281, 283
Segal, B., 33
Self-actualized persons, 158-159
Self-disclosure, 165-167
Self-fulfilling prophecy effect, 51
Self theory, 159-160
Sells, L. W., 44
Semantic Differential questionnaire, 63
Sequential Tests of Educational Progress, 53
Serbin, L. A., 16, 50, 168
"Sesame Street," 16
Sex and the Professional, 262
Sex education courses, 45-46
Sex Equality in Guidance Opportunities (SEGO)
    Project, 209, 283-284
Sex Information and Education Council of the
    United States (SIECUS), 265
Sex Role Development, 262
Sex roles, defined, 6
Sex Role Stereotype Questionnaire (SRSQ), 29,
    288
Sex Role Stereotyping and Socialization in Educa-
    tion (course), 249, 250, 253-255
Sex Role Stereotyping in Schools Series, 263
Sex role transcendence, defined, 156
Sexton, P., 40
Sex typing, defined, 6
Sexual behavior, students' views on, 80
Sexuality, Human (course), 249, 250, 255-257
Shapiro, J., 62
Sherfey, M. J., 257
Sherman, J., 43, 44, 258
Shertzer, B., 72-73
Shoben, E. J., Jr., 174